THE NEW CAMBRIDGE SHAKESPEARE

FOUNDING GENERAL EDITOR
Philip Brockbank

GENERAL EDITOR
Brian Gibbons, *Professor of English Literature, University of Münster*

ASSOCIATE GENERAL EDITORS
A. R. Braunmuller, *Professor of English, University of California, Los Angeles*
Robin Hood, *Senior Lecturer in English, University of York*

THE THIRD PART OF KING HENRY VI

A series of outstanding productions by the Royal Shakespeare Company and others has recently demonstrated the theatrical vitality of Shakespeare's plays about the reign of Henry VI.

In the *Third Part* Shakespeare extends his essay on monarchical politics by contrasting the good but ineffective Henry VI with his rival, the sensual and victorious Edward IV. He also offers more evidence of the perils of aristocratic factionalism in a series of scenes that display the grievous wounds caused by the Wars of the Roses. Here we watch the savage death of the Duke of York at the hands of Queen Margaret, the moving lament of King Henry as he witnesses the slaughter of the battle of Towton where the Lancastrians were defeated, and, finally, Henry's death at the hands of Richard of Gloucester, later King Richard III.

THE NEW CAMBRIDGE SHAKESPEARE

Romeo and Juliet, edited by G. Blakemore Evans
The Taming of the Shrew, edited by Ann Thompson
Othello, edited by Norman Sanders
King Richard II, edited by Andrew Gurr
A Midsummer Night's Dream, edited by R. A. Foakes
Hamlet, edited by Philip Edwards
Twelfth Night, edited by Elizabeth Story Donno
All's Well That Ends Well, edited by Russell Fraser
The Merchant of Venice, edited by M. M. Mahood
Much Ado About Nothing, edited by F. H. Mares
The Comedy of Errors, edited by T. S. Dorsch
Julius Caesar, edited by Marvin Spevack
The Second Part of King Henry IV, edited by Giorgio Melchiori
King John, edited by L. A. Beaurline
King Henry VIII, edited by John Margeson
The First Part of King Henry VI, edited by Michael Hattaway
Antony and Cleopatra, edited by David Bevington
The Two Gentlemen of Verona, edited by Kurt Schlueter
Measure for Measure, edited by Brian Gibbons
The Second Part of King Henry VI, edited by Michael Hattaway
The Third Part of King Henry VI, edited by Michael Hattaway
The Poems, edited by John Roe
King Henry V, edited by Andrew Gurr
King Lear, edited by Jay L. Halio

THE THIRD PART OF
KING HENRY VI

Edited by
MICHAEL HATTAWAY
Professor of English Literature,
University of Sheffield

CAMBRIDGE
UNIVERSITY PRESS

Published by the Press Syndicate of the University of Cambridge
The Pitt Building, Trumpington Street, Cambridge CB2 1RP
40 West 20th Street, New York, NY 10011–4211, USA
10 Stamford Road, Oakleigh, Victoria 3166, Australia

© Cambridge University Press 1993

First published 1993

Printed in Great Britain at the University Press, Cambridge

A catalogue record for this book is available from the British Library

Library of Congress cataloguing in publication data

Shakespeare, William, 1564–1616.
[King Henry VI. Part 3]
The third part of King Henry VI / edited by Michael Hattaway.
    p.   cm. – (The New Cambridge Shakespeare)
Includes bibliographical references.
ISBN 0-521-37331-X (hardback) – ISBN 0-521-37705-6 (paperback)
1. Henry VI, King of England, 1421–1471 – Drama. I. Hattaway,
Michael. II. Title. III Series: Shakespeare, William, 1564–1616.
Works. 1984. Cambridge University Press.
PR2816.A2H38   1993
822.3′3 – dc20   92-965 CIP

ISBN 0521 37331 X hardback
ISNB 0521 37705 6 paperback

THE NEW CAMBRIDGE SHAKESPEARE

The *New Cambridge Shakespeare* succeeds *The New Shakespeare* which began publication in 1921 under the general editorship of Sir Arthur Quiller-Couch and John Dover Wilson, and was completed in the 1960s, with the assistance of G. I. Duthie, Alice Walker, Peter Ure and J. C. Maxwell. *The New Shakespeare* itself followed upon *The Cambridge Shakespeare*, 1863–6, edited by W. G. Clark, J. Glover and W. A. Wright.

The New Shakespeare won high esteem both for its scholarship and for its design, but shifts of critical taste and insight, recent Shakespearean research, and a changing sense of what is important in our understanding of the plays, have made it necessary to re-edit and redesign, not merely to revise, the series.

The *New Cambridge Shakespeare* aims to be of value to a new generation of playgoers and readers who wish to enjoy fuller access to Shakespeare's poetic and dramatic art. While offering ample academic guidance, it reflects current critical interests and is more attentive than some earlier editions have been to the realisation of the plays on the stage, and to their social and cultural settings. The text of each play has been freshly edited, with textual data made available to those users who wish to know why and how one published text differs from another. Although modernised, the edition conserves forms that appear to be expressive and characteristically Shakespearean, and it does not attempt to disguise the fact that the plays were written in a language other than that of our own time.

Illustrations are usually integrated into the critical and historical discussion of the play and include some reconstructions of early performances by C. Walter Hodges. Some editors have also made use of the advice and experience of Maurice Daniels, for many years a member of the Royal Shakespeare Company.

Each volume is addressed to the needs and problems of a particular text, and each therefore differs in style and emphasis from others in the series.

PHILIP BROCKBANK
Founding General Editor

CONTENTS

ILLUSTRATIONS

Illustrations 1 and 2 are reproduced by permission of the National Portrait Gallery, London; 3 and 4 by permission of the British Library; 6, 12 (Tom Holte Photographic Collection) 9, 10, 11, 13 (photograph Gordon Goode), 16 by permission of the Shakespeare Centre Library, Stratford-upon-Avon); 14 by permission of Joe Cocks Photography, Stratford-upon-Avon; 15 photograph Nicole Audibert.

PREFACE

Henry VI Part 3 brings to a close Shakespeare's epic account of the Wars of the Roses. He had begun the sequence with his account of the loss of England's empire in France during the Hundred Years War, and in *Part 2* shown how, in a respite from battles waged abroad, 'civil butchery'[1] took an even fiercer toll of the fabric of England. In *Part 3* we witness the final degradation of chivalry: this play contains some of the most horrific scenes in the canon as England's warlords sacrifice their honour to a remorseless ethic of revenge. Here we see the ignominious death of York, taunted in his agony by Henry's fearsome consort, Margaret of Anjou, the deaths of Henry's adversary Clifford and of Clifford's adversary Warwick 'the kingmaker', the slaughtering of Henry by Richard of Gloucester, shortly to become Richard III, and of Henry's young son Prince Edward, by his namesake Edward – King Edward IV of England.

The play has come into its own in this century only after it was experienced in the theatre: modern theatre-goers have sometimes had the opportunity of seeing it as the last sequence of a 'cycle' in which its pageant of violence and suffering has provided a climax to a demonstration of the evils of the civil broils unleashed by dynastic rivalries. The celebrated scene (2.5) in which King Henry, from a molehill, watches a father discover he has killed his son and a son discover he has killed his father, seems neither primitive nor static but rather placed crucially as a still point within the welter of carnage that surrounds it.

In the decades since the last major editions, those of John Dover Wilson (The New Shakespeare, 1952) and Andrew S. Cairncross (New Arden, 1964), Stratford and London have seen major productions of versions of this history cycle (1964 and 1977), a shortened version went on a national tour (1987–8), and a shortened version appeared at Stratford in late 1988. Reviews of those productions have turned into some of the most perceptive critical appraisals of these plays.

The editions of Wilson and Cairncross, along with that of Norman Sanders (New Penguin, 1981), created major advances in our knowledge of these texts. To these editors I owe a debt for their major work on the lexical problems of the text, although I have been surprised how much there was still to do. Cairncross's edition offered challenging but unendorsable views of the history of the text. The Oxford edition of *The Complete Works* (1986), wherein *3 Henry VI* (known there as *Richard Duke of York*) was prepared by William Montgomery and Gary Taylor, along with the apparatus in *William Shakespeare: A Textual Companion* (1987), appeared after my own work was well advanced. The work of these editors has

1 *1 H4* 1.1.13

been perpetually stimulating, often provocative. My own edition, however, will be found to be far less interventionist than theirs. I had prepared a draft of this edition and of *2 Henry VI* before turning to my final work on *1 Henry VI*. Working on the plays in this order persuaded me that critical arguments exist in plenty for the case that Shakespeare wrote his plays in the order of history, arguments that have not been taken sufficient note of by those scholars who have approached the problems of authorship and composition from textual propositions alone.

To the late Philip Brockbank I am grateful for much encouragement and the loan of his PhD thesis which not only records pioneering work on the sources of the sequence, but which generated a series of articles that were really the first to treat the plays as a major achievement. These stood virtually alone and certainly unchallenged for a critical generation. My own work supports Brockbank's pioneering but not yet accepted contention that Shakespeare drew far more from Holinshed than from Hall.

Librarians at the Universities of Kent, Sheffield, Texas, and at the British and London Libraries have been consistently helpful; so have the staff of the Oxford Text Archive who provided me with electronic copies of the Folio and Quarto texts which were an invaluable aid in checking the text I had established. Mary White and Sylvia Morris at the Shakespeare Centre Library in Stratford could not have been more helpful in guiding me through their archives and, in particular, helping me with the choice of illustrations. To colleagues at Kent and Sheffield I am grateful for sabbatical leaves which hastened the advancement of this work. Professor Brian Gibbons, general editor, entrusted this volume to his colleague, Professor A. R. Braunmuller, but the advice and encouragement he gave me while I was working on the first two volumes hastened the completion of this. Al Braunmuller's advice was pointed and pertinent. Professor Martin Dodsworth and Dr Mark Greengrass gave me some useful references and Professors Jonathan Bate and Andrew Gurr shared some unpublished fruits of their research. My colleague Professor Norman Blake found time in the middle of a busy year to scrutinise my typescript and impelled me to clarify my thinking on several linguistic and other related points. Thanks to Sarah Stanton of Cambridge University Press for her patience and sage suggestions. C. Walter Hodges' drawings served, as always, to stimulate and not just to illustrate.

University of Sheffield   M.H.

ABBREVIATIONS AND CONVENTIONS

Shakespeare's plays, when cited in this edition, are abbreviated in a style modified slightly from that used in the *Harvard Concordance to Shakespeare*. Other editions of Shakespeare are abbreviated under the editor's surname (Cairncross, Dyce) unless they are the work of more than one editor. In such cases, an abbreviated series name is used (Cam., Johnson Var.) When more than one edition by the same editor is cited, later editions are discriminated with a raised figure (Collier[2]). All quotations from Shakespeare, except those from *1–3 Henry VI*, use the lineation of *The Riverside Shakespeare*, under the textual editorship of G. Blakemore Evans.

1 Shakespeare's plays

Ado	*Much Ado About Nothing*
Ant.	*Antony and Cleopatra*
AWW	*All's Well That Ends Well*
AYLI	*As You Like It*
Cor.	*Coriolanus*
Cym.	*Cymbeline*
Err.	*The Comedy of Errors*
Ham.	*Hamlet*
1H4	*The First Part of King Henry the Fourth*
2H4	*The Second Part of King Henry the Fourth*
H5	*King Henry the Fifth*
1H6	*The First Part of King Henry the Sixth*
2H6	*The Second Part of King Henry the Sixth*
3H6	*The Third Part of King Henry the Sixth*
H8	*King Henry the Eighth*
JC	*Julius Caesar*
John	*King John*
LLL	*Love's Labour's Lost*
Lear	*King Lear*
Mac.	*Macbeth*
MM	*Measure for Measure*
MND	*A Midsummer Night's Dream*
MV	*The Merchant of Venice*
Oth.	*Othello*
Per.	*Pericles*
R2	*King Richard the Second*
R3	*King Richard the Third*
Rom.	*Romeo and Juliet*
Shr.	*The Taming of the Shrew*
STM	*Sir Thomas More*
Temp.	*The Tempest*

TGV	*The Two Gentlemen of Verona*
Tim.	*Timon of Athens*
Tit.	*Titus Andronicus*
TN	*Twelfth Night*
TNK	*The Two Noble Kinsmen*
Tro.	*Troilus and Cressida*
Wiv.	*The Merry Wives of Windsor*
WT	*The Winter's Tale*

2 Other works cited and general references

Abbott	E. A. Abbott, *A Shakespearian Grammar*, 1878 edn (references are to numbered paragraphs)
Alexander	*William Shakespeare, The Complete Works*, ed. Peter Alexander, 1951
Arber	E. Arber, *A Transcript of the Registers of the Company of Stationers of London 1554–1640*, 5 vols., 1875–94
Armstrong	Edward A. Armstrong, *Shakespeare's Imagination*, 1963
Baldwin	T. W. Baldwin, *Shakspere's 'Small Latine & Lesse Greeke'*, 2 vols., 1944
Bell	*Shakespeare's Plays*, ed. J. Bell, 9 vols., 1774
Bentley	G. E. Bentley, *The Jacobean and Caroline Stage*, 7 vols., 1941–68
Boswell-Stone	W. G. Boswell-Stone, *Shakespeare's Holinshed: The Chronicle and the Historical Plays Compared*, 1896
Brewer	E. C. Brewer, *The Dictionary of Phrase and Fable*, n.d.
Brockbank	J. P. Brockbank, 'Shakespeare's historical myth: a study of Shakespeare's adaptations of his sources in making the plays of *Henry VI* and *Richard III*', unpublished PhD dissertation, University of Cambridge, 1953
Bullough	Geoffrey Bullough, *Narrative and Dramatic Sources of Shakespeare*, 8 vols., 1957–75
Cairncross	*3 Henry VI*, ed. Andrew S. Cairncross, 1964 (New Arden)
Cam.	*Works*, ed. William Aldis Wright, 9 vols., 1891–3 (Cambridge Shakespeare)
Capell	*Mr William Shakespeare his Comedies, Histories, and Tragedies*, ed. Edward Capell, 10 vols., 1767–8
Cartwright	Robert Cartwright, *New Readings in Shakespeare*, 1866
Cercignani	F. Cercignani, *Shakespeare's Works and Elizabethan Pronunciation*, 1981
Chambers	E. K. Chambers, *The Elizabethan Stage*, 4 vols., 1923
Collier	*Works*, ed. John P. Collier, 8 vols., 1842–4
Collier[2]	*Works*, ed. John P. Collier, 1853
Collier MS	Perkins' Second Folio, 1632 (Huntington Library)
Colman	E. A. M. Colman, *The Dramatic Use of Bawdy in Shakespeare*, 1974
conj.	conjecture
Crane	*Henry VI, Part Three*, ed. Milton Crane, 1968 (Signet)
Dekker, *ND*	Thomas Dekker, *Non Dramatic Works*, 5 vols., 1884–6
Delius[2]	*Werke*, ed. Nicolaus Delius, 7 vols., 1854–[61]

Dent	R. W. Dent, *Shakespeare's Proverbial Language: An Index*, 1981 (references are to numbered proverbs)
DNB	*Dictionary of National Biography*
Drayton	Michael Drayton, *Works*, ed. J. W. Hebel *et al.*, 5 vols., 1951
Dyce	*The Works of William Shakespeare*, ed. Alexander Dyce, 6 vols., 1857
Dyce^2	*The Works of William Shakespeare*, ed. Alexander Dyce, 9 vols., 1864–7
Eds.	Various editors
ELR	*English Literary Renaissance*
ES	*English Studies*
F	*Mr William Shakespeares Comedies, Histories, and Tragedies*, 1623 (First Folio)
F2	*Mr William Shakespeares Comedies, Histories, and Tragedies*, 1632 (Second Folio)
F3	*Mr William Shakespear's Comedies, Histories, and Tragedies*, 1664 (Third Folio)
F4	*Mr William Shakespear's Comedies, Histories, and Tragedies*, 1685 (Fourth Folio)
Fabyan	Robert Fabyan, *The New Chronicles of England and France*, 1516, reprinted 1811
Farmer	Richard Farmer, in Johnson Var. (see below)
FQ	Edmund Spenser, *The Faerie Queene*, ed. A. C. Hamilton, 1977
Grafton	Richard Grafton, *A Chronicle at Large of the History of The Affayres of England*, 1569, reprinted in 2 vols., 1809
Griffiths	Ralph A. Griffiths, *The Reign of Henry VI*, 1981
Hall	Edward Hall, *The Union of the . . . Families of Lancastre and Yorke*, 1548, reprinted 1809 (page references are to the 1809 edn)
Halliwell	*The Complete Works of Shakespeare*, ed. James O. Halliwell, 16 vols., 1853–65
Hanmer	*The Works of Shakspear*, ed. Thomas Hanmer, 6 vols., 1743–4
Hart	*3 Henry VI*, ed. H. C. Hart, 1910 (Arden)
Hattaway	Michael Hattaway, *Elizabethan Popular Theatre*, 1982
Henslowe	*Henslowe's Diary*, ed. R. A. Foakes and R. T. Rickert, 1961
HLQ	*The Huntington Library Quarterly*
Holinshed	Raphael Holinshed, *Chronicles of England, Scotland, and Ireland*, second edition, 1587, reprinted in 6 vols., 1808 (unless otherwise specified, page references are to vol. III of the 1808 edn)
Hudson	*The Complete Works of William Shakespeare*, ed. Henry N. Hudson, 11 vols., 1851–6
Hulme	Hilda M. Hulme, *Explorations in Shakespeare's Language*, 1962
Irving	*The Works of William Shakespeare*, ed. Henry Irving and Frank A. Marshall, 8 vols., 1888–90
Johnson	*The Plays of William Shakespeare*, ed. Samuel Johnson, 8 vols., 1765
Johnson Var.	*The Plays of William Shakespeare*, ed. Samuel Johnson and George Steevens, 10 vols., 1773
Jonson	*The Works of Ben Jonson*, ed. C. H. Herford and P. and E. Simpson, 11 vols., 1925–52

Keightley	*The Plays of Shakespeare*, ed. Thomas Keightley, 6 vols., 1864
Kittredge	*The Complete Works of Shakespeare*, ed. George Lyman Kittredge, 1936
Kökeritz	Helge Kökeritz, *Shakespeare's Pronunciation*, 1953
Long	John H. Long, *Shakespeare's Use of Music: The Histories and Tragedies*, 1971
Mahood	M. M. Mahood, *Shakespeare's Wordplay*, 1957
Malone	*The Plays and Poems of William Shakespeare*, ed. Edmond Malone, 10 vols., 1790
Marlowe	*The Works of Christopher Marlowe*, ed. C. F. Tucker Brooke, 1910
Mason	John Monck Mason, *Comments on . . . Shakespeare's Plays*, 1785
McKerrow	Unpublished edition of *3 Henry VI*, cited in Wells and Taylor (see below)
Metamorphoses	Ovid, *Metamorphoses*, trans. Arthur Golding (1567), ed. J. F. Nims, 1965
Mirror	*The Mirror for Magistrates*, ed. Lily B. Campbell, 1938
Munro	*The London Shakespear*, ed. John Munro, 6 vols., 1958
Nashe	Thomas Nashe, *Works*, ed. R. B. McKerrow, 5 vols., 1904–10, revised by F. P. Wilson, 1958
Neilson	*The Complete Dramatic and Poetic Works of William Shakespeare*, ed. William Alan Neilson, 1906
Noble	Richmond Noble, *Shakespeare's Biblical Knowledge*, 1935
NQ	*Notes and Queries*
O	[William Shakespeare], *The true Tragedie of Richard Duke of Yorke, and the death of good King Henrie the Sixt . . .*, 1595, (Octavo), Shakespeare Quarto Facsimiles, No. 11, 1958
obs.	obsolete
OED	*Oxford English Dictionary*
Onions	C. T. Onions, *A Shakespeare Glossary*, revised by Robert D. Eagleson, 1986
Oxford	*William Shakespeare: The Complete Works*, ed. Stanley Wells and Gary Taylor, 1986
Partridge	Eric Partridge, *Shakespeare's Bawdy*, 1968 edn
PBSA	*Papers of the Bibliographical Society of America*
Pelican	*The Second and Third Parts of King Henry the Sixth*, ed. Robert K. Turner Jr and George Walton Williams, 1967
Plutarch	*The Lives of the Noble Grecians and Romanes*, trans. Thomas North, 8 vols., 1928 edn
PMLA	*Publications of the Modern Language Association of America*
Pope	*The Works of Shakespear*, ed. Alexander Pope, 6 vols., 1723–5
PQ	*Philological Quarterly*
Q2	[William Shakespeare], *The True Tragedie of Richarde Duke of Yorke . . .*, 1600
Q3	*The Whole contention betweene the two Famous Houses, Lancaster and Yorke*, 1619; prepared in facsimile by Charles Praetorius, 1886
Rann	*Dramatic Works*, ed. Joseph Rann, 6 vols., 1786–94
Reed	*The Plays of William Shakspeare*, [ed. Isaac Reed], 10 vols., 1785

Ren. Drama	*Renaissance Drama*
RES	*Review of English Studies*
Riverside	*The Riverside Shakespeare*, ed. G. Blakemore Evans, 1974
RORD	*Research Opportunities in Renaissance Drama*
Rowe	*The Works of Mr William Shakespear*, ed. Nicholas Rowe, 6 vols., 1709
Rowe[2]	*The Works of Mr William Shakespear*, ed. Nicholas Rowe, 2nd edn, 6 vols., 1709
Rowe[3]	*The Works of Mr William Shakespear*, ed. Nicholas Rowe, 3rd edn, 8 vols., 1714
Sanders	*3 Henry VI*, ed. Norman Sanders, 1981 (New Penguin)
SB	*Studies in Bibliography*
Schmidt	Alexander Schmidt, *Shakespeare-Lexicon*, 1886 edn
Scott-Giles	C. W. Scott-Giles, *Shakespeare's Heraldry*, 1950
SD	stage direction
SEL	*Studies in English Literature*
Seymour	E. H. Seymour, *Remarks... upon the Plays of Shakespeare*, 2 vols., 1805
SH	speech heading
Shakespeare's England	*Shakepeare's England: An Account of the Life and Manners of his Age*, ed. Sidney Lee and C. T. Onions, 2 vols., 1916
Singer	*The Dramatic Works of William Shakespeare*, ed. Samuel Weller Singer, 10 vols., 1826
Singer[2]	*The Dramatic Works of William Shakespeare*, ed. Samuel Weller Singer, 10 vols., 1856
Sisson	*Works*, ed. C.J. Sisson, 1954
Sisson, *New Readings*	C. J. Sisson, *New Readings in Shakespeare*, 2 vols., 1956
SP	*Studies in Philology*
SQ	*Shakespeare Quarterly*
S.St.	*Shakespeare Studies*
S.Sur.	*Shakespeare Survey*
Staunton	*The Plays of William Shakespeare*, ed. Howard Staunton, 3 vols., 1858–60
Steevens	*The Plays of William Shakespeare*, ed. George Steevens and Isaac Reed, 4th edn, 15 vols., 1793
Stow	John Stow, *The Survey of London*, 1603 edn, reprinted in Everyman Library, n.d.
subst.	substantively
Sugden	E. H. Sugden, *A Topographical Dictionary to the Works of Shakespeare and his Fellow Dramatists*, 1925
Theobald	*The Works of Shakespeare*, ed. Lewis Theobald, 7 vols., 1733
Theobald[2]	*The Works of Shakespeare*, ed. Lewis Theobald, 8 vols., 1740
Thomas	K. V. Thomas, *Religion and the Decline of Magic*, 1971
Thomson	W. H. Thomson, *Shakespeare's Characters: A Historical Dictionary*, 1951
Tilley	M. P. Tilley, *A Dictionary of the Proverbs in England in the Sixteenth and Seventeenth Centuries*, 1950 (references are to numbered proverbs)
TLN	Through line numbering

Vaughan Henry H. Vaughan, *New Readings and Renderings of Shakespeare's Tragedies*, 3 vols., 1886

Walker William S. Walker, *Critical Examination of the Text of Shakespeare*, 3 vols., 1860

Warburton *The Works of Shakespear*, ed. William Warburton, 8 vols., 1747

Wells and Taylor Stanley Wells and Gary Taylor, *William Shakespeare: A Textual *Textual Companion* Companion*, 1987

White *Works*, ed. Richard Grant White, 12 vols., 1857–66

Williams Penry Williams, *The Tudor Regime*, 1979

Wilson *3 Henry VI*, ed. J. Dover Wilson, 1952 (New Shakespeare)

Unless otherwise specified, biblical quotations are given in the Geneva version (1560).

INTRODUCTION

Henry VI: the reign and the plays

> Far better it were to loose a piece of right,
> Than limbs and life in sousing for the same.
>
> William Baldwin, 'Richard Plantagenet', 155–6, in *The Mirror for Magistrates*, 1559[1]

Thus was the principality posted over sometimes to Henry, sometimes to Edward, according to the sway of the party prevailing: ambition and disdain still casting faggots on the fire whereby the heat of hatred gathered the greater force, to the consumption of the peers and the destruction of the people.

Raphael Holinshed, *Chronicles of England, Scotland, and Ireland*, 1587[2]

THE PROMISED END?

The opening shot of Jane Howell's 1983 television version of *3 Henry VI* is a close-up of a wounded corpse, the disposition of the body suggesting the dead Christ, a kind of *pietà*. The camera then withdraws, revealing that this corpse is but one of a whole heap of corpses. There is, it turns out, no transfiguration, only a holocaust. Spectators or readers coming to *3 Henry VI* after their experience of the first two parts of the play may, justly perhaps, be expecting an ending that is a conclusion, a redemptive or tragic vision to set against their overall experience of political duplicity and martial carnage. They will not, however, find it: just a relentless demonstration of political degradation as the turbulent warlords who rule England destroy what is left of the commonweal.[3] Horror, moral horror, rather than Aristotelian 'terror' might be the appropriate reaction. *1 Henry VI* concentrated on war, war between England and France. *2 Henry VI* focussed on the extinction of justice and equity by political intrigue and popular rebellion.[4] The struggle continues, but, given the absence of monarchical power and authority in *3 Henry VI*, 'rebellion' does not seem to be an appropriate label for the cause of the Yorkists. What we have instead is ritualised anarchy. As Francis Bacon wrote, 'For many a man's strength is in opposition, and, when that faileth, he groweth out of use.'[5] The 'case of truth'[6] has dissolved, the opposing

---

1 *Mirror*, p. 190; 'sousing' means swooping (like a hawk) or striking blows.
2 Holinshed, p. 301.
3 Judith Hinchcliffe, *King Henry VI, Parts 1, 2, and 3*, Garland Shakespeare Bibliographies, 1986, provides an annotated survey of criticism. For a bibliographical essay, see Edward Berry, 'Twentieth-century Shakespeare criticism: the histories', in Stanley Wells (ed.), *The Cambridge Companion to Shakespeare Studies*, 1986, pp. 249–56. For other plays of the period dealing with the iniquities of civil war see Michael Hattaway (ed.), *1H6*, 1990, p. 33 n.; for an eloquent passage from Holinshed against the iniquities of the English peers for unleashing civil war, see Appendix 1, p. 210.
4 See Michael Hattaway (ed.), *2H6*, 1991, pp. 14–17.
5 W. A. Wright (ed.), *Bacon's Essays*, 1865, 'Of faction', p. 208.
6 *1H6* 2.4.2.

1 Henry VI (artist unknown)

rights of York and Lancaster have been suppressed, suppressed by a struggle of might that serves only to establish men in positions of power.

This last play depicts the consequences of that primal act of faction-forming that occurred in the Temple Garden in 2.4 of *Part 1*, and, like the first play in the sequence, it concentrates on battles: the play moves from slaughter to slaughter on the battlefield – and elsewhere. In its first scene Henry declares that the very Parliament House, filled with bloodstained warriors, has become a 'shambles' (1.1.71) or butcher's shop: the motif of butchery is ironically echoed in Henry's lines to Gloucester, his murderer, as he faces him in his prison cell:

> So first the harmless sheep doth yield his fleece
> And next his throat unto the butcher's knife.   (5.6.8–9)

Edward's last line, the last line of the play, 'For here, I hope, begins our lasting joy', expresses a wish and not a certainty.

Between opening and close Shakespeare fills the bulk of his chronicle history with the representation of four battles: Wakefield where York was butchered, Towton where Henry was given his emblematic vision of the horrors of inter-necine conflict, Barnet where Warwick was slain, and Tewkesbury where the Lancastrians were finally defeated. Is there anything of a theodicy here, a justification of the ways of God to man, or is it rather a story of what Yeats called 'blind ambitions, untoward accidents, and capricious passions'?[1] There are some signs that in *3 Henry VI* Shakespeare was laying down markers that were to be taken up in *Richard III* where the intrigue and murder goes on, although in another (Senecan) dramatic mode.[2] Does the play depict a divided kingdom or, by implication at least, the agonised throes of a society fatally divided between monarchy and aristocracy? Does the play demonstrate that royal prerogative is mere fiction, necessarily subject, to use a term from Holinshed, to 'imbeciling' by the nobles?[3] It is up to a critic or director to find transfiguration – if that can be done.

Rather than beginning with a description of the 'transgressions against history'[4] of which Shakespeare has been deemed to be guilty in his Henry VI plays – his account, that is, of the period from the funeral of Henry V in 1422 to the murder of Henry VI in 1471 and the ransoming of Queen Margaret in 1475 – or a rehearsal of arguments over what parts of the plays Shakespeare may or may not have written,[5] let us consider what might have drawn him to this complicated chapter in the history of fifteenth-century England. Complicated it is, and so it was inevitable that its very wealth of incident led the dramatist to begin his career as a writer of 'history plays' by concentrating as much on actions and their outcomes as on personalities and their motives: he could not avoid investigating politics and the secular as well as morality and the theological.

Unlike the reigns of Henry V and Richard III, that of Henry VI was not dominated by the personality of its monarch – Edward IV's rule during the last years of Henry's 'reign' is stark evidence of this. Rather it was a period of war

---

1 'At Stratford-on-Avon' (1901), in *Essays and Introductions*, 1961, pp. 106–7.
2 See Dominique Goy-Blanquet, *Le Roi mis à nu*, 1986, pp. 366–79.
3 Holinshed, p. 272; for a succinct discussion of the debate over the royal prerogative in Tudor times, see G. R. Elton, *The Tudor Constitution*, 1960, pp. 17–20.
4 Theobald, IV, 390 n.
5 The play is first attributed to Shakespeare in the Pavier Quarto of 1619 (see Textual analysis, p. 201). The evidence summarised in Wells and Taylor, *Textual Companion*, p. 112, does little to dislodge the tradition that the play is by Shakespeare.

between nations (the Hundred Years War) and within the kingdom (the Wars of the Roses). It was also a time of dynastic strife which manifested itself in both aristocratic factionalism and popular insurrection, a sequence of contests between allegiance to the monarchy and alliance among peers. Shakespeare offered to the playhouse audiences of sixteenth-century London a deliberate rearrangement of historical events into dramatic themes. For this reason, therefore, the plays are best regarded not simply as 'adapted history' or as vehicles for dramatic biography but as a set of complex essays on the *politics* of the mid-fifteenth century – essays which, of course, also offer reflections on Shakespeare's own times. For it was only after he had in this way learned to convert chronicle into political analysis that he turned to the kind of history that thrusts personality out into the foreground of the action: *Richard II*, *Henry IV*, and *Henry V* were written after the Henry VI plays and *Richard III*. The great sequence of studies of the history and politics of England was not composed in the order of the chronology of her Plantagenet rulers.

THE LOSS OF FRANCE AND THE WARS OF THE ROSES
Henry VI came to the throne as a nine-months-old infant in 1422,[1] and, while he was a minor, England was ruled through a council, his uncle 'good' Duke Humphrey of Gloucester being Protector. Henry's reign began with some military success: John Talbot, first Earl of Shrewsbury, displayed conspicuous heroism on the field of battle, and the champion of the French, Joan, la Pucelle, was overthrown and burned alive (*1 Henry VI* 5.3–4). However, by 1453 the French territory won back for England by virtue of his father Henry V's heroic victory at Agincourt in 1415 (*Henry V* 4.1–8) had been recovered for the French by their king Charles VII, Henry VI's maternal uncle.

In *1 Henry VI*, Shakespeare moved from the funeral of Henry V through to the marriage of his son. He took us through a sequence of battles – at Orléans (*1 Henry VI* 1.2 ff.), Rouen, and Bordeaux (3.2 ff. and 4.2 ff.) – which led to a truce which was called at Tours in 1444 (5.4) and which centred on a politic marriage for Henry (arranged with an eye to his own benefit by the Earl of Suffolk) with Margaret of Anjou, a cousin to King Charles. Although *1 Henry VI* thus ended, unhistorically, with success for the English, Shakespeare demonstrated *en route* that the empire had been irremediably weakened and that this was principally caused by internal sedition.

Part 1, therefore, constituted a historical prologue, a demonstration of the way in which the Hundred Years War affected the Wars of the Roses which are dramatised in *Parts 2* and *3*. The title of the 'bad Quarto' of *Part 2*, *The First Part of the Contention betwixt the two Famous Houses of York and Lancaster*, therefore,

---

1 Ralph Griffiths, *The Reign of King Henry VI*, 1981, offers a modern history of the reign; see also K. B. McFarlane, *England in the Fifteenth Century*, 1982. W. G. Boswell-Stone, *Shakespeare's Holinshed, the Chronicle and the Historical Plays Compared*, 1896, reprints passages from the sources in the order Shakespeare deployed them; Peter Saccio, *Shakespeare's English Kings*, 1977, offers a modern account of the dramatic chronicle provided by Shakespeare.

EDWARDVS·   IIII·

2   Edward IV (artist unknown)

need not suggest that Shakespeare might have begun writing his sequence with the second play, but simply that he was following Holinshed, who clearly announced his intention of attending to happenings in England after he had completed his account of the Treaty of Tours:

Whilst the wars between the two nations of England and France ceased . . . the minds of men were not so quiet, but that such as were bent to malicious revenge sought to compass their prepensed purpose, not against foreign foes and enemies of their country, but against their own countrymen and those that had deserved very well of the commonwealth.[1]

The coronation, in 1445, of Margaret of Anjou as Queen of England marks the beginning of *2 Henry VI*. That play concentrated largely on the conspiracy of Buckingham, Somerset, and Cardinal Beaufort, Bishop of Winchester, to take power from Humphrey of Gloucester, Protector of the kingdom and father-figure to the king, and on the civil tumult of the Wars of the Roses. These had begun when Henry's cousin Richard, third Duke of York, laid claim to the throne. The claim was based on the grounds that York was the maternal great-great-grandson of Lionel, Duke of Clarence, third son of Edward III (1327–77), whereas Henry was great-grandson of John of Gaunt, Duke of Lancaster, the fourth son.[2] York chose as his badge a white rose, while the Lancastrians, led by York's enemy Somerset, wore red roses (*1 Henry VI* 2.4). (Henry VI's claim was further weakened by the fact that his grandfather Henry IV – 'Bullingbrook' – was commonly held to have usurped the throne and murdered the childless Richard II in 1400.) Moreover, rebellion broke out in Ireland, and York, who was assigned to put it down, took the opportunity to make his army serve his own ambition (*2 Henry VI* 3.1), winning the first battle of St Albans on 22 May 1455. This is depicted in the final sequence of *2 Henry VI*.

Part 3 begins when Henry is compelled to acknowledge York as heir apparent to the crown (1.1),[3] but York is defeated and savagely killed at the battle of Wakefield two months later (1.3–4), a battle in which the barbarous Cliffords played a prominent part on the Lancastrian side. The Yorkists were defeated again at the second battle of St Albans in February 1461 (2.1), but the Lancastrians then withdrew north while York's eldest son Edward was proclaimed as King Edward IV in London. The next month Edward marched northwards and won the battle of Towton, which established him on the throne (2.3–6),[4] and Henry took refuge in Scotland (his wife and son going into exile in France) until he was captured (3.1). He was imprisoned in the Tower (3.2) from 1465 until 1470 when he was restored to the throne by the 'kingmaker', Earl of Warwick (4.2 and 4.6). Warwick had been enraged by the news that Edward, 'taking counsel of his own desire',[5] had made an impolitic marriage with the widow Elizabeth, Lady Grey (3.2) while Warwick was abroad negotiating for the hand of a French princess for the new king. In April 1471, after losing the battle of Barnet, in which Warwick was killed (5.2–3), Henry fell into the hands of Edward again, and Queen Margaret was defeated by Edward's younger brother

1 Holinshed, p. 210.
2 See the genealogical table, pp. 224–7.
3 Historically this happened on 24 October 1460, but the play fuses the events of 1455 with this political capitulation by King Henry five years later.
4 The famous scene (*3H6* 2.5) in which the king sees a father who has killed his son and a son who has killed his father is fictitious.
5 Hall, p. 366.

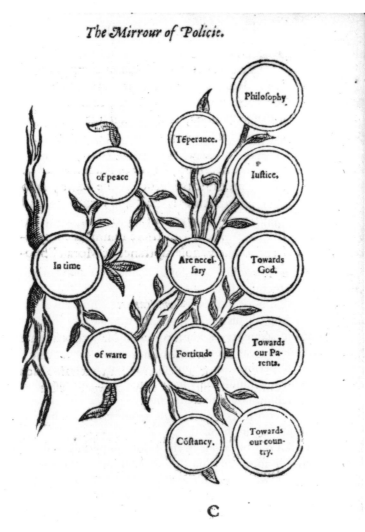

The Mirrour of Policie.

3 Kingly ideals. Engraving from the anonymous translation of G. de la Perrière, *The Mirror of Policy*, 1598

Richard of Gloucester at the battle of Tewkesbury the next month (5.4–5). Henry was recommitted to the Tower, where, on the night of Edward's return, he was murdered (5.6) – it is supposed by Gloucester.[1] The sequence ends with a brief appearance by Edward's twelve-year-old son, later Edward V, who, along

1 Contemporaries suspected that the murder was done at the behest of Edward: see A. B. Hinds (ed.), *Calendar of State Papers, Milan*, 1912, I, 157. Modern historians do not doubt that Henry died violently, possibly by order of Edward, but not necessarily at the hands of Richard of Gloucester (see Griffiths, p. 892).

with his brother Richard and at Gloucester's instigation, was also to be murdered in the Tower.[1]

The reign, then, was a pattern of disorder, a mirror for Shakespeare's contemporaries of the disastrous effect of dynastic strife, centred on personal ambition rather than any desire for reform, which could so easily have broken out upon the death of Elizabeth. Francis Bacon was to rejoice at the succession of King James, fearing that without it:

after Queen Elizabeth's decease, there must follow in England nothing but confusions, interreigns, and perturbations of estate, likely far to exceed the ancient calamities of Lancaster and York.[2]

Not only were there 'vertical' divisions between the noble factions: the reign witnessed division between the populace and the élite in the Jack Cade rebellion.[3] In his handling of this event, Shakespeare suggested that the rebellion could be construed as an attempt at revolution rather than as just a riot,[4] although the text also demonstrates the way in which political conflagration occurred when the horizontal divisions manifest in popular discontent were exacerbated by aristocratic dissension.[5]

To dramatise all this was massively ambitious, innovative – there were no popular plays on English history before the Armada in 1588 – and potentially radical. A dramatic sequence as long as this must also have created distinctive theatrical conventions – as modern revivals have demonstrated. It would have been expensive to perform in sequence without recourse to a standardised repertory style with some uniformity in costumes and with doubling – which may itself have made telling political comments on the action. These plays are not vehicles for star performers – although modern actors have amassed great reputations from playing in them.

Political plays fell out of favour in the Jacobean period, and in the eighteenth century the plays disappeared almost completely from the canon of performed works. Perhaps they were too radical and anti-establishment; the female characters, moreover, were not objects of sentiment but seekers after power.[6] The

---

1 See *R3* 4.3; Richard III, of course, was to be defeated and killed by Queen Elizabeth's Tudor grandfather, Henry VII, at the Battle of Bosworth in 1485, so uniting the white rose with the red.

2 *The Beginning of the History of Great Britain*, in James Spedding, R. L. Ellis and D. D. Heath (eds.), *Works*, 15 vols., 1857–74, VI, 276–7.

3 See *2H6* 4.2–3, 5–9.

4 See Hattaway (ed.) *2H6*, pp. 21–34.

5 For an account of the military power of aristocratic magnates in the 1590s, see J. A. Sharpe, *Early Modern England: A Social History, 1550–1760*, 1987, p. 160.

6 So we read in the introduction to Bell's *Edition of Shakespeare's Plays*, 1774: 'National transactions, however important they may be in their nature and consequences, are not likely to have a very popular effect, as they tend chiefly to indulge political reflection, but have very little to gratify taste. Such pieces as this are also very barren of female characters and affecting circumstances, without which the drama is too defective. Shakespeare has herein adhered to facts, and maintained just preservation of character, without producing one striking scene: it is not therefore to be recommended for representation' (VII, 89).

nineteenth century found them unsuited for performance with the naturalistic sets that were in vogue – and perhaps their analysis of empire was too extreme. In our own times literary critics have found them disappointingly based on narrative rather than significant structure, lacking both psychologically complex characters and the kind of verbal density that Shakespeare was to attain in his later plays. But this is to ignore the particular theatrical qualities – bold dramatic patterns, strong theatrical rhythms, the cumulative effects of deeply etched stage images – that modern directors have found in them, and their tough-minded anatomy of the political nation of England.

The play: 'what should be the meaning of all those foughten fields?'[1]

Part 3 will always be remembered for its scenes of death: those of the children Rutland[2] and Prince Edward, that of York,[3] those of the arch-enemies Clifford and Warwick the kingmaker, and that, finally, of King Henry. It may be that Shakespeare had in mind the chronicles of the falls of great men recorded in *The Mirror for Magistrates* – figures from the period of the Wars of the Roses count for about half the *exempla* found in the 1559 edition – but Shakespeare's treatment of their 'tragedies' is generally more complicated than that of William Baldwin and his collaborators.[4] As he has done throughout the sequence, Shakespeare explores not just the moral but the political dimensions of these noble lives. For despite the way that many die with a quotation or rhetorical figure on their lips, thus turning event into occasion, image into moral emblem, they may be simply cheering themselves up, dramatising themselves *in extremis* in a way that is not categorically different from the way their political antagonists had disguised their true motives under rhetorical shows of honour or com-passion. A political theme is announced in the second line of the play's second scene when Edward claims to be best at 'playing the orator': the proverbial phrase will be repeated on two other occasions.[5] Rhetoric was traditionally distrusted: in this play eloquence, like prowess in battle, is always seen as a means to power and, as we have hinted, a way of giving understanding at least to an audience exposed, through spectacle, to what is almost intolerable.

Part 2 of the sequence was much concerned with trials: significantly the word 'trial' does not appear in *Part 3* which is largely a succession of battles that stem

1 Holinshed, p. 273; compare Appendix 1, p. 210.
2 See plate 11, p. 37.
3 York's death scene was obviously celebrated and probably suggested the title of the octavo version of the play *The True Tragedy of Richard, Duke of York*. It is unlikely, however, that Shakespeare would have accorded the play this title, given that Richard dies in its first act (compare Textual analysis, p. 201 below). It was from this scene that Greene recalled the line 'O tiger's heart wrapped in a woman's hide' (1.4.137).
4 The title of Tragedy 13, for example, reads 'How Richard Plantagenet, Duke of York, was slain through his over-rash boldness, and his son, the Earl of Rutland, for his lack of valiance' (*Mirror*, p. 182). Baldwin ascribes the fact that it was a headless arrow that killed Clifford to divine justice (p. 195), and holds Henry responsible for his own misfortunes by virtue of his betrayal of Duke Humphrey (p. 218).
5 2.2.43, 3.2.188.

(a)

4(a and b)   Two emblems from George Wither, *A Collection of Emblems Ancient and Modern*, 1635, pp. 3 and 163. The mottoes on 4a read 'The law reigns and arms protect' and 'God is close[st]', on 4b 'By laws and arms'. Their implications are explored in Ernst H. Kantorowicz, 'On transformations of Apolline Ethics', *Selected Studies*, 1965, 399–408

from feuds. Ethical systems have been suppressed by political mechanisms of the crudest variety. In 2.4 and 2.6, for example, where we see the last fight and the death of Clifford, Shakespeare departs from the chroniclers who report that Warwick 'remitted the vengeance and punishment [for his brother's death[1]] to God'.[2] A few lines thereafter we read of the death of Clifford, shot through the neck by 'an arrow without a head': it is at least implied by Holinshed that his death is no accident but an act of divine retribution.[3] Shakespeare, however, has Clifford confront his Yorkist adversary Richard of Gloucester, and thereby

1 See 2.3.14–15.
2 Hall, p. 255; Holinshed, p. 277.
3 The text of Holinshed offers a marginal comment, 'Cruelty paid with sudden mischief' (p. 277); for other examples of these sardonic marginalia see Hattaway (ed.), *2H6*, pp. 31–2. Many were probably written by the antiquary Abraham Fleming (1552?–1607) whose name often appears in the margins.

(b)

suggests that his death depends not on a divine pattern but on the fortunes of war.[1] Even pious King Henry, who acts as a chorus to one of the central scenes of the play, that which offers a perspective upon the battle of Towton (2.5), and who views the world in idealised pastoral terms, does not, as we might expect in a pastoral, see the battle as a trial by combat,[2] but rather as an incursion of

1 The chroniclers also considered that Edward's perjury at York (4.7) was the cause why 'the issue of this king suffered (for the father's offence) the deprivation not only of lands and worldly possessions but also of their natural lives by their cruel uncle, King Richard III' (Holinshed, p. 305; compare Hall, p. 292). Shakespeare, however, makes Edward more of a machiavel than a perjurer and does not hint that this act will have great consequences. For an example from Hall of a providential explanation of Henry's misfortunes characteristically set sceptically against a secular one, see Appendix 1, p. 208.

2 For trials by combat, see Hattaway (ed.), *2H6*, pp. 14–15; J. Huizinga, *Homo Ludens*, 1950, pp. 93–5; Julian Pitt-Rivers, *The Fate of Shechem*, 1977, pp. 8–11; G. Holderness, N. Potter, and J. Turner, *Shakespeare: The Play of History*, 1988, pp. 16–32; Bacon, at the opening of his essay, 'Of seditions and troubles', uses a conceit that is strikingly similar to the one Shakespeare gives to Henry: 'Shepherds of people had need know the calendars of tempests in state; which are commonly greatest when things grow to equality' (*Essays*, p. 54).

violence from a hostile 'natural' world into the world of art inhabited by his imagination:

> This battle fares like to the morning's war
> When dying clouds contend with growing light,
> What time the shepherd, blowing of his nails,
> Can neither call it perfect day nor night.
> Now sways it this way, like a mighty sea
> Forced by the tide to combat with the wind;
> Now sways it that way, like the selfsame sea,
> Forced to retire by fury of the wind.
> Sometime the flood prevails and then the wind;
> Now one the better, then another best,
> Both tugging to be victors, breast to breast
> Yet neither conqueror, nor conquerèd:
> So is the equal poise of this fell war.　　　　　　　　　(2.5.1–13)

Warwick charges Edward IV with being a traitor (5.1.109), an action that, in a chivalric world, would draw an immediate challenge and a fight to the death. In this play, however, the battle between Edward and Warwick occurs, significantly, off-stage, and Edward comes from it to dump his dying adversary on the ground with as much ceremony as would be accorded a slaughtered wolf.[1] Family loyalties may have been the initial cause of the feuds, but an audience watching *3 Henry VI* is likely to feel that individual ambition rather than family honour is what fuels the vendettas that inform the play.[2] Both Henry and York seem to have forgotten that the quarrel between their families originally was a dynastic one: their claims to legitimacy and authority in this play are now validated only by the forces they can muster. Shakespeare suppresses the role of the great Council of lords spiritual and temporal which, upon consideration of both Edward's claim and Henry's abilities, and after consulting the Commons, decided that Edward ought to be king:[3] in the play the forces of the rival claimants simply slug it out.

Few characters in *3 Henry VI* seem possessed of the conscience exhibited by the antagonists in the later plays concerning the reign of Henry IV: Clifford, descendant of the Harry Percy (Hotspur) who appears in *Henry IV*, possesses none of his forebear's brio – he backs Henry, careless of whether his title is 'right or wrong' (1.1.159). Edward IV, praised by Sir Thomas More as a good and politic king[4] and beloved of the people, appears here only as an ambitious and lascivious warrior. Only Gloucester, the avatar of cruelty on the Yorkist side, a monster whose deformity is an index (and possible cause) of his sadism and

---

1 See 5.2.1–4.
2 See Alexander Leggatt, *Shakespeare's Political Drama*, 1988, p. 12.
3 Holinshed p. 272 (Hall, p. 253); see Appendix 1, pp. 213–14. There may, however, be memories of this in 3.3.117–18.
4 See Appendix 1, pp. 214–15; for a survey of Edward IV's reputation, see Charles Ross, *Edward IV*, 1974, pp. 418–26.

perverted will to power,[1] does offer hints of the psychological ruin that comes
from dreaming upon the crown. As in *Richard III* we find in his soliloquies
(especially that of 3.2.124–95) some material from which we might impute
a connection between his appearance and his personality (as opposed to his
motives). His sense of self is validated by no honour system based on ethics or
status, so that his proud proclamation at the end of the play might be regarded
ambivalently, as a kind of apotheosis, or as a register of the terrible toll his
ambition has wrought in him:

> I had no father, I am like no father;
> I have no brother, I am like no brother;
> And this word 'love', which greybeards call divine,
> Be resident in men like one another
> And not in me: I am myself alone.   (5.6.80–4)

'A mind courageously vicious may happily furnish itself with security, but she
cannot be fraught with this self-joying delight and satisfaction', wrote Montaigne
in his essay 'Of Repenting' ('Du repentir') – this seems to catch the tone of the
speech which may move as much towards wistfulness as well to 'Stoic self-
reliance'.[2] Richard's soliloquy, in fact, is one of the first examples in the canon
of a soliloquy which serves as a developed interior monologue and not just a
device for conveying information. He is moving from a sense of his own malice to
a sense of his own vice, defined thus by Montaigne: 'Malice sucks up the greatest
part of her own venom, and therewith empoisoneth herself. Vice leaveth, as an
ulcer in the flesh, a repentance in the soul which still scratcheth and bloodieth
itself.'[3] However, only in *Richard III* in his 'I am I' soliloquy[4] does Richard
exhibit that full conscience or repentance.

Deformity may give Richard a psychic energy, but it is his self-fashioning
Protean quality that gives him political power,[5] what he terms 'advantages'
(3.2.192).[6] In this play he addresses the audience directly after he has murdered
Henry (5.6.72 ff.), laying the ground plans for the schemes he will bring to
fruition in *Richard III*.[7] Ancient and Renaissance writers often addressed
themselves to the problem of tyrants and the politics of resistance against them.[8]
Having demonstrated throughout this trilogy that 'the elementary disease in rule
results . . . not from excess of authority in king or tribune, but from a loss of

---

1 Richard is not a diabolic character (compare E. M. W. Tillyard, *Shakespeare's History Plays*,
  1944, p. 195) or, necessarily deformed and to be read as an embodiment of 'the common
  Renaissance neo-Platonic notion that the physical body was a mirror of the soul' (G. L.
  Kittredge (ed.), *3H6*, 1969, p. xv).
2 John D. Cox, *Shakespeare and the Dramaturgy of Power*, 1989, p. 176; see Pitt-Rivers, p. 2, for a
  discussion of the meaning of the heroic formula *Soy quién soy* (I am who I am) in the plays of
  Calderón in the seventeenth century.
3 'Of repenting', *Essays*, trans. J. Florio, Everyman edn, III, 25.
4 *R3* 5.3.177–206.
5 See Leggatt, pp. 28–9.
6 Henry refers to him as Roscius, the great Roman actor (5.6.10).
7 Gloucester's rise to power in this play follows that of Suffolk in *1H6* and York in *2H6*.
8 See G. H. Sabine, *A History of Political Theory*, 1951 edn, pp. 322–7 and *passim*.

hierarchical identity, or rank, in the ruler',[1] Shakespeare begins to plot the emergence of a tyrant. The play ends with the birth of a new prince, seeming to portend future happiness but, after what we have seen of Richard, that ending and that happiness can only be provisional.

CHIVALARY, FEUDALISM, AND THE MONARCHY

The play, like its predecessors, begins with ceremony, two linked ceremonies in fact: Gloucester's violation of the head of Somerset, cut off in battle,[2] and Henry's entailing of the crown to York. These both have to do with rituals of honour; the former to do with the removal of honour, the latter to do with the bestowing of it.[3] Gloucester's act of desecration signifies the extinguishing of the residual chivalric code of conspicuous virtue, the eclipsing of honour by main force. It is a prologue to a play in which many more heads will roll, including, before long, that of Gloucester's own father York. The second, political, ritual, the entailing of the crown, registers an analogous cultural shift. York provokes the sequence by the ambiguous affront,[4] at once a threat and a theatricalised taunt, of sitting in Henry's chair of state, and the climax of this part of the scene comes with Warwick's line 'Resolve thee, Richard: claim the English crown' (1.1.49) – which acts as the cue for King Henry's entrance.

Now the word 'crown' occurs sixty times in this text, more than in any other play in the canon.[5] In Elizabethan English, the word 'ceremony' could mean both a ceremonial occasion and a talismanic object used therein. The process of entailing the crown (1.1.196–7)[6] takes away from any mystery or sanctity the object might have. It is desacralised, reified, no longer a metonym (here the adjunct of power) but merely a synecdoche (a part for the whole), a badge representing the material forces that sustain the king, an index of power rather than authority.[7] The scene in fact is yet another index of a change in a whole style of political thought, change from a sacred to secular concept of monarchy.[8] The king becomes not a man apart, but simply *primus inter pares*, and, as we see in the penultimate scene of the play when Gloucester stabs King Henry, this act

---

1 Alan Hager, *Shakespeare's Political Animal*, 1990, p. 10.

2 See *2H6* 5.2.65 SD.2–3.

3 See Pitt-Rivers, pp. 4–5, on the anthropology of these two rituals which have to do with the head (the word occurs twenty-nine times in the play); for a reading of the *kalos thanatos*, the beautiful death which Hal bestows on Hotspur in *1H4*, see Ann Lecercle, 'Epics and ethics in *1 Henry IV*', in J. P. Teissedou (ed.), *Henry the Fourth . . . pouvoir et musique*, 1990, pp. 191–218.

4 Pitt-Rivers, p. 7.

5 The word 'father' occurs sixty-eight times, far more often than in any other play in the canon.

6 Compare the way that, according to Francis Bacon, Henry VII avoided any act of entail to secure his right to the crown in 1485 (J. R. Lumby (ed.), *Bacon's History of the Reign of King Henry VII*, 1881, pp. 14–15); for a reading of the play that centres on the idea of the kingdom as property see F. W. Brownlow, *Two Shakespearean Sequences*, 1977, pp. 44–59.

7 See Michael Hattaway, 'For now a time is come to mock at form: *Henry IV* and ceremony' in Teissedou (ed.), *Henry the Fourth*, pp. 147–74.

8 See Ernst H. Kantorowicz, 'Mysteries of state: an absolutist concept and its late mediaeval origins', *Selected Studies*, 1965, pp. 381–99, and Robert Eccleshall, *Order and Reason in Politics*, 1978.

5   Act 1, Scene 1: York on Henry's throne by C. Walter Hodges. The scene shown here as
originally mounted at the Rose Theatre, Southwark, in 1592–3. Conjectural reconstruction based
upon the size and shape of the theatre's foundation, discovered and excavated in 1989

of killing a king is stripped of the sense of sacrilege[1] that we find in *Macbeth* or
even *Richard II*. Shakespeare's vision of late medieval England owes little to
romance, nostalgia, or any desire to evoke an idealised concept of order. It is a
sketch of a political world that is very little different from the anatomy of ancient
Rome that he was to return to later – as was Ben Jonson. 'Rome is but a
wilderness of tigers', proclaims Titus Andronicus:[2] so, in this play, is England.
(It was from ancient Rome that Bacon took most of his *exempla* for his essay
'Of Faction'.)

Just as in public life honour has declined into valour, virtue into *virtù*, so, in
private life, love and chastity have been supplanted by lust and lechery. As in

1 Pitt-Rivers, p. 14.
2 *Tit.* 3.1.54.

Titus Andronicus and *King Lear* images of political chaos are infused by images of animality and sexual licentiousness.[1] Edward who, according to certain modern historians, married the Lady Grey in order to build up an alliance that would check the power of Warwick and the Nevilles, is presented by the chroniclers and by Shakespeare as merely promiscuous and licentious.[2] Edward here plays the role of the dauphin who starts to seduce Joan La Pucelle shortly after their first encounter.[3] Likewise Margaret of Anjou (who, in *Part 1*, seemingly stepped into Joan's role after the latter was led off to be burned as a witch[4]) is scarcely a paragon of femininity but rather a virago, 'a manly woman, using to rule and not to be ruled',[5] one who empowers the vendetta, mocks York's grief for the murder of his son Rutland (1.4.84–93) and, as 'the better captain [than the king]',[6] is to be found at the centre of those 'foughten fields' that brought such chaos to the commonwealth. Joan had been hailed as 'Astraea's daughter' (*1 Henry VI* 1.6.4): Margaret too is associated with 'justice', but despite the lapidary weight of her rhetoric at Tewkesbury, a playhouse audience, having seen her cruelty in action, knows that this is indeed but rhetoric and comprehends the chilling truth that 'justice' can mean nothing without the firm politic control her husband was unable to impose:

> Lords, knights, and gentlemen, what I should say
> My tears gainsay: for every word I speak
> Ye see I drink the water of my eye.
> Therefore, no more but this: Henry, your sovereign,
> Is prisoner to the foe, his state usurped,
> His realm a slaughter-house, his subjects slain,
> His statutes cancelled, and his treasure spent:
> And yonder is the wolf that makes this spoil.
> You fight in justice: then, in God's name, lords,
> Be valiant, and give signal to the fight. (5.4.73–82)

A third recollection of *1 Henry VI* is provided by Clarence who, at Coventry, seeing perhaps that the sands of Henry are running out, justifies his defection to Edward on the grounds of kinship (5.1.81–102). It is significant that an act of 'perjury'[7] begins the act in which Edward will triumph, and we remember Joan

---

1 See, for example, York's diatribe against the queen (1.4.111–20) and the flyting match between Gloucester and Margaret (2.2.133–49).

2 See 2.1.41–2 and 3.2. Ross however, argues that Edward was led by desire rather than politics (*Edward IV*, pp. 84–8).

3 *1H6* 1.2.118–23.

4 See Hattaway (ed.), *1H6*, pp. 27–8.

5 Hall, p. 249; compare Holinshed, p. 268; Margaret may have served to evoke the sentiments aroused by John Knox against (Catholic) queens at the beginning of Elizabeth's reign: 'To promote a woman to bear rule, superiority, dominion, or empire above any realm, nation, or city, is repugnant to nature, contumely to God, a thing most contrarious to His revealed will and approved ordinance, and finally it is the subversion of good order, of all equity and justice' (*The First Blast of the Trumpet against the Monstrous Regiment of Women*, 1558, p. 9).

6 Holinshed, p. 260 marginal note; for Margaret, see Phyllis Rackin, 'Patriarchal history and female subversion', in *Stages of History: Shakespeare's English Chronicles*, 1990, pp. 157–8.

7 See 2.2.81 n. and 5.5.40 n.

6   Act 1, Scene 1: York on Henry's throne. David Warner, Donald Sinden, and Brewster Mason in
Peter Hall's 'Edward IV', 1964

la Pucelle's twitting of Burgundy ('Done like a Frenchman: turn and turn
again.'[1])

The extinction of justice in England, as we have seen, was one of the major
themes of *Part 2*: 'Set justice aside then, and what are kingdoms but fair thievish
purchases [pursuits]? For what are thieves' purchases but little kingdoms, for
in thefts the hands of the underlings are directed by the commander, the con-
federacy of them is sworn together, and the pillage is shared by the law amongst
them' – so St Augustine in *The City of God*,[2] laying down a tradition of Christian
political realism which, according to John D. Cox,[3] has been neglected by
literary and cultural critics who have sought to generate simple oppositional and
'radical' readings of Shakespeare. Whether Shakespeare was drawing upon the
historiography of St Augustine or reacting against idealising forms of political
thought from his own age, he was offering a suggestion that an examination of
the relationship between *feudal* ideals and opportunistic political behaviour might
tell us more about an age than, say Spenser's romanticising evocation of *chivalric*

1 *1H6* 3.3.85.
2 Trans. John Healey, 1610, 4.4, Everyman edn, I, 115.
3 *Shakespeare and the Dramaturgy of Power*, pp. 12–15.

ideals.[1] The sequence had begun with an invocation of Henry V, later to be celebrated as 'this star of England'.[2] Talbot was introduced in *Part 1* as an old-fashioned idealised chivalric warrior,[3] a champion of the nation rather than a champion simply of the monarch, the role adopted by Sir John Montgomery in 4.7 of this play. By *Part 3*, as we have seen, this kind of honour has declined into mere valour, and courtesy has been replaced by militarism. Edward laments that in killing York, his father, Clifford has 'slain/The flower of Europe for his chivalry' (2.1.70–1). However, the act provokes no justice in the form of trial by combat but the cold-blooded pursuit of revenge – the nobles become like Pyrrhus in Seneca's *Troades*. Now Hamlet considers the figures of Pyrrhus only to reject it as a model:[4] Clifford, Gloucester, and Edward have no such compunction. Their virtues are 'reckless courage, personal pride and self-respect... and on the other hand savage ferocity, deliberate cruelty, anger indulged in almost to the point of madness... the virtues and vices of Homeric heroes, not of Christian paladins as imagined in the ideal pictures of Tasso and Spenser'.[5] Warwick names Henry as a man 'In whose cold blood no spark of honour bides' (1.1.186), but the play gives the lie to the fancy that the honour of the war-lord has anything to offer the commonweal.[6]

The play's second scene sets out Gloucester's sophistical arguments which cause York to forget the oath he had sworn to Henry in the scene before:[7] this scene is the obverse of 2.2 where Clifford tries to get Henry to forget his oath and restore his son as his heir. Principle gives way to politics, and chivalry, in the context of this play, fosters the shedding rather than the saving of blood – it serves only to sustain a fiction of feudalism. Honour deriving from virtue has given way completely to honour as status: the king is he who wears the crown. It is significant in this context that Edward is denied a coronation scene: that would have raised, legitimated, and resanctified his authority. As Julian Pitt-Rivers writes:

1 See Malcolm Vale, *War and Chivalry: Warfare and Aristocratic Culture in England, France and Burgundy at the End of the Middle Ages*, 1981. Vale begins his study with a critique of the romanticising tendencies in Huizinga's *The Waning of the Middle Ages*, 1919; see also Maurice Keen, *Chivalry*, 1984, and Mervyn James, *Society, Politics and Culture in Early Modern England*, 1986. For Elizabethan neo-medievalism, see Michael Leslie, *Spenser's 'Fierce Warres and Faithfull Loves'*, 1983.
2 *H5* Epilogue 6
3 See Hattaway (ed.), *1H6*, pp. 28–31; for Elizabethan political chivalry, see Frances A. Yates, 'Elizabethan chivalry: the romance of the Accession Day tilts', in her *Astraea*, 1975, pp. 88–111.
4 See Michael Hattaway, *Hamlet*, 1987, pp. 88–90; for the *Troades* and *Richard III*, see A. Hammond (ed.), *R3*, 1981, pp. 80–1; for general resemblances between *3H6*, Senecan tragedies, and Elizabethan revenge plays, see David Riggs, *Shakespeare's Heroical Histories: Henry VI and its Literary Tradition*, 1971, pp. 131–9.
5 These phrases derive from the description by F. Warre Cornish of the history of the Crusades; see his *Chivalry*, 1901, pp. 24–5.
6 Compare Huizinga: 'Even if it were not more than a fiction, these fancies of war as a noble game of honour and virtue have still played an important part in developing civilization, for it is from them that the idea of chivalry sprang and hence, ultimately, of international law' (*Homo Ludens*, 1950, p. 96).
7 See Appendix 1, p. 213; compare Frances A. Shirley, *Swearing and Perjury in Shakespeare's Plays*, 1979.

thanks to its duality, honour does something which the philosophers say they cannot do: derive an *ought* from an *is*; whatever *is* becomes *right*, the *de facto* is made *de jure*, the victor is crowned with laurels, the war-profiteer is knighted, the tyrant becomes the monarch, the bully, a chief. The reconciliation between the social order as we find it and the social honour which we revere is accomplished thanks to the confusion which hinges upon the duality of honour and its associated concepts. It is a confusion which fulfils the function of social integration by ensuring the legitimation of established power.[1]

In *Part 2*, moreover, the effects of vendettas between the war-lords included the popular uprising which was taken over by Cade. *Part 2* gave us a rebellion which contained some elements of revolution.[2] In *Part 3*, however, the 'people' scarcely appear: constitutional change can take only one form, that of a *coup d'état*. York wants a coup: the moment when Warwick stamps his foot (1.1.169 SD) to summon the Yorkist forces is a Brechtian *Gestus* that demonstrates, by its theatricality, the paltriness of the moral and political issues at play. Chivalry is dead, justice extinct, and, as under the tyrant Ninus of Assyria, 'the people [have] no law but the king's will'.[3] The political community of England is no more.[4]

POLITICS IN THE THEATRE

History mediates between two worlds, that of the Plantagenets and that of the Tudors: Edward's embarrassed utterance 'And for this once my will shall stand for law' (4.1.50), made in the context of providing the Lord Hastings with a wife, obliquely gestures towards the problem, to become a vexed question in Tudor times, of proclamations which were *prima facie* instruments of absolute rule.[5] This play is conspicuous for the absence of both parliaments and people, the institutional and pragmatic checks on monarchical absolutism, and demonstrates the complete unsuitedness to kingly authority of any of the claimants to regal power. 'For when the authority of princes is made but an accessary to a cause', wrote Francis Bacon about 1597, 'and that there be other bands that tie faster than the band of sovereignty, kings begin to be put almost out of possession.'[6] It is as though Shakespeare was demonstrating by his epic of cruelty that the aristocracy needed either to be constrained by a strong monarchy or that a joint hegemony of monarchy and aristocracy was worthy of neither absolute power nor any kind of partnership in a political contract.[7] An extreme view would see the play as a plea for republicanism of the sort we find proposed in La Perrière's neo-machiavellian *Le miroir politique* (1555) which sets out in a schematic way patterns of political degradation: 'to live under the rule of one king or prince is a dangerous thing, in as much as it is a matter very difficult here in this world to

---

1 Pitt-Rivers, p. 16.
2 Hattaway (ed.), *2H6*, pp. 21–34.
3 Augustine, *City of God*, 4.6, 1, 117; Ninus was the 'Ninny' of *MND* 3.1.97.
4 Compare Edward Berry, *Patterns of Decay: Shakespeare's Early Histories*, 1975.
5 On proclamations see Williams, *passim*, and compare the wish of Dick the Butcher that the laws of England may come out of Cade's mouth (*2H6* 4.7.5).
6 Bacon, 'Of seditions and troubles', *Essays*, p. 56.
7 No one in Shakespeare's histories, however, argues against the institution of monarchy.

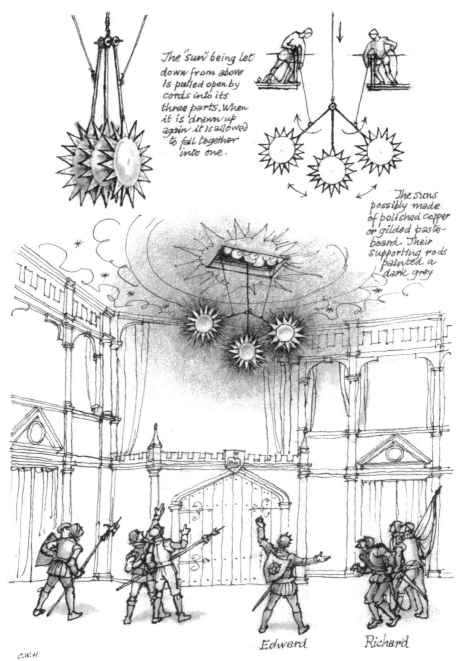

The 'sun' being let down from above is pulled open by cords into its three parts. When it is drawn up again it is allowed to fall together into one.

The suns possibly made of polished copper or gilded pasteboard. Their supporting rods painted a dark grey

Edward   Richard

C.W.H.

7   Act 2, Scene 1: the three suns by C. Walter Hodges. From the stage direction and following narrative description, it seems likely that the effect of the three suns which eventually merge into one was actually shown on the stage. The illustration here is conjectural.

find one so perfect in every respect as is fit and convenient for him that taketh the name upon him'.[1]

The play, however, could not sustain itself without, on occasion, turning from politics and switching to other modes, to elements of comedy and tragedy. Like *Richard III*, it contains a vein of black comedy. This tone is established in that opening ritual when Richard wins a vaunting match with his brothers in the first scene of the play, giving a cue to his father to taunt the remains of his adversary:

> RICHARD   Speak thou for me, and tell them what I did.
>   [*Throwing down the Duke of Somerset's head*]
> YORK   Richard hath best deserved of all my sons. –
>   But is your grace dead, my Lord of Somerset?   (1.1.16–18)

Later in the scene Henry, after the entailing ceremony ends with some pathetic self-dramatisation, plays the part of the hen-pecked husband:

> KING HENRY   And I with grief and sorrow to the court.
>   [*King Henry and Exeter turn to leave*]
>   *Enter the* QUEEN [MARGARET *and* PRINCE EDWARD]
> EXETER   Here comes the queen, whose looks bewray her anger.
>   I'll steal away.
> KING HENRY   Exeter, so will I.
> MARGARET   Nay, go not from me, I will follow thee.
> KING HENRY   Be patient, gentle queen, and I will stay.   (1.1.212–16)

As for tragedy, the vaunting politicians do not have the steeliness of will that marks a true tragical hero: after winning great victories over Henry at St Albans and Northampton,[2] York, perhaps a more reluctant rebel than he is sometimes portrayed,[3] settles for a political compromise,[4] and Edward, led by his desire, makes a politically disastrous match. His courtship of the Lady Grey is casual and flippant – the tone is caught by the equivocal asides of his brothers and his retort: 'Brothers, you muse what chat we two have had' (3.2.109). Nowhere in the play, unlike the Henry IV plays, do we find characters at ease with themselves and each other. Even in his death scene Henry treats Richard his murderer as a fustian player: 'What scene of death hath Roscius now to act?' (5.6.10): Richard, at his entrance, had set the tone by mocking Henry's piety: 'Good day, my lord. What, at your book so hard?' (5.6.1). The theatricalised dialogue suggests that

---

1 G. de la Perrière, *The Mirror of Policy*, trans. anon., 1598, sig. Bi[r].
2 See above, p. 6, and 1.1 n. below.
3 See Hattaway (ed.), *2H6*, pp. 40–1; notice how, in the first scene, he calls for support from his political allies three times in fifteen lines (1.1.28, 31, 43). Retitling the play *Richard Duke of York*, as the Oxford editors do (following the title of the unauthoritative Octavo version), has critical as well as textual implications.
4 Perhaps in the play he is cowed into compromise by the indomitable Clifford (see 1.1.159–62). Historically the lords seem to have been unwilling to accept the enormity of York's claim. The chroniclers report that his speech to the parliament was attended by 'prodigious tokens' when a crown which was designed to set lights upon in the Commons crashed to the ground as did the crown which stood on top of Dover Castle (Holinshed, p. 264; Hall, p. 248).

8   Act 5, Scene 1: the powers at Coventry, by C. Walter Hodges. For elaborate productions such as
the Henry VI plays, the available actors, apprentices, stage-hands, etc. probably totalled not more
than thirty persons. So in this scene the different contingents of the opposed armies are each
represented symbolically by the commander, his drum and flag, and perhaps one or two soldiers.
They enter and exit separately and are not seen all together at one time – there might therefore have
been opportunity for doubling

both men know that this act of killing a king is to be sordid murder and not a tragic ceremony.

Henry, in this fallen world, dies as a prophet (5.6.57), not as a tragic hero, paying the price for what made him good as a man but prevented him from being great as a king.[1] His peaceableness contrasts with the valour of the war-lords, his willingness to find a legal compromise to end the dynastic conflicts contrasts with their proclivities to summary executions. However, according to a long tradition, valour and justice largely defined 'what majesty should be',[2] and Henry was totally lacking in the first[3] and convinced that judgement ought to be remitted to God. Holinshed compared him with Julius Caesar – the similarities between their régimes were implicit in *Part 2*:[4] 'he was induced with those qualities of mind which the poet [Ovid, *de Ponto* lib. 1] ascribed unto Caesar (namely slow to punish, and sad when he was constrained to be severe, sith the one commended his lenity, the other savoured of tyranny)'.[5] When we see Henry as a political animal, he is either an ineffectual pacifist – 'frowns, words, and threats / Shall be the war that Henry means to use' (1.1.72–3) – or, in the Towton scene, one who has withdrawn into the contemplative life. As Alan Hager writes:

Warnings about the dangers of self-deposition of monarchs, contained in political parables in Sidney's *Arcadia* or in a number of Shakespeare's plays from *Henry VI* and *Love's Labour's Lost* to *Richard II*, *King Lear*, and *The Tempest*, appear throughout Elizabethan literature and political tracts. Such allegorical and expository animadversion aims, in part, I suspect, at the Spanish rulers' tendency to retire to religious retreat, in part, at a fear that Elizabeth may end up in doubtful deliberation with her own deputies in a time of crisis, such as during Philip II's long-planned invasion.[6]

But, to be fair, like Warwick in *1 Henry VI* and like Hamlet, Henry finds himself in a 'case of truth',[7] a dilemma which is impossible. Entailing the crown to York is a fine tactical device to prevent civil war, but it means disinheriting his son and losing the political support of his wife. Later he vacillates into passivity and puts the battle of Towton into God's hands, seeing it as a theodicy rather than as a power struggle, just as as he did in the Horner episode of *Part 2*. (Perhaps Henry felt some guilt: he, after all, had threatened that war would 'unpeople his realm' before he surrendered the throne to York.[8])

1 Compare Hattaway (ed.), *2H6*, pp. 11–14; at the time of the play's composition and first performances, Henri IV of France, the 'gallic Hercules', offered to Europe an image that contrasted completely with that of Shakespeare's Henry VI (see Yates, *Astraea*, pp. 208–14).
2 *Ham.* 2.2.87; see Ernst Kantorowicz, 'On transformations of Apolline ethics', in his *Selected Studies*, 1965, pp. 399–408.
3 In the chronicles it is different: between St Albans and Northampton (1455 and 1460), for example, Henry seems an active politician, a good tactician, and a stern judge. (After Bloreheath 'the king pardoned all the poor soldiers, saving certain ringleaders; for the which some he punished and fined, and some he hanged and quartered' (Holinshed, p. 253; Hall, p. 242).
4 See Hattaway (ed.), *2H6*, p. 69.
5 Holinshed, p. 256; compare Griffiths, p. 249.
6 Hager, p. 139 n. 4.
7 See Hattaway (ed.), *1H6*, p. 32.
8 See 1.1.126–30.

Hall and Holinshed also wrote of Henry's saintliness[1] and later in the play he proclaims himself if not a saint at least a peacemaker or comforter, reminding us of 'the life which has so often disappeared behind the mayhem of battle':[2]

> KING HENRY   Here at the palace will I rest awhile.
> Cousin of Exeter, what thinks your lordship?
> Methinks the power that Edward hath in field
> Should not be able to encounter mine.
> EXETER   The doubt is that he will seduce the rest.
> KING HENRY   That's not my fear; my meed hath got me fame:
> I have not stopped mine ears to their demands
> Nor posted off their suits with slow delays;
> My pity hath been balm to heal their wounds,
> My mildness hath allayed their swelling griefs,
> My mercy dried their water-flowing tears;
> I have not been desirous of their wealth,
> Nor much oppressed them with great subsidies,
> Nor forward of revenge – though they much erred.
> Then why should they love Edward more than me?
> No, Exeter, these graces challenge grace:
> And when the lion fawns upon the lamb
> The lamb will never cease to follow him.   (4.8.33–50)

The trouble is, of course, that while as a moral strategy these values might win the assent of the spectators, as a tactical device they are quite ineffective – as is revealed by the coup that follows immediately:

> *Shout within*, 'A Lancaster! A Lancaster!'
> EXETER   Hark, hark, my lord! What shouts are these?
> *Enter* [KING] EDWARD *and his Soldiers* [, *with* GLOUCESTER, *and others*]
> KING EDWARD   Seize on the shame-faced Henry, bear him hence;
> And once again proclaim us King of England. –
> You are the fount that makes small brooks to flow:
> Now stops thy spring, my sea shall suck them dry
> And swell so much the higher by their ebb. –
> Hence with him to the Tower; let him not speak.   (4.8.50 SD–7)

Henry was presumably captured by a ruse, breathtaking in its swiftness and signalling the extinction of a dynasty.

Shakespeare made much of the scene in which Richard murdered Henry, building upon rumour and Tudor propaganda. Yet again we cannot know his intention: it could be that dying at the hands of Richard, who fills the role of a scourge of God, is some retribution on Henry for his weakness as king.[3] It could equally be that Shakespeare simply wanted to register the power of the 'Machiavel' who, by studying men and occasions, was able, with the end of

---

1 See Appendix 1, pp. 208–10.
2 Leggatt, p. 26.
3 See Anthony Brennan, *Shakespeare's Dramatic Structures*, 1986, pp. 108–9, who points out that Henry is 'prominent almost by his absence', appearing in only twenty-two of the eighty scenes that comprise the sequence.

achieving the sole felicity of an earthly crown, to triumph remorselessly over the goodness of a true king. Henry, as we have seen, does not really achieve tragic status – there is no still point of recognition – although his death is moving. Margaret survives him. Of her Edward had exclaimed, 'A wisp of straw were worth a thousand crowns / To make this shameless callet know herself' (2.2.144–5), and it is doubtful whether she too achieves any recognition through her tribulations. At the end, however, she does portray the 'natural' feelings of a woman when she bemoans the murder of her son in terms that are refractions of those of York in 1.4.[1]

HISTORIOGRAPHY

Concerning history plays, Coleridge wrote:

The transitional link between the Epic and the Drama is the Historic Drama. In the Epic poem a pre-announced Fate gradually adjusts and employs the will and the Incidents as instruments ... while the Drama places Fate & Will in opposition [to each other, and is] then most perfect when the victory of fate is obtained in consequence of imperfections in the opposing Will, so as to leave a final impression that the Fate itself is but a higher and a more intelligent Will.[2]

Critics as well as characters have, however, cheered themselves up by seeing this 'historic drama' as possessed of a tragic dimension, perhaps an act in the theatre of a world in which 'Fate' or even a pattern of divine retribution is to be perceived.[3] Shakespeare's principal source, however, the chronicle of Raphael Holinshed, tended to read the events of the reign of Henry VI as part of a political and not a theological lesson. Holinshed, for example, reflecting after his account of the Duke of York, writes of

the rent regiment of King Henry, who (besides the bare title of royalty and naked name of king) had little appertaining to the port of a prince. For whereas the dignity of princedom standeth in sovereignty, there were of his nobles that imbeciled [dishonestly took away] his prerogative by sundry practices, specially by main force, as seeking either to suppress, or to exile, or to make him away: otherwise what should be the meaning of all those foughten fields from time to time, most miserably falling out both to prince, peer, and people?[4]

---

1 See Susan Bassnett, 'Sexuality and power in "Henry VI"', *Shakespeare Jahrbuch* (Weimar) 124 (1988), 183–91.
2 S. T. Coleridge (on *Richard II*), *Lectures 1808–1819 on Literature*, ed. R. A. Foakes, 2 vols., 1987, I, 283.
3 E. M. W. Tillyard, for example, sees Edward IV committing three major crimes (urging his father York to break his oath to Henry, lying to the Mayor of York, and stabbing his prisoner, the young Prince Edward) each of which, he argues, is 'enough to imperil himself and his posterity' (*Shakespeare's History Plays*, p. 189). For an account of a different kind of structural pattern see Sherman Hawkins, 'Structural pattern in Shakespeare's histories', *SP* 88 (1991), 16–45.
4 For Holinshed's secularising comments on the reign, see Appendix 1, p. 210; it might be contrasted with Sir Walter Ralegh's old-fashioned providentialist account (C. A. Patrides (ed.) *Sir Walter Ralegh: The History of the World* [1614], 1971, pp. 52–4), My reading of Holinshed and of Shakespeare's refractions of Holinshed make him much more 'modern' than he seems to F. J. Levy – see his 'Hayward, Daniel, and the beginnings of politic history in England', *HLQ* 50 (1987), 1–34; for a general survey of Shakespeare's chronicle plays and the new Renaissance historiography, see Rackin, *Stages of History*.

Shakespeare's history, like that of Holinshed, derives from the new historio-
graphical methods of the Renaissance.[1] It serves as an art of demonstration,
rather than, as it had been in the hands of medieval chroniclers, an art of inter-
pretation. The period was itself one of transition, and history, for Shakespeare,
was not a reproduction of 'truth' but was itself productive of truths, political
truths. Characters in the play interpret, ascribing the course of history to powers
beyond themselves – the word 'fortune' and its derivatives occurs twenty times in
the text – but these stand as exclamations not explanations. The text contains in
fact a multiplicity of histories.

Montaigne notes, in his essay 'Of Prognostications', that 'in public confusions,
men amazed at their own fortune, give themselves head-long, as it were, to all
manner of superstition, to search in heaven the causes and ancient threats of
their ill luck'.[2] Spenser, translating Joachim du Bellay's *Les Antiquitez de Rome*,
is tossed between two conflicting explanations of civil wars in Rome:[3] that
offered by Horace[4] that a bitter fate pursued the Romans as a consequence of
Romulus' slaying of his brother Remus, and another, more secular explanation:
that the desolation is caused by the blind frenzy of ambition:

> If the blinde furie, which warres breedeth oft,
> Wonts not t'enrage the hearts of equal beasts,
> Whether they fare on foote, or flie aloft,
> Or armèd be with clawes, or scalie creasts;
> What fell *Erynnis* with hot burning tongs,
> Did grype your hearts, with noysome rage imbew'd,
> That each to other working cruell wrongs,
> Your blades in your own bowels you embrew'd?
> Was this (ye *Romanes*) your hard destinie?
> Or some old sinne, whose unappeasèd guilt
> Powr'd vengeance forth on you eternallie?
> Or brothers blood, the which at first was spilt
> Upon your walls, that God might not endure,
> Upon the same to set foundation sure?[5]

The fall of great men in Shakespeare, however, is not inevitable – as in the
medieval writings that derive from Boccaccio's *De Casibus virorum illustrium* –
but unequivocally the consequence of political machination. Shakespeare makes
this plain by giving Richard of Gloucester, as he gave York,[6] a soliloquy in
which he sets out his political ambitions. For Richard in this play is a true
Machiavellian, 'a jolly statesman' who studies the conditions of men and their
fortunes, teaches 'how to tie / The sinews of a city's mystic body';[7] in *Richard*

---

1 For the secularism of the first two parts of the trilogy, see Hattaway (ed.), *1H6*, pp. 14–16 and
  2H6, pp. 7–14.
2 *Essays*, III.xi, p. 56
3 For texts dealing with civil war contemporary with *1–3H6*, see Hattaway (ed.), *1H6*, p. 33 n.
4 *Epodes*, 7.
5 William A. Oram *et al.* (eds.), *The Yale Edition of the Shorter Poems of Edmund Spenser*, 1989,
  p. 399, 323–36; see also 'Date and occasion', p. 54 n. 2.
6 *2H6* 1.1.211–56.
7 Donne, 'Satyre 1', 7–8.

III he plays a similar role but in a very different, providentially ordered, world, with the result that he is reduced to the bogyman role of the 'murderous Machiavel' (3.2.193) he designates for himself in this earlier play.[1] Many sixteenth-century writers of history were not interested in mystification or in letting chronicles remain as annals – as William Baldwin, writing a dramatic monologue for John Tiptoft,[2] Earl of Worcester, who served as Edward IV's 'butcher' when he was consolidating his position after the flight of Henry to Scotland, made clear:

> Unfruitful Fabyan followed the face
> Of time and deeds, but let the causes slip;
> Which Hall hath added, but with double [deceitful] grace
> For fear, I think, lest trouble might him trip:
> For this or that (sayeth he) he felt the whip.
> Thus story [history] writers leave the causes out,
> Or so rehearse them as they were in doubt.
>
> But seeing causes are the chiefest things
> That should be noted of the story writers,
> That men may learn what ends all causes brings,
> They be unworthy the name of chroniclers
> That leave them clean out of their registers
> Or doubtfully report them: for the fruit
> Of reading stories standeth in the suit.
>
> And therefore, Baldwin, either speak upright
> Of our affairs or touch them not at all:
> As for myself, I weigh all things so light
> That nought I pass how men report my fall.
> The truth whereof yet plainly show I shall
> That thou mayst write and other thereby read
> What things I did, whereof they should take heed.[3]

Shakespeare's political radicalism can be seen by comparing *3 Henry VI* with the *De Casibus* plays to which an earlier generation of critics likened it.[4] The anonymous *The Lamentable Tragedy of Locrine* (*c.* 1594) and *The True Chronicle History of the whole Life and Death of Thomas Lord Cromwell* (*c.* 1600), for example, provide appropriate comparisons.[5] Their subject and style are manifest in the dying aria of Estrild, beloved of the heroic but amorously fickle Locrine, just after her hero has killed himself:

---

1 On the two types of stage machiavel in the period, see Hattaway, pp. 143–4.
2 Although Shakespeare does not name him, Tiptoft may be identified as the Lieutenant of the Tower (4.6).
3 *Mirror*, 'John, Earl of Worcester', 22–42; for examples of Hall playing at 'this and that', offering alternative kinds of historical explanation, see Hattaway (ed.), *2H6*, p. 8.
4 The Henry VI plays are placed in this tradition by Willard Farnham, *The Medieval Heritage of Elizabethan Tragedy*, 1936, pp. 385–7.
5 For a study that examines the 'truth' of such texts, see G. K. Hunter, 'Truth and art in history plays', *S.Sur. 42* (1990), 15–24.

O fickle fortune! O unstable world!
What else are all things that this globe contains
But a confused chaos of mishaps,
Wherein, as in a glass, we plainly see
That all our life is but as a tragedy?
Since mighty kings are subject to mishap –
Ay, mighty kings are subject to mishap!   (5.4.116–22)[1]

Shakespeare eschews the moralising prologues found in both plays, the re-
venging ghosts,[2] or the series of allegoric dumbshows that centre on Ate, the
goddess of Revenge who appears in the former, nor does he place in the mouths
of his protagonists anything as patently choric as the following:

But whatsoe'er the Fates determined have,
It lieth not in us to disannul;
And he that would annihilate his mind,
Soaring with Icarus too near the sun,
May catch a fall with young Bellerophon:
For when the fatal sisters have decreed
To separate us from this earthly mould,
No mortal force can countermand their minds.   (*Locrine* 1.1.33–40)[3]

The language in these plays is generally heroical bombast mingled with the
conceits of clownage, and the characters are heroes or villains, constant lovers or
inconstant betrayers. *Cromwell*, the subject of which is described by the Chorus
as the Lord Chamberlain's 'height of rising and his sudden fall',[4] arranges
its characters in obvious categories of the good and the bad rather than, as
Shakespeare does, in political factions: the scholarly, generous, and charit-
able Cromwell is set against the scheming of Stephen Gardiner, Bishop of
Winchester. There is no such opposition between Henry and York or even
Gloucester.

As in *1 Henry VI*,[5] mythic ideals in speech are, in this last play, set against
the realities of conflict in action. A Messenger narrates the capture of York:

Environèd he was with many foes
And stood against them, as the hope of Troy
Against the Greeks that would have entered Troy.
But Hercules himself must yield to odds;
And many strokes, though with a little axe,
Hews down and fells the hardest-timbered oak.
By many hands your father was subdued,

---

1 Modernised from the text in C. F. Tucker Brooke (ed.), *The Shakespeare Apocrypha*, 1908. The
  theatrum mundi figure that appears in *3H6* 2.3.27–8, serves, paradoxically, to reinforce the sense
  of *agency* of the characters to which it is related.
2 The ghosts that appear in *R3* seem to me to be, like the witches in *Macbeth*, as much projections
  of the consciousness of the antagonists as instigators of the action.
3 Modernised from Brooke. The reference to Icarus in *3H6* 5.6.21 significantly works the myth into
  a political allegory.
4 4. Chorus. 9, modernised from Brooke.
5 See Hattaway (ed.) *1H6*, pp. 5–6.

> But only slaughtered by the ireful arm
> Of unrelenting Clifford and the queen . . . (2.1.50–8)

However, the audience has already seen the capture of York and it would be appropriate for a director to make that sequence far less heroic in the showing than in the telling.

STRUCTURE AND DRAMATIC STYLES

This is a play without a hero, a political essay that must, by virtue of its secularising point of view, remain a chronicle. In the event it is an extraordinarily deft shaping of shapeless material that might to a lesser talent than Shakespeare have seemed completely intractable for the theatre. Inevitably the story of the play is centred on its battles: on the first confrontations between York and Lancaster at St Albans, Northampton, and then Wakefield. The battle of Towton, as we have seen, marks a turning point where Henry, before defeat, shares with the audience his awareness of the horror of civil war. With that battle Henry loses the name but not necessarily the authority of king, and the next set of battles maps the practices and fortunes of rival nobles supporting rival monarchs. Although, after Towton, Edward has the ascendancy, *his* authority is weakened by his alliance with Lady Grey which not only costs him the loyalty of Warwick and Clarence but gives his brother Gloucester opportunities to cause even more factions to germinate. The Yorkists' decline is prefigured by 2.1 in which their vision of apotheosis, the three suns, is interrupted by news of their father's death.[1] Warwick the kingmaker achieves his apotheosis in Act 4 but his authority is quickly eclipsed when Edward soon escapes his clutches.

The symmetry of the conflict is marked by scenic quotation and juxtapositions which create simple dramatic ironies. The first line of Act 1, spoken by Warwick, 'I wonder how the king escaped our hands' is echoed by the first line of Act 2, 'I wonder how our princely father scaped', a moment when Edward does not yet know of the death of his father. In 4.5 Edward is sprung from captivity in Yorkshire by Gloucester and in the next scene Henry is released from the Tower of London through the agency of Warwick.

Tewkesbury marks a 'period of tumultuous broils' (5.5.1) and the extinction of the house of Lancaster. There is, of course, no 'restoration of order': 5.5 is notable for its combination of the customary rituals of revenge as Oxford and Somerset are led off to execution and the naked savagery that is displayed as a king stabs a child,[2] the heir to his rival. The scene that follows is given to Henry's final moments: it is notable that he is not given a still point for a rhetorical meditation that leads to recognition like Richard III or a long dying aria like Richard II. Instead he is cut off by Gloucester in the midst of an

---

1 See Hereward T. Price on the device of the interrupted ceremony in 'Construction in Shakespeare', *University of Michigan Contributions in Modern Philology* 17, 1951, and Hattaway (ed.), *1H6*, pp. 11–12.

2 It should be noted, however, that Prince Edward taunts the brothers York into killing him (5.5.33–7).

uncharacteristic curse. Richard then delivers his speech of recognition ('I am myself alone' (5.6.84)): Henry is denied even the consolation of tragedy.

After this pattern of conflict had been established, Shakespeare could, as he did in *1 Henry VI*,[1] resort to theatrical shorthand. As an example, let us take the eloquent dumbshow and noise of the episode when Edward is captured:

Warwick and the rest cry all, 'Warwick, Warwick!' *and set upon the guard, who fly, crying*, 'Arm, Arm!', *Warwick and the rest following them. The Drum playing and Trumpet sounding, enter* WARWICK, SOMERSET, *and the rest, bringing the* KING *out in his gown, sitting in a chair.* RICHARD [*of* GLOUCESTER] *and* HASTINGS *fly over the stage.*

This is followed by a passage of dialogue that contains many of the elements that are to be found throughout the sequence:

SOMERSET   What are they that fly there?
WARWICK   Richard and Hastings. Let them go; here is the duke.
KING EDWARD   'The duke'? Why, Warwick, when we parted
      Thou call'dst me king.
WARWICK   Ay, but the case is altered.
    When you disgraced me in my embassade,
    Then I degraded you from being king
    And come now to create you Duke of York.
    Alas, how should you govern any kingdom
    That know not how to use ambassadors,
    Nor how to be contented with one wife,
    Nor how to use your brothers brotherly,
    Nor how to study for the people's welfare,
    Nor how to shroud yourself from enemies?
KING EDWARD   Yea, brother of Clarence, art thou here too?
    Nay then I see that Edward needs must down. –
    Yet, Warwick, in despite of all mischance,
    Of thee thyself and all thy complices,
    Edward will always bear himself as king:
    Though Fortune's malice overthrow my state,
    My mind exceeds the compass of her wheel.
WARWICK   Then, for his mind, be Edward England's king,
                    Takes off his crown
    But Henry now shall wear the English crown
    And be true king indeed: thou but the shadow.   (4.3.27 SD–50)

Here is a rich mine of political game and verbal play: the setting of the name of duke against that of king, the play with notions of the 'shadow' and substance of authority,[2] Warwick's formal catalogue of complaints, Edward's self-deluding and self-dramatising invocation of Fortune[3] when it is obvious that he has lost his power through politic practice, and, finally, the Brechtian *Gestus* when

1 See, for example, *1H6* 3.3.28–36.
2 Compare *1H6* 2.3.35–7.
3 Edward, like so many others, exhibits the fundamental error of any sort of determinism, the supposition that because an event was historically caused to happen, it was bound to happen before it was caused.

Warwick removes the crown, a simple and brutal motion that undoes the opening ceremony of the play and symbolises the way in which authority rests upon material power. Marlowe made the point succinctly:

> But what are kings, when regiment is gone,
> But perfect shadows in a sunshine day? (*Edward II* 5.1.25–6)

The play dramatises an important constitutional question: is a subject's loyalty to the person or to the office of the sovereign? It is brought into focus, characteristically, in a short emblematic sequence where Henry VI, fleeing from the victorious Edward IV, is, like a stricken deer, captured by two forest keepers:

> My father and my grandfather were kings
> And you were sworn true subjects unto me:
> And tell me, then, have you not broke your oaths?
> 1 KEEPER No, for we were subjects but while you were king. (3.1.77–80)

On other occasions the style is equally rhetorical. Here Shakespeare deploys the figures of anaphora (repetition) and anthypophora (what Puttenham calls 'the response'[1]):

> 'Tis beauty that doth oft make women proud:
> But God He knows thy share thereof is small.
> 'Tis virtue that doth make them most admired:
> The contrary doth make thee wondered at.
> 'Tis government that makes them seem divine:
> The want thereof makes thee abominable.
> Thou art as opposite to every good
> As the Antipodes are unto us
> Or as the south to the Septentrion.
> O tiger's heart wrapped in a woman's hide,
> How couldst thou drain the life-blood of the child
> To bid the father wipe his eyes withal
> And yet be seen to bear a woman's face? (1.4.128–40)

This all takes place in an extended *vituperatio* which, with the lament,[2] is the pattern of extended speech most prevalent in the play.

The play is remembered not only for its chronicle of broils and deaths but for moments when Shakespeare turns from writing that tends to documentary towards highly patterned scenes or, as A. P. Rossiter once called them,

---

1 George Puttenham, *The Arte of English Poesie*, 1589, pp. 165 and 170–1. For a general analysis of the style of the play see Percy Simpson, *Studies in Elizabethan Drama*, 1955, pp. 64–9; Riggs, *Shakespeare's Heroical Histories*; G. R. Hibbard, 'The forced gait of a shuffling nag', in C. Leech and J. M. R. Margeson (eds.), *Shakespeare 1971*, 1972, pp. 76–88; Carol M. Kay, 'Traps, slaughters, and chaos: a study of Shakespeare's *Henry VI* plays', *Studies in the Literary Imagination* 5 (1972), 1–26; Ronald Watkins, 'The only Shake-scene', *PQ* 54 (1975), 47–67; L. C. Knights, 'Rhetoric and insincerity', and Wolfgang Clemen, 'Some aspects of style in the *Henry VI* plays', in P. Edwards. I-S. Ewbank, G. K. Hunter (eds.), *Shakespeare's Styles: Essays in Honour of Kenneth Muir*, 1980, pp. 1–8 and 9–24; James C. Bulman, *The Heroic Idiom of Shakespearean Tragedy*, 1985, *passim*.

2 See Wolfgang Clemen, *English Tragedy before Shakespeare*, 1961, pp. 211–86.

9   Act 2, Scene 5: the battle of Towton. An engraving by H. François Gravelot, in Hanmer, 1743,
IV, 194

'rituals'.[1] The most notable of these is the sequence at the battle of Towton (2.5) where the king witnesses a double recognition scene, that of a father who has killed his son and that of a son who has killed his father. (The pattern here of long speeches followed by single lines spoken in turn by each of the characters recalls effects more familiar in opera.[2]) Perhaps Shakespeare intended his audience to remember a sequence way back in *1 Henry VI* (4.5–7) where Talbot and his son fought and died together – that sequence was ritualised by being written largely in heroic couplets. For Henry, who needs no persuasion, Towton is yet another example of the pathos generated by war; for the audience it is set in a double perspective. They too share the misery of the survivors but also recognise how Henry's piety and yearning for the pastoral life are no fit qualities for a king.

There is a similar double perspective on the death of the Duke of York. The sequence was quoted visually at Towton: York died on a 'molehill', Henry viewed the battle from a molehill.[3] York's death was handled in different ways by the chroniclers, Hall confining himself to the 'facts' of the case, and Holinshed embellishing his narrative with details that turned York into a figure of Christ.[4] There may therefore have been specific allusions in productions with which Shakespeare was associated to the schematic figuration of mystery plays, possibly to Christian iconology. (The scene also contains echoes of the scene in Seneca's *Medea* where Medea confronts Jason with his dead sons.[5]) York's ascent to Henry's throne earlier in the play (1.1.49) may also have reminded audiences of Lucifer ascending God's throne in the mystery plays, and his death may have recalled scenes depicting the buffeting and scourging of Christ. Recognition of a scriptural or dramatic allusion, however, does not determine critical or theatrical tone. An alternative reading of York's ascent to the throne is that this simple, almost banal theatrical act turns a claim by right into a claim by possession[6] – we do not know to what degree these religious images were displaced from a religious to a secular level, just as we do not know whether Shakespeare conceived of York as a principled rebel or as a dogged fighter, driven by a combination of ambition and revenge.

In an analysis of these scenes, John D. Cox argues for a kind of transcendence,[7] but the scene worked quite differently in the production that started the modern interest in the plays: in 1963 Peter Hall's production for the Royal Shakespeare Company turned this into a moment of distilled cruelty as Margaret

1 A. P. Rossiter, 'The structure of *Richard the Third*', *Durham University Journal* 31 (1938), 44–75.
2 They are also to be found in Kyd's *The Spanish Tragedy* (see Hattaway, p. 121).
3 See notes to 1.4.76 and 2.5.14.
4 See Appendix 1, p. 213.
5 See Inga-Stina Ewbank, 'The fiend-like queen: a note on *Macbeth* and Seneca's *Medea*', *S.Sur. 19* (1966), 82–92.
6 Compare *John* 1.1.39–40.
7 See Cox, *Shakespeare and the Dramaturgy of Power*, pp. 94–5.

10   Act 5, Scene 6: Gloucester arrives to murder Henry. An engraving by H. Fuseli in Riverton's 1805 edition

and Clifford, in 'a deadly blood-supper',[1] smeared York's face with the blood of Rutland, his murdered son.[2]

The distinction between chronicle and ritual in the Elizabethan theatre may, in fact, be factitious. Rossiter argued that this sort of patterning really emerged in *3 Henry VI*, as a prelude to the formality of *Richard III*, the play that was to follow. But 'ritual' was present in *1 Henry VI*, in the scenes, written largely in couplets, that depict the deaths of Talbot and his son (4.5–4.7), and, less obviously perhaps, in the twin scenes in *2 Henry VI* which depict the deaths of Gloucester and Winchester. The distinction rests on the false premise that there was a degree of naturalistic representation in Elizabethan playhouses.

Modern spectators of *3 Henry VI* have in fact had two different kinds of experience of the play. They may have seen it on its own, or they may have seen it as part of a dramatisation of what has been called 'the first tetralogy' or even, somewhat misleadingly, 'Shakespeare's history cycle'. To those experiencing the play as part of a sequence, the conclusion to a long day of play-watching, the play might appear as something akin to a prolonged movement in a symphony, a remorseless exposition – or recapitulation – of a mood or thesis, coming before the highly patterned and more readily explicable *Richard III*. That is indeed part of the play's effect, but to stress its spectacular violence, its bouts of self-serving oratory, is to suppress its concentration on the nature of political groups and its continued anatomy of the relationship between political action and moral value. Does loyalty to a dynasty supersede loyalty to a country, can authority be retained in the presence of overwhelming power, can justice be preserved in a factionalised kingdom and, if not, is totalitarianism justified? These are some of the questions asked by the play.

Stage history

After performances which we presume to have taken place in Shakespeare's lifetime from March 1592[3] we know of no further performances before the closing of the theatres. In 1681 John Crowne's expanded adaptation of Acts 1–3 of *2 Henry VI* was produced by the Duke's Company at Dorset Garden Theatre with the title of '*Henry the Sixth, the First Part, With the Murder of Humphrey Duke of Glocester [sic]*'.[4] Crowne followed that with *The Misery of Civil War*, an adaptation of *3 Henry VI* which includes the Cade Rebellion of *Part 2*.[5] In July 1723 Theophilus Cibber produced a further compilation at Drury Lane made from material from Act 5 of *2 Henry VI* and Acts 1–2 of *3 Henry VI*,[6] and in

1 Hall, p. 251; for feasts of death in the second part, see Hattaway (ed.), *2H6*, pp. 31–2.
2 For the pattern of fathers and sons in the trilogy, see Hattaway (ed.), *1H6*, pp. 30–1.
3 See p. 53 below.
4 John Genest, *Some Account of the English Stage from the Restoration in 1660 to 1830*, 10 vols., 1832, I, 302–4; George C. D. Odell, *Shakespeare from Betterton to Irving*, 2 vols., 1920, I, 63–7; see also Hazelton Spencer, *Shakespeare Improved*, 1927, pp. 310–13.
5 Odell, I, 66–7.
6 Odell, I, 250–2; C. B. Hogan, *Shakespeare in the Theatre, 1701–1800*, 2 vols., 1952–7, II, 202–3.

11   Act 1, Scene 3: the death of Rutland. From the Boydell Collection

1795 Richard Valpy wrote a version of Acts 2–5 of *3 Henry VI*, entitled *The Roses*.[1]

The play was produced by Edmund Kean as part of J. H. Merivale's five-act adaptation, *Richard Duke of York*, 1817, a compilation of the three parts of the play performed at Drury Lane (with passages from Chapman, Marston, and Webster thrown in) from 15 December in that year.[2] Kean took the star part of York. Another abridgement of the three parts into three acts was made by Charles Kemble (1775–1854, younger brother to John Philip Kemble) but there is no evidence that it was published or performed in his lifetime.[3]

There were productions in Germany and Austria in the nineteenth century including a notable version at the Burgtheater in Vienna in 1873.[4] More recently German audiences have seen a performance of the trilogy as part of a 'cycle' by Franz Dingelstedt at Weimar,[5] a Brechtian production by Peter Palitzsch (*Der Rosenkriege*) in Berlin,[6] and a collage version of the three parts done by Georgio Strehler in Salzburg and Vienna.[7]

F. R. Benson produced the three parts of the play at Stratford on 2, 3, and 4 May, 1906,[8] *3 Henry VI* being performed for the first time in many years as 'the revival play' of the season.[9] The director used a permanent set which could yet be deployed in the service of illusion. So an anonymous reviewer wrote: 'There was no changing of scenery, except of portable furniture, the action was continuous, and the auditors were expected to exercise not only their attention but their imagination. "The Player's House" served for all castles and battlements and balconies: the arras and painted cloths for all backgrounds; curtains gave opportunities for concealment, and ordinary exits and entrances allowed a continuous stream of performers to pass over the proscenium.'[10] Another

---

1 See the reprint with an introduction by T. J. B. Spencer, 1971; for this and the earlier adaptations, see George C. Branan, *Eighteenth-Century Adaptations of Shakespearian Tragedy*, 1956.

2 Charles H. Shattuck, *The Shakespeare Promptbooks* 1965, p. 154; accounts are given in Genest, VIII, 636–41 and Odell, II, 128–30. It was not well received: see the review in *The Times*, 23 December, 1817, and L. L. and C. W. Houtchens (eds.), *Leigh Hunt's Dramatic Criticism*, 1949, pp. 180–2. A contemporary review from *The European Magazine* is reprinted by Gāmini Salgādo, *Eyewitnesses of Shakespeare*, 1975, pp. 86–7.

3 It is printed in *The Henry Irving Shakespeare*, 8 vols., 1888, III, 201–46. Sprague describes an uncut amateur production of *Parts 2* and *3* by the Hovenden Theatre Club in August 1959 that used only ten men and three women (A. C. Sprague, *Shakespeare's Histories: Plays for the Stage*, 1964, pp. 114–16); it was later performed at Cambridge (see 'Notice of production of *2* and *3 Henry VI*', *SQ* 13 (1962), 109.

4 See E.L. Stahl, *Shakespeare und das Deutsche Theater*, 1947.

5 See Robert K. Sarlos, 'Dingelstedt's celebration of the tercentenary: Shakespeare's histories as a cycle', *Theatre Survey* 5 (1964), 117–31.

6 See Anthony Vivis, 'Shakespeare without the shadows', *Gambit* 3 (1965), 96–9.

7 See Christian Jauslin, 'Das Spiel der Mächtigen: Georgio Strehlers Einrichtung von *Henry VI*', *Shakespeare Jahrbuch* (Heidelberg) 112 (1976), 15–22.

8 Benson's interpretative note is given by Sprague, p. 112 who also notes that the production is reviewed at length in *The Athenaeum*, 12 May 1906.

9 See Mrs C. C. Stopes, 'The acting possibilities of Henry VI – Part III', *Stratford-upon-Avon Herald*, 20 April 1906.

10 *Stratford-upon-Avon Herald*, 11 May 1906.

reviewer wrote: 'A conspicuous feature of the present revival is the care which has been bestowed upon what may be termed the historical and archeological side of the production. With an Irving-like minuteness of study of detail, Mr F. R. Benson has gone into this deeply and he has wisely secured the best of aid in transporting the atmosphere and colour of a brilliant period of history on to the stage.'[1] Benson himself took the part of Richard of Gloucester. A reviewer noted: 'even yet we have not fully seen the revival play performed, because modern stage methods and scenery take up so much time that the work of Shakespeare is cut, and we do not see the whole . . . After the play and the enthusiastic recalls, Mr Benson came before the footlights and made a short speech, apologising for any defects, and reminding the audience that the cycle had never been presented as a whole as yet on consecutive nights. He explained that we must read into it not so much of Shakespeare's dramatic construction as his philosophy of History and his patriotic desire to point out the evils of civil war.'[2]

In the United States Gilmor Brown directed the play for the first time at the Pasadena Community Playhouse in California from 25–27 July 1935 as part of a season which saw productions of all ten histories.[3]

A sequence of notable modern revivals began when, under Sir Barry Jackson, the whole sequence was directed by Douglas Seale at the Birmingham Repertory Theatre from 1951.[4] The sequence was played in London on successive nights at the Old Vic in 1953.[5] 'Douglas Seale was a director who knew what a clean thrusting style could do for a crowded chronicle. Hence the ultimate triumph at the Vic in Finlay James's setting of triple Gothic arches.'[6] Jack May played the king and Rosalind Boxall Queen Margaret. Seale brought the production again to the Old Vic, where it was played with *Parts 1* and *2* condensed into one performance from 16 October 1957.[7] In that season *The Times* reviewer

---

1 *Birmingham Express*, 2 May 1906.
2 *Stratford-upon-Avon Herald*, 11 May 1906.
3 Louis Marder describes a production of the three parts of the sequence condensed by Arthur Lithgow into a single one-act play and performed in August 1952 at Antioch Area Theatre, Yellow Springs, Ohio: 'History cycle at Antioch College', *SQ* 4 (1953), 57–8. See Peter D. Smith, 'The 1966 festivals at Ashland, Oregon and San Diego, California', *SQ* 17 (1966), 407–17 for a production of *3H6* by Jerry Turner; J. H. Crouch, 'The Colorado Shakespeare Festival, 1969', *SQ* 20 (1969), 455–8 for a production of *3H6* by Michael Addison; Foster Hirsch, 'The New York Shakespeare Festival, 1970', *SQ* 21 (1970), 477–80, for an account of a production of the trilogy by Stuart Vaughn; Alan C. Dessen, 'The Oregon Shakespeare Festival, 1977', *SQ* 29 (1978) for an account of a production of *3H6* by Pat Patton; and Joseph H. Stodder and Lillian Wilds, 'Shakespeare in Southern California and Visalia', *SQ* 31(1980), 254–74 for an account of productions of *2H6* and *3H6* by Keith Lawrence in Los Angeles.
4 Seale had begun with *2H6* in 1951; *3H6* followed in 1952 (22 July) and *1H6* in 1953 (14 July). See Sir Barry Jackson, 'On producing *Henry VI*', *S.Sur.* 6 (1953), 49–52; T. W. Kemp, 'Acting Shakespeare: modern tendencies in playing . . .', *S.Sur.* 7 (1954), 121–7; Kenneth Tynan, *Curtains*, 1961, pp. 181–3; J. C. Trewin, *Going to Shakespeare*, 1978, p. 20.
5 The whole sequence was reviewed in *The Times*, 15–17 July 1953.
6 J. C. Trewin, *Shakespeare on the English Stage, 1900–1964*, 1964, p. 225.
7 The reviewer in *The Times* felt that the London performances did not match the original ones (17 October 1957).

contrasted the magnificent declamation of 'the notable speech by the captured York' as it had been done earlier and as it was now delivered with 'quiet realism' by John Arnatt. He went on: 'The most lovely scene in the play is that in which the mild Henry meditates on the woeful mischance of war ... It is exquisitely lighted under an arrangement of Gothic arches which gives full effect to the symbolic figures of fathers and sons who have fallen in opposite sides in civil strife.'[1]

In 1963 part of the text furnished the final acts of the Royal Shakespeare Company's *'Edward IV'*, the second part of *The Wars of the Roses* adapted from *1–3 Henry VI* by John Barton and directed at Stratford by Peter Hall.[2] This was designed to be part of a revival of all of the history plays mounted to celebrate the Shakespeare centenary the following year. Barton not only cut passages, but added material of his own, usually derived from the chronicles.[3] In the programme, John Barton and Peter Hall wrote: 'We are sure that these early plays produced in an unadapted form would show to a modern audience the force of their political and human meaning.' The intention, moreover, was not to create star vehicles, but to establish a unified company style, played on a set that eschewed any kind of historical accuracy or theatrical glamour. The influence of Brecht's notions of history and the theatrical style of his Berliner Ensemble was manifest: 'Hall's policy? To fashion a company that can play together, to and with each other, with only the occasional use of stars with ready-made reputations ... Whatever distant historical ends these kings and nobles may be carrying out, it is their individual actions that are determining the sway of the struggle.'[4]

Although the conception of the productions was widely praised, many reviewers found the violence of the later parts of the sequence distasteful or disturbing – the sequence was revived at Stratford in 1964, the year in which the Royal Shakespeare Company first performed Peter Weiss' *The Persecution and Assassination of Marat ... under the Direction of the Marquis de Sade*. The kind of work the company was doing led to the season being associated not only with Brecht but with a 'theatre of cruelty'. 'In the second of the plays, *Edward IV*, the violence grows to a kind of white heat of blood lust as Yorkists and Lancastrians,

1 *The Times*, 17 July 1953.
2 For a general review, see John Russell Brown, *Shakespeare's Plays in Performance*, 1966, pp. 195–202, and for a pictorial record, see Harold Matthews, 'The Wars of the Roses', *Theatre World* 59 (1963), 11–14. A television version of this production was broadcast by the BBC: see Alice B. Griffin, 'Shakespeare through the camera's eye', *SQ* 17 (1966), 383–7. Barton's text *'Henry VI'* was performed at the Stratford Festival Theatre in Ontario in 1966: see Arnold Edinborough, 'The Canadian Shakespeare Festival', *SQ* 17 (1966), 399–402.
3 The text is given in J. Barton and P. Hall, *The Wars of the Roses: Adapted for the Royal Shakespeare Company from William Shakespeare's 'Henry VI, Parts I, II, III and Richard III'*, 1970; see Barbara Hodgdon, 'The Wars of the Roses: scholarship speaks on the stage', *Shakespeare Jahrbuch* (Heidelberg) 108 (1972), 170–84.
4 Bernard Levin, *Daily Mail*, 18 July 1963; compare Bernard Crick, 'The political in Britain's two national theatres', in James Redmond (ed.), *Themes in Drama I: Drama and Society*, 1979, pp. 169–94, who argues that Barton displayed politics as merely a desire for power and did not sufficiently explore notions of loyalty and honour.

12   Act 3, Scene 2: the wooing of Lady Grey in Peter Hall's '*Edward IV*', 1963

abandoning the council table, join the fight in earnest on the battle field where every battle ends in an orgy of savagery.'[1] 'Warwick, instead of merely commanding the beheading of Clifford [see 2.6], is given an axe and does the deed himself, flinging the head to Edward, so that it can take the place of his father's on the walls.'[2] '"*Henry VI*" with its string-pulling, power-balancing scenes, is a subtler diversion than "*Edward IV*" which is mainly carnage and cutlery.'[3]

Yet it was felt that the sequence had provided exemplary evidence of the Royal Shakespeare Company's economic and aesthetic ideals: 'The important overall qualities of the production, which would not have been possible under anything but a long-term plan and settled . . . conditions, are complete balance in atmosphere and performance; a sense of unity in aim and ambition; narrative swiftness and lucidity arising from common interest and integrity of purpose; and the force of performances that have an immediate effectiveness individually and in relationship to each other.'[4]

David Warner's much celebrated performance as the monkish king contrasted with that of Roy Dotrice who, as Edward IV, was clad in sun-covered golden

1 T. C. Worsley, *Financial Times*, 18 July 1963.
2 Charles Graves, *Scotsman*, 31 July 1963.
3 Kenneth Tynan, *Observer*, 21 July 1963.
4 R. B. Marriott, *Stage and Television Today*, 25 July 1963.

drapes. As Henry, Warner matched the high expectations raised by the earlier play: '[his] weak face twists self-depreciatingly as he slouches across the stage in apathy – and all the while Margaret's determination and despair are growing proportionately'.[1] 'One of the finest moments comes at his death, stabbed by the young Crook-back, with whom he exchanges a dying kiss: an inexplicably moving invention.'[2] Tynan described Henry's 'kind of wry affection for his assassin. I have seen nothing more Christ-like in modern theatre.'[3] One reviewer noted that Warner then quoted a visual moment from *2 Henry VI*: 'Mr Warner has two spectacular pieces of business – his fall down the steps of the throne after the announcement of Duke Humphrey of Gloucester's death[4] and his fall from the table on which he has been murdered by the newly created Duke.'[5] The forgiving kiss was also to be quoted: 'The gesture of forgiveness later became a curse; in *Richard III* Henry's ghost kissed Richard again, and Richard went into his final battle wearing the mark of Cain.'[6]

Peggy Ashcroft as Margaret playing amidst a wilderness of tigers continued to draw plaudits from the critics as she acted 'the wanton queen already despising the saintly king she has married . . . Among many superb moments . . . I shall long remember the speech she makes to her dispirited followers making their last stand. She summons some inner strength from out of the weariness of defeat and, though she speaks like a lioness, the beast in her, you can feel, is already dead. Marvellous.'[7] 'Hardly an actor left the stage alive without a wound draining down his face; some were beheaded on the spot and their unreal looking heads exhibited. York's death, the most bloody of them all, drawn out by Margaret's taunting – Dame Peggy Ashcroft wriggles and chortles with joyful revenge here – is the beginning of the play's downward drop to bloodbath level.'[8]

In this play the Yorkists occupy centre stage. Alan Brien described 'the three ravenous wolf-cub sons of the Yorkist claimant baying and snapping at each other in savage mock-battle around their castle rumpus-room . . . Roy Dotrice plays [Edward IV] with all stops out – a lecherous, brutal roaring whelp whose animal energy glows as hotly in his golden armour on the battlefield as naked in bed with his whore . . . Mr [Ian] Holm's Gloucester avoids any comparison with Olivier's. This is a reasonable, winning, personable boy, despite the withered hand, the buckled back and club foot, whose acrid humour is expressed in deadpan politeness rather than sardonic snarls. He has a past as well as a present – you can feel that he has been so smothered with affection at home that his

1 David Pryce-Jones, *Spectator*, 26 July 1963.
2 *The Times*, 18 July 1963.
3 Kenneth Tynan, *Observer*, 21 July 1963.
4 *2H6* 3.2.
5 Charles Graves, *Scotsman*, 31 July 1963.
6 Leggatt, p. 247 n. 35.
7 T. C. Worsley, *Financial Times*, 18 July 1963; see also Peggy Ashcroft, 'Margaret of Anjou', *Shakespeare Jahrbuch* (Heidelberg) 109 (1973), 7–9.
8 *Guardian Journal* (Nottingham), 18 July 1963.

13   Act 5, Scene 6: Ian Holm (Gloucester) and David Warner (Henry) in Peter Hall's '*Edward IV*', 1964

relatives no longer see the crippled body let alone the distorted mind.'[1] '[He] gives promise of an original King Richard III, a kind of manic-depressive, *un triste personnage* as the French crime reports would say.'[2] 'At the finish, where Shakespeare concludes with Edward's optimistic "For here, I hope, begins our lasting joy" Stratford has Richard Crook-back giving a snort of derision as he sits apart in contemptuous solitude.'[3]

Part of the acclaim won for the production derived from the set: 'It is a hard world – shaped in steel, John Bury, the present designer says. He has told us how he has tried to mark the English court by "thick enclosing walls", the English countryside by trees, and France by the use of copper. All is stern, metallic, and ringing. The stage is wide and bare, a sounding-board for fierce words and fierce deeds.'[4] The stage was backed by steel trellis work, and the 'walls' were great triangular structures faced with a pattern of rivetted plates, which could be moved like massive city gates. 'We seem to be claustrophobically caught between two swinging metal wings that crush us first from one side then

1   Alan Brien, *Sunday Telegraph*, 21 July 1963.
2   David Pryce-Jones, *Spectator*, 26 July 1963.
3   B. A. Young, *Punch*, 24 July 1963.
4   J. C. Trewin, *Birmingham Post*, 18 July 1963.

from the other.'[1] Prominent was a large council table which could be thrust out over matching stylised flagstones to the front of the stage, suggesting the domination of lords over monarch. 'The play is admirably produced to show us how behind the scenes decisions are cooked up to be ratified later at this table.'[2] 'The endless succession of sorties and sieges with clanking figures wrestling in half-light actually became restful interludes between the far more dramatic and exciting clashes of ambition and policy.'[3] Also thrust out was a 'push-on-push-off throne and dais... itself a miniature architectural masterpiece, oddly contemporary yet not without the dignity of history. It would have graced Coventry Cathedral or the Shell Building.'[4]

Instead of historical costumes actors wore uniform greys, blacks, and browns flecked with gold: '[the barons] are nicely differentiated but not in a fancy Guthrie fashion'.[5] Instead therefore of appearing as heroes in a divinely appointed saga they were operators within a specific political milieu.

The complete sequence of three plays was directed by Terry Hands at Stratford-upon-Avon for the Royal Shakespeare Company from 12 July 1977.[6] They were staged in conjunction with a revival of Hands's very successful 1975 Stratford production of *Henry V*: Alan Howard played both kings, father and son, to great acclaim. The productions were revived at the Aldwych Theatre in London in April 1978. The style of production, which was designed by Farrah, was again, like that of *Henry V*, epic in the Brechtian manner. The bare stage with stark simple properties but bold costumes was much praised.[7] The grass which had appeared on the bare stage for *2 Henry VI* disappeared: instead this text was played against a setting of camouflage. The director wrote of it: 'It seems to be taking place in a kind of Arthurian forest – light coming through the branches. Certain colours – like the roses – are constant, but in fact the productions are very simple in a scenic sense.'[8] The music by Guy Woolfenden did not always please: 'The speeches for the son who has killed his father and

1 T. C. Worsley, *Financial Times*, 18 July 1963.
2 T. C. Worsley, *Financial Times*, 18 July 1963.
3 Alan Brien, *Sunday Telegraph*, 21 July 1963.
4 Ken Griffith, *South Wales Evening Argus*, 19 July 1963.
5 T. C. Worsley, *Financial Times*, 18 July 1963.
6 The first night of *3 Henry VI* was 2 July. The story of the productions is told by Sally Beauman, *The Royal Shakespeare Company*, 1982, pp. 338–42; see also M. Billington, 'Shakespeare's dance to the broken music of time', *Guardian*, 17 April 1978, p. 8; B. Nightingale, '*Henry VI*', *New Statesman*, 94 (22 July 1977); J-M. Maguin, 'Review of Terry Hands' RSC Stratford production of Henry VI', *Cahiers élisabéthains* 12 (1977), 77–80; G. K. Hunter, 'The Royal Shakespeare Company plays Henry VI', *Ren. Drama* 9 (1978), 91–108; G. M. Pearce, Review of Terry Hands' RSC London production of *Henry VI*, *Cahiers élisabéthains* 14 (1978), 107–9; D. Daniell, 'Opening up the text: Shakespeare's Henry VI plays in performance', in Redmond (ed.), *Drama and Society*, pp. 247–77; H. D. Swander, 'The rediscovery of Henry VI', *SQ* 29 (1978), 146–63; R. Warren, 'Comedies and histories at two Stratfords, 1977', *S.Sur. 31* (1978), 141–53; J. C. Trewin, 'Shakespeare in Britain', *SQ* 29 (1978), 212–22; Carol A. Chillington, '*Henry VI, Parts I, II, III*. Produced by the Royal Shakespeare Company', *Educational Theatre Journal* 29 (1977), 566–9.
7 See Hattaway (ed.), *1H6*, pp. 50–1.
8 Simon Trussler (ed.), *Royal Shakespeare Company 1978*, 1979.

the father who has killed his son are accompanied by sad, woodwind music which, to my mind, distracts attention from their pathos, rather than amplifies it.'[1]

'[Hands] hasn't found an overpowering single image for the three plays, like the diamond shaped council-table that dominated *The Wars of the Roses* [see above]. But he has ... evoked a style that admirably suits chronicle plays. It's based on a minimal setting, roving spotlights, and a bold frontal style of playing that gives the actors a chance to establish direct lines of contact with the audience.'[2] Benedict Nightingale claimed that the productions succeeded 'without that editorializing, moralizing touch with has sometimes spoiled promising productions at Stratford'.[3] After the London revival, the critic of *The Financial Times* wrote: 'To my mind this is the best Shakespeare production I have ever seen. There is no scenery, no more than a token growth of grass [in *2 Henry VI*]; but there is a spare yet powerful use of props – cannon mostly in *Part 1* where the war is on an international scale, the Throne and the benches of Parliament in the other parts – and there are fine costumes devised so that the wearer is always recognizable.'[4]

Critics quickly singled out Anton Lesser's Gloucester for praise: 'Elfin-featured with a bright boyish grin, he becomes a deadly hobgoblin in action, radiating ecstasy on the battlefield, and relapsing into twisted dejection, compulsively scratching his leg, when he is unemployed. The great scene in this version is the killing of the king, staged against a raised metallic trapdoor and played as a verbal duel between Alan Howard, the prisoner, who has happily relaxed into contemplative inactivity, and an assassin whose only pleasure is in savage action.'[5]

Howard's performance continued to please: 'At first [Henry's] fractious nobles puzzle and pain him, but by the end he finds them almost amusing: their shenanigans are so easy to see through, and matter so much less than they suppose. He dies smiling, or trying to, a tattered, white-haired preview of the regenerate Lear ... Altogether, Mr Howard has brought off a perilous feat, not only to represent an unsentimental, unpretentious virtue, but to show it developing, maturing, deepening.'[6]

John Baker wrote of the Yorkists: 'It was a brilliant idea to equate treachery and perfidy with hopeless social gaucherie – one of the many felicities of Terry Hands' production.'[7] 'Emrys James's York, an increasingly balletic performance, expires almost in a dance of death. Julian Glover's Warwick now assumes the full authority of the kingmaker, a gold-armoured giant snatching the crown from the unworthy Edward's head as if it were a paper hat. Less convincing is

1 B. A. Young, *Financial Times*, 15 July 1977.
2 Michael Billington, *Guardian*, 17 April 1978.
3 Benedict Nightingale, *New Statesman*, 22 July 1977.
4 B. A. Young, *Financial Times*, 17 April 1978.
5 Irving Wardle, *The Times*, 15 July 1977.
6 Benedict Nightingale, *New Statesman*, 22 July 1977.
7 John Barber, *Daily Telegraph*, 15 July 1977.

14   Helen Mirren and Alan Howard in Terry Hands's 1977 Stratford production

the development of Helen Mirren's Margaret, which remains as flirtatious as
ever . . . and relies too predictably on the fatal erotic approach, cradling York's
head in her lap before she impales him, and even pleading for her own death in
the style of a bedroom invitation.'[1] 'Alfred Lynch plays lecherous Edward, his
love of luxury denoted in his fine white costume and the public caresses of his
queen (Anne Raitt), who sits on his lap while he occupies the throne.'[2]

A French adaptation – of the three Henry VI plays and Richard III – was
prepared and directed by Denis Llorca in 1978. It was entitled *Kings, ou les
adieux à Shakespeare*, comprised three parts, 'L'été', 'L'automne' and 'L'hiver'
(with a preliminary adaptation of the deposition of Richard II by Bullingbrook,
'Le printemps') and took the form of a twelve-hour performance that was
remarkable for its spectacle and symbolic structure. It was performed at the
Maison des arts André Malraux at Créteil near Paris in May 1979 after being the
centrepiece of the festival at Carcassonne the previous summer.[3]

The BBC's television version of the play was broadcast on 17 January 1983. It
was produced by Shaun Sutton[4] and directed by Jane Howell. For this, the
other two parts of the plays, and *Richard III*, a constructivist, anti-illusionist set
was used, a seemingly circular playing space – or playground – surrounded by
walls and galleries made of old doors and timber, suggesting perhaps the rickety
and improvised structures of institutions as Shakespeare portrayed them. The
director 'worked with her designers [Oliver Bayldon and John Peacock] to
produce a set suggestive of a brightly coloured playground, with Playcraft props,
"dressing up" costumes, and armour inspired by the shoulder pads of American
football'.[5] It worked well, far better in my opinion than those productions shot
on location or which used an illusionistic set.[6] In this play the stockade stood
blackened by fire, ravaged in the civil broils of the first two parts. The anti-
illusionist tendency was further marked by having soliloquies spoken directly to
the camera and by having Henry acting as an unseen presenter at the pageants of
the Battle of Towton (2.5).

This production was particularly notable for its battle sequences where
effective use was made of slow cross-fades, concentration on details like fallen
helmets, and balletic movement (particularly effective during the snow–fall of
the final battle at Tewkesbury (5.4–5)). The Battle of Towton was amplified by

---

1 Irving Wardle, *The Times*, 15 July 1977.
2 B. A. Young, *Financial Times*, 15 July 1977.
3 See Marie-Claude Rousseau's account of the discussion on the play at the Société Française
  Shakespeare (*Actes du congrès*, 1979), and reviews in *Midi Libre*, 18 and 19 July 1978; *La Dépêche
  du Midi*, 17 July 1978, *Les Nouvelles littéraires*, 20 July 1978; *Le Monde*, 5 August 1978 and 16
  May 1979.
4 Jonathan Miller had produced the first two plays in the sequence.
5 Robert Hapgood, 'Shakespeare on film and television', in Wells (ed.), *The Cambridge Companion
  to Shakespeare Studies*, p. 278; see also Henry Fenwick, 'The Production', *The BBC TV
  Shakespeare: Henry VI Part One*, 1983, pp. 22–3; reviews are collected in J. C. Bulman and H. R.
  Coursen (eds.), *Shakespeare on Television*, 1988, pp. 292–6.
6 See Graham Holderness, 'Radical potentiality and institutional closure: Shakespeare in film and
  television', in J. Dollimore and A. Sinfield (eds.), *Political Shakespeare*, 1985, pp. 192 ff.

15   Act 1, Scene 4: the end of York in the French adaptation by Denis Llorca (1978). Anne Alvaro plays Margaret and Jean Claude Drouot plays York

the use of mirrors:[1] long files of soldiers and cannon appeared effectively in painterly perspective. York and his crew entered startlingly by hacking their way into the playing arena, but York (Bernard Hill) had lost his panache. He limped in on a leg stiffened by wounds. Clifford (Oengus Macnamara) was an untheatrical warrior – more a pathological case – a short man who, unlike the others, wore a sweat-band round his forehead which gave him the appearance of an Indian brave: he bore an axe instead of a shield. Richard of Gloucester (Ron Cook) was also short but only mildly deformed. Mark Wing-Davey was a thoughtful plain-spoken Warwick, and Julia Foster a diminutive Margaret as fierce as a ferret at the beginning of the play, but increasingly tired and drawn, until, towards the end of the play, she was reduced to the clamorous but impotent choric figure she becomes in *Richard III*. The production ended with Edward IV and his warriors dancing triumphantly in a circle around Gloucester. He broke out from the revels, and the last shot was of him disappearing ominously through a blackened door.

In 1986 the English Shakespeare Company under the artistic direction of Michael Pennington and Michael Bogdanov began to mount, for a national tour,

1 See Jane Howell, Dominique Goy-Blanquet, and Michael Hattaway, 'Représentations télévisuelles de la guerre', in M. T. Jones-Davies (ed.), *Shakespeare et la guerre*, 1990, pp. 161–9.

seven of Shakespeare's histories under the title of *The Wars of the Roses*. The Henry VI plays were condensed into two texts: *Henry VI: House of Lancaster*, and *Henry VI: House of York*, the latter part of which contained *3 Henry VI*. The play received its first performance on 15 December 1987 at the Theatre Royal in Bath. Bogdanov directed and John Castle played York.[1] The plays were performed in a box formed by black screens, and much use was made of recorded music. The productions were notable for plain delivery of the verse and the clarity with which the action was delineated. (Scenes from the end of *2 Henry VI* and *3 Henry VI* were spliced together: the death of Old Clifford (*2 Henry VI*, 5.2) and Rutland (*3 Henry VI*, 1.3), for example, being juxtaposed.) None of the characters was manic, but all were morally blinkered. In the first play costumes and a certain amount of weaponry were taken from styles of the First World War although swords were also occasionally used. The second play evoked the styles of the Second World War – *Richard III* was to be set in Edwardian England. The men at the court of Edward IV wore white tuxedos and those scenes were punctuated by cool jazz: in contrast Clarence and Gloucester, along with many of the warlords, spoke with Yorkshire accents marking, as in the Hands production, a division between court and country. Elegiac music accompanied some of the most violent sequences of the production. Paul Brennen, a tall, thin, and almost totally bald actor played a lonely unpious king, dressed in a morning coat and quite ineffectual against the new militarists in their modern army uniforms. June Watson, dressed for the most part in the uniform of an officer from the Women's Army Corps, was a Margaret who was no vixen or harridan, simply an iron lady for whom there was no alternative to her own cause.[2] Charles Dale was an energetic Young Clifford, John Castle a bluff and sturdy York confident of the merit of his claim, and Richard Duke of Gloucester was played by Andrew Jarvis. He was a malign elf with pointed ears, completely bald (thus showing an eerie visual resemblance to his victim Henry in the penultimate scene), and dressed, for the most part, in a camouflage jacket. He played as a witty bovver-boy, by far the best performance of the sequence. The play ended with his coming downstage and speaking the first line of *Richard III* – after the infant Edward V had been brought on, 'this sun of York' was heard by the audience as 'this son of York'.

The Royal Shakespeare Company produced another adaptation, *The Plantagenets*, at Stratford in 1988, directed by Adrian Noble and designed by Bob Crowley. The three parts of *Henry VI* were condensed into two plays, '*Henry VI*' and '*The Rise of Edward IV*', in an adaption of a version by Charles Wood, the plays being performed as a trilogy along with *Richard III*.[3] The first half of '*Henry VI*' ran from the beginning of Shakespeare's *1 Henry VI*: the second half

1 The company released an excellent video of the production, recorded at a live performance.
2 Like Peggy Ashcroft, however, she smeared York's face with Rutland's blood in 1.4.
3 '*Henry VI*' was first performed on 29 September 1988, '*The Rise of Edward IV*' on 6 October 1988, and the trilogy on one day on 22 October 1988. In the programme for the production, Alan Sinfield offers an analysis of the ideological assumptions which informed the previous RSC productions by Hall and Hands.

from the last scene of *1 Henry VI* through to the end of Act 3 of *2 Henry VI*. *'Edward IV'* began with Cade (the Horner scenes having been cut), and the first half ended with the Battle of Towton (*3 Henry VI*, 2.5)

Design took a high profile in the production. A raked deep stage was used, covered with a grill from which smoke wafted up throughout most of the production, thus enhancing the elaborate lighting effects (by Chris Parry) that were deployed throughout. 'Huge bannered walls at the start of *The Plantagenets* blaze with lilies, lozenges, and lions in blue, red, black and gold, but the punctured floor steams like the sidewalks of Manhattan, as though . . . fifteenth-century English history . . . were one long dash across the crust of hell'.[1] During the short interlude occupied by the reign of Edward IV the stage was covered by a cloth and the stage was adorned with beautiful women.[2] The director said: 'One of the most interesting aspects of working on the plays has been looking at the way a human being of almost supreme power can recreate the world in his image. This can either result in the spiritual world which Henry VI tries to achieve in his rather naïve way, or the sensuous world which Edward IV appears to create.'[3] Under the iron influence of Richard Duke of Gloucester, the stage became black, white and grey and the savagery grew in intensity: Clifford's head was hacked off on-stage, an image that ended the first half of the play. Snow fell on the refugee queen, her women and children, at Tewkesbury and the cloth was to be pulled up the back to form a cruel white backdrop down which crimson splats of blood dripped into stark patterns. Michael Billington wrote: 'I had never noticed before how much these plays are about prophecy: everyone has a nightmare vision of the impending chaos they seem powerless to prevent.'[4] The costumes were elaborate and, generally, historically accurate, unlike the uniform styles devised for the earlier Stratford productions by Hall and Hands.

Although the cast was not consistently strong there were some fine performance among the supporting roles. 'David Lyon's Warwick is a steely study in expediency goaded beyond endurance . . . and [David] Calder's York passes from eager lithe aristocrat to grizzled warrior: he acquires the remote, impersonal look that comes with power, but retains a massive, craggy dignity to the end.'[5]

Ralph Fiennes' Henry attained a classic stature. When he was captured by the Keepers in 3.1 he was dressed as a pilgrim, still striving energetically for grace to be restored to his country. 'Instead of a holy simpleton he is a king with a stained-glass profile, a melodic voice and a passionate belief in the need for order: he is a militant pacifist hopelessly at sea in personal relationships',[6] 'a

1 Michael Ratcliffe, *Observer*, 30 October 1988.
2 They doubled as soldiers in the battle scenes which, because of cutting, reduced the dramatic contours of much of the rest of the play to a relentless parade of militaristic barbarity.
3 See Adrian Noble (talking to Michael Romain), 'Shakespeare on the war-path', *Observer*, 23 October 1988.
4 *Guardian*, 24 October 1988.
5 John Peter, *Sunday Times*, 30 October 1988.
6 *Guardian*, 24 October 1988.

16   Act 1, Scene 4: Penny Downie in Adrian Noble's 1988 Stratford production

man whose fatal flaw is not weakness but goodness'.[1] He died in the cage
beneath the throne occupied by Mortimer in 'Henry VI', executed by Anton
Lesser's Gloucester whose role in this play, 'a deadly urchin with a personality in

1 Francis King, Sunday Telegraph, 30 October 1988.

permanent overdrive',[1] turned into that of a sardonic psychopath as Richard III
– the role he had also played in 1977. Lesser was 'unfashionably (for a Richard
of today) indifferent to sex. Uncorrupted by social vices, he despises the idle
pleasures of his lewd, smirking brother, Edward (Ken Bones), flinging a flagon
of wine at the great sun, his mind always racing faster than the tongue can
speak.'[2] The audience laughed uneasily at King Edward's question 'Where's
Richard gone?' (5.5.83), knowing full well that nothing could stop his brother
murdering the king. This was no death in love: their actions were projected as
huge shadows by footlight spots onto the backcloth behind, making actual the
metadrama inscribed in Henry's question 'What scene of death hath Roscius
now to act?' (5.6.10). Henry's body was taken down in the cage as by a miners'
lift, and a huge white Yorkist sun was lowered to cover the blood behind. Penny
Downie as the queen who had been dressed in gold in her sensual youth, now
was dressed in shiny black, a jaguar-like Queen of the Night who, unable to
perceive that her husband's responsibility to his country had led him to dis-
possess his own son in favour of York, played the role of exultant executioner
when the capture of York enabled her to torment him with the death of his son
Rutland. 'This woman makes Lady Macbeth look like Mother Theresa, but you
can never quite hold her at arm's length. It is somehow possible to feel com-
passion for her, when her little son is butchered before her eyes [5.5], even
though you remember that the same woman was capable of daubing York's
face in the blood of his own dead boy.'[3] In fact the queen faints when Richard
offers to kill her in that scene (5.5.44). The last scene began with Prince
Edward brought in as a new-born babe: it ended, as has become customary, with
Gloucester ascending the throne and shouting 'Now . . . !'

Date and occasion

1 Henry VI, or a version of it, would seem to have been written and performed by
8 August 1592, the date of entry in the Stationers' Register of Thomas Nashe's
Pierce Penilesse his Supplication to the Divell.[4] There, in the course of a defence
of drama, the author offers a description of theatrical heroism as a 'reproof to
these degenerate effeminate days of ours'. He continues:

How would it have joyed brave Talbot (the terror of the French) to think that after he
had lain two hundred years in his tomb, he should triumph again on the stage, and have
his bones new embalmed with the tears of ten thousand spectators at least (at several
times), who, in the tragedian that represents his person, imagine they behold him fresh
bleeding.[5]

1 John Peter, *Sunday Times*, 30 October 1988.
2 Michael Ratcliffe, *Observer*, 30 October 1988.
3 Paul Taylor, *Independent*, 24 October 1988.
4 Arber, II, 292.
5 Nashe, I, 212.

This would seem to indicate that Nashe had seen, in a public playhouse, a play with Talbot as a central figure. It is reasonable to assume that this was a performance of the text that the compilers of the Folio present to us as being by Shakespeare,[1] because in 1593, when Nashe wrote another pamphlet, *The Terrors of the Night*, he included a number of expressions and images found in that text.[2] (Nashe might well, indeed, have written part of the play himself.[3])

On 2 September of the same year (1592), another pamphleteer and dramatist, Robert Greene, lay dying.[4] Later that month and shortly after his death another pamphlet was printed, *Greenes Groats-worth of Witte... Written before his death and published at his dyeing request,*[5] which contains a famous warning to gentlemen play-makers, the so-called university wits, to distrust the fickle nature of players, especially one:

> Yes, trust them not; for there is an upstart crow, beautified with our feathers that, with his 'Tiger's heart wrapped in a player's hide', supposes he is as well able to bombast out a blank verse as the best of you: and being an absolute *Iohannes fac totum*, is in his own conceit the only Shake-scene in a country. (sig. FI‍ʳ)[6]

The reference is obviously to Shakespeare who was, as may be inferred from this mock invective, serving as a player as well as a playwright – the phrase 'beautified with our feathers' means, probably, that he appeared in plays by Greene and his fellows. (The problem is whether Greene was pillorying Shakespeare's pride or alleging plagiarism – taking 'beautified with our feathers' to mean the latter.[7]) Moreover, the pastiche of the line from *3 Henry VI*, 'O tiger's heart wrapped in a woman's hide' (1.4.137), indicates that the third play of the trilogy was at least written by this date, and there is evidence, from verbal echoes of *3 Henry VI* in the anonymous *Troublesome Reign of King John*,[8] that Shakespeare had seen his trilogy performed by the time of the publication of that play in 1591.

As for the *terminus a quo* for the play's composition, there is very little evidence.[9] Now that the opinion of Chambers that Shakespeare made a 'late start' in his writing career has been strongly challenged,[10] it has seemed possible

---

1 For the authorship of *1H6* see Hattaway (ed.), pp. 41–3.
2 See C. G. Harlow, 'A source for Nashe's *Terrors of the Night* and the authorship of *1 Henry VI*', *SEL* 5 (1965), 31–47 and 269–81.
3 See Hattaway (ed.), *1H6*, p. 42.
4 The date comes from a pamphlet entitled *The Repentance of Robert Greene*, 1592, sig. D2ʳ.
5 Entered in the Stationers' Register 20 September 1592 (Arber, II, 620).
6 The controversies raised by this passage since Malone are reviewed by D. Allen Carroll, 'Greene's "vpstart crow" passage: A survey of commentary', *RORD* 28 (1985), 111–27.
7 We cannot tell whether Greene was alluding to vain or ostentatious crows described in Macrobius, Martial, and Aesop or, far less likely, a thieving crow in Horace's third *Epistle*; see S. Schoenbaum, *William Shakespeare, A Compact Documentary Life*, 1977, pp. 151 ff.; D. Allen Carroll, '*Johannes Factotum* and Jack Cade', *SQ* 40 (1989), 491–2 argues that there is a second allusion to Shakespeare in that Cade was known as 'Mend-all'.
8 See E. A. J. Honigmann, *Shakespeare's Impact on his Contemporaries*, 1982, p. 80.
9 For some circumstantial evidence see Hattaway (ed.), *1H6*, 4.7.61–70 n.
10 Honigmann, *Shakespeare's Impact*, pp. 70 ff.

that Shakespeare may have begun to write plays as early as 1584, and that the Henry VI plays may have been written soon after the publication of the second edition of Holinshed's *Chronicles* in 1587. Honigmann is prepared to conjecture that *1 Henry VI* could have been written as early as 1589.[1] I am inclined to believe that play was written before the other two parts of the sequence, at some date between 1589 and 1591,[2] although recent work, based on rare-word tests, suggests that it may have been written after them.[3]

The problem of when exactly *1 Henry VI* was first *performed* and by whom has given rise to a vast amount of enquiry and is intricately bound up with the question of the theatrical genesis of the other two plays in the sequence. The following account is the most probable: it is based on the premise that Shakespeare wrote the whole of the trilogy and in the order of the events it portrays.[4] (The part of the argument that follows concerning the play's theatrical provenance, however, is not invalidated by a proof that the play was written and performed after *2* and *3 Henry VI*.) It assumes that the Folio texts derive from holographic copy (see Textual analysis) and admits the possibility of some revision. It assumes that Shakespeare wrote the trilogy for performance by Lord Strange's Men.

On 3 March 1592 Philip Henslowe recorded taking £3 16*s* 8*d* at a performance of '*harey the vj*' put on by Lord Strange's Men at the Rose.[5] Ferdinando, Lord Strange, who succeeded his father as fifth Earl of Derby in

---

1 Honigmann, *Impact*, p. 88. Chambers argued that *1 Henry VI* 'was put together in 1592, to exploit an earlier theme which had been successful' in *2* and *3 Henry VI* (*William Shakespeare*, 2 vols., 1930, I, 292–3).

2 Charles W. Hieatt, 'Dating *King John*: the implications of the influence of Spenser's *Ruins of Rome* on Shakespeare's text', *NQ* 233 (1988), 458–63 finds a source for 5.1.83–4 in lines from *Ruins of Rome*, 24 (published in Spenser's *Complaints* between 29 December 1590 and 19 March 1591; see p. 27); however, the resemblance between the two passages does not seem to me to be sufficient to argue that Shakespeare's lines derive from Spenser.

3 See Wells and Taylor, p. 217.

4 Arguments concerning the authorship of *3H6* are reviewed by Wells and Taylor, *Textual Companion*, p. 112. My findings in respect of chronology are supported by Antony Hammond, the most recent editor of *R3* (see his New Arden edition, 1981, pp. 54–61), although it is possible that *R3* was written after the playhouses had reopened late in 1592, even after Shakespeare had worked on the Senecan material in *Tit.* (Wells and Taylor, *Textual Companion*, pp. 115–16). Wilson centred his contention that *1 Henry VI* must have been written after the other two parts of the sequence on two observations: that the six months between March and September offered Shakespeare insufficient time to write and have performed *2H6* and *3H6*, and that Talbot, the 'hero' of Part 1, is not mentioned in the latter plays (p. xiii). But this latter observation is predicated on a misleading literary premise, that plays must have heroes and that Talbot is here 'the' hero. It is also unlikely that Shakespeare would have conflated (as he did in *1H6*) two generations of the houses of Warwick and Somerset (see notes in the 'List of Characters'). Wells and Taylor also argue that the play was written after *2* and *3H6*: 'Internal evidence has suggested to most editors that *Part One* assumes a familiarity with *Contention* and *Duke of York*, which in turn require no familiarity with *Part One*. Rare vocabulary in the portions most securely attributable to Shakespeare link them most strongly (in order) with *Duke of York* [i.e. *3H6*], *Richard III*, *Titus*, and *Two Gentlemen*' (p. 113). Rare vocabulary tests, however, surely point only to possible near contiguities with, say, *3H6* and *R3*, which could obviously have been as easily written soon *after 1H6* as *before*. The Taylor chronology also rests on the assumption that *2H6* and *3H6* had already been written and *performed* before March 1592.

5 Henslowe, p. 16; for the company see Chambers, II, 118–27.

1593 was a patron of Shakespeare[1] and a descendant of the Lord Talbot who appears in that play.[2] As we know of no other play about Henry VI, it is reasonable to assume that this note refers to one of the plays from Shakespeare's sequence. Henslowe's entry bears a marginal note 'ne', but it is not certain that this designates a new play rather than one newly licensed by the Master of the Revels[3] – or else substantially revised. (It was unlikely to have been a performance of 2 Henry VI or 3 Henry VI since Henslowe regularly registered the first parts of multi-part plays only by their main titles, and indicated parts only for later plays in these sequences.[4]) There is, however, some external evidence to support the very reasonable conjecture that this entry records receipts for a play by Shakespeare. Nashe's Pierce Penilesse (which contains the passage about Talbot) is dedicated to Lord Strange, and contains an encomium of Edward Alleyn who at the time was the leading player of Lord Strange's Men.[5] The play, moreover, may well have been newly written – or, equally plausibly, revived – for events in the play parallel recent contemporary history: in the period from 1589 until 1591 three forces of English soldiers were sent to France in support of the Huguenot Henry of Navarre.[6] From October 1591 until January 1592 Englishmen under the command of the Earl of Essex participated in another, unsuccessful, siege of Rouen.[7] (It is extremely unlikely, furthermore, that there was a rival Henry VI play performing at the same time of which no record has survived.[8])

After this (first?) performance 'harey the vj' was performed fourteen more times until 19 June.[9] The comparatively high receipts for these performances compared with those from the plays that are not marked 'ne' in this sequence of the diary could further confirm the conjecture that the play was newly written or

---

1 E. A. J. Honigmann, Shakespeare: The 'Lost Years', 1985, pp. 59 ff.; Honigmann's findings contest the long-held and influential view that Shakespeare did not have anything to do with Strange's Men before 1594. For this see Peter Alexander, Shakespeare's 'Henry VI' and 'Richard III', 1929, pp. 188 ff. Sidney Thomas, 'On the dating of Shakespeare's early plays', SQ 39 (1988) contests Honigmann's findings but does not consider the evidence that derives from a comparison of the texts of the Henry VI plays (see below, pp. 59–61).

2 One of Talbot's titles is 'Lord Strange of Blackmere' (1H6 4.7.65).

3 Henslowe, p. xxx; Honigmann, Impact, 76–7, is extremely sceptical about taking 'ne' to mean 'new'. It could even be that the Privy Council Order of 12 November 1589 to the Archbishop of Canterbury, the Lord Mayor of London, and the Master of the Revels asking them to scrutinise all plays performed in and about the City of London because the players had taken 'upon them without judgement or decorum to handle in their plays matters of divinity and state' 'unfit to be suffered' (Chambers, IV, 306) made relicensing in 1592 necessary.

4 See Roslyn L. Knutson, 'Henslowe's naming of parts', NQ 228 (1983), 157–60.

5 Chambers, II, 120.

6 See 1H6 4.7.61 n; for a general account of possible topical interest see Bullough, III, 24–5 who on these grounds argues for composition in autumn 1591 or winter 1591–2.

7 See J. E. Neale, Queen Elizabeth I, 1979 edn, pp. 326 ff.; Bullough, III, 80–6, reprints extracts from the journal kept at the siege by Sir Thomas Coningsby. These historical analogues, however, offer no proof of the chronology of Shakespeare's early works and there is no reason not to postulate, as Honigmann does, a date of composition and performance as early as 1589.

8 See Hanspeter Born, 'The date of 2, 3 Henry VI', SQ 25 (1974), 323–34, and Peter Alexander's revised opinion, Shakespeare, 1964, p. 80.

9 Henslowe, pp. 16–19.

of topical interest. (It is worth recording that Strange's Men were performing Greene's *A Looking-Glass for London and England* and *Friar Bacon and Friar Bungay* during this same season,[1] which may explain that author's jealousy. (Greene therefore must have known *3 Henry VI*, from which he parodied the 'tiger's heart' line, from performances. It is unlikely that he would have quoted the line, given his satirical intent, if he knew it only from manuscript, or even, if the play was newly written, from rehearsal.)

Unfortunately these inconclusive entries are the only documentary material that would associate Shakespeare with Strange's Men, although Honigmann has recently adduced strong circumstantial evidence that would point to a long association with that company.[2] This helps to dispose of claims, made by those theatre historians who were uneasy about the Henslowe evidence, that there is a stronger probability that at this time Shakespeare was working for the rival Queen's Men with whom Greene also had an association.[3] (A recent advocate of this theory, G. M. Pinciss, argued his case from the presence of verbal similarities between lines of Shakespeare and lines from plays known to have belonged to the Queen's Men.[4] However, an author's knowledge of a company's repertoire does not imply that the author was a member of that company. Then as now players and playwrights presumably saw each other's offerings.)

Henslowe's season came to an end in June, for on 23 June 1592 the Privy Council forbade theatrical performances until Michaelmas[5] of that year, because of an outbreak of the plague[6] and the players were kept out of their theatres. About July – the documents are undated – Strange's Men, supported by the Watermen of the Bankside (who ferried members of the audience across the Thames) petitioned the Privy Council for leave to return from provincial touring to the Rose: 'forasmuch ... our company is great, and thereby our charge intolerable in travelling the country, and the continuance thereof will be a mean to bring us to division and separation'.[7] By 29 December, more entries in Henslowe's *Diary* indicate that they were installed in their playhouse again, and the relevant run of entries includes receipts from two more performances of '*harey the vj*' before it ceases on 1 February,[8] all theatrical performances having been again prohibited because of the plague.[9]

The arguments of many scholars who have investigated the problems of the Henry VI sequence have rested on the assumption that it would have been impossible for Strange's Men to have prepared all three plays for performance in the period between February (Henslowe records his first takings from what we

1 Henslowe, pp. 16–17.
2 Honigmann, '*Lost Years*', pp. 59–76.
3 See Pollard's introduction to Alexander's *Shakespeare's 'Henry VI'*, pp. 13–21.
4 'Shakespeare, Her Majesty's Players, and Pembroke's Men', *S.Sur. 27* (1974), 129–36.
5 Chambers, IV, 310–11.
6 Chambers, IV, 347–8.
7 Chambers, IV, 311–12.
8 Henslowe, pp. 19–20; the epilogue to *H5* (1599) notes that the Henry VI plays were 'oft' shown on the stage (13).
9 Chambers, IV, 313.

may now presume to have been *1 Henry VI* on 3 March) and 2 September, when Greene lay dying. (This is the nub of Dover Wilson's argument[1] and would seem to have been taken over by Cairncross who argues that all of the plays must have been *written* before the first was *performed*.[2]) However, as Bernard Beckerman, working from Henslowe's *Diary*, pointed out, 'the time between final purchase of the manuscript and the first indication of production extends from three to fifty-one days, the average duration being a little over twenty days'.[3] If the plays had not been written and performed before 1592, this would still have allowed ample time for the company to have prepared if not performed the whole of the sequence before Greene's death – that is between March and early September, 1592. Shakespeare may well have been finishing *2* and *3 Henry VI* during the spring of that year in preparation for a summer production which had to be cancelled because of the plague.[4]

There is confirmation for both these schedules in the Folio texts, which indicate that the manuscripts from which they derive were at least prepared for performance in a London playhouse rather than for the scantier theatrical resources of a provincial tour. All three parts of the sequence demand that scenes be played 'aloft': *1 Henry VI*, 1.4.21 (*on the turrets*), 1.6.0, 3.2.40, and 5.3.130 (*on the walls*), 3.2.25 (*on the top*), 4.2.2 (*aloft*); *2 Henry VI*, 1.4.11 (*aloft*), 4.9.0 (*on the tarras* [terrace]); *3 Henry VI*, 5.1.0 and 5.6.0 (*on the walls*). All three plays contain references that imply the use of tiring-house doors that could signify the gates to a city[5] or serve to build up a symmetrical stage image.[6]

But some time in the latter half of 1592 it seems that what Lord Strange's Men had feared did happen: while they were exiled from the Rose it appears that they divided,[7] and one group, under the patronage of the Earl of Pembroke, embarked on a provincial tour that began in October and lasted about ten months until the group had to return to London, pawn their costumes, and sell their playbooks.[8]

The fact that the 1594 quarto version of *2 Henry VI* is entitled *The First Part of the Contention betwixt the Two Famous Houses of Yorke and Lancaster* has encouraged some scholars to endorse the view that *2 Henry VI* was the first play in the sequence to be written. However, there are various equally conjectural arguments that can be set against this. Perhaps *The First Part of the Contention . . .* was

---

1 J. Dover Wilson (ed.), *1 Henry VI*, 1952, p. xiv.
2 A. S. Cairncross (ed.), *1 Henry VI*, 1962, p. xxxv; this is also the view of Bullough, III, 23–4.
3 B. Beckerman, *Shakespeare at the Globe*, 1962, p. 10.
4 This is also the conclusion of Born, pp. 328 ff. It seems legitimate to infer from 3.1.133 that in *1H6* the part of the king was taken by a boy player who would have surrendered his role to an adult for the later plays of the sequence. This might account for the way in which *2H6* and *3H6* were associated as a two-part 'Contention' play.
5 *1H6* 1.3.14 and 28 ('*the Tower gates*'), 2.1.38 ('*Enter several ways*' (indicating that each character was to use a different entrance)).
6 *2H6* 1.1.0 SD. 3–4, 2.3.58 SD. 1–3; *3H6* 2.5.54 SD and 78 SD.
7 Chambers, II, 129; however, Karl P. Wentersdorf, 'The origin and personnel of the Pembroke Company', *Theatre Research International*, 5 (1979–80), 45–68, argues that Pembroke's Men had belonged to the Queen's Men.
8 Chambers, II, 128; *Diary*, p. 280.

chosen as a more interesting title and one more likely to attract an audience than '*The Second Part of King Henry VI*'. It might also have been judged uneconomical to attempt the mounting of a three-part sequence in the provinces. Given that Henry has a small part in *1 Henry VI*, and a part likely to have been taken by a boy player rather than the adult who presumably took the role in the later two plays, *Parts 2* and *3* might have been rehearsed together. The sources also make a thematic distinction between their account of the Hundred Years War and the Wars of the Roses, even though in chronicle terms the two overlapped. After their accounts of the death of Talbot (see *1 Henry VI*, 4.7) both Hall and Holinshed make it apparent that they have finished with the wars in France and are picking up their pens to begin a new sequence, in effect, the contention of the houses of York and Lancaster.[1] There is no reason to deny that Shakespeare may well have thought of the play as *The First Part of the Contention* but equally no reason to disturb tradition and rename it for modern audiences. The title, in other words, seems to record the beginning of a sequence rather than the beginning of the trilogy. As Dr Johnson wrote: 'It is apparent that this play begins where the former ends, and continues the series of transactions, of which it presupposes the first part already known. This is a sufficient proof that the second and third parts were not written without dependence on the first, though they were printed as containing a complete period of history.'[2]

The name of Pembroke's company is on the title-page of the 'bad quarto' of *3 Henry VI*, *The True Tragedy of Richard Duke of York*[3] (1595) an octavo, on that of *Titus Andronicus* (1594), and *The Taming of A Shrew* (1594) – a bad quarto of *The Taming of the Shrew*[4] – as well as of Marlowe's *Edward II* (1592). *The First Part of the Contention* does not bear the name of a company on its title-page although the compilers of Q1 included in their text recollections of several plays Pembroke's Men owned including some of the above.[5] The Shakespearean texts, moreover, all show evidence of having been shortened and adapted for a smaller number of players. The presence of three of his plays in this group would confirm Shakespeare's association with the new company as well as the association of Pembroke's Men with the parent group, Strange's Men – which confirms in turn the preliminary assumption of this argument that '*harey the vj*' was probably *1 Henry VI*. It seems, however, that Shakespeare was not acting with the new touring group, for his name does not figure among those of the six sharers of the company.[6]

Further confirmation that *2 Henry VI* and *3 Henry VI* were written for performance by Strange's Men comes from the appearance of actors' names

---

1 Hall, p. 231; compare Holinshed, p. 237; reprinted in Hattaway (ed.), *2H6*, p. 225.
2 Johnson, v, 3.
3 This again suggests an attempt to disguise the fact that the play was part of a sequence.
4 See Ann Thompson (ed.), *The Taming of the Shrew*, 1984, pp. 1–3.
5 See Hattaway (ed.), *2H6* 1.4.23 n. and Appendix 2, p. 225.
6 See Mary Edmond, 'Pembroke's Men', *RES* 25 (1974), 129–36. Edmond shows that two of the other sharers had earlier associations with Henslowe. See also D. George. 'Shakespeare and Pembroke's Men', *SQ* 32 (1981), 305–23.

in speech headings. (There is no way of telling whether these derive from Shakespeare or the book-holder.) John Holland is named in *2 Henry VI*, 4.2 and Sincklo in *3 Henry VI*, 3.1. These in all probability were the same J. Holland and John 'Sincler' whose names appear in the 'plot' of *2 Seven Deadly Sins* which Greg conjectures to have been performed by Strange's Men at the Curtain, probably in 1590.[1] A third player is named in *3 Henry VI*, 3.1 simply as 'Humphrey'. The only known player of the period with this name is Humphrey Jeffes whose name occurs frequently in Henslowe's diary, but only from 1597. Recently W. Schrickx found a record of the date of his birth (23 December 1576) and conjectures that he was abroad from 1592.[2] This small piece of evidence would push back the beginning of the period of composition to some time before that date and confirm the conjecture that although the three plays may all have been written for Strange's Men, only the first part was performed by them for the reasons given above.

The hypothesis that would follow from this arugment would be that *The First Part of the Contention* and *The True Tragedy* which are adaptations of *2 Henry VI* and *3 Henry VI*, were designed for the provincial tour. Strange's Men would have retained ownership of the 'books' of these plays but may have allowed some of their ex-members to prepare the abridgements. David George has accumulated a list of fifteen players who could have been included in the 1592 Pembroke company;[3] the number of players required for 2.3 of *The First Part of the Contention* is eighteen, the same number as that required for 1.1 of *The True Tragedy*[4] and the Quarto version of *Richard III*.[5] (This number allows for only two extras and includes two boys' parts.[6]) It is possible, then, that there were at least three more players in the group who have left no trace. This would have been a slightly larger group than usual: a text like the 1600 Quarto of *Henry V* that may derive ultimately from a touring performance requires fifteen players.[7]

---

1 W. W. Greg, *Elizabethan Dramatic Documents*, 1931, p. 113; see also B. Morris (ed.), *The Taming of the Shrew*, 1981, pp. 49–50. George Bevis, who appears in 4.2. and 4.7 of *2H6*, does not appear in this 'plot'. Andrew Gurr notes that 'There is also a "Nicke" in that list who may be the same as the "Nicke" named in the Cade scene in the pirated text of *2 Henry VI* [*1 Contention* TLN 1551 etc.] and in *The Taming of the Shrew* (3.1.82)', *The Shakespearean Stage 1574–1642*, 1970, p. 26. He may be the Nicholas Tooley named among the players listed at the beginning of the First Folio. Saunder (Simpcox) of *2H6* may have been played by Alexander Cooke whose name also appears in the 'plot' – 'Saunder' being an abbreviated form of 'Alexander'.
2 W. Schrickx, 'English actors at the courts of Wolfenbüttel . . .', *S.Sur. 33* (1980), 153–68.
3 David George, 'Shakespeare and Pembroke's Men', p. 313.
4 A. C. Sprague, *Shakespeare's Histories*, calculated that thirteen players were needed for *1H6* (p. 114).
5 See Hammond (ed.), *R3*, p. 65; twenty-seven players are required for *Titus Andronicus* – see E. Waith (ed.), *Tit.*, 1984, pp. 216–17.
6 The arguments of Scott McMillin, 'Casting for Pembroke's Men: the *Henry VI* quartos and *The Taming of A Shrew*', *SQ* 23 (1972), 141–59 must be considered invalid as he inexplicably discounts 'bit' parts, 'defined as roles of [less] than ten lines altogether'. His article does contain, however, useful descriptions of the regrouping of Strange's Men as Pembroke's Men.
7 A calculation communicated to me privately by Andrew Gurr. However, Gary Taylor argues for only eleven players: see Stanley Wells and Gary Taylor, *Modernizing Shakespeare's Text*, 1979, pp. 72 ff.

But a largish company *is* conceivable, given the fact that many players would have been driven out of the metropolis by the plague.

There is, however, some evidence in the stage directions of *The First Part of the Contention* which might suggest that the text *recalls* performance in a London playhouse:[1] two doors are stipulated in 1.1, 2.3, 4.10, and 5.1 (TLN 1, 4; 847, 850; 1927; 2062, 2063); there is a possible reference to a discovery space in 3.2, alarms are sounded 'within' in 4.1 (TLN 1463), and 1.4 demands three levels since Dame Eleanor goes *up to the tower* (TLN 488) and exits *above* (TLN 533), while a spirit *riseth up* (TLN 507), presumably from a cellarage. Likewise *The True Tragedy* seems to demand a tiring-house: two entrances are called for (2.4.0 SD),[2] a post is sounded *within* (3.3.160 SD), a functional door is required (*The Mayor opens the door and brings the keys in his hand* [4.7.34 SD]), and 'chambers' are discharged (5.4.82.1 SD).[3] Other stage directions suggest a stage gallery: 'three suns' appear presumably lowered from above (2.1.20 SD) and an upper playing area is used in 5.1 and in 5.6 which are set '*on the walls*' and '*in the Tower*'[4] respectively. Unless *2* and *3 Henry VI* had in fact been performed at the Rose by June we have to conjecture that the compilers of these texts were players recalling actions worked out in rehearsals – or that the stage directions are the relics of performances designed for halls. The recollections of *1 Henry VI* which appear in the texts of both the second and third plays,[5] also allow us to conjecture that these texts were compiled while memories of London performances of *Part 1* were still fresh.

The conclusion must be that the whole sequence was *written* some time before March 1592. If it was written late, circumstances may have conspired to prevent the *production* in that season of the second and third parts of the play. The quartos may represent a condensation of Shakespeare texts for performance in one afternoon, either planned but not performed for London, or planned and performed in the provinces.

Sources

In *1 Henry VI*, it could be demonstrated, Shakespeare used the 1587 edition of Holinshed[6] as his main source with some recourse to Hall, Fabyan, and others. The material he covered ran from the funeral of Henry V in 1422 to the

---

1 My arguments are confirmed by William Montgomery's Oxford D. Phil. thesis, *The Contention of York and Lancaster: A Critical Edition*, 1985; see also Wells and Taylor, *Textual Companion*, p. 176, and William Montgomery, 'The original staging of *The First Part of the Contention* (1594)', *S.Sur. 41* (1988), 13–22. This article also contains a detailed analysis of problems of doubling.

2 'Alarmes, and then enter *Richard* at one dore and *Clifford* at the other' (O, sig. C2ʳ).

3 See Hattaway (ed.), *1H6*, Illustration 5, p. 19.

4 See 5.6 0 SD n.

5 See Hattaway (ed.), *2H6*, p. 237, and Appendix 2, p. 221.

6 For an account of the way that edition was censored, see Elizabeth Story Donno, 'Some aspects of Shakespeare's Holinshed', *HLQ* 50 (1987), 229–48.

betrothal of Henry VI in 1446, and included the death of Talbot which historically occurred seven years later, in 1453. In *2 Henry VI* he doubled back a
little to include Eleanor's penance which was imposed in 1442, but took the
action forward from Margaret's arrival in England to York's victory at the first
battle of St Albans in 1455.[1] The action of *3 Henry VI* telescopes the first battle
of St Albans into the battle of Northampton in 1461 (omitting the treaty concluded at Westminster in 1458[2]) and bridges over another gap in the action,
that between the murder of the king in 1471 and the paying by Reignier in 1475
of the ransom demanded by Edward IV for Queen Margaret (5.7.37–40).[3]
The play concentrates on the opposition between the scions of the houses
of York and Lancaster and the political relationships between Margaret and
Warwick: it omits, for example, the important London rising against Edward, led
by Thomas Neville, bastard son of Lord Thomas Falconbridge, which occurred
in 1471 between the battle of Tewkesbury and the murder of Henry VI.[4]
Including the episode would, presumably, have given Edward a political motive
for the assassination of Henry. Likewise the battle of Barnet (5.2) follows hard
upon the confrontation between Warwick and Edward at Coventry (5.1), thus
giving the impression that Barnet is not near London but in Warwickshire.

In this play five scenes (1.1, 1.2, 1.4, 3.2, and, probably, 5.1) are, by and large,
more closely indebted to Holinshed than to Hall and five more to Hall than to
Holinshed (1.3, 2.5, 4.1, 4.7, 4.8).[5] There is no evidence that Shakespeare
consulted Grafton for this play.[6] However, he derived the queen's long
amplification of the rhetorical figure of the ship of state (5.4.1–31) from Arthur
Brooke's *Tragical History of Romeus and Juliet* (1562).[7]

I have dealt earlier in the introduction with Shakespeare's tendency not to
endorse any supernatural explanation of the sorts that are to be found in
Holinshed and Hall. Although certain episodes bear a striking resemblance
to sequences in medieval mystery plays (York's ascent of the throne in 1.1
resembles Lucifer's occupation of God's throne, and his humiliation before
death in 1.4 resembles the buffeting of Christ), Shakespeare seems to have
deliberately secularised these archetypes.[8] He also seems to have, presumably
for dramatic reasons, heightened the contrast between Henry and Edward,
making the latter, unusually for the period, opportunist and lascivious.[9]

---

1 See Hattaway (ed.), *1H6* and *2H6*, pp. 27–8 and 68 respectively.
2 Holinshed, pp. 247–9 gives the articles in full.
3 For a full account of the relationship between play and chronicles see Bullough, pp. 157–71.
4 Holinshed, pp. 321–4.
5 See Appendix 1, pp. 208–17, the headnotes to these scenes, and Brockbank, pp. 32 ff. and
   p. 310 n. 146.
6 Compare Brockbank, p. 33; he may, however, have read Fabyan (see 3.1.1 n. and 4.7.0 SD n.).
7 See Appendix 1, p. 217.
8 See John D. Cox, 'Inventing secular history', chapter 5 of his *Shakespeare and the Dramaturgy of
   Power*, pp. 82–103.
9 Hall, for example, notes (p. 341) that 'from the pleasure of the body, to the which he was prone
   and much given, he did much abstain and forbear'. For the history of Edward's reputation see
   Charles Ross, *Edward IV*, 1974, pp. 418–26.

NOTE ON THE TEXT

The principal authoritative text for this play is that provided by the 1623 First Folio (F). The nature and provenance of F – it derives basically from Shakespeare's manuscript – are discussed in the Textual analysis (pp. 201–7) below. The first edition of the play, which appeared almost thirty years earlier, the octavo of 1595 (O), does derive from theatrical performances, but by a process of memorial reconstruction.[1] This means that when there are substantive differences between passages of dialogue in F and O it is seldom possible to regard the octavo reading as being authoritative. The octavo stage directions, however, deriving as they do from performances, often help to supply F's omissions or to amplify what is unspecific in what Shakespeare probably set down in his 'study'. The 'editor' of the Second Folio (F2) made a lot of corrections, especially corrections to metre. Some of these have been accepted, although they have no special authority. The second and third Quartos (1600 and 1619) derive (independently) from O and equally have no special authority.

The collation in this edition (immediately below each page of text) records all significant departures from F, including variants in lineation and variants in the wording and placing of stage directions as well as in speech headings. It does not record corrections of misprints or modernisations of spellings except where these may be of some consequence. In the format of the collation, the authority for this edition's reading follows immediately after the quotation from the text. Other readings, if any, follow in chronological order. Readings offered by previous editors are registered only if they must be considered in relationship to recent discussions of the play's textual cruces, or if they offer a challenging alternative where no certainty is possible. When, as is usually the case, the variant or emendation adopted has been used by a previous editor or suggested by a textual commentator, those authorities are cited in the abbreviated forms *Rowe* and *conj. Vaughan* respectively. *Subst.* stands for *substantively*, and indicates that I have not transcribed part of the Folio or a later emendation literally – see pp. xi–xvi above for an explanation of the abbreviations and a full list of the editions and commentaries cited. The form *Eds.* is used for insignificant and obvious editorial practices (minor clarifications and expansions of stage directions or modernisations of proper names, for example, which do not need to be ascribed to one originator), and the form *This edn* is used for innovations of my own. Significant additions to the Folio stage directions are enclosed in square brackets – there is a comparatively large number of these because of the fact that the Folio text derives from an authorial manuscript and because the octavo directions provide

1 See Textual analysis, p. 203.

a useful quarry of information concerning early staging (see above). In the commentary an asterisk in the lemma (the key word or phrase printed in bold type) is used to call attention to an emendation in the text; the collation should be consulted for further information.

I have, according to the convention of this edition, modernised and regularised proper names. Where past forms of verbs require an accentuation that they would not receive in modern speech, they are marked with a *grave* accent ('fixèd', 'tunèd'). Unmarked '-ed's' can be assumed to have been elided.

I have tried to keep punctuation as light as is consistent with the clarification of sense, often removing line-end commas from F's text, for the reason that a line-ending can itself provide a subtle and flexible pause or break in the sense. The rhythms surpass what Nashe derided as 'the spacious volubility of a drumming decasyllabon'.[1] Previous editors who punctuated heavily gave us texts that impose rhythmic monotony for readers and actors – there is more enjambment in early Shakespeare than might be supposed from some modern editions. Any substantive departure from the F punctuation, however, is recorded in the collation. I have not attempted to purge the text of short or half-lines, or automatically to expunge metrical irregularity, believing that players can use these for special emphases or effects.[2] Consistency in this area is both impossible and undesirable: if I have regularised metre, I have done so only when I would have made the decision as an actor. Given that there is a lot of metrical irregularity in this text, however, I have recorded in the collation further regularisations that players or readers may care to adopt. I have, however, often followed Pope and restored paired half-lines to whole lines.

I have followed traditional act and scene divisions. These were determined by eighteenth-century editors – the divisions registered in F are irregular and inconsistent. I have not, however, recorded the location of any scenes, as it seems to me that all scenes in the drama of the English renaissance 'take place' on the stage not at 'Waddington Hall' or 'near Towton', and that localisation encourages readers at least to impose expectations appropriate only to naturalist drama. The very first scene of the play is nicely problematic: the opening dialogue suggests a dialogue on the field of battle, but the protagonists then move to Henry's throne which, presumably, stood in a parliament chamber.

Headnotes to scenes in the commentary give references to source material in both Holinshed and Hall. Headnotes also relate the action, where this is possible, to actual places and historical events.

---

1 Epistle prefixed to Greene's *Menaphon*; see Nashe, I, 311.
2 For short lines, see John Barton, *Playing Shakespeare*, 1984, pp. 30–2; for the neo-Augustan regularising of the recent Oxford edition see David Bevington, 'Determining the indeterminate', *SQ* 38 (1987), 501–19.

*The Third Part of
King Henry VI*

LIST OF CHARACTERS

KING HENRY THE SIXTH
QUEEN MARGARET OF ANJOU, *daughter of Reignier, King of Naples*
EDWARD, *Prince of Wales, son of Henry and Margaret*
DUKE OF EXETER
DUKE OF SOMERSET
EARL OF NORTHUMBERLAND
EARL OF WESTMORLAND   } *Lancastrians*
EARL OF OXFORD
LORD CLIFFORD
SIR JOHN SOMERVILLE
A SON *that has killed his father*
A HUNTSMAN *who guards King Edward*

HENRY, EARL OF RICHMOND, *distant cousin to Henry VI and Edward IV, later King Henry VII*

DUKE OF YORK, *Richard Plantagenet, son of Richard, late Earl of Cambridge*
EDWARD, *Earl of March, son of York and later Duke of York and* KING EDWARD IV
GEORGE, *later* DUKE OF CLARENCE, *son of York*
RICHARD, *son of York, later* DUKE OF GLOUCESTER *and King Richard III*
Edmund, EARL OF RUTLAND, *son of York*
TUTOR *to Rutland*
SIR THOMAS SOMERVILLE
SIR JOHN MORTIMER, *uncle to the Duke of York*
SIR HUGH MORTIMER, *uncle to the Duke of York*
DUKE OF NORFOLK
MARQUESS OF MONTAGUE
EARL OF WARWICK, *Richard Neville, son of the Earl of Salisbury*   } *Yorkists*
EARL OF PEMBROKE
LORD STAFFORD
LORD HASTINGS
SIR WILLIAM STANLEY
SIR JOHN MONTGOMERY
A NOBLEMAN
A FATHER *that has killed his son*
Two KEEPERS

LADY ELIZABETH GREY, *later wife to Edward IV and*
   QUEEN ELIZABETH
PRINCE EDWARD, *infant son to Edward and Queen Elizabeth*
NURSE *to Prince Edward of York*
LORD RIVERS, *brother to Lady Elizabeth*

LIEUTENANT *of the Tower of London*
MAYOR OF YORK   *Office holders*
MAYOR OF COVENTRY

KING LEWIS THE ELEVENTH, *King of France*
LADY BONA, *his sister-in-law*   *The French*
LORD BOURBON, *the French High Admiral*

Attendant lords, soldiers, aldermen, watchmen, servants, messengers

Notes

F does not supply a list of characters; an imperfect one was first given by Rowe.

KING HENRY THE SIXTH (1421–71) Son of Henry V (1387–1422) whom he succeeded when nine months old. The part might have been taken by a boy in *1H6* (see Hattaway (ed.), *1H6*, p. 38 n. 9).

QUEEN MARGARET (1430–82) Daughter of Reignier, who married Henry VI by proxy at Nancy in 1445, Suffolk standing as proxy for the king. She courted unpopularity by allying herself with Suffolk and then Somerset, both of whom were held responsible for the loss of territories in France – an alliance that York was able to exploit. For an account of her reputation that offers much useful information on her husband's reign and considers her in regard to the positive icons of queenship created by Elizabeth I, see Patricia-Ann Lee, 'Reflections of power: Margaret of Anjou and the dark side of queenship', *Renaissance Quarterly*, 39 (1986), 183–217.

EDWARD (1453–71) Prince of Wales and only son of Henry VI and Margaret. Present at the second Battle of St Albans, 1461 and knighted that year. Supported by Louis XI and René of Lorraine. Betrothed to Warwick's younger daughter Anne who appears in *R3* 1.2. Defeated at Tewkesbury and murdered by the Yorkists.

DUKE OF EXETER (?–1473) Henry Holland, son of John Holland, Earl of Huntingdon. (Thomas Beaufort, the 'Exeter' of *1H6*, left no issue.) Although the brother-in-law of Edward IV, he supported the Lancastrians, and was left for dead at Barnet. He recovered, only to be attainted by Edward IV. He died in poverty.

DUKE OF SOMERSET As in *1* and *2H6*, Shakespeare seems to have deliberately conflated (see below 5.1.73–5) two members of this family: Henry Beaufort (1436–64), the third duke, son of the Edmund Beaufort whose head is thrown down by Gloucester at 1.1.16, and his younger brother Edmund Beaufort (1438–71), the fourth duke. Henry Beaufort was made Captain of Calais by

Queen Margaret in 1459. By 1462 he was in favour with Edward IV (see 4.1), but he rejoined Margaret at Hexham where, after the Lancastrian defeat, he was executed. Edmund was brought up in France, returning to England after Warwick's defection. He fought at Barnet but was taken prisoner at Tewkesbury and beheaded by order of Edward IV (see 5.5.3).

EARL OF NORTHUMBERLAND (1421–61) Henry Percy, the third earl, grandson of Hotspur and son of the Henry Percy whose death is reported in 1.1.4–9. He was knighted as a child in 1426 along with the infant Henry VI; he attended the parliament in Coventry where the Yorkist leaders were attainted, defeated and killed York at Wakefield (compare 1.4.169–71), but died himself at Towton.

EARL OF WESTMORLAND (?–1484) Ralph Neville, second Earl of Westmorland, who married Hotspur's daughter Elizabeth, the widow of John Clifford. In fact it was his younger brother John who fought for the Lancastrians, but Holinshed (p. 278) and Hall (p. 256) mistakenly have him slain at Towton.

EARL OF OXFORD (1443–1513) John de Vere, the thirteenth earl. His father (John) and elder brother Aubrey were attainted and executed in 1462. He was with Warwick in France and helped to restore Henry VI in 1470. He defeated Hastings at Barnet, but after the battle was lost he fled to France. After a second return to England he was defeated at St Michael's Mount and sent back to France and captivity near Calais. He escaped to join Richmond and fought with him at Bosworth.

LORD CLIFFORD (1435–61) John, thirteenth Baron Clifford, son of Old Clifford who was the son-in-law of Hotspur and who appears in *2H6* and was, like his father, a determined foe of the Duke of York. He survived the second Battle of St Albans but was killed at Ferrybridge on the eve of the Battle of Towton.

SIR THOMAS SOMERVILLE No first name is given to the character in F or O. He does not appear in Holinshed or Hall. There was a Sir Thomas Somerville (?–1500) of Aston-Somerville, four miles south of Evesham (see Thomson, p. 275).

HENRY, EARL OF RICHMOND (1457–1509) Son of Edmund Tudor, Earl of Richmond, and Margaret Beaufort, the great-grand-daughter of John of Gaunt. He was brought up in Wales. In 1470, during the brief restoration of Henry VI, he is reported to have been presented to the king (see 4.6). He had to take refuge in France when Edward IV was restored, and remained there until 1485 when he landed in England and defeated Richard III at Bosworth. He married Elizabeth of York, daughter of Edward IV, in 1486, thus uniting the white rose with the red.

DUKE OF YORK (1411–60) Descended through his mother from the Mortimer line, which derived from Lionel Duke of Clarence, third son of Edward III. His father, who was descended from Edmund of Langley, fifth son of Edward III and first Duke of York, had been executed in 1415 for conspiring against Henry V. He was restored to his title of Duke of York in *1H6* 3.1.

EDWARD (1442–83) Son of Richard Duke of York and his wife Cicely Neville. Born at Rouen, he became Earl of March and was attainted as a Yorkist in 1459. Defeated Henry VI's forces at Northampton in 1460 and proclaimed King Edward IV in 1461 after defeating the Lancastrians at Towton. His death is reported in *R3* 2.2.

GEORGE (1449–78) Sixth son of York, born in Dublin while his father was Lord Lieutenant of Ireland. After his father's death in 1460 sent with Richard to Utrecht, but returned on accession of Edward in 1461 to be created Duke of Clarence. Married Warwick's elder daughter Isabella against Edward's wishes. Joined Warwick in invasion of England and captured Edward at Edgecote but had to release him to appease public opinion. Fled to France but returned to England again in 1470 to assist Warwick restore Henry VI. When Edward landed in 1471 Clarence deserted to him at Coventry and fought with him at Barnet and Tewkesbury. Quarrelled violently with his brother Richard over latter's desire to marry Anne Neville. In *R3* 1.4 Shakespeare portrays the rumoured manner of his death, in a butt of malmsey.

RICHARD (1452–85) Eleventh son of York, born at Fotheringay Castle. Created Duke of Gloucester 1461; commanded the vanguard at Barnet and Tewkesbury. Murdered Henry VI and contrived to have himself proclaimed king in 1483. His nickname 'Crouchback' or 'Crook-back' derived from a real but possibly minor deformity: Sir Thomas More reports that his left shoulder was much higher than his right (Hall, pp. 342–3). The fact that historically he was only three years old at the opening of the play where he appears as the killer of Somerset suggests that Shakespeare thought of him not only as Henry's enemy but his anti-type, and intended from an early stage to write a play about him.

RUTLAND (1443–60) Edmund Earl of Rutland, second son of York, although treated in the play as the youngest of the family (Hall, p. 251, says he was twelve at the time of his death).

TUTOR Robert Aspall, chaplain and tutor to Rutland (Hall, p. 251; Holinshed does not give his name).

SIR JOHN MORTIMER, SIR HUGH MORTIMER Both these 'bastard uncles' (Holinshed, p. 268; Hall, p. 250) of the Duke of York died at Wakefield in 1460. They were presumably illegitimate brothers of York's mother, Anne Mortimer.

DUKE OF NORFOLK John Mowbray (1415–61), third Duke of Norfolk and hereditary Earl Marshal of England. Supported the Duke of York who was his uncle by marriage, although his influence with the duke did not match that of the Nevilles. Defeated with Warwick at St Albans and fought at Towton.

MONTAGUE John Neville (?–1471), third son of the Richard Neville, Earl of Salisbury who appears in *2H6*. He was brother to Warwick and nephew to York (but see 1.1.14 n.). He was raised to the peerage in 1465, imprisoned by York after the second Battle of St Albans but freed by Edward after Towton in 1461. Defeated the Lancastrians at Hexham in 1464 but after a dispute over the estates and earldom of Northumberland fought on the Lancastrian side at Barnet where he was killed.

EARL OF WARWICK (1428–71) Shakespeare had conflated two personages. The 'Warwick' of *1H6* was Richard de Beauchamp, Earl of Warwick (1382–1439). He had accompanied Henry V to France, was present at his funeral in 1422 (see *1H6* 1.1), was charged with the education of the infant Henry VI in 1428, and was dead by the time of the truce signed at Tours (see *1H6* 5.4). The 'Warwick' of this play is his son-in-law Richard Neville, known as the 'kingmaker'. Son of the Earl of Salisbury, he succeeded in 1449 to the title and estates of Richard de Beauchamp whose daughter Anne he had married.

EARL OF PEMBROKE William Herbert (?–1469), first Earl of Pembroke. Knighted in 1449 by Henry VI. Fought on the side of the Yorkists and captured and executed at Edgecote.

LORD STAFFORD Humphrey Stafford (1439–69), knighted by Edward IV at Towton and created Lord Stafford in 1464. A quarrel with Pembroke led to a defeat in a battle with Robin of Redesdale for which Edward IV had him executed.

LORD HASTINGS William Hastings (1430?–83), Sheriff of Leicestershire and Warwickshire, made a peer by Edward after his coronation in 1461. When Edward V succeeded he opposed Rivers and, without a trial, was beheaded by Richard of Gloucester (see *R3* 3.4).

SIR WILLIAM STANLEY (1435–95) Attainted as a Yorkist but then made Chamberlain of Chester by Edward IV in 1461. Supported Richmond against Richard III at Bosworth in 1485 but was executed after joining the Perkin Warbeck conspiracy.

MONTGOMERY (?–1495) He appears in the text (4.7.40) as 'Sir John' but the chroniclers call him 'Sir Thomas' (Holinshed, p. 306; Hall, p. 292). He was an Esquire of the Body to Henry VI, but joined Edward at Nottingham (not at York as in 4.7) with a large body of men. He escorted Margaret into exile in France in 1475, and later served Richard III.

NOBLEMAN Sir James Harrington, who captured Henry VI at Waddington Hall (see 3.2.118–19).

LADY ELIZABETH GREY (1437?–92) Daughter of Sir Richard Woodville, later Earl Rivers, by Jacquetta of Luxembourg, widow of John, Duke of Bedford. She married Sir John Grey (see 3.2.2 n.) who was killed at St Albans in 1461. The Woodvilles and Rivers were Lancastrians, and the accession of Edward IV led to her losing her inheritance. She secretly married the king in 1464 and was crowned in 1465. The advancement of her relatives alienated her from the court of Richard III and she was not better treated by her son-in-law Henry VII. She died at Bermondsey Abbey. See J. R. Lander, 'Marriage and politics: the Nevilles and the Wydevilles', *Bulletin of the Institute of Historical Research*, 36 (1963), 119–52.

PRINCE EDWARD (1470–83) Eldest son of Edward IV and Elizabeth Woodville, created Prince of Wales in 1471, two months after the murder of Edward Plantagenet. His father entrusted him to a Council of Control which centred on Clarence, Gloucester, and Earl Rivers. Succeeded to the throne in

1483 and reigned as Edward V for two months, a period of struggles for power between the Woodvilles and Gloucester. Sent to the Tower by Gloucester along with his brother where the two boys were murdered – by order of Gloucester, according to Sir Thomas More.

LORD RIVERS (1442?–83) Anthony Woodville, brother to Elizabeth, became the second earl in 1469. He helped Edward IV at Barnet, and in 1473 became Chief Butler of England. He was suspected of treason by Gloucester, the Protector after Edward's death, and was beheaded, probably without trial, at Pontefract.

LIEUTENANT At the time of 4.6, the Lieutenant of the Tower was John Tiptoft (1427?–70), Earl of Worcester. He was known as the 'butcher of England' after hanging and impaling twenty of Clarence's party and was himself executed after the flight of Edward IV (Holinshed, p. 301). His successor who held office during the time of 5.6 was John Sutton (1401?–87), sixth Baron Dudley.

MAYOR OF YORK In 1471 the mayor was Thomas Beverley, merchant of the Staple.

MAYOR OF COVENTRY In 1470–1, just before the battle of Barnet, the mayor was John Brett. 'For his adherence to Henry VI he was deprived of his sword of state by Edward IV and the citizens were compelled to pay a fine of 500 marks to recover the sword and their franchise' (Thomson, p. 202).

KING LEWIS (1423–83) Louis XI, son of Charles VII (who appears as the Dauphin in *1H6*) and Marie of Anjou (the aunt of Queen Margaret). In 1436 married the daughter of James I of Scotland, Margaret, and then, after her death, Charlotte of Savoy. Succeeded to the throne in 1461.

LADY BONA (?–1485) The third daughter of Louis, first Duke of Savoy, and sister-in-law to Louis XI. She married the Duke of Milan in 1468.

LORD BOURBON Jean, Count of Rousillon and Admiral of France, bastard son of Charles, Duke of Bourbon, and husband of Joan, bastard daughter of Louis XI.

THE THIRD PART OF HENRY THE SIXTH

[1.1] [*A chair of state.*] *Alarum. Enter* [RICHARD] PLANTAGENET, [DUKE OF YORK], EDWARD, [EARL OF MARCH], [CROOK-BACK] RICHARD [*bearing a severed head*], [*the* EARL OF RUTLAND], [*the* DUKE OF] NORFOLK, [*the* MARQUESS OF] MONTAGUE, [*and the* EARL OF] WARWICK, [*with Drum*] *and Soldiers* [*with white roses in their hats*]

WARWICK I wonder how the king escaped our hands.
YORK While we pursued the horsemen of the north,
    He slyly stole away and left his men;
    Whereat the great Lord of Northumberland
    Whose warlike ears could never brook retreat   5

Title] The third Part of Henry the Sixt, with the death of the Duke of Yorke F; The true Tragedie of Richard *Duke of Yorke, and the death of* good King Henrie the Sixt, *with the whole contention betweene* the two Houses Lancaster and Yorke, as it was sundrie times acted by the Right Honourable the Earle of Pembrooke his seruants. O
Act 1, Scene 1   1.1] *Eds.; Actus Primus. Scæna Prima.* F   0 SD.1 *A chair of state.*] *Oxford (following 5t); not in* F
0 SD.2 CROOK-BACK] O *subst.; not in* F   0 SD.3 *bearing . . . head*] *This edn; not in* F   0 SD.3 RUTLAND] O; *not in* F
0 SD.4 MONTAGUE] F *subst.;* FALCONBRIDGE. *Cairncross (throughout scene)*   0 SD.5 *with Drum*] O; *not in* F   0 SD.5 *with white . . . hats*] O; *not in* F   2 SH] O *subst.;* Pl. *(or Plant.)* F *(until 43; thereafter/Yorke)*

Act 1, Scene 1

1.1 'This play is only divided from the former for the convenience of exhibition; for the series of action is continued without interruption, nor are any two scenes of any play more closely connected than the first scene of this play with the last of the former' (Johnson). The play begins with an allusion to the first battle of St Albans, fought on 22 May 1455 (Holinshed, pp. 240–2; Hall, pp. 232–4). The king's flight (line 1) is fictitious: Henry in fact remained in the town before being taken to London. In November York was appointed Protector after Henry had become imbecile. He recovered in 1456. Hostilities broke out in 1458–9, and in 1460 the Yorkists took Henry prisoner at Northampton whence he was conveyed to London for a Parliament called on 7 October. Shakespeare seems to have read York's oration in Holinshed (pp. 262–4) see 26 and 29 n. York was declared heir apparent on 24 October (Holinshed, pp. 262–8; Hall, pp. 245–9).

0 SD.1 *A chair of state This scene and 3.3 require a 'state' or chair equipped with a canopy (see *OED* State *sb* 20 a and b) which was prob-

ably placed on an elevated platform. The chair and, conceivably, the platform could have been brought out where necessary or 'discovered' but they may have remained on stage throughout the play as an index of the play's concern with power. The platform might well have served as Henry's 'molehill' (2.5.14) at the battle of Towton.

0 SD.1 *Alarum* A drum or trumpet call to direct troops on the battlefield (Long, pp. 4–5).

0 SD.3 *RUTLAND F does not indicate an entrance for this character nor is he assigned any lines before 1.3 where he is killed. However, O indicates that he might have been brought on in 1.1 to swell the scene, and it would help an audience to recognise him immediately he appears in 1.3.

0 SD.4 *white roses the badge of the Yorkists; see *1H6* 2.4.

1 **wonder** am amazed.

4 **Lord of Northumberland** Henry Percy (1394–1455), the second Earl and the son and heir to Hotspur.

5 **brook retreat** obey the sound of the trumpet's call for retreat.

Cheered up the drooping army; and himself,
Lord Clifford, and Lord Stafford, all abreast,
Charged our main battle's front and, breaking in,
Were by the swords of common soldiers slain.
EDWARD Lord Stafford's father, Duke of Buckingham,   10
Is either slain or wounded dangerous:
I cleft his beaver with a downright blow.
That this is true, father, behold his blood.
MONTAGUE And, brother, here's the Earl of Wiltshire's blood,
Whom I encountered as the battles joined.   15
RICHARD Speak thou for me, and tell them what I did.
[*Throwing down the Duke of Somerset's head*]
YORK Richard hath best deserved of all my sons. –
But is your grace dead, my Lord of Somerset?
NORFOLK Such hope have all the line of John of Gaunt!
YORK Thus do I hope to shake King Henry's head.   20

6 himself,] F2; himselfe. F   11 dangerous] F; dangerouslie O   14 brother] F *subst.*; cousin *Pelican* (*following* O *at*
1.2.1)   16 SD] *Theobald; not in* F   18 But] F; What O   19 hope] F; hap *Dyce*²

6 **Cheered up** revived – as the sun revives a
drooping plant (see Schmidt).
7 **Lord Stafford** Humphrey, the eldest
surviving son of Humphrey, first Duke of
Buckingham. 'He was "greatly hurt" (Paston
Letters) in the first battle of St Albans, and died
not long after' (Thomson, p. 277).
8 **battle's** battalion's (*OED* Battle *sb* 9).
9 In *2H6* (5.2.27) Clifford was in fact slain by
York: this is the pretext offered by Clifford at
1.3.5 for killing Rutland (compare Hall, p. 251).
1.1.55 and 162, 1.3.5 and 47, 1.4.31–2 and 175
also have Clifford slain by York. However,
Holinshed (p. 240; Hall, p. 233) lists 'John,
Lord Clifford' among the dead at the first battle
of St Albans.
10 Humphrey Stafford, the first Duke of
Buckingham (1402–60), grandson of Thomas
of Woodstock and killed at the battle of
Northampton five years later.
11 **dangerous** dangerously (Abbott 1) – the
reading of O, which may be preferable.
12 **beaver** helmet or visor of the helmet,
often pushed up over the top of the helmet.
12 **downright** vertically downwards (*OED* sv
1).
14 **brother** In Act 1 (compare 1.1.116, 1.2.4,
36, 55, and 60) Montague (John Neville, third
son of Richard Neville, Earl of Salisbury) is
designated as York's brother in error. In fact he
was brother to Warwick (also Richard Neville),
and is called such in 2.1.166 and thereafter.

The source of the error may be that York was
married to Cicely, Richard Neville's sister. If
Shakespeare thought that Richard (Earl of
Salisbury) and John Neville were brothers rather
than father and son, he might have used
'brother' in its customary sense of 'brother-in-
law'. O uses the designation 'cosen Montague'
(1.2.1 etc.) which may represent an (authorial?)
revision. Cairncross, however, (p. xxi) used this
as evidence that Falconbridge, York's actual
brother-in-law, disappeared from the text during
revision, his lines being reallocated to Montague
(see 211 n. and 240 n.).
14 James Butler, Earl of Wiltshire (1420–
61), was captured at Towton and after beheaded
at Newcastle.
16 **thou** here expressing contempt; compare
the 'your' in 18.
17 In fact Richard was only three at the time
of the battle of St Albans in 1455.
19 **line . . . Gaunt** The Lancastrians were all
descended from John of Gaunt, Duke of
Lancaster, and father of Henry IV. Edmund,
second Duke of Somerset was his grandson,
Henry VI his great-grandson.
19 **hope** expectation (*OED* sv *sb* 3); some
editors after Dyce amend to 'hap' on the
grounds that hap/hope quibbles are common in
the period.
19 **have** (expresses a wish).
20 **hope** expect.

WARWICK And so do I, victorious Prince of York.
    Before I see thee seated in that throne
    Which now the house of Lancaster usurps,
    I vow by heaven these eyes shall never close.
    This is the palace of the fearful king   25
    And this the regal seat: possess it, York,
    For this is thine, and not King Henry's heirs'.
YORK Assist me then, sweet Warwick, and I will,
    For hither we have broken in by force.
NORFOLK We'll all assist you; he that flies shall die.   30
YORK Thanks, gentle Norfolk. – Stay by me, my lords;
    And, soldiers, stay and lodge by me this night.
                They go up
WARWICK And when the king comes, offer him no violence
    Unless he seek to thrust you out perforce.
                      [Exeunt soldiers]
YORK The queen this day here holds her parliament,   35
    But little thinks we shall be of her council.
    By words or blows here let us win our right.
YORK Armed as we are, let's stay within this house.
WARWICK The Bloody Parliament shall this be called,
    Unless Plantagenet, Duke of York, be king   40
    And bashful Henry deposed, whose cowardice
    Hath made us by-words to our enemies.
YORK Then leave me not. – My lords, be resolute:
    I mean to take possession of my right.
WARWICK Neither the king nor he that loves him best,   45

---

21 York.] F *subst.;* Yorke, O   24 heaven] F *subst.;* heauens O; Heauen Q3   27 heirs'] *Warburton;* Heires F   34
SD]*This edn, conj. Walker; not in* F   36 council] *Pope;* counsaile F   43 not.] *This edn;* not, F   43 lords,] *Eds.;*
Lords F

23 Bullingbrook, son of John of Gaunt, Duke of Lancaster, deposed Richard II to become Henry IV.

25 **fearful** timorous.

26 **regal seat** The phrase occurs in Holinshed (p. 262); Hall reads 'throne royal' (p. 245).

28 **will** used here instead of 'shall' (Abbott 316), and expressing mere volition.

29 **broken . . . force** The account of this does not occur in Hall (see Holinshed, p. 262).

32 **lodge** lie, sleep.

32 SD This would seem to indicate that the 'state' or throne stood on a dais. The dialogue is

continuous, so it is improbable that the tiring-house balcony would have been used.

34 **perforce** forcibly (*OED* 1a).

*34 SD It is clear that the soldiers must exit at some point before 169 when they enter again.

36 **of her council** (1) privy to the deliberations, (2) in her confidence (counsel).

41 **bashful** shamefaced (Schmidt).

41 **Henry** Possibly trisyllabic here (Cercignani, p. 358) as in Q2's version of 1.1.139.

42 **by-words** proverbial for our cowardice; compare Ps. 44.14: 'Thou makest us to be a by-word among the heathen' (Bishops' Bible).

The proudest he that holds up Lancaster,
Dares stir a wing, if Warwick shake his bells.
I'll plant Plantagenet: root him up who dares.
Resolve thee, Richard: claim the English crown.

[*York seats himself on the throne*]

Flourish. Enter KING HENRY, CLIFFORD, NORTHUMBERLAND,
WESTMORLAND, EXETER, *and the rest* [, *with red roses in their hats*]

KING HENRY My lords, look where the sturdy rebel sits   50
   Even in the chair of state. Belike he means,
   Backed by the power of Warwick that false peer,
   To aspire unto the crown and reign as king.
   Earl of Northumberland, he slew thy father,
   And thine, Lord Clifford; and you both have vowed
      revenge   55
   On him, his sons, his favourites, and his friends.
NORTHUMBERLAND If I be not, heavens be revenged on me!
CLIFFORD The hope thereof makes Clifford mourn in steel.
WESTMORLAND What, shall we suffer this? Let's pluck him down;
   My heart for anger burns: I cannot brook it.   60
KING HENRY Be patient, gentle Earl of Westmorland.
CLIFFORD Patience is for poltroons such as he.

---

46 he] F *subst;* burd O   49 SD.1] *This edn (following Johnson); not in* F   49 SD.3 *with ... hats*] O; *not in* F   55
Clifford, and] F *subst.;* Clifford; *conj Cairncross*   62 poltroons] F *subst.;* Poultroones, and F2

46 The most fearless supporter of the
Lancastrians.
   46 he O's 'burd', i.e. 'bird' or young upstart, is
attractive, offering a pun in the context of 'wing'
in the next line.
   47 shake ... bells Falcons wore bells above
their feet which served, it was believed, to terrify
their prey (*Shakespeare's England*, II, 357–8).
   48 plant install, establish, quibbling on
'Plantagenet'; compare 3.3.198.
   49 Resolve thee Take the decision (*OED*
Resolve *v* 19a).
   49 SD.2 *Flourish* A trumpet fanfare, calling
attention to the presence of the monarch (Long,
p. 10), but here placed so that, as well as
signalling the processional entrance of Henry, it
seems to amplify Warwick's proclamation of
Richard (compare 275 SD and see Long,
pp. 27–8).
   49 SD.3 *and the rest* This phrase, common
in F but generally represented by '*with soldiers*' in
O, designates soldiers to support Westmorland,
Northumberland, and Clifford and who would
leave the stage with their masters at 186–90.

   49 SD.3 *red roses* the badge of the
Lancastrians.
   50 sturdy rough, refractory (*OED* sv 4 and
5).
   51 chair of state See O SD n.
   51 Belike It is likely that.
   57 not i.e. not revenged.
   58 hope expectation.
   58 steel armour (rather than in the conventional mourning cloaks).
   59 shall ... suffer must we put up with.
   60 heart With the liver and the brain, one of
the three 'sovereign thrones' (*TN* 1.1.37). 'The
heart is the seat of life and of affections, and
perturbations of love or hate, like or dislike
of such things as fall within the compass of
sense ...' (T. Bright, *A Treatise of Melancholy*,
1586, p. 46); compare 1.4.87.
   61 gentle noble.
   62 Patience Pronounced with three syllables
(Cercignani, p. 309).
   62 poltroons wretches, cowards (probably
accented on the first syllable).

He durst not sit there, had your father lived.
My gracious lord, here in the parliament
Let us assail the family of York.   65
NORTHUMBERLAND Well hast thou spoken, cousin: be it so.
KING HENRY Ah, know you not the city favours them
    And they have troops of soldiers at their beck?
EXETER But when the duke is slain, they'll quickly fly.
KING HENRY Far be the thought of this from Henry's heart,   70
    To make a shambles of the parliament house!
    Cousin of Exeter, frowns, words, and threats
    Shall be the war that Henry means to use. –
    Thou factious Duke of York, descend my throne
    And kneel for grace and mercy at my feet: 75
    I am thy sovereign.
YORK   I am thine.
EXETER For shame come down: he made thee Duke of York.
YORK It was my inheritance, as the earldom was.
EXETER Thy father was a traitor to the crown.
WARWICK Exeter, thou art a traitor to the crown   80
    In following this usurping Henry.
CLIFFORD Whom should he follow but his natural king?
WARWICK True, Clifford; that's Richard, Duke of York.
KING HENRY And shall I stand and thou sit in my throne?
YORK It must and shall be so: content thyself.   85
WARWICK Be Duke of Lancaster; let him be king.
WESTMORLAND He is both king and Duke of Lancaster:
    And that the Lord of Westmorland shall maintain.

---

66 cousin:] *Cambridge;* Cousin F   69 SH] O *subst., Theobald; Westm.* F   76] F *subst.;* I am thy soueraigne. / York.
Thou art decciu'd: I am thine. O   78 It was] F; 'Twas O   78 earldom was] F *subst.;* kingdome is O   83
Clifford] F *subst.;* Clifford, and Q3

---

63 **your father** Henry V.

66 **cousin** kinsman.

67 **city** London (as distinct from the court). In *2H6* the queen claims that the city supports Henry (5.2.81), but the chroniclers note that Henry feared to fight York near London because the duke 'had too many friends' there (Holinshed, p. 238; Hall, p. 232).

68 **beck** command.

*69 SH O's attribution of this speech to Exeter is probably correct, given that Henry's next speech is addressed to him.

71 **shambles** slaughter-house.

72 **Cousin** Used by a sovereign to address a nobleman.

74 **factious** seditious (*OED* sv 1).

77 **he ... York** see *1H6* 3.1.

78 **earldom** of March, by virtue of which he claimed the throne through his mother Anne Mortimer; compare 2.1.179 and *2H6* 2.29–52. However, O's 'kingdom' makes a line that would be clearer to a playhouse audience.

79 The Earl of Cambridge, father of York, was executed during the reign of Henry V (see *H5* 2.2).

82 **natural** rightful by virtue of his birth (*OED* sv *adj* 10b).

85 **It ... so** Compare the phrase 'I must and will' (Dent M1330.1).

WARWICK And Warwick shall disprove it. You forget
    That we are those which chased you from the field   90
    And slew your father and, with colours spread,
    Marched through the city to the palace gates.
NORTHUMBERLAND Yes, Warwick, I remember it to my grief;
    And, by his soul, thou and thy house shall rue it.
WESTMORLAND Plantagenet, of thee and these thy sons,   95
    Thy kinsmen and thy friends, I'll have more lives
    Than drops of blood were in my father's veins.
CLIFFORD Urge it no more, lest that, instead of words,
    I send thee, Warwick, such a messenger
    As shall revenge his death before I stir.   100
WARWICK Poor Clifford; how I scorn his worthless threats!
YORK Will you we show our title to the crown?
    If not, our swords shall plead it in the field.
KING HENRY What title hast thou, traitor, to the crown?
    Thy father was as thou art, Duke of York;   105
    Thy grandsire, Roger Mortimer, Earl of March:
    I am the son of Henry the Fifth,
    Who made the dauphin and the French to stoop
    And seized upon their towns and provinces.
WARWICK Talk not of France sith thou hast lost it all.   110
KING HENRY The Lord Protector lost it and not I:

---

91 father] O; Fathers F   93 Yes] F; No O   102 SH] O; *Plant.* F (*throughout the rest of the scene*)   105 Thy] O;
My F   106 grandsire] *Cairncross;* Grandfather F   108 dauphin] *Eds.;* Dolphin F

91 *father O's reading is justified by the 'his'
of 94; F's 'Fathers' was probably caught from
'colours'.

91 colours flags, banners.

94, 100 his my father's.

96 have . . . lives kill more of them.

97 John Neville, Westmorland's father who
died in 1423, was not in fact killed on the
battlefield.

97 blood were For the omitted relative see
Abbott 244.

99 messenger an exterminating angel; for
angels as God's messengers see Heb. 1.7.

102 title legal right.

103 plead speak for, defend.

***105** York's father was in fact Earl of
Cambridge (see 79 n.); he inherited his title
from his father's elder brother Edward who died
at Agincourt. Edward appears as the Duke of
Aumerle in *R2.*

106 *grandsire I accept Cairncross's suggestion that F's 'grandfather' may well have been

caught from the line before, so destroying the
metre.

107 'The military reputation of Henry the
Fifth is the sole support of his son. The name of
Henry the Fifth dispersed the followers of Cade
[*2H6* 4.8.16]' (Johnson Var.).

108 dauphin Louis, eldest son of Charles VI,
who appears in *H5.* F's spelling, 'Dolphin',
indicates the pronunciation (Cercignani, p. 354;
compare *1H6* 1.1.92 n.)

108 stoop submit.

109 seized upon captured.

110 The loss of the English empire in France
was one of the themes of *1H6* and Henry's
surrender, on the occasion of his marriage, of
Anjou and Maine to Margaret's father Reignier
was one of the main causes for contention in
2H6.

110 sith since.

111 Lord Protector Humphrey, Duke of
Gloucester, whose downfall is portrayed in *2H6.*

When I was crowned, I was but nine months old.

RICHARD You are old enough now and yet, methinks, you lose. –
Father, tear the crown from the usurper's head.

EDWARD Sweet father, do so: set it on your head.   115

MONTAGUE Good brother, as thou lov'st and honourest arms,
Let's fight it out and not stand cavilling thus.

RICHARD Sound drums and trumpets and the king will fly.

YORK Sons, peace!

KING HENRY Peace, thou, and give King Henry leave to speak!   120

WARWICK Plantagenet shall speak first: hear him, lords,
And be you silent and attentive too,
For he that interrupts him shall not live.

KING HENRY Think'st thou that I will leave my kingly throne
Wherein my grandsire and my father sat?   125
No: first shall war unpeople this my realm;
Ay, and their colours, often borne in France –
And now in England to our heart's great sorrow –
Shall be my winding-sheet. Why faint you, lords?
My title's good and better far than his.   130

WARWICK Prove it, Henry, and thou shalt be king.

KING HENRY Henry the Fourth by conquest got the crown.

YORK 'Twas by rebellion against his king.

KING HENRY [*Aside*] I know not what to say, my title's weak. –
Tell me, may not a king adopt an heir?   135

YORK What then?

KING HENRY And if he may, then am I lawful king:
For Richard, in the view of many lords,
Resigned the crown to Henry the Fourth

113] Pope; You...now, / And...loose F   116] Pope; Good Brother, / As...Armes F   120 SH] *This edn;*
Henry. F; *Northum.* O   124] F; Ah *Plantagenet,* why seekest thou to depose me? / Are we not both *Plantagenets* by
birth, / And from two brothers lineallie discent? / Suppose by right and equitie thou be king, / Thinkst thou that I
will leave my kingly seate O   131 Prove] F *subst.;* But prove F2 *subst.*   134, 151 SD] *Capell; not in* F   135 Tell
me, may] F; May *conj. Cairncross*

112 Henry disingenuously confuses his
succession (30 August 1422) with his coronation
(November 1431); see Introduction p. 57 n. 4;
compare 3.1.76 and see *1H6* 4.1.
  113 **yet** even now.
  117 **stand** delay.
  117 **cavilling** disputing.
  118 **Sound** An optative (i.e. let sound).
  120–4 For O's version of these lines (which
suggest a much less confident Henry) see
Appendix 2, p. 218; see also Textual analysis,
p. 204.
  120 SH O's attribution of this line to
Northumberland may be correct.

129 **winding-sheet** shroud.
  129 **faint** do you lose heart (*OED* sv *v* 1).
  132 **by conquest** Henry, disingenuously
perhaps, evokes in this context the legal sense of
the phrase, 'by acquisition' rather than 'by
inheritance', with no reference to the mode (see
OED Conquest *sb* 7, and headnote).
  133 **his king** Richard II.
  136 **then?** if he did?
  137 **And if** If (Abbott 103).
  138–9 For Shakespeare's portrayal of
Richard II's abdication, see *R2* 4.1.
  139 **Henry** Again possibly trisyllabic – see
41 n. above.

Whose heir my father was, and I am his.   140
YORK He rose against him, being his sovereign,
    And made him to resign his crown perforce.
WARWICK Suppose, my lords, he did it unconstrained,
    Think you 'twere prejudicial to his crown?
EXETER No, for he could not so resign his crown   145
    But that the next heir should succeed and reign.
KING HENRY Art thou against us, Duke of Exeter?
EXETER His is the right, and therefore pardon me.
YORK Why whisper you, my lords, and answer not?
EXETER My conscience tells me he is lawful king.   150
KING HENRY [*Aside*] All will revolt from me and turn to him.
NORTHUMBERLAND Plantagenet, for all the claim thou lay'st,
    Think not that King Henry shall be so deposed.
WARWICK Deposed he shall be, in despite of all.
NORTHUMBERLAND Thou art deceived. 'Tis not thy southern
    power   155
    Of Essex, Norfolk, Suffolk, nor of Kent,
    Which makes thee thus presumptuous and proud,
    Can set the duke up in despite of me.
CLIFFORD King Henry, be thy title right or wrong,
    Lord Clifford vows to fight in thy defence.   160
    May that ground gape and swallow me alive
    Where I shall kneel to him that slew my father.
KING HENRY O Clifford, how thy words revive my heart.
YORK Henry of Lancaster, resign thy crown –
    What mutter you, or what conspire you, lords?   165
WARWICK Do right unto this princely Duke of York

---

144 his crown] F *subst.;* his son *conj. Johnson;* the crown *Capell*   **155**] *Pope;* Thou ... deceiu'd: / 'Tis ... power
F   **164** thy] F; the *Hudson*

141 him Richard II.
142 perforce by force.
144 'The phrase "prejudicial to his crown", if it be right, must mean "detrimental to the general rights of hereditary royalty"; but I rather think that the transcriber's eye caught "crown" from the line below, and that we should read "prejudicial to his *son*, to his *next heir*"' (Johnson).
146 But Without bringing it about (Abbott 120).
150 conscience reason, understanding (*OED*

sv 3); the moment quotes Salisbury's revelation through conscience that York was the rightful heir to the crown (*2H6* 5.1.177–8).
  154 despite spite.
  155 deceived mistaken.
  155 southern Northumberland speaks from the vantage point of a northern earl.
  155 power army.
  161 ground ... me Compare Num. 16.30: 'And the earth opened her mouth and swallowed them up', also Ps. 106.17, Dent GG2.
  166 right justice.

Or I will fill the house with armèd men
And over the chair of state, where now he sits,
Write up his title with usurping blood.

He stamps with his foot, and [a Yorkist Captain and] the soldiers show
themselves

KING HENRY My Lord of Warwick, hear but one word: 170
Let me for this my lifetime reign as king.
YORK Confirm the crown to me and to mine heirs,
And thou shalt reign in quiet while thou liv'st.
KING HENRY Convey the soldiers hence, and then I will.
WARWICK Captain, conduct them into Tuttle fields.   175
                                    [*Exit Captain and Yorkist soldiers*]
KING HENRY I am content. – Richard Plantagenet,
Enjoy the kingdom after my decease.
CLIFFORD What wrong is this unto the prince your son!
WARWICK What good is this to England and himself!
WESTMORLAND Base, fearful, and despairing Henry!   180
CLIFFORD How hast thou injured both thyself and us!
WESTMORLAND I cannot stay to hear these articles.
NORTHUMBERLAND Nor I.
CLIFFORD Come, cousin, let us tell the queen these news.
WESTMORLAND Farewell, faint-hearted and degenerate king   185
In whose cold blood no spark of honour bides.   [*Exit*]
NORTHUMBERLAND Be thou a prey unto the house of York
And die in bands for this unmanly deed!   [*Exit*]
CLIFFORD In dreadful war mayst thou be overcome
Or live in peace abandoned and despised!   [*Exit*] 190
WARWICK Turn this way, Henry, and regard them not.
EXETER They seek revenge and therefore will not yield.

168 over] F *subst.*; o'er F2 *subst.*   169 SD.1 *a . . . and*] *This edn; not in* F   170 hear] F *subst.*; hear me
F3   174–5] O *subst.; not in* F   175 Tuttle] *This edn;* Tuthill O; *not in* F   175 SD] *This edn; not in* F   186, 188,
190 SD] O; *not in* F

169 **usurping blood** i.e. King Henry's.
170 **hear** The metre suggests that this is
disyllabic (Cercignani, p. 147), unless F3's 'hear
me' is adopted.
*174–5 It is likely that these lines were
skipped by the compositor (or perhaps were
added by the author to show Henry refusing to
act under duress).
*175 **Tuttle fields** Open ground in Westminster, used for tournaments and a training
ground for troops.
178 **wrong** a great wrong.

182 **articles** terms of agreement.
186 **cold** passionless.
*186–90 SD These stage directions occur
only in O. It is not certain whether soldiers
accompany their masters here (see 49 SD n.).
188 **bands** bonds, confinement.
189 **dreadful** terrible, awful.
192 'They go away not because they doubt
the justice of this determination, but because
they have been conquered, and seek to be
revenged. They are not influenced by principle
but passion' (Johnson).

KING HENRY Ah, Exeter!
WARWICK   Why should you sigh, my lord?
KING HENRY Not for myself, Lord Warwick, but my son
    Whom I unnaturally shall disinherit.   195
    But be it as it may. – [*To York*] I here entail
    The crown to thee and to thine heirs for ever,
    Conditionally, that here thou take an oath
    To cease this civil war and, whilst I live,
    To honour me as thy king and sovereign,   200
    And neither by treason nor hostility
    To seek to put me down and reign thyself.
YORK This oath I willingly take and will perform.
WARWICK Long live King Henry! Plantagenet, embrace him.
    [*York comes down and he and the king embrace*]
KING HENRY And long live thou, and these thy forward sons!   205
YORK Now York and Lancaster are reconciled.
EXETER Accursed be he that seeks to make them foes!
    Sennet. Here [*York's train*] *come down*
YORK Farewell, my gracious lord; I'll to my castle.
    [*Exeunt York and his sons with soldiers*]
WARWICK And I'll keep London with my soldiers.
    [*Exit with soldiers*]
NORFOLK And I to Norfolk with my followers.   210
    [*Exit with soldiers*]
MONTAGUE And I unto the sea from whence I came.
    [*Exit with soldiers*]

---

196 SD] *Collier MS; not in* F 204 SD] *This edn; not in* F 207 SD *Here . . . down*] *Oxford; Here they come downe.* F; *after 203 / Pelican* 208] F *subst.;* My lord Ile take my leaue, for Ile to *Wakefield* / To my castell. O **208, 209, 210, 211** SD] O *subst.; not in* F

195 unnaturally against the law of nature.
196 be . . . may Compare the proverb 'Be as be may' (Dent B65).
196 entail bestow as an inalienable possession (*OED* sv *v* 2a).
*204 SD I have conjectured that York here leaves the 'state' to embrace Henry; it could be, however, that, as part of his play for power, he compels Henry to climb up to him.
205 forward (1) zealous (*OED* sv *adj* 6c), (2) presumptuous, bold (*OED* sv *adj* 8).
207 SD Sennet Music used for processions of dignitaries.
208 See collation. O's version seems to contain a detail (the location of the castle) anticipated from 2.1.107.
208 castle Sandal Castle, near Wakefield.
209 keep remain in.
211 There is no reason to connect Montague with the sea – in 1.2 he is with York at Sandal (see 208). He seems to have been confused in Shakespeare's mind here with Falconbridge – see 241; compare 1.1.14 n. Alternatively, Shakespeare may have confused him with Sir Simon Montford who, having been assigned to keep the Kent coast and the Cinque Ports, was captured by Falconbridge in 1460 (Holinshed, p. 256).

KING HENRY And I with grief and sorrow to the court.
[*King Henry and Exeter turn to leave*]

Enter the QUEEN [MARGARET *and* PRINCE EDWARD]

EXETER Here comes the queen, whose looks bewray her anger.
    I'll steal away.
KING HENRY   Exeter, so will I.
MARGARET Nay, go not from me; I will follow thee.   215
KING HENRY Be patient, gentle queen, and I will stay.
MARGARET Who can be patient in such extremes?
    Ah, wretched man, would I had died a maid
    And never seen thee, never borne thee son,
    Seeing thou hast proved so unnatural a father!   220
    Hath he deserved to loose his birthright thus?
    Hadst thou but loved him half so well as I
    Or felt that pain which I did for him once
    Or nourished him, as I did with my blood,
    Thou wouldst have left thy dearest heart-blood there,   225
    Rather than have made that savage duke thine heir
    And disinherited thine only son.
PRINCE EDWARD Father, you cannot disinherit me:
    If you be king, why should not I succeed?
KING HENRY Pardon me, Margaret. – Pardon me, sweet son,   230
    The Earl of Warwick and the duke enforced me.
MARGARET Enforced thee! Art thou king and wilt be forced?
    I shame to hear thee speak. Ah, timorous wretch,
    Thou hast undone thyself, thy son, and me,
    And given unto the house of York such head   235
    As thou shalt reign but by their sufferance.
    To entail him and his heirs unto the crown,
    What is it but to make thy sepulchre
    And creep into it far before thy time?

---

212 SD.1] *Oxford; not in* F   212 SD.2 MARGARET . . . EDWARD] O *subst.; not in* F   213] *Pope subst.;* Heere . . .
Queene, / Whose . . . anger: F   214 Exeter, so] F *subst.;* so, Exeter *Pope*   220 so unnatural a father] F *subst.;* a
father so unnatural *conj. Hudson*

213 **bewray** reveal (*OED* sv 6).
216 **gentle** (1) noble, (2) tender – here ironic.
225 **there** (on the throne).
229 At the time of events represented here, Edward was seven years old.
233 **shame** am ashamed (*OED* sv *v* 1).
235 **head** freedom; the metaphor is from riding (*OED* sv *sb* 57).

236 **sufferance** permission.
237–8 'The queen's reproach is founded on a position long received among politicians, that the loss of a king's power is soon followed by loss of life' (Johnson).
237 **entail** appoint as heir (*OED* sv *v* 2b).

> Warwick is chancellor and the Lord of Calais,   240
> Stern Falconbridge commands the Narrow Seas,
> The duke is made Protector of the realm,
> And yet shalt thou be safe? Such safety finds
> The trembling lamb environèd with wolves.
> Had I been there, which am a silly woman,   245
> The soldiers should have tossed me on their pikes
> Before I would have granted to that act.
> But thou preferr'st thy life before thine honour:
> And seeing thou dost, I here divorce myself
> Both from thy table, Henry, and thy bed,   250
> Until that act of parliament be repealed
> Whereby my son is disinherited.
> The northern lords, that have forsworn thy colours,
> Will follow mine if once they see them spread;
> And spread they shall be, to thy foul disgrace   255
> And utter ruin of the house of York!
> Thus do I leave thee. – Come, son, let's away,
> Our army is ready: come, we'll after them.

KING HENRY Stay, gentle Margaret, and hear me speak.
MARGARET Thou hast spoke too much already: get thee gone.   260
KING HENRY Gentle son Edward, thou wilt with stay me?

---

240 Calais] *Eds.;* Callice F   241 Falconbridge] F *subst.;* Montague *conj. Oxford*   245 silly] F; seely *Oxford*   255
thy] F; the *conj. Keightley*   256 And] F; And the *Oxford*   261 with] O; *not in* F

240 According to Holinshed (p. 242; Hall, p. 233), it was in fact Richard Neville, first Earl of Salisbury, who was appointed Lord Chancellor and Warwick Captain of Calais. Cairncross argues that 'the text was probably altered here before performance to eliminate the part of Salisbury' (p. 15 n.).
  241 **Stern** Cruel (*OED* sv *adj* 3).
  241 **Falconbridge** William Neville (d. 1463), husband of the daughter of the last baron Faulconberg and uncle of Warwick; Admiral of the Channel fleet in 1462 (see Thomson, pp. 114–16). There is mention in the chroniclers, however, of two other Nevilles: Thomas who was appointed 'vice-admiral of the sea', but much later, after the battle of Tewkesbury (Holinshed, p. 321; Hall, p. 301); and then his father 'the Lord Thomas Falconbridge ('who had lately before been sent to the sea by the Earl of Warwick and after fallen to practise piracy' (Holinshed, p. 321). Falconbridge does not appear in the play, and Oxford's conjecture 'Montague' is attractive, given that lord's

connection with the sea at 211. He may have been in an earlier version of the text of which this is a survival, to be later fused with Montague. Compare A. S. Cairncross, 'An "inconsistency" in *3 Henry VI*', *MLR*, 4 (1955), 492–4.
  241 **Narrow Seas** Straits of Dover.
  242 **The duke** York.
  244 **environèd** surrounded.
  245 **silly** 'seely' or helpless (*OED* sv 1b and c, 'esp. as a conventional . . . epithet of sheep').
  246 **tossed** brandished (*OED* Toss *v* 10).
  246 **pikes** lances with axe-like heads, the chief weapons of a large part of the infantry.
  247 **granted** assented (*OED* Grant *v* 1).
  247 **act** decision, decree.
  249–50 **I . . . bed** The queen is referring to divorce *a mensa et thoro* – see D. H. Phillips, *Shakespeare and the Lawyers*, 1972, p. 13.
  258 **come** pay heed now.
  261 ***with** O's reading is justified by both sense and metre, although F's 'stay' could mean 'support'.

MARGARET Ay, to be murdered by his enemies.
PRINCE EDWARD When I return with victory from the field
          I'll see your grace: till then, I'll follow her.
MARGARET Come, son, away; we may not linger thus.   265
                              [Exit with Prince Edward]
KING HENRY Poor queen! How love to me and to her son
          Hath made her break out into terms of rage.
          Revenged may she be on that hateful duke
          Whose haughty spirit, wingèd with desire,
          Will 'cost my crown and, like an empty eagle,   270
          Tire on the flesh of me and of my son.
          The loss of those three lords torments my heart:
          I'll write unto them and entreat them fair.
          Come, cousin, you shall be the messenger.
EXETER And I, I hope, shall reconcile them all.   275
                              [Flourish.] Exeunt

[1.2] *Enter* RICHARD, EDWARD [EARL OF MARCH], *and* [*the*
MARQUESS OF] MONTAGUE

RICHARD Brother, though I be youngest, give me leave.
EDWARD No, I can better play the orator.
MONTAGUE But I have reasons strong and forcible.

---

263 from] O; to F   265 SD] *Rowe subst.; not in* F   266] *Pope subst.;* Poore Queene, / How … Sonne, F   270 'cost] *This edn;* cost F; souse *conj.* Dyce   275 SD] *Wilson subst.; Exit. / Flourish. (part of* 1.2.0 SD) F   **Act 1, Scene 2**   1.2] *Capell; not in* F   1] F *subst.; Edw.* Brother, and cosen *Montague,* giue mee leaue to speake. O   2 SH] F *subst.; Rich.* O

265–71 If, as seems likely, Margaret and the prince exit at 265 (see collation), these lines may constitute a long aside or soliloquy.
   267 terms words.
   269 wingèd with impelled by.
   270 'cost F's 'cost' is probably a variant of 'coast' = accost, attack, assail (*OED* sv *v* 9); or may be a hawking metaphor = keep at a distance from (*OED* sv *v* 10) – or simply = 'cost me'. Wilson glosses as 'rob [me] of', citing Greene's *Alphonsus King of Aragon,* 158 where the word obviously means 'robbery', a sense unrecorded in *OED.* Dyce's conjecture 'souse' (=swoop upon like a falcon; compare *John* 5.2.150) is attractive.
   270 empty ravenous
   271 Tire on Tear ravenously from, like a hawk (*OED* Tire *v*² II. 2).
   272 those three lords 'That is, of Northumberland, Westmorland, and Clifford, who had left him in disgust [see 186–90]' (Johnson).

273 **entreat them fair** treat them kindly (*OED* Treat *v* 1).
   274 cousin Henry Holland, Duke of Exeter, had married Anne Plantagenet, the sister of Edward IV, but remained faithful to Henry VI (Thomson).
   275 SD *Flourish* Sounded by trumpeters and a sign of the presence of authority (Long, pp. 10–11). In F it is placed before the entrance of Yorkists at the beginning of the next scene. As at 49 SD, therefore, and placed as above, it may sound ambiguously, ironically proclaiming both the decline of Henry and the rise of his protagonists.

Act 1, Scene 2
1.2 The chroniclers report how, in 1461, York moved north to his castle at Sandal near Wakefield after hearing that the Lancastrians were assembling 'a great army' in the north (Holinshed, p. 268; Hall, p. 250). Holinshed (p. 269; see Appendix 1, p. 213) reflects on

Enter the DUKE OF YORK

YORK Why how now, sons and brother, at a strife?
        What is your quarrel? How began it first?   5
EDWARD No quarrel, but a slight contention.
YORK About what?
RICHARD About that which concerns your grace and us:
        The crown of England, father, which is yours.
YORK Mine, boy? Not till King Henry be dead.   10
RICHARD Your right depends not on his life or death.
EDWARD Now you are heir: therefore enjoy it now.
        By giving the house of Lancaster leave to breathe,
        It will outrun you, father, in the end.
YORK I took an oath that he should quietly reign.   15
EDWARD But for a kingdom any oath may be broken:
        I would break a thousand oaths to reign one year.
RICHARD No; God forbid your grace should be forsworn.
YORK I shall be, if I claim by open war.
RICHARD I'll prove the contrary, if you'll hear me speak.   20
YORK Thou canst not, son; it is impossible.
RICHARD An oath is of no moment, being not took
        Before a true and lawful magistrate
        That hath authority over him that swears.
        Henry had none, but did usurp the place.   25

---

4 brother] F; brothers F3; cousin *Capell*   6 slight] F; sweete O

whether York's death was due to the oath he is
seen breaking in this scene. Hall gives York a
speech from which details in 68 and 73–5 may
derive (p. 250; see Appendix 1, p. 211).
    0 SD.1 EDWARD According to the chroniclers,
Edward, having been ordered by York to follow
him north, never reached Sandal and did not
fight at Wakefield. He was at Gloucester when
he heard of the deaths of his father and brother
(Holinshed, p. 269; Hall, p. 251).
    1, 2 SHH O's reversal of the attributions of
these two lines may be correct, given that
Richard is given the long speech below (22–34).
    1, 55 Brother See 1.1.14 n.
    1 give me leave allow me to speak.
    2 play the orator proverbial (Dent O74.1).
    6 contention verbal altercation (*OED* sv 2).
    11 right just title.

13 breathe rest.
14 outrun elude (*OED* sv 2b).
15 quietly in peace.
16 Compare Cicero, *De Officiis*, III.c.21: 'Nam
si violandum est ius, regnandi gratia violandum
est', and compare the proverb 'For a kingdom
any law may be broken' (Tilley K90).
18 be forsworn commit perjury.
22–5 'The obligation of an oath is here
eluded by very despicable sophistry. A lawful
magistrate alone has the power to exact an oath,
but the oath derives no part of its force from the
magistrate. The plea against the obligation of an
oath obliging to maintain an usurper, taken from
the unlawfulness of the oath itself in the foregoing play, was rational and just' (Johnson).
    22 moment consequence.
    22 being . . . took if it is not sworn.

Then, seeing 'twas he that made you to depose,
Your oath, my lord, is vain and frivolous.
Therefore to arms! And, father, do but think
How sweet a thing it is to wear a crown,
Within whose circuit is Elysium   30
And all that poets feign of bliss and joy.
Why do we linger thus? I cannot rest
Until the white rose that I wear be dyed
Even in the lukewarm blood of Henry's heart.

YORK Richard, enough: I will be king, or die. –   ,   35
[*To Montague*] Brother, thou shalt to London presently
And whet on Warwick to this enterprise. –
Thou, Richard, shalt to the Duke of Norfolk
And tell him privily of our intent. –
You, Edward, shall unto my Lord Cobham   40
With whom the Kentishmen will willingly rise;
In them I trust, for they are soldiers
Witty, courteous, liberal, full of spirit.
While you are thus employed, what resteth more
But that I seek occasion how to rise,   45

36 SD] *This edn; not in* F   36 Brother] F; *cosen* O   40 unto my Lord] F; *to Edmund Brooke* Lord O; unto my Lord *of Hanmer*   41 rise;] *This edn; rise* F   43 Witty] F; *Wealthy and Theobald*   44 more] *Eds.;* more? F

26 **depose** swear upon oath (*OED* sv 5c).
27 **vain** worthless.
27 **frivolous** a legal term = manifestly insufficient or futile (*OED* sv 1b).
29–31 Echoes the content and stagey rhythms of Marlowe's *1 Tamburlaine* 2.5.57–61: 'A god is not so glorious as a king. / I think the pleasure they enjoy in heaven / Cannot compare with kingly joys in earth: / To wear a crown enchased with pearl and gold, / Whose virtues carry with it life and death . . .' and 2.7.27–9: 'the ripest fruit of all, / That perfect bliss and sole felicity, / The sweet fruition of an earthly crown'.
30 **circuit** circumference.
30 **Elysium** The abode of the spirits of the blessed in Greek mythology.
31 **feign** invent, imagine.
33 **white rose** the badge of the house of York (see *1H6* 2.4.30).
36 **Brother** See 1.1.14 n.
36 **presently** immediately.
39 **privily** secretly.
40 **Cobham** Sir Edward Brooke, a fierce Yorkist, who fought at the first battle of St Albans. Holinshed (p. 238) and Hall (p. 232) note that he was among York's 'special friends'.

An incorrect version of his full name appears in the text of O (see collation) and it is probable that this was censored out – or tactlessly inserted by a reporter. In Shakespeare's time his descendants, who numbered among their ancestors Sir John Oldcastle, a prototype of Falstaff, were unhappy to hear their name from the mouths of players (see S. Schoenbaum, *William Shakespeare: A Compact Documentary Life*, 1977, pp. 192–6).
41 **Kentishmen** Holinshed (p. 259) and Hall (p. 243) note how the men of Kent supported the Yorkist cause before the battle of Northampton earlier in 1460.
41 **rise** rebel.
42 **them** Warwick, Norfolk, and Cobham.
43 Compare the report of Caesar's praise of Kentishmen in *2H6*: 'The people liberal, valiant, active, wealthy' (4.7.52).
43 **Witty** Wise.
43 **liberal** gentlemanly (*OED* sv *adj.* 1).
44 **resteth** remains (*OED* Rest v^2 3).
44 **more** else.
45 **occasion** opportunity.
45 **rise** become great, an 'awkward echo of 41' (Wilson).

And yet the king not privy to my drift
Nor any of the house of Lancaster?

Enter [a MESSENGER]

But stay: what news? Why com'st thou in such post?
MESSENGER The queen with all the northern earls and lords
    Intend here to besiege you in your castle.   50
    She is hard by with twenty thousand men;
    And therefore fortify your hold, my lord.
YORK Ay, with my sword. What, think'st thou that we fear them? –
    Edward and Richard, you shall stay with me;
    My brother Montague shall post to London;   55
    Let noble Warwick, Cobham, and the rest,
    Whom we have left protectors of the king,
    With powerful policy strengthen themselves,
    And trust not simple Henry nor his oaths.
MONTAGUE Brother, I go; I'll win them, fear it not: 60
    And thus most humbly I do take my leave.   *Exit*

Enter [SIR JOHN] MORTIMER and his brother
[SIR HUGH MORTIMER]

YORK Sir John and Sir Hugh Mortimer, mine uncles,
    You are come to Sandal in a happy hour:
    The army of the queen mean to besiege us.
SIR JOHN She shall not need; we'll meet her in the field.   65
YORK What, with five thousand men?

47 SD *a* MESSENGER] O; *Gabriel* F   49] *Pope subst.;* The Queene, / With . . . Lords, F   49 SH] O *subst; Gabriel*
F   53] *Pope;* I . . . Sword, / What . . . them? F   55 brother] F *subst.;* Cosen O   60 Brother] F; Cousin *Capell*
61 SD.2–3 SIR JOHN . . . SIR HUGH MORTIMER] O; *not in* F

46 **drift** purpose.
* 47 SD F's 'Enter Gabriel' indicates authorial
copy and designates Gabriel Spencer, later a
member of the Admiral's Men and killed by Ben
Jonson in a duel on 22 September 1598.
48 **post** haste.
49–53 'I know not whether the author
intended any moral instruction, but he that reads
this has a striking admonition against that pre-
cipitancy by which men often use unlawful
means to do that which a little delay would put
honestly in their power. Had York but stayed a
few moments he had saved his cause from the
stain of perjury' (Johnson).
52 **hold** stronghold (*OED* sv *sb*[1] 10).

56–7 In Holinshed, York, himself 'Protector
of the realm, . . . assigned the Duke of Norfolk
and Earl of Warwick, his trusty friends, to be
about the king' (p. 268; Hall, pp. 249–50).
58 **policy** stratagem, cunning.
59 **simple** witless.
60 **fear** doubt.
62 **uncles** York's mother Anne was a
Mortimer, daughter to Roger Mortimer, fourth
Earl of March. The chroniclers note they were
bastard brothers (Holinshed, p. 268; Hall,
p. 250).
63 **Sandal** Sandal Castle, near Wakefield.
63 **happy** opportune.

RICHARD Ay, with five hundred, father, for a need;
    A woman's general: what should we fear?
       A march afar off
EDWARD I hear their drums; let's set our men in order
    And issue forth and bid them battle straight.   70
YORK Five men to twenty! Though the odds be great,
    I doubt not, uncle, of our victory.
    Many a battle have I won in France
    When as the enemy hath been ten to one:
    Why should I not now have the like success?   75
                  Alarum. Exeunt

[1.3] *[Alarums and then] enter [the* EARL OF *]* RUTLAND *and his*
TUTOR

RUTLAND Ah, whither shall I fly to scape their hands?

      Enter CLIFFORD *[and Soldiers]*

    Ah, tutor, look where bloody Clifford comes.
CLIFFORD Chaplain, away! Thy priesthood saves thy life.
    As for the brat of this accursèd duke,
    Whose father slew my father, he shall die.   5
TUTOR And I, my lord, will bear him company.
CLIFFORD Soldiers, away with him!

69] *Pope;* I...Drummes: / Let's...order, F   72 uncle] F *subst.;* uncles *Hudson*   75 SD *Exeunt]* Q2; *Exit.*
F   **Act 1, Scene 3**   1.3] *Capell; not in* F   0 SD *Alarums...then]* O *subst.; not in* F   1 SD] *Placed as in* O; *after*
2 *in* F   1 SD *and Soldiers]* *Theobald (after 2); not in* F   5 Whose] F; *His* Capell   7] F *subst.;* Soldiers awaie and
drag him hence perforce: Awaie with the villaine. O

67 for a need if need be.
68, 73–5 These lines may derive from a
speech given to York in Hall (p. 250; see
Appendix 1, p. 211).
68 woman's woman is.
68 SD *march* a march rhythm played on
drums.
68 SD *afar off* i.e. within the tiring-house.
70 straight straightway.
74 When as When (Abbott 116).

Act 1, Scene 3
*****1.3** The account of Rutland's death at the
battle of Wakefield on 30 December 1460
(Boswell-Stone, p. 298 n. 4) is given in
Holinshed (p. 269; Hall, pp. 251 – see
Appendix 1, p. 212). Again, Shakespeare seems

to have followed a speech reported by Hall (see
5 n. and 12–15 n.).
   0 SD *Alarums* This detail from O suggests
that this scene is linked with that preceding by
the sounds of an off-stage battle (see 1.1.0 SD).
*****1 SD** The stage direction is placed thus in O,
after 2 in F.
   4 brat child: 'sometimes used without contempt, though nearly always implying insignifi-
cance' (*OED*).
   5 Hall (and not Holinshed) gives a speech to
Clifford which includes the words 'Thy father
slew mine' (p. 251); compare 1.1.7 n.
   5 Whose Refers to 'brat' and not 'duke'.
   7 O's version of the line (see collation)
suggests that the Tutor put up a struggle.

TUTOR Ah, Clifford, murder not this innocent child,
　　　　Lest thou be hated both of God and man!
　　　　　　　　　　　　　　　Exit [, *dragged off by soldiers*]
CLIFFORD How now, is he dead already? Or is it fear   10
　　　　That makes him close his eyes? I'll open them.
RUTLAND So looks the pent-up lion o'er the wretch
　　　　That trembles under his devouring paws;
　　　　And so he walks, insulting o'er his prey,
　　　　And so he comes, to rend his limbs asunder.   15
　　　　Ah, gentle Clifford, kill me with thy sword
　　　　And not with such a cruel threat'ning look.
　　　　Sweet Clifford, hear me speak before I die:
　　　　I am too mean a subject for thy wrath:
　　　　Be thou revenged on men, and let me live.   20
CLIFFORD In vain thou speak'st, poor boy: my father's blood
　　　　Hath stopped the passage where thy words should enter.
RUTLAND Then let my father's blood open it again:
　　　　He is a man and, Clifford, cope with him.
CLIFFORD Had I thy brethren here, their lives and thine   25
　　　　Were not revenge sufficient for me;
　　　　No, if I digged up thy forefathers' graves
　　　　And hung their rotten coffins up in chains,
　　　　It could not slake mine ire nor ease my heart.
　　　　The sight of any of the house of York   30
　　　　Is as a fury to torment my soul;
　　　　And, till I root out their accursèd line
　　　　And leave not one alive, I live in hell.
　　　　Therefore –   [*Lifting his hand*]
RUTLAND O let me pray before I take my death!   35
　　　　[*Kneels*] To thee I pray, sweet Clifford: pity me!
CLIFFORD Such pity as my rapier's point affords.

---

9 SD *dragged ... soldiers*] *Theobald; not in* F; *Exit* the Chaplein O   10–11] *Pope;* How ... alreadie? / Or ... eyes? / Ile ... them. F   21–22] *Pope;* In ... Boy: / My ... passage / Where ... enter. F   34 SD] *Johnson; not in* F   36 SD] *This edn (conj. Walker); not in* F

9 **of** by.
9 SD ***dragged ... soldiers*** O's text (see collation here and at 52) seems to indicate that all the soldiers exit here so that Rutland's death is unwitnessed. Hall, however, has Clifford kill Rutland before the eyes of the tutor (p. 251).
12–15 The epic simile seems to derive from Hall (p. 251; see Appendix 1, p. 212).
12 'That is, the lion that hath been long "confined" without food, and is let out to devour a man condemned' (Johnson).

14 **insulting** triumphing insolently (*OED* Insult *v* 1).
16 **gentle** noble.
19 **mean** unworthy.
24 **cope** fight (*OED* sv v^2 2).
26 **sufficient** pronounced with four syllables (Cercignani, p. 309).
31 An allusion to the classical Furies who caused grievous mental torments in murderers etc; compare *Metamorphoses*, IV, 614–15.
*36 SD Both Holinshed (p. 269) and Hall (p. 251) note that Rutland met his death when kneeling before Clifford.

RUTLAND I never did thee harm: why wilt thou slay me?
CLIFFORD Thy father hath.
RUTLAND   But 'twas ere I was born.
    Thou hast one son: for his sake pity me   40
    Lest in revenge thereof, sith God is just,
    He be as miserably slain as I.
    Ah, let me live in prison all my days
    And when I give occasion of offence
    Then let me die, for now thou hast no cause.   45
CLIFFORD No cause?
    Thy father slew my father: therefore die.   [*Stabs him*]
RUTLAND *Di faciant laudis summa sit ista tuae!*   [*Dies*]
CLIFFORD Plantagenet, I come, Plantagenet!
    And this thy son's blood cleaving to my blade   50
    Shall rust upon my weapon till thy blood,
    Congealed with this, do make me wipe off both.
                                    Exit [*with Rutland's body*]

[**1.4**] *Alarum. Enter* RICHARD, DUKE OF YORK

YORK The army of the queen hath got the field,
    My uncles both are slain in rescuing me,

46–7] *Eds.; No cause? thy . . . dye* F   47 SD] *Rowe (after 48); not in* F   48 *Di*] *Eds.; Dij* F   48 SD] *Theobald; not
in* F   52 this] F; *his* O   52 SD *Exit*] F, O; *Exit . . . with . . . soldiers / Oxford*   52 SD *with . . . body*] *Oxford; not in*
F   Act 1, Scene 4   1.4] *Capell; not in* F

39 ere . . . born York killed Clifford's father
at the first battle of St Albans (1455) at the end
of *2H6*, placed in dramatic time only a few
weeks earlier, although historically five years
before the time of this scene. Rutland had in fact
been born in 1443 although Holinshed (p. 269)
and Hall (p. 251) make him twelve years old at
the time of his death.
    41 sith since.
    48 'May the gods cause this to be the height
of your glory!' – so Phyllis taunts Demophoon
for seducing her in Ovid's *Heroides*, II, 66.
    49 Plantagenet The Duke of York.

Act 1, Scene 4
***1.4** See 1.3 n. York's capture and death on
the battlefield at Wakefield (30 December 1460)
is recounted in Holinshed (pp. 268–9) and Hall
(p. 250), as is the queen's order to have the
heads of her adversaries displayed at York.

Holinshed in fact gives two versions of York's
death: in the second of these, translated from
Johannes   Whethamstede   (Boswell-Stone,
p. xx), it is reported that York was alive when
tormented by Clifford (see Appendix 1, p. 213
and 67 n.). Hall has him dead when crowned
with the paper-crown (p. 251; compare *Mirror*,
pp. 189 and 194; and see 95 SD). Shakespeare
invented the detail of the blood-stained handkerchief at 79–83. The scene may derive in a
general way from the episode of the buffeting
and scourging of Christ found in all of the extant
mystery cycles.
    1–6 For O's very different version of these
lines which may indicate a censor's intervention,
see Appendix 2, p. 218.
    1 got the field won the battle.
    2 uncles Sir John and Sir Hugh Mortimer of
1.2.

And all my followers to the eager foe
Turn back and fly, like ships before the wind,
Or lambs pursued by hunger-starvèd wolves.   5
My sons, God knows what hath bechancèd them:
But this I know, they have demeaned themselves
Like men borne to renown by life or death.
Three times did Richard make a lane to me
And thrice cried, 'Courage, father, fight it out!'   10
And full as oft came Edward to my side
With purple falchion, painted to the hilt
In blood of those that had encountered him;
And when the hardiest warriors did retire,
Richard cried, 'Charge, and give no foot of ground!'   15
Ned cried, 'A crown, or else a glorious tomb!
A sceptre, or an earthly sepulchre!'
With this we charged again. But, out alas,
We budged again – as I have seen a swan
With bootless labour swim against the tide   20
And spend her strength with over-matching waves.
          A short alarum within
Ah, hark! The fatal followers do pursue,
And I am faint and cannot fly their fury;
And were I strong, I would not shun their fury.
The sands are numbered that makes up my life;   25
Here must I stay and here my life must end.

8 borne] F; born *Eds.*   16 Ned] *conj. Collier;* And F; And Edward *conj. Oxford*   19 budged] *conj. Johnson;* bodg'd
F   25 makes] F; make F2

3 **eager** ardent, fierce (*OED* sv 5).
4 **Turn back** Turn their backs (Wilson).
5 **hunger-starved** starvèd here means 'emaciated' (*OED ppl adj.* 3); compare *1H6* 1.5.16.
6 **My sons** The chroniclers report the presence at Wakefield only of Rutland: George and Richard were actually younger.
6 **bechancèd** happened to.
8 **borne** F's reading (meaning 'carried' or 'impelled') makes more sense than the customary emendation to 'born'.
9 **make a lane** cut his way through.
12 **purple** blood-stained (*OED* sv 2d).
12 **falchion** a single-edged curved sword.
14 **retire** retreat.
16 ***Ned** Collier's emendation of F's 'And' is justified by the omission of mention of him and

by the fact that, as heir to York, Edward would inherit the crown. There may be a line missing which reported the battle-cry of George. Retaining 'And', however, makes for a nice irony, given Richard's regal ambitions (a point made privately by Norman Blake).
18 **out, alas** expresses indignant reproach (*OED* Out *int* 2).
19 ***budged** flinched, gave way (*OED* Budge v^2 1b).
20 **bootless** fruitless.
21 **spend** use up.
21 **with** against.
21 **over-matching** of superior strength; compare 64 below.
22 **fatal** deadly.
25 **sands** in an hourglass.
25 **makes** make (Abbott 333).

Enter the QUEEN [MARGARET], CLIFFORD,
NORTHUMBERLAND, *the young* PRINCE [EDWARD], *and Soldiers*

Come, bloody Clifford, rough Northumberland,
I dare your quenchless fury to more rage:
I am your butt and I abide your shot.
NORTHUMBERLAND Yield to our mercy, proud Plantagenet.   30
CLIFFORD Ay, to such mercy as his ruthless arm
    With downright payment showed unto my father.
    Now Phaëthon hath tumbled from his car
    And made an evening at the noontide prick.
YORK My ashes, as the Phoenix, may bring forth   35
    A bird that will revenge upon you all;
    And in that hope I throw mine eyes to heaven,
    Scorning whate'er you can afflict me with.
    Why, come you not? What, multitudes and fear?
CLIFFORD So cowards fight when they can fly no further;   40
    So doves do peck the falcon's piercing talons;
    So desperate thieves, all hopeless of their lives,
    Breathe out invectives 'gainst the officers.
YORK O, Clifford, but bethink thee once again
    And in thy thought o'errun my former time;   45
    And, if thou canst for blushing, view this face
    And bite thy tongue that slanders him with cowardice
    Whose frown hath made thee faint and fly ere this.
CLIFFORD I will not bandy with thee word for word

---

26 SD *the . . .* PRINCE] F *subst.; not in* O   33 Phaëthon] *Eds.; Phaeton* F   46 And, . . . blushing,] *Eds.; And . . .
canst, for blushing,* F

27 **rough** violent, harsh.
29 **butt** target (in archery).
29 **abide** endure.
31 **ruthless** pitiless.
32 **downright** a quibble on 'downright' as
applied to a vertical blow – see 1.1.12.
33 **Phaëthon** (three syllables) son of
Phoebus who, by driving his father's chariot of
the sun, would have destroyed the earth had
not Zeus killed him with a thunderbolt – see
Metamorphoses, I, 944-II, 415 and compare 2.6.12.
The sun was a Yorkist badge – see 2.1.25.
33 **car** chariot.
34 **noontide prick** the mark for noon on a
sundial.
35–6 The Phoenix, a fabulous bird said to
live in Arabia, was born again from its own ashes
every 500 years; compare *1H6* 4.7.93 n.; for the

Phoenix as a symbol of everlasting political
power, see Ernst H. Kantorowicz, *Selected
Studies*, 1965, p. 396.
36 **bird** son (*OED* sv 1c), i.e. Edward IV.
37 **throw** cast.
40 Compare the proverb 'Despair makes
cowards courageous' (Tilley, D216).
41 Clifford virtually repeats the line at 2.2.18
when urging the king to revenge.
43 **Breathe out** Speak vehemently (*OED*
12b).
44 **but . . . thee** just reflect.
45 **o'errun** review.
46 **for** because of.
47 **bite** silence (Dent T400.1).
48 **faint** lose heart (*OED* sv *v* 1).
49 **bandy** exchange.

But buckler with thee blows twice two for one.   [*Draws*]   50
MARGARET Hold, valiant Clifford. For a thousand causes
    I would prolong a while the traitor's life. –
    Wrath makes him deaf. – Speak thou, Northumberland.
NORTHUMBERLAND Hold, Clifford; do not honour him so much
    To prick thy finger, though to wound his heart.   55
    What valour were it, when a cur doth grin,
    For one to thrust his hand between his teeth,
    When he might spurn him with his foot away?
    It is war's prize to take all vantages
    And ten to one is no impeach of valour.   60
    [*They fight and take York, who struggles*]
CLIFFORD Ay, ay: so strives the woodcock with the gin.
NORTHUMBERLAND So doth the cony struggle in the net.
YORK So triumph thieves upon their conquered booty;
    So true men yield, with robbers so o'er-matched.
    [*Drops his sword*]
NORTHUMBERLAND What would your grace have done unto him
    now?   65
MARGARET Brave warriors, Clifford and Northumberland,
    Come make him stand upon this molehill here,
    That raught at mountains with outstretchèd arms
    Yet parted but the <u>shadow</u> with his hand.

---

50 buckler] F; buckle O, *Theobald*   50 SD] *Johnson; not in* F   60 SD] *This edn; not in* F; Fight and take him O;
They lay hands on York, who struggles. / Johnson   64 yield, with robbers] F2; yeeld with Robbers, F   64 SD] *Capell
subst.; not in* F

---

50 buckler ward or catch with a shield (*OED*
sv *v* 2; compare 3.3.99) – although O's 'buckle'
= 'join in close fight', may be the correct
reading.
53 Wrath … deaf Emrys Jones, *The Origins
of Shakespeare*, 1977 p. 184 n. traces the phrase
back to Erasmus' 'fevore surdus', translated in
Sherry's *Treatise of Schemes and Tropes*, 1550.
53 him Clifford.
55 Compare the proverb 'The pricking of thy
finger is the piercing of his heart' (Dent P571.1).
56 grin bare its teeth.
58 spurn kick.
59 'All vantages are in war lawful prize'; that
is 'may be lawfully taken and used' (Johnson).
59 prize privilege (*OED* sv *sb*[1] 3b).
59 vantages opportunities.
60 So that for ten to attack one is no disgrace.
60 impeach calling in question (*OED* sv *sb*
3).
*60 SD It will be a critical decision for a
director whether to make this fight match the

epic description of it offered láter (2.1.50–8) by
a Messenger.
61–2 Both the woodcock and the rabbit
were easily snared and so became emblems of
stupidity.
61 gin snare.
62 cony rabbit, also a dupe or gull (*OED*
sv 6).
63 triumph exult.
64 true honest.
66 Brave Fine.
67 molehill recalls Calvary; compare also the
proverb 'Better to be king of a molehill than a
kaiser's slave' (Tilley K55); the detail of York's
death on a molehill is taken from Holinshed
(p. 269) and is not in Hall.
68 raught reached.
68 mountains commonly antithetic with
molehills (Tilley M1035).
69 parted took as his share (*OED* Part *v* 10).
69 but only.

What, was it you that would be England's king? 70
Was't you that revelled in our parliament
And made a preachment of your high descent?
Where are your mess of sons to back you now,
The wanton Edward and the lusty George?
And where's that valiant crook-back prodigy, 75
Dickie your boy, that with his grumbling voice
Was wont to cheer his dad in mutinies?
Or, with the rest, where is your darling, Rutland?
Look, York: I stained this napkin with the blood
That valiant Clifford with his rapier's point 80
Made issue from the bosom of the boy:
And if thine eyes can water for his death
I give thee this to dry thy cheeks withal.
                    [*Throwing it to him*]
Alas, poor York, but that I hate thee deadly
I should lament thy miserable state. 85
I prithee grieve to make me merry, York.
What, hath thy fiery heart so parched thine entrails
That not a tear can fall for Rutland's death?
Why, art thou patient, man? Thou should'st be mad;
And I, to make thee mad, do mock thee thus. 90
Stamp, rave, and fret, that I may sing and dance.
Thou wouldst be feed, I see, to make me sport:
York cannot speak unless he wear a crown. –
A crown for York! and, lords, bow low to him.

Marginal annotations: INSULT; SLOW; INFLICTING PAIN?; FAST SARCASM; SOUR/SWEET

73 back] F; bail *conj. Cambridge*   81 the] F; thy O   83 SD] *Collier²; not in* F   91] F *subst.; after 86* O

71 **revelled** 'led your party of riotous masquers' (Wilson).

72 **preachment** wearisome sermon.

73 **mess** literally a party of four at a banquet.

75 **prodigy** 'portentous monstrosity' (Wilson).

76 **grumbling** querulous.

77 **cheer** urge on.

77 **mutinies** rebellions.

79 **stained...blood** This may recall the sponge filled with vinegar offered to Christ at the crucifixion (Matt. 27. 48).

79 **napkin** handkerchief (*OED* sv 2); for an exploration of the significance of blood-stained napkins in English Renaissance drama, see Marion Lomax, *Stage Images and Traditions: Shakespeare to Ford*, 1987, pp. 35–7.

83 1.4.158 indicates that Margaret may have here smeared his face with blood as was done in Hall's 1964 production at Stratford.

84 **hate...deadly** This echoes Perseda's line to Soliman before she turns to revenge 'A kiss I grant thee, though I hate thee deadly' (Kyd (?), *Soliman and Perseda*, 5.4.67).

87 **fiery heart** see 1.1.60n.

87 **entrails** 'the inward parts regarded as the seat of the emotions = "heart", "soul"' (*OED* Entrail 4).

89 **mad** angry (*OED* sv 5).

91 O's placing of this line after 86 may be felt to improve the contours of the speech.

92 **feed** paid (like an entertainer), or bribed.

94 A possible parody of the mockery of Christ with the crown of thorns at the crucifixion (see Matt. 27. 29) – as Holinshed (p. 269, Appendix 1, p. 213) makes explicit; compare 2.5.69 ff.

Hold you his hands whilst I do set it on.   95
[*Putting a paper crown on his head*]
Ay, marry, sir, now looks he like a king!
Ay, this is he that took King Henry's chair,
And this is he was his adopted heir.
But how is it that great Plantagenet
Is crowned so soon and broke his solemn oath?   100
As I bethink me, you should not be king
Till our King Henry had shook hands with death.
And will you pale your head in Henry's glory
And rob his temples of the diadem
Now, in his life, against your holy oath?   105
O, 'tis a fault too too unpardonable. –
Off with the crown and, with the crown, his head:
And, whilst we breathe, take time to do him dead.
CLIFFORD That is my office for my father's sake.
MARGARET Nay, stay: let's hear the orisons he makes.   110
YORK She-wolf of France, but worse than wolves of France,
Whose tongue more poisons than the adder's tooth,
How ill-beseeming is it in thy sex
To triumph like an Amazonian trull
Upon their woes whom Fortune captivates!   115
But that thy face is vizard-like, unchanging,

95 SD] *Rowe; not in* F   107 crown,] F *subst.;* crown, *She knocks it from his head* / *Oxford*   111] *Pope;* Shee-
Wolfe . . . France, / But . . . France, F   115 their] F; his O

95 SD *paper crown* That this detail was in fact part of the stage business may be deduced from *R3* 1.3.174 ('When thou did'st crown his warlike brows with paper'). The paper crown is mentioned in Hall (p. 251; Holinshed says it was made of 'sedges or bulrushes' (p. 269)).
96 **marry** a mild oath ('by the Virgin Mary').
97 **chair** throne.
100 **broke . . . oath** 1.2.1–47 record the discussion over whether York should break his oath to Henry. Holinshed (but not Hall) reports it was believed by many that York's breaking of the oath was the cause of his 'miserable end' (p. 269).
102 **shook hands with** encountered: proverbial (Dent ss6).
103 **pale** encompass (*OED* sv *v* 1b).
105 **in his life** during his lifetime.
106 **fault** offence.
106 **too too** a common intensive.
107 Margaret may knock the crown from

York's head here, or, at 164, take it from his head and hand it back.
108 **breathe** rest.
108 **take . . . dead** seize the opportunity to kill him; compare *Ant.* 2.6.23.
109 **office** particular duty.
110 **orisons** prayers.
112 Compare Ps. 140. 3: 'They have sharpened their tongues like a serpent; adder's poison is under their lips.'
114–15 **triumph . . . Upon** exult, gloat . . . Over.
114 **an . . . trull** a warlike prostitute. The reference may be an allusion 'to Tomyris triumphing over the captive Cyrus (compare *1H6* 2.3.6); the Amazons being regarded as Scythians' (Wilson); compare *FQ*, 2, 10, 56. The classical source is Herodotus, 1, 214.
115 **captivates** subdues.
116 **vizard-like** expressionless like a mask; but also alluding to the habit of prostitutes of wearing masks (*OED* Vizard *sb* 1a).

Made impudent with use of evil deeds,
I would assay, proud queen, to make thee blush.
To tell thee whence thou cam'st, of whom derived,
Were shame enough to shame thee, wert thou not
    shameless.   120
Thy father bears the type of King of Naples,
Of both the Sicils and Jerusalem,
Yet not so wealthy as an English yeoman.
Hath that poor monarch taught thee to insult?
It needs not, nor it boots thee not, proud queen,   125
Unless the adage must be verified
That beggars mounted run their horse to death.
'Tis beauty that doth oft make women proud:
But God He knows thy share thereof is small.
'Tis virtue that doth make them most admired: 130
The contrary doth make thee wondered at.
'Tis government that makes them seem divine:
The want thereof makes thee abominable.
Thou art as opposite to every good
As the Antipodes are unto us   135
Or as the south to the Septentrion.
O tiger's heart wrapped in a woman's hide,
How couldst thou drain the life-blood of the child
To bid the father wipe his eyes withal
And yet be seen to bear a woman's face?   140
Women are soft, mild, pitiful, and flexible:

---

117 deeds,] F2; deedes. F   120] *Pope*; Were . . . thee, / Wert . . . shamelesse. F   120 wert thou] F; wert *conj. S. Walker*   137 tiger's] F (Tygres); Tygers O, Greene, *Groatsworth of witte*, 1592, sig. F1'; tigress' *Capell*

117 **impudent** shameless (*OED* sv 1).
117 **use** the constant practice.
118 **assay** try.
119 **derived** descended.
121 **type** sign, i.e. the crown (*OED* sv *sb* 3), with a quibble on 'tipe' = the highest honour (*OED* 2) but here ironic; compare *Lucr.* 1050.
122 **the Sicils** Naples and Sicily of which Reignier, Margaret's father, was titular king (compare *2H6* 1.1.6).
123 **yeoman** a freeholder of country land to the value of 40 shillings a year.
124 **insult** triumph in a scornful way (*OED* sv *v* 1).
125 **boots** avails.
126 **verified** proved true (*OED* Verify 1b).
127 Compare the proverb 'Set a beggar on

horseback and he will ride a gallop' (Tilley B238).
132 **government** 'evenness of temper and decency of manners' (Johnson).
135 **Antipodes** people living on the other side of the globe (*OED* sv 1); the idea 'was embodied in the Ptolemaic cosmology' (J. A. K. Thomson, *Shakespeare and the Classics*, 1952, p. 92).
136 **Septentrion** the north – referring to the seven stars in the 'Great Bear' constellation.
137 The line parodied by Greene in *A Groatsworth of Wit*; see Introduction, p. 53.
137 **hide** skin (*OED* sv *sb* 2).
139 **withal** with it.
141 **pitiful** compassionate (*OED* sv 2).
141 **flexible** tractable (*OED* sv 3a).

Thou stern, obdurate, flinty, rough, remorseless.
Bid'st thou me rage? Why, now thou hast thy wish.
Wouldst have me weep? Why, now thou hast thy will,
For raging wind blows up incessant showers   145
And, when the rage allays, the rain begins.
These tears are my sweet Rutland's obsequies
And every drop cries vengeance for his death
'Gainst thee, fell Clifford, and thee, false Frenchwoman.
NORTHUMBERLAND Beshrew me, but his passion moves me so   150
    That hardly can I check my eyes from tears.
YORK That face of his the hungry cannibals
    Would not have touched, would not have stained with blood;
    But you are more inhuman, more inexorable –
    O, ten times more – than tigers of Hyrcania.   155
    See, ruthless queen, a hapless father's tears.
    This cloth thou dipp'd'st in blood of my sweet boy,
    And I with tears do wash the blood away.
    Keep thou the napkin and go boast of this;
    And if thou tell'st the heavy story right,   160
    Upon my soul, the hearers will shed tears:
    Yea, even my foes will shed fast-falling tears
    And say, 'Alas, it was a piteous deed!'
    There, take the crown and, with the crown, my curse;
    And in thy need such comfort come to thee   165
    As now I reap at thy too cruel hand. –
    Hard-hearted Clifford, take me from the world,
    My soul to heaven, my blood upon your heads.

---

142 obdurate] F; indurate O   150 passion] *Cambridge;* passions F   150 moves] F *subst.;* moue O   152–3] O
(*reading* Could not have tucht); That . . . his, / The . . . Toucht, / Would . . . blood: F   153 with blood] F; the roses
just with F2; the roses juic'd with blood *Theobald*   154 inhuman] *Rowe;* inhumane F   166 too cruel hand] F
subst.; two cruell hands O, Q2; too cruell hands Q3

142 **obdurate** hard-hearted; O's 'indurate'
had the same meaning in the period.
   142 **rough** violent, cruel (*OED* sv 7).
   145–6 Compare the proverbs 'Small rain lays
great winds' (Tilley R16) and 'After wind comes
rain' (Tilley T275).
   146 **allays** abates.
   147 **obsequies** funeral rites.
   149 **fell** fierce.
   150 **Beshrew** Curse.
   150 ***passion** F's 'passions' is almost certainly
a compositorial error as Shakespeare does not
use the plural in this sense elsewhere.
   152 **cannibals** a general term for the recently
discovered natives of America who were held to

eat human flesh (see *Shakespeare's England,*
I, 176–7).
   154 ***inhuman** brutal, cruel (*OED* sv 1).
   155 **Hyrcania** A province on the south
shores of the Caspian, associated with tigers; see
Dido's speech to Aeneas in Virgil, *Aeneid,* IV,
366–7.
   156 **ruthless** pitiless.
   156 **hapless** luckless.
   160 **heavy** sorrowful.
   164 See 107 n.
   167–8 **take . . . heads** 'me', 'my soul', and
'my blood' are all objects of 'take'.
   168 **my . . . heads** you are responsible for my
death; compare *H5* 1.2.96.

NORTHUMBERLAND Had he been slaughterman to all my kin,
                I should not for my life but weep with him   170
                To see how inly sorrow gripes his soul.
MARGARET What, weeping-ripe, my Lord Northumberland?
          Think but upon the wrong he did us all
          And that will quickly dry thy melting tears.
CLIFFORD Here's for my oath; here's for my father's death.   175
                                                    [*Stabbing him*]
MARGARET And here's to right our gentle-hearted king.
                                                    [*Stabbing him*]
YORK Open Thy gate of mercy, gracious God,
      My soul flies through these wounds to seek out Thee. [*Dies*]
MARGARET Off with his head and set it on York gates –
          So York may overlook the town of York.   180
                                                    Flourish. Exeunt

[2.1] *A march. Enter* EDWARD [EARL OF MARCH], RICHARD,
[*with Drum and Soldiers*]

EDWARD I wonder how our princely father scaped
        Or whether he be scaped away or no
        From Clifford's and Northumberland's pursuit.
        Had he been ta'en, we should have heard the news;
        Had he been slain, we should have heard the news: 5
        Or had he scaped, methinks we should have heard

---

172 weeping-ripe] *Theobald;* weeping ripe F   175 SD] *Pope; not in* F   176 king] F; kind O   176 SD] *Rowe; not in* F   178 SD] *Rowe; not in* F   180 SD *Exeunt*] O *subst.; Exit.* F   **Act 2, Scene 1   2.1**] *Rowe; not in* F   0 SD *with Drum and Soldiers*] O; *and their power* F

---

169 **slaughterman** killer.
171 **inly** (*adj.*) inward, heartfelt.
171 **gripes** embraces (*OED* Gripe *v* 3c), afflicts (*OED* 7).
172 **weeping-ripe** ready to weep.
174 **melting** 'arising from a softened heart' (Pelican).
176 **gentle-hearted** noble-hearted.

Act 2, Scene 1
*2.1 The prodigy of the appearance after the battle of Wakefield of three suns to the Earl of March is reported in Holinshed (p. 270; Hall, p. 251). Historically, however, Edward was not in Wakefield but at Mortimer's Cross where he defeated a group of Welsh Lancastrians. The

account of the Yorkist defeat at the second battle of St Albans fought on 17 February 1461 (Boswell-Stone, p. 301) and which is narrated in the scene is found in Holinshed (p. 270; Hall, p. 252). The detail of the return of Richard and George from Utrecht (see 143–8) where their mother had sent them after their father's death (Holinshed, p. 272; Hall, p. 253) is also un-historical: Shakespeare probably wanted to create foils for Edward.
0 SD.2 *Drum* Drummer. This detail from O again probably records a detail of performance.
1 The line almost repeats, ironically, the first words of the play when the Yorkists were in the ascendant: now the Lancastrians are triumphant.
4 **ta'en** captured.

> The happy tidings of his good escape.
> How fares my brother? Why is he so sad?

RICHARD I cannot joy until I be resolved
> Where our right valiant father is become.   10
> I saw him in the battle range about
> And watched him how he singled Clifford forth.
> Methought he bore him in the thickest troop
> As doth a lion in a heard of neat,
> Or as a bear encompassed round with dogs,   15
> Who, having pinched a few and made them cry,
> The rest stand all aloof and bark at him:
> So fared our father with his enemies,
> So fled his enemies my warlike father;
> Methinks 'tis prize enough to be his son.   20
>
> *[Three suns appear in the air.]*
> See how the morning opes her golden gates
> And takes her farewell of the glorious sun:
> How well resembles it the prime of youth
> Trimmed like a younker prancing to his love!

EDWARD Dazzle mine eyes or do I see three suns?   25

RICHARD Three glorious suns, each one a perfect sun;
> Not separated with the racking clouds
> But severed in a pale clear-shining sky.
> See, see! They join, embrace, and seem to kiss

---

19 my] F; from our Q3   20 SD] O; *not in* F; *after 24* Cairncross   28 sky] F *subst.*; sky. *The three suns begin to join /*
Oxford

---

9 resolved satisfied (*OED* Resolve *v* 2).

10 is become has betaken himself, gone (*OED* Become 1).

12 singled . . . forth selected out (a hunting term).

13 him himself.

14 neat cattle.

16 pinched bitten; for the image see Armstrong, p. 42.

17 aloof at a distance (*OED* sv 3).

20 prize privilege (*OED* sb¹ 3b).

*20 SD The fact that the reported text O contains these words suggests that property suns were flown above the stage (see p. 60). These may have been fireworks (see Chambers, III, 76–7; Hattaway, pp. 13, 31, 60). Holinshed remarks on this event that 'men imagined that [Edward] gave the sun in his full brightness for his badge' or cognisance (p. 270; Hall, p. 251).

21–2 'Aurora takes for a time her farewell of the sun when she dismisses him to his diurnal course' (Johnson).

21–6 Compare Ps. 19. 4–5: 'Their line is

gone forth through all the world, and their words into the ends of the world: in them he hath set a tabernacle for the sun. Which cometh forth as a bridegroom out of his chamber and rejoiceth like a mighty man to run his race'; also *FQ*, 1, 5, 2: 'At last the golden Orientall gate / Of greatest heauen gan to open faire, / And Phoebus fresh, as bridegroom to his mate, / Came prauncing forth, shaking his deawie haire.'

22 sun another allusion to the Yorkist badge.

24 Trimmed Dressed up.

24 younker fashionable young man.

25 Dazzle . . . eyes . . . ? Do my eyes blur . . . ?

27 with by.

27 racking fleeting.

29 There is no way of telling whether there was some device which made the properties move in the manner Richard describes or whether Shakespeare intended him to be deluded. The chroniclers report that the suns 'suddenly joined altogether into one' (Holinshed, p. 270; Hall, p. 251).

As if they vowed some league inviolable;   30
Now are they but one lamp, one light, one sun:
In this the heaven figures some event.
EDWARD 'Tis wondrous strange, the like yet never heard of.
I think it cites us, brother, to the field
That we, the sons of brave Plantagenet,   35
Each one already blazing by our meeds,
Should notwithstanding join our lights together
And overshine the earth as this the world.
Whate'er it bodes, henceforward will I bear
Upon my target three fair-shining suns.   40
RICHARD Nay, bear three daughters: by your leave I speak it,
You love the breeder better than the male.

Enter [a MESSENGER] *blowing [a horn]*

But what art thou whose heavy looks foretell
Some dreadful story hanging on thy tongue?
MESSENGER Ah, one that was a woeful looker-on   45
When as the noble Duke of York was slain,
Your princely father and my loving lord!
EDWARD O speak no more, for I have heard too much.
RICHARD Say how he died, for I will hear it all.
MESSENGER Environèd he was with many foes   50
And stood against them, as the hope of Troy
Against the Greeks that would have entered Troy.
But Hercules himself must yield to odds;

33] *Pope;* 'Tis . . . strange, / The . . . of. F   40 fair-shining] *Eds.;* faire shining F   41] *Pope;* Nay . . . Daughters: /
By . . . it, F   42 SD *a* MESSENGER] Q3; *one* F   42 SD *a horn*] *Eds.; not in* F   45 looker-on] *Eds.;* looker on F

32 **figures** foreshows (*OED* Figure *v* 5).
34 **cites** calls.
36 **by . . . meeds** because of our merits (*OED*
Meed *sb* 3).
38 **overshine** illuminate.
38 **this** this phenomenon.
40 **target** light shield.
41–2 'The first snarl given to Crook-back'
(Wilson). Richard alludes to his brother's
lasciviousness and also possibly suggests that
daughters would be easier to remove from the
throne were his brother to die.
42 **breeder** female.
42 SD **blowing** i.e. sounding a horn – the
sound of a 'post' or express rider; see *MV* 5.1.47;
alternatively it might mean 'out of breath'
(compare *Wiv.* 3.3.86).

43 **heavy** sombre.
46 **When as** When.
48–9 'The generous tenderness of Edward,
and savage fortitude of Richard, are well dis-
tinguished by their different reception of their
father's death' (Johnson).
50 **Environèd** Surrounded.
51 **the . . . Troy** Hector; compare Virgil,
Aeneid II, 281: 'O lux Dardaniae! spes O
fidissima Teucrum'; Henry uses the same
phrase to Warwick at 4.8.25.
53 Compare the proverb 'Hercules himself
cannot deal with two' (Tilley H436), and see
Textual analysis, p. 202.

And many strokes, though with a little axe,
Hews down and fells the hardest-timbered oak.   55
By many hands your father was subdued,
But only slaughtered by the ireful arm
Of unrelenting Clifford and the queen,
Who crowned the gracious duke in high despite,
Laughed in his face and, when with grief he wept,   60
The ruthless queen gave him to dry his cheeks
A napkin steepèd in the harmless blood
Of sweet young Rutland, by rough Clifford slain;
And after many scorns, many foul taunts,
They took his head and on the gates of York   65
They set the same; and there it doth remain,
The saddest spectacle that e'er I viewed.
EDWARD Sweet Duke of York, our prop to lean upon,
Now thou art gone we have no staff, no stay.
O Clifford, boisterous Clifford! Thou hast slain   70
The flower of Europe for his chivalry,
And treacherously hast thou vanquished him,
For hand to hand he would have vanquished thee.
Now my soul's palace is become a prison:
Ah, would she break from hence that this my body   75
Might in the ground be closèd up in rest!
For never henceforth shall I joy again,
Never, O never, shall I see more joy!
RICHARD I cannot weep, for all my body's moisture
Scarce serves to quench my furnace-burning heart;   80

---

80 heart] F *subst.;* hate Q3

54–5 Compare the proverb 'Many strokes fell great oaks' (Tilley s941).
55 Hews...fells For the singular terminations see Abbott 333.
57 ireful wrathful.
59 in high despite with haughty contempt.
60 Laughed...face This detail comes from the chroniclers: 'they laughed then that shortly after lamented' (Holinshed, p. 269; Hall, p. 251).
62 napkin handkerchief.
62 harmless innocent (*OED* sv 3).
63 rough cruel.
69–70 Compare Marlowe, *The Massacre at Paris* 23.4–5: 'Sweet Duke of Guise, our prop to lean upon, / Now thou art dead, here is no stay for us.'
69 stay support.
70 boisterous savage (*OED* sv 9).

71 The chroniclers apply the phrase 'flower of chivalry' to the future Edward IV (Holinshed, p. 272; Hall, p. 253)
71 chivalry prowess in war (*OED* sv 3b).
74 Compare the proverb, derived ultimately from Plato, 'The body is the prison of the soul' (Dent B497).
74 soul's palace i.e. the body.
75 she his soul.
78 more joy happiness again.
79 moisture the liquid 'humours' inherent in all animals and plants (*OED* sv 2c).
80 furnace-burning heart Anger caused the heart to become over-heated – see 1.4.87, *1H6* 2.4.108 n; however, Q3's 'hate' for 'heart' is attractive, especially since 'heart's' appears in the next line (compare *John* 3.1.341–2).

Nor can my tongue unload my heart's great burden,
For selfsame wind that I should speak withal
Is kindling coals that fires all my breast
And burns me up with flames that tears would quench.
To weep is to make less the depth of grief: 85
Tears then for babes, blows and revenge for me!
Richard, I bear thy name: I'll venge thy death
Or die renownèd by attempting it.

EDWARD His name that valiant duke hath left with thee;
His dukedom and his chair with me is left.   90

RICHARD Nay, if thou be that princely eagle's bird,
Show thy descent by gazing 'gainst the sun:
For 'chair and dukedom', 'throne and kingdom' say,
Either that is thine or else thou wert not his.

March. Enter WARWICK, MARQUESS [*of*] MONTAGUE, [*with
Drum, Ancient, and Soldiers*]

WARWICK How now, fair lords? What fare, what news abroad?   95

RICHARD Great lord of Warwick, if we should recompt
Our baleful news and, at each word's deliverance,
Stab poniards in our flesh till all were told,
The words would add more anguish than the wounds:
O valiant lord, the Duke of York is slain!   100

EDWARD O Warwick, Warwick, that Plantagenet
Which held thee dearly as his soul's redemption
Is by the stern Lord Clifford done to death.

---

81 burden] *Johnson;* burthen F   83 fires] F; fires up F3   94 SD MONTAGUE] O; *Mountacute* F   94 SD
with . . . *Soldiers*] O *subst.; and their Army* F   95 fare] O; faire F   96 recompt] F2; tecompt F; recount F3; report O

82 **wind** breath.
83 **fires** For the singular see Abbott 333.
88 **renownèd** made famous.
90 **chair** seat of authority (*OED* sv *sb* 3).
91–2 **if . . . sun** It was believed that eagles
tested their young by getting them to gaze at the
sun. If a chick's eyes watered, it was killed
(Pliny, *Nat. Hist.*, XXIX, 6; Tilley E3). The sun
probably symbolises the king; the 'princely eagle'
was highest in the hierarchy of birds – with a
probable reference to York's badge of a falcon
(see 5.2.12).
91 **bird** chick.
94 **that** the sun, i.e. the power and authority
of the king.

94 SD.1 **March** i.e. the sound of fifes and
drums (Long, p. 6).
94 SD.2 *****Ancient** A standard-bearer or
'ensign' (see *Shakespeare's England*, I, 117–8 and
Gary Taylor, 'Ancients and moderns', *SQ* 36
(1985), 525–7). The detail comes again from O
(see collation).
95 **fare** cheer.
95 **abroad** in the world.
96 **recompt** obsolete variant of 'recount'.
97 **baleful** painful (*OED* sv 2a).
98 **poniards** daggers.
102 **held** prized.
102 **redemption** salvation.
103 **stern** fierce, cruel.

WARWICK Ten days ago I drowned these news in tears
        And now, to add more measure to your woes,   105
        I come to tell you things sith then befall'n.
        After the bloody fray at Wakefield fought
        Where your brave father breathed his latest gasp,
        Tidings, as swiftly as the posts could run,
        Were brought me of your loss and his depart.   110
        I, then in London, keeper of the king,
        Mustered my soldiers, gathered flocks of friends,
        And very well appointed, as I thought,
        Marched toward Saint Albans to intercept the queen,
        Bearing the king in my behalf along;   115
        For by my scouts I was advertisèd
        That she was coming with a full intent
        To dash our late decree in parliament
        Touching King Henry's oath and your succession.
        Short tale to make, we at Saint Albans met,   120
        Our battles joined, and both sides fiercely fought:
        But whether 'twas the coldness of the king,
        Who looked full gently on his warlike queen,
        That robbed my soldiers of their heated spleen,
        Or whether 'twas report of her success,   125
        Or more than common fear of Clifford's rigour
        Who thunders to his captives blood and death,
        I cannot judge: but, to conclude with truth,
        Their weapons like to lightning came and went;

113] O *subst.; not in* F   127 captives] *Rowe subst.*; Captiues, F; captaines O; captives – *Capell*

104–6 The text proclaims the difference between theatrical and dramatic time, the time of the action.
  105 **measure** quantity (*OED* sv *sb* 14).
  106 **sith** since.
  108 **latest** last.
  109 **posts** mounted messengers.
  110 **depart** death (*OED* sv *sb* 1b).
  111 **keeper** custodian.
  *113 This line from O, not in F, was probably a compositorial omission; its restoration improves the syntax of the sentence.
  113 **appointed** equipped.
  115 **Bearing . . . along** taking with me.
  115 **in . . . behalf** in my own interest (*OED* Behalf 4).
  116 **advertisèd** informed (accented on the second syllable: Cercignani, p. 46).

  118 **dash** confound.
  118 **late** recent.
  119 **Touching** Concerning.
  120 **Short . . . make** proverbial (Dent ss8).
  121 **battles** battalions.
  122 **coldness** lack of zeal.
  124 **spleen** courage (*OED* sv 5).
  126 **rigour** harshness.
  127 **thunders** proclaims; compare *TN* 1.5.256.
  127 **captives . . . death** O's reading, 'captains' (see collation), may well be correct, in which case we should read 'Blood and death', Clifford's war-cry.
  129 **like . . . went** compare the proverb 'As swift as lightning' (Tilley L279).

Our soldiers', like the night-owl's lazy flight,   130
Or like an idle thresher with a flail,
Fell gently down, as if they struck their friends.
I cheered them up with justice of our cause,
With promise of high pay and great rewards,
But all in vain: they had no heart to fight   135
And we, in them, no hope to win the day;
So that we fled: the king unto the queen,
Lord George, your brother, Norfolk, and myself
In haste, post-haste, are come to join with you;
For in the Marches here we heard you were,   140
Making another head to fight again.

EDWARD Where is the Duke of Norfolk, gentle Warwick?
And when came George from Burgundy to England?

WARWICK Some six miles off the duke is with the soldiers;
And, for your brother, he was lately sent   145
From your kind aunt, Duchess of Burgundy,
With aid of soldiers to this needful war.

RICHARD 'Twas odds belike when valiant Warwick fled:
Oft have I heard his praises in pursuit,
But ne'er till now his scandal of retire.   150

WARWICK Nor now my scandal, Richard, dost thou hear:
For thou shalt know this strong right hand of mine
Can pluck the diadem from faint Henry's head
And wring the awful sceptre from his fist,
Were he as famous and as bold in war   155
As he is famed for mildness, peace, and prayer.

RICHARD I know it well, Lord Warwick; blame me not:
'Tis love I bear thy glories makes me speak.
But in this troublous time what's to be done?

---

130 soldiers'] *Capell;* Souldiers F   131 an idle] O; a lazie F   144 the soldiers] F *subst.;* his power O   158
makes] F2; make F

131 *an idle F's 'a lazie' was presumably
caught from 130.
   133 cheered...up revived them (see
1.1.6 n.)
   139 post-haste with all possible speed.
   140 Marches Borders (of Wales).
   141 Making...head Raising another force.
   142 gentle noble.
   143–8 See headnote.
   144 the soldiers O's 'his power' may be a
better reading, 'soldiers' having been caught
from 147, unless it refers to the army whose
defeat is narrated in 135–7 above.

145 for as for.
   146 aunt...Burgundy The Duchess Isabel,
wife of Duke Philip the Good, was daughter of
King John I of Portugal by the eldest daughter
of John of Gaunt. She was therefore third cousin
and not aunt to Edward.
   147 needful needy, requiring aid.
   147 war attack (*OED* sv 4b).
   148 'Twas odds They lost the advantage.
   150 scandal of retire notoriety for
retreating.
   153 faint faint-hearted.
   154 awful awe-inspiring.

Shall we go throw away our coats of steel   160
And wrap our bodies in black mourning gowns,
Numb'ring our Ave-Maries with our beads?
Or shall we on the helmets of our foes
Tell our devotion with revengeful arms?
If for the last, say ay, and to it, lords.   165
WARWICK Why, therefore Warwick came to seek you out
And therefore comes my brother Montague. –
Attend me, lords: the proud insulting queen
With Clifford and the haught Northumberland
And of their feather many more proud birds   170
Have wrought the easy-melting king like wax.
He swore consent to your succession,
His oath enrollèd in the parliament;
And now to London all the crew are gone
To frustrate both his oath and what beside   175
May make against the house of Lancaster.
Their power, I think, is thirty thousand strong:
Now if the help of Norfolk and myself
With all the friends that thou, brave Earl of March,
Amongst the loving Welshmen canst procure,   180
Will but amount to five and twenty thousand,
Why, *via*! To London will we march
And once again bestride our foaming steeds
And once again cry 'Charge!' upon our foes,

---

170 more] *Eds.;* moe F   181 five and twenty] F *subst.;* forty eight O *subst.*   182 march,] F; march amaine
O   184 'Charge . . . foes] *Staunton;* Charge vpon our Foes F; 'Charge . . . foes' *Eds.*

---

161 mourning gowns worn at funerals: for
an illustration see Hattaway (ed.), *1H6*, p. 6.
162 Compare *2H6* 1.3.50–1 where Margaret
says her husband's mind is 'bent . . . To number
Ave-Maries on his beads'.
162 Numb'ring Counting.
162 Ave-Maries Prayers (Hail Maries).
162 beads rosary beads.
164 Tell Proclaim (*OED* sv 3b), with a
quibble on 'tell one's beads' (*OED* 21c).
166, 167 therefore for that reason.
167 my . . . Montague This is the correct
relationship; in Act 1, Montague is designated as
York's brother (see 1.1.14 n.).
168 Attend Listen to (*OED* sv 1).
168 insulting triumphantly insolent (*OED*
sv 1).
169 haught haughty.
170–1 Compare the proverb 'To work (upon
one) like wax' (Dent W138), and there is probably a latent Icarus image embedded in the lines

(see Armstrong, p. 37); see 5.6.18 n.
170 of . . . feather Compare the proverb
'Birds of a feather will flock together' (Tilley
B393).
173 enrollèd entered on the records (rolls)
(*OED* Enrol *v* 5).
174 crew gang (*OED* sv *sb* 4).
175 frustrate annul (*OED* sv 2b).
175 what beside anything else.
176 make militate (*OED* sv *v* 76).
177–81 thirty . . . thousand O's equivalent
figures 'fifty thousand' and '48 thousand' may
derive from the chroniclers who offer sixty
thousand and forty-eight thousand, six hundred
and sixty (Holinshed, pp. 277–8; Hall, p. 255).
177 power army.
179 Earl of March The title of Edward
before York's death (see 192).
180 loving friendly, loyal.
182 via forward (It.).

But never once again turn back and fly.   185
RICHARD Ay now methinks I hear great Warwick speak:
　　　　Ne'er may he live to see a sunshine day
　　　　That cries 'Retire!', if Warwick bid him stay.
EDWARD Lord Warwick, on thy shoulder will I lean;
　　　　And when thou fail'st – as God forbid the hour! –   190
　　　　Must Edward fall, which peril heaven forfend!
WARWICK No longer Earl of March but Duke of York!
　　　　The next degree is England's royal throne:
　　　　For king of England shalt thou be proclaimed
　　　　In every borough as we pass along;   195
　　　　And he that throws not up his cap for joy
　　　　Shall, for the fault, make forfeit of his head.
　　　　King Edward, valiant Richard, Montague,
　　　　Stay we no longer dreaming of renown,
　　　　But sound the trumpets and about our task.   200
RICHARD Then, Clifford, were thy heart as hard as steel,
　　　　As thou hast shown it flinty by thy deeds,
　　　　I come to pierce it, or to give thee mine.
EDWARD Then strike up, drums! God and Saint George for us!

Enter a MESSENGER

WARWICK How now, what news?   205
MESSENGER The Duke of Norfolk sends you word by me
　　　　The queen is coming with a puissant host;
　　　　And craves your company for speedy counsel.
WARWICK Why then, it sorts: brave warriors, let's away.

Exeunt

---

190 fail'st] F; faints O; faint'st Q2; fall'st *Steevens*   198 Richard,] O *subst.; Richard* F   204 up,] *Cairncross;* up
F   207 host;] *Eds.;* Hoast, F   209 sorts:...let's] *Theobald subst.;* sorts, braue Warriors, let's F; sorts braue
Lordes. Lets O   209 SD] *Eds.; Exeunt Omnes.* F; *March. Exeunt / Oxford*

185 **back** away (*OED* Turn *v* 48).
187 **he** anyone.
187 **sunshine** sunny, happy.
188 **stay** stand one's ground (*OED* sv *v* 7).
191 **forfend** forbid.
193 **degree** step.
197 **fault** default, neglect (*OED* sv *sb* 2).

201 **were...steel** proverbial (Dent H310.1,
H311).
204 **Saint George** the patron saint of
England and hence of a claimant to its throne.
207 **puissant host** powerful army.
209 **it sorts** things are as they should be
(*OED* Sort *v* 18b).

[2.2] *Flourish. Enter the* KING, *the* QUEEN [MARGARET], CLIFFORD, NORTHUMBERLAND, *and young* PRINCE [EDWARD], *with Drum and Trumpets* [*and Soldiers*]

MARGARET Welcome, my lord, to this brave town of York.
    Yonder's the head of that arch-enemy
    That sought to be encompassed with your crown.
    Doth not the object cheer your heart, my lord?
KING HENRY Ay, as the rocks cheer them that fear their wrack: 5
    To see this sight it irks my very soul.
    Withhold revenge, dear God! 'Tis not my fault
    Nor wittingly have I infringed my vow.
CLIFFORD My gracious liege, this too much lenity
    And harmful pity must be laid aside.   10
    To whom do lions cast their gentle looks?
    Not to the beast that would usurp their den.
    Whose hand is that the forest bear doth lick?
    Not his that spoils her young before her face.
    Who scapes the lurking serpent's mortal sting?   15
    Not he that sets his foot upon her back.
    The smallest worm will turn, being trodden on,
    And doves will peck in safeguard of their brood.
    Ambitious York did level at thy crown:
    Thou smiling while he knit his angry brows.   20

Act 2, Scene 2   2.2] *Capell; not in* F   0 SD.1 *Flourish*] F; *York's head is thrust out above. Flourish / Oxford*   0
SD.3 *and Soldiers*] O *subst.; not in* F   8 wittingly] F; *willingly* Walker

---

Act 2, Scene 2
*2.2 The scene is largely unhistorical and serves to establish personalities and motives in the opposing forces before the battle of Towton. Edward was in fact knighted the day after the second battle of Saint Albans (Holinshed, p. 271; Hall, p. 252)

0 SD.3 *Drum and Trumpets* Drummer and trumpeters.

1 brave splendid.

2 Yonder's Margaret had ordered York's head set above the gates of York (1.4.179), and it is possible that a property head was displayed from the gallery over the stage (until 2.6.85 – see 2.6.85–6 n.); the player could equally, however, have gestured towards the back of the playhouse yard.

2 the arch-enemy Richard, Duke of York.

4 object sight (*OED* sv *sb* 3b).

5 wrack shipwreck (*OED* sv *sb*² 2).

8 wittingly on purpose.

8 infringed my vow see 1.1.195–202. Henry's conscience is wrung by the possibility that he has committed perjury, an agony of which the queen and Clifford are oblivious.

9 lenity mildness.

13 forest wild, 'as opposed to the tame bear often exhibited in cities' (Kittredge).

14 spoils seizes as prey (*OED* Spoil *v* 4).

15 lurking...sting Like Error in *FQ* (1, 1, 15), the serpent is imagined to have a sting in her tail.

17 Compare the proverb 'Tread on a worm and it will turn' (Tilley w909).

18 in...of for the protection of; compare 1.4.41.

19 level aim.

He, but a duke, would have his son a king
And raise his issue like a loving sire;
Thou, being a king, blest with a goodly son,
Didst yield consent to disinherit him,
Which argued thee a most unloving father.   25
Unreasonable creatures feed their young;
And though man's face be fearful to their eyes,
Yet, in protection of their tender ones,
Who hath not seen them, even with those wings
Which sometime they have used in fearful flight,   30
Make war with him that climbed unto their nest,
Offering their own lives in their young's defence?
For shame, my liege, make them your precedent!
Were it not pity that this goodly boy
Should lose his birthright by his father's fault   35
And long hereafter say unto his child,
'What my great-grandfather and grandsire got
My careless father fondly gave away'?
Ah, what a shame were this! Look on the boy
And let his manly face, which promiseth   40
Successful fortune, steel thy melting heart
To hold thine own and leave thine own with him.
KING HENRY   Full well hath Clifford played the orator,
        Inferring arguments of mighty force:
        But, Clifford, tell me, didst thou never hear   45
        That things ill got had ever bad success?
        And happy always was it for that son
        Whose father, for his hoarding, went to hell?

---

30 in] O; with F   **35** lose] O; loose F   **37** great-grandfather] *Capell;* great Grandfather F   **48** hell?] O; hell: F

22 raise his issue elevate the rank of his sons.

25 argued proved.

26 Unreasonable Not endowed with reason (*OED* sv 1).

27 fearful frightening.

28 tender young, beloved.

30 *in O's reading seems preferable to F's 'with' which was probably caught from the preceding or following line.

30 fearful terrified.

37 great-grandfather and grandsire Henry IV and Henry V.

38 careless heedless (*OED* sv 2).

38 fondly foolishly.

39 shame disgrace (*OED* sv 3b).

41 melting softened with feeling.

43 played the orator proverbial (Dent O74.1).

44 Inferring Adducing (*OED* Infer 2).

46 things . . . success Compare the proverb 'Evil-gotten goods never prove well' (Tilley G301).

46 success outcome (*OED* sv 1).

47–8 happy . . . hell Compare the proverb 'Happy is the child whose father goes to the devil' (Tilley C305).

47 happy fortunate.

48 for because of.

I'll leave my son my virtuous deeds behind:
And would my father had left me no more!   50
For all the rest is held at such a rate
As brings a thousandfold more care to keep
Than in possession any jot of pleasure.
Ah, cousin York, would thy best friends did know
How it doth grieve me that thy head is here!   55
MARGARET My lord, cheer up your spirits: our foes are nigh
And this soft courage makes your followers faint.
You promised knighthood to our forward son:
Unsheathe your sword and dub him presently. –
Edward, kneel down.   60
KING HENRY Edward Plantagenet, arise a knight;
And learn this lesson: draw thy sword in right.
PRINCE EDWARD My gracious father, by your kingly leave,
I'll draw it as apparent to the crown
And in that quarrel use it to the death.   65
CLIFFORD Why, that is spoken like a toward prince.

Enter a MESSENGER

MESSENGER Royal commanders, be in readiness:
For with a band of thirty thousand men
Comes Warwick backing of the Duke of York;
And in the towns, as they do march along,   70
Proclaims him king – and many fly to him:
Darraign your battle for they are at hand.
CLIFFORD I would your highness would depart the field:
The queen hath best success when you are absent.
MARGARET Ay, good my lord, and leave us to our fortune.   75
KING HENRY Why, that's my fortune too: therefore I'll stay.

62 lesson:] F *subst.*; lesson boy O   66 SH] F *subst.*; *Northum.* O

51 **rate** cost.
57 **courage** disposition (*OED* sv 1).
57 **faint** lose heart (*OED* sv *v* 1).
58 **forward** eager, bold (*OED* sv *adj.* 6c).
59 **presently** immediately.
62 **in right** for just causes.
64 **apparent** heir apparent.
65 **quarrel** cause (*OED* sv *sb*³ 2d).
66 **toward** promising (*OED* sv *adj* 3).
69 **backing** in support.
69 **the Duke of York** Edward.
72 **Darraign ... battle** Set your troops in fighting array.

72 **at hand** In the previous scene Warwick had announced that the Lancastrians had gone to London and that he proposed to follow them (2.1.174–85), but at the end of that scene (207) he learns that they have returned north.
73–4 Compare Holinshed: 'Thus was the queen fortunate in her two battles, but unfortunate was the king in all his enterprises: for where his person was present, the victory still fled from him to the contrary part' (p. 271; Hall p. 252).
74 **success** fortune (*OED* sv 2).

NORTHUMBERLAND Be it with resolution then to fight.
PRINCE EDWARD My royal father, cheer these noble lords
      And hearten those that fight in your defence:
      Unsheathe your sword, good father; cry, 'Saint George!'   80

March. Enter EDWARD [EARL OF MARCH], WARWICK,
RICHARD, [GEORGE], NORFOLK, MONTAGUE, *and Soldiers*

EDWARD Now, perjured Henry, wilt thou kneel for grace
      And set thy diadem upon my head
      Or bide the mortal fortune of the field?
MARGARET Go rate thy minions! Proud insulting boy,
      Becomes it thee to be thus bold in terms   85
      Before thy sovereign and thy lawful king?
EDWARD I am his king and he should bow his knee:
      I was adopted heir by his consent.
      Since when his oath is broke, for, as I hear,
      You that are king, though he do wear the crown,   90
      Have caused him by new act of parliament
      To blot out me and put his own son in.
CLIFFORD And reason too:
      Who should succeed the father but the son?
RICHARD Are you there, butcher? O I cannot speak!   95
CLIFFORD Ay, Crook-back, here I stand to answer thee
      Or any he the proudest of thy sort.
RICHARD 'Twas you that killed young Rutland, was it not?
CLIFFORD Ay, and old York, and yet not satisfied.

80 SD.2 GEORGE] *Eds.; Clarence* F   89 Since] F2; *Cla.* Since F; *George.* Since O, *Oxford subst.*   92 out me] F; *our
brother out* O   93 too] F; *George* O

78 **cheer** encourage.
80 **Saint George** see 2.1.204 n.
80 SD.2 *GEORGE F reads 'Clarence' although George does not receive that title until
2.6.104.
81 **perjured** because he has reneged on his
oath concerning the succession of the Yorkists;
the accusation is ironic in the extreme, given
that, in 1.2, Edward's father had deliberately
committed perjury, the violation of a promise
made on oath (*OED* sv b).
81 **grace** pardon.
83 **bide** await.
83 **mortal fortune** deadly outcome.
84 **rate** berate, chide.
84 **minions** favourites, 'creatures' (*OED*
Minion 1c).

84 **boy** (an insult).
85 **terms** words.
*89–92 Both F and O assign these lines to
George, and O makes subsequent changes to
92–3 (see collation). This agreement suggests
that F derives here from contaminated copy in O
(see Textual analysis, p. 207).
90 **You** i.e. Margaret.
92 **blot out me** obliterate my name from the
records.
93 **reason** rightly.
97 Compare the proverb 'The proudest of
you all' (Dent P614.1).
97 **he** one.
97 **sort** crew, gang (*OED* sv *sb* 17).

RICHARD For God's sake, lords, give signal to the fight.   100
WARWICK What say'st thou, Henry, wilt thou yield the crown?
MARGARET Why how now, long-tongued Warwick, dare you speak?
        When you and I met at Saint Albans last
        Your legs did better service than your hands.
WARWICK Then 'twas my turn to fly, and now 'tis thine.   105
CLIFFORD You said so much before and yet you fled.
WARWICK 'Twas not your valour, Clifford, drove me thence.
NORTHUMBERLAND No, nor your manhood that durst make you
        stay.
RICHARD Northumberland, I hold thee reverently.
        Break off the parley, for scarce I can refrain   110
        The execution of my big-swoll'n heart
        Upon that Clifford, that cruel child-killer.
CLIFFORD I slew thy father: call'st thou him a child?
RICHARD Ay, like a dastard and a treacherous coward,
        As thou didst kill our tender brother Rutland.   115
        But ere sun set I'll make thee curse the deed.
KING HENRY Have done with words, my lords, and hear me speak.
MARGARET Defy them then, or else hold close thy lips.
KING HENRY I prithee give no limits to my tongue:
        I am a king and privileged to speak.   120
CLIFFORD My liege, the wound that bred this meeting here
        Cannot be cured by words; therefore be still.
RICHARD Then, executioner, unsheathe thy sword.
        By Him that made us all, I am resolved
        That Clifford's manhood lies upon his tongue.   125
EDWARD Say, Henry, shall I have my right or no?
        A thousand men have broke their fasts today
        That ne'er shall dine unless thou yield the crown.

101] *Pope;* What . . . *Henry,* / Wilt . . . *Crowne?* F   108 SH] O *subst.; Nor.* F   110 parley] F; parle *Hudson*   116
sun set] O *subst;* Sunset F

102 **long-tongued** proverbial (Dent LL6), babbling.
  104 Compare the proverb 'One pair of legs is worth two pair of hands' (Dent P34).
  109 **hold** esteem.
  109 **reverently** with veneration.
  110 **refrain** check (*OED* sv *v* 1).
  111 **The execution** Turning the passion into action.
  111 **big-swoll'n** with anger: see Primaudaye, *The French Academie*, 1594 edn, p. 308.
  112 **child-killer** Historically Richard was nine years younger than Rutland.

114–15 (Richard ignores Clifford's taunt).
  114 **dastard** sneaking coward.
  115 **tender** young (*OED* sv *adj* 4).
  119 **give** set.
  119 **limits** restrictions.
  121 **wound** Clifford would seem to be thinking of the death of his father (see *2H6* 5.2).
  122 **still** silent.
  124 **resolved** convinced (*OED* Resolve *v* 16a).
  125 That Clifford's tongue is mightier than his sword.

WARWICK If thou deny, their blood upon thy head,
    For York in justice puts his armour on.   130
PRINCE EDWARD If that be right which Warwick says is right,
    There is no wrong but every thing is right.
RICHARD Whoever got thee, there thy mother stands,
    For well I wot thou hast thy mother's tongue.
MARGARET But thou art neither like thy sire nor dam,   135
    But like a foul misshapen stigmatic
    Marked by the Destinies to be avoided,
    As venom toads or lizards' dreadful stings.
RICHARD Iron of Naples, hid with English gilt,
    Whose father bears the title of a king –   140
    As if a channel should be called the sea –
    Sham'st thou not, knowing whence thou art extraught,
    To let thy tongue detect thy base-born heart?
EDWARD A wisp of straw were worth a thousand crowns
    To make this shameless callet know herself.   145
    Helen of Greece was fairer far than thou,
    Although thy husband may be Menelaus;
    And ne'er was Agamemnon's brother wronged

133 SH] O; *War.* F

129 deny refuse.
129 upon be upon.
***133 SH** The speech that follows indicates
the F's assignment of these lines to Warwick is
an error; this is confirmed by O.
133, 139, 147 Recalling Margaret's alliance
with Suffolk in *2H6*.
133 got begot.
134 wot know.
135 dam mother (contemptuous since the
word was used mainly of beasts).
136 stigmatic 'one branded by nature with
deformity' (Onions).
137 Marked Branded.
137 Destinies The three Fates of classical
mythology, Clotho, Lachesis, and Atropos.
138 venom poisonous: the erroneous notion
that toads are venomous goes back to Pliny,
Natural History, XXV; compare Tilley T360.
138 lizards'...stings Because of the
medieval translation of Latin *anguis* as 'lizard', it
was erroneously believed that lizards had stings.
139 Base Neapolitan woman, concealed by
English gold – with a possible punning allusion
to the 'guilt' generated by the relationship with

Suffolk. Naples was famous for the manufacture
of armour (Sugden, p. 359). Margaret was
daughter to King Reignier of Naples.
    141 channel rivulet (*OED* sv 2), sewer (*OED*
sv 3).
    142–3 knowing...heart 'To show thy
meanness of birth by the indecency of language
with which thou railest at my deformity'
(Johnson)
    142 extraught extracted.
    143 detect reveal.
    144 wisp of straw The reference is to the
habit of making scolds wear a garland of straw
(see R. Nares, *Glossary*, 1859 ed., for examples)
or to making a figure of straw for them to rail at
(*OED* Wisp *sb*¹ 2b).
    145 callet harlot.
    147 Menelaus brother of Agamemnon,
husband of Helen, cuckolded by Paris; compare
133 above. The insult implies that Prince
Edward may not have been Henry's son, a
suspicion reported in the chroniclers who note
that the 'common people... had an opinion that
the king was not able to get a child' (Holinshed,
p. 236; Hall, p. 230).

By that false woman as this king by thee.
His father revelled in the heart of France   150
And tamed the king and made the dauphin stoop:
And had he matched according to his state,
He might have kept that glory to this day;
But when he took a beggar to his bed
And graced thy poor sire with his bridal day,   155
Even then that sunshine brewed a shower for him
That washed his father's fortunes forth of France
And heaped sedition on his crown at home.
For what hath broached this tumult but thy pride?
Hadst thou been meek, our title still had slept,   160
And we, in pity of the gentle king,
Had slipped our claim until another age.
GEORGE But when we saw our sunshine made thy spring
And that thy summer bred us no increase,
We set the axe to thy usurping root,   165
And though the edge hath something hit ourselves,
Yet know thou, since we have begun to strike,
We'll never leave till we have hewn thee down
Or bathed thy growing with our heated bloods.
EDWARD And in this resolution I defy thee;   170
Not willing any longer conference

---

151 dauphin] *Rowe subst.;* Dolphin F   163 SH] O *subst.;* Clarence F *subst. (throughout)*

149 **that ... woman** Helen.
150 **His father** Henry V.
150 **revelled** had his will, acted wantonly, with a possible secondary meaning 'drew back blood' (*OED* Revel *v²*).
151 **the king** Charles VI of France.
151 **the dauphin** Charles, later Charles VII.
151 **stoop** submit.
152 **he** Henry VI.
152 **matched** married.
152 **state** rank, social position.
154–5 Suffolk had arranged the marriage of Margaret to Henry according to terms whereby she brought him no dowry (see *2H6* 1.1.56–9).
155 Honoured your father (Reignier) by marrying his daughter; see *2H6* 1.1.42–8.
155 **his** Henry VI's.
156 **brewed** brought about (*OED* Brew *v* 4c).
157 **forth of** out of.
159 **broached** tapped, initiated.
160 **title** claim to the crown (*OED* sv *sb* 7c).
160 **still** always.
162 **Had slipped** Would have left in abeyance (*OED* Slip *v* 21b).

163–6 'When we saw that by favouring thee we made thee grow in fortune, but that we received no advantage from thy fortune flourishing by our favour, we then resolved to destroy thee, and determined to try some other means, though our first efforts have failed' (Johnson).
164 **increase** harvest.
165 Compare Luke 3.9: 'Now also is the axe laid unto the root of the trees: therefore every tree which bringeth not good fruit shall be hewn down and cast into the fire.'
165 **usurping** because the Yorkists regarded Lancastrian Henry as a usurper.
165 **root** possibly an obscene reference to her husband's penis (see Colman, p. 212).
166 **something** somewhat.
168 **leave** cease.
169 **bathed** watered (continuing the tree metaphor); alternatively the word in this context might, ironically, mean 'drown'.
170 **resolution** certainty (*OED* sv 13b).
171 **conference** talk (*OED* sv 4).

Since thou deniest the gentle king to speak. –
Sound, trumpets! Let our bloody colours wave;
And either victory, or else a grave!
MARGARET Stay, Edward.   175
EDWARD No, wrangling woman, we'll no longer stay:
These words will cost ten thousand lives this day.
[*Flourish. March. Exeunt Edward and his men at one door and Queen*
Margaret and her men at another door]

[2.3] *Alarum. Excursions. Enter* WARWICK

WARWICK Forspent with toil, as runners with a race,
I lay me down a little while to breathe;
For strokes received and many blows repaid
Have robbed my strong-knit sinews of their strength,
And, spite of spite, needs must I rest awhile.   5

Enter EDWARD [EARL OF MARCH] *running*

EDWARD Smile, gentle heaven, or strike, ungentle death,
For this world frowns, and Edward's sun is clouded.
WARWICK How now, my lord, what hap? What hope of good?

Enter GEORGE

GEORGE Our hap is loss, our hope but sad despair,
Our ranks are broke and ruin follows us.   10

172 deniest] o; denied'st F   177 SD] *Oxford; Exeunt omnes* F   Act 2, Scene 3   2.3] *Capell; not in* F   1
Forspent] F *subst.*; Sore spent o   6 strike,] *Eds.*; strike F   8 SD GEORGE] o; *Clarence* F; *George, running / Oxford*

172 *deniest** forbid; F's 'denied'st' is a
common e/ed misreading.
176 wrangling brawling.
177 words altercations (*OED* Word 5).
*177 SD This exit by 'several (i.e. separate)
ways' was suggested by Oxford and reflects
common staging practice (see 2.4.0 SD, 2.5.54,
78 SD, *1H6* 2.1.38 SD, and Hattaway, p. 24).

Act 2, Scene 3
*2.3 2.3 to 2.6 dramatise the fighting which
ended at Towton (near Leeds in Yorkshire) on
29 March 1461. Shakespeare passes over the
proclamation of Edward as king in London
(Holinshed, p. 272; Hall, p. 253 – see Appendix
1, pp. 213–14) and in this scene magnifies a
preliminary skirmish at Ferrybridge where Warwick's bastard brother was killed (Holinshed,

p. 277; Hall, p. 255) into a serious set-back for
the Yorkists. The chroniclers, however, make
much of Warwick's fury at the death of his
bastard brother (Holinshed, p. 277; Hall, p. 255).
0 SD *Excursions* attacks and counter attacks.
1 Forspent Exhausted.
2 breathe rest.
5 spite of spite come what may (Dent ss8).
6 ungentle ignoble.
7–13 For o's different version of these lines
which may indicate that Salisbury was originally
in the text, see Appendix 2, p. 218.
7 sun Edward's badge was the sun – see
2.1.20 SD n.
8 hap fortune.
8 SD George may, like his brothers, enter
'running' (see 6 and 13); alternatively he might
walk on in despair (see 9).

What counsel give you? Whither shall we fly?
EDWARD Bootless is flight, they follow us with wings;
    And weak we are and cannot shun pursuit.

Enter RICHARD [*running*]

RICHARD Ah, Warwick, why hast thou withdrawn thyself?
    Thy brother's blood the thirsty earth hath drunk,   15
    Broached with the steely point of Clifford's lance;
    And in the very pangs of death he cried,
    Like to a dismal clangour heard from far,
    'Warwick, revenge! Brother, revenge my death!'
    So, underneath the belly of their steeds   20
    That stained their fetlocks in his smoking blood,
    The noble gentleman gave up the ghost.
WARWICK Then let the earth be drunken with our blood:
    I'll kill my horse because I will not fly.
    Why stand we like soft-hearted women here,   25
    Wailing our losses whiles the foe doth rage,
    And look upon, as if the tragedy
    Were played in jest by counterfeiting actors?
    Here on my knee I vow to God above
    I'll never pause again, never stand still,   30
    Till either death hath closed these eyes of mine
    Or fortune given me measure of revenge.
EDWARD O Warwick, I do bend my knee with thine,
    And in this vow do chain my soul to thine. –
    And, ere my knee rise from the earth's cold face,   35
    I throw my hands, mine eyes, my heart to Thee,

---

13 SD *running*] O; *not in* F

12 **Bootless** Useless.
13 **shun** avoid.
15–19 Compare Gen. 4.10: 'the voice of thy brother's blood crieth unto me from the ground'.
15–20 For O's version of these lines, compare 1.1.240 n. and see Appendix 2, pp. 218–19.
15 **brother's blood** O offers an account of the death of Warwick's 'father' at this point. This seems more likely to be a mistake than a recollection of an unrevised passage since Holinshed (p. 277) notes that the 'Bastard of Salisbury, brother to the Earl of Warwick' was killed at Ferrybridge, and that this kindled his resolution to stay and fight (Hall, p. 255).
16 **Broached with** Set flowing by.
18 **dismal** ill-boding.

20–3 Compare Judith 6.4: 'For we will tread them under feet with them, and their mountains shall be drunken with their blood'.
21 **fetlocks** the tufts of hair that grow above horses' hooves.
21 **smoking** steaming.
24 The chroniclers note that Warwick actually killed his horse in the presence of King Edward in token that he would not flee (Hall, p. 255; Holinshed, p. 277).
25 **stand we** do we hang about.
26 **whiles** while.
27 **upon** on.
32 **measure** satisfaction (*OED* sv *sb* 10).
36 Compare Ps. 25.1: 'Unto Thee, O Lord, lift I up my soul.'

Thou setter up and plucker down of kings,
Beseeching Thee, if with Thy will it stands
That to my foes this body must be prey,
Yet that Thy brazen gates of heaven may ope   40
And give sweet passage to my sinful soul. –
Now, lords, take leave until we meet again
Where'er it be, in heaven or in earth.

RICHARD Brother, give me thy hand; and, gentle Warwick,
Let me embrace thee in my weary arms.   45
I, that did never weep, now melt with woe
That winter should cut off our spring-time so.

WARWICK Away, away! Once more, sweet lords, farewell.

GEORGE Yet let us all together to our troops
And give them leave to fly that will not stay,   50
And call them pillars that will stand to us,
And if we thrive, promise them such rewards
As victors wear at the Olympian games.
This may plant courage in their quailing breasts,
For yet is hope of life and victory.   55
Forslow no longer, make we hence amain!

                                              Exeunt

[2.4] [*Alarums*] *Excursions. Enter* RICHARD [*at one door*] *and*
CLIFFORD [*at the other*]

RICHARD Now, Clifford, I have singled thee alone:
Suppose this arm is for the Duke of York,

44] *Pope; Brother, / Giue . . . Warwicke,* F   48] O; *Away, away: / Once . . . farwell.* F   49 all together] *Rowe;*
altogether F   53 wear] F (weare); ware *Hudson*   **Act 2, Scene 4**   2.4] *Capell; not in* F   o SD] O *subst.;*
Excursions. Enter Richard and Clifford. F   1] F; *Rich. A Clifford a Clifford. / Clif. A Richard a Richard. / Rich. Now*
Clifford, for *Yorke* & *young Rutlands death,* O

---

37 Compare Dan. 2.21: 'He taketh away
kings: He setteth up kings', as well as 3.3.157
and 5.1.26 where similar phrases refer to
Warwick.

  38 stands accords.
  40 Yet Even.
  40 brazen strongly made, everlasting (*OED*
sv *adj* 1b).
  43 in earth on earth.
  44 gentle noble.
  47 winter i.e. death; compare the 'sunshine'
of 2.2.163 and *R3* 1.1.1 ('Now is the winter of
our discontent'.)
  51 pillars main and valued supporters (compare *2H6* 1.1.72).
  51 to by.

52 rewards Wreaths of wild olive were
awarded at the ancient Olympic games, but
victors might also win rewards from their native
states.
  54 quailing faltering.
  56 Forslow Delay.
  56 amain at full speed.

Act 2, Scene 4
  *2.4 Shakespeare invents this confrontation
between Richard and Clifford.
  o SD–1 O's SD and the war-cries of the two
fighters (see collation) probably derive from early
performances.
  1 singled singled out from the herd (a term
used in hunting).

And this for Rutland; both bound to revenge,
Wert thou environed with a brazen wall.
CLIFFORD Now, Richard, I am with thee here alone: 5
This is the hand that stabbed thy father York,
And this the hand that slew thy brother Rutland,
And here's the heart that triumphs in their death
And cheers these hands that slew thy sire and brother
To execute the like upon thyself;   10
And so, have at thee!

> [*Alarums.*] *They fight.* WARWICK *comes* [*and rescues*
> *Richard*]. *Clifford flies*

RICHARD Nay, Warwick, single out some other chase,
For I myself will hunt this wolf to death.

> *Exeunt*

[2.5] *Alarum. Enter* KING HENRY *alone*

KING HENRY This battle fares like to the morning's war
When dying clouds contend with growing light,
What time the shepherd, blowing of his nails,
Can neither call it perfect day nor night.

---

8 death] F; deathes O   11 SD] *This edn following* O (Alarmes. They fight, and then enters *Warwike* and rescues
Richard, & then *exeunt omnes*. Alarme still, and then enter *Henry solus*.); They Fight. *Warwicke comes, Clifford flies.*
F   Act 2, Scene 5   2.5] *Capell; not in* F   2 dying] F; dyeing *conj. this edn*   2 contend] *Eds.*; contend, F

4 brazen impenetrable (*OED sv adj* 1b).
8 triumphs exalts.
9 cheers incites.
12 chase object of pursuit, quarry (*OED sv sb*¹ 14).

Act 2, Scene 5
*2.5 Shakespeare seems to have taken the idea for this scene from Hall who ends his account of the battle with the reflection, 'This conflict was in manner unnatural, for in it the son fought against the father, the brother against the brother...' (p. 256; compare 5–8 n.). Both chroniclers report Henry's flight to Berwick (128) and thence to Scotland (Holinshed, p. 278; Hall, p. 256). D. J. Womersley, '*3 Henry VI*: Shakespeare, Tacitus, and parricide', *NQ* 230 (1985), 468–73, links the passage to the *topos* of sons who have killed fathers and vice versa

found in Tacitus' *Historiae*, III, xxv. This may have been known to Shakespeare from Savile's translation (licensed 15 May 1591). However, Shakespeare may equally have recalled the Tudor homily against rebellion: 'countrymen ... disturb the public peace of their country ... the brother ... [seeks] the death of his brother; the son of the father, the father ... [seeks] the death of his sons' (*Certain Sermons or Homilies*, 1844 edn, p. 511).
  0 SD It is more likely that Henry surveyed the battle from upstage than from the gallery above the stage – see 14 n. below.
  2 dying possibly punning on 'dyeing' (see collation).
  3 What time At the time when.
  3 blowing ... nails in patient idleness; compare *Shr.* 1.1.107 n. (New Arden).
  3 of on.

Now sways it this way, like a mighty sea   5
Forced by the tide to combat with the wind;
Now sways it that way, like the selfsame sea
Forced to retire by fury of the wind.
Sometime the flood prevails and then the wind;
Now one the better, then another best,   10
Both tugging to be victors, breast to breast,
Yet neither conqueror nor conquerèd:
So is the equal poise of this fell war.
Here on this molehill will I sit me down.
To whom God will, there be the victory!   15
For Margaret my queen and Clifford too
Have chid me from the battle, swearing both
They prosper best of all when I am thence.
Would I were dead, if God's good will were so:
For what is in this world but grief and woe?   20
O God, methinks it were a happy life
To be no better than a homely swain;
To sit upon a hill, as I do now,
To carve out dials quaintly, point by point,
Thereby to see the minutes how they run: 25
How many makes the hour full complete,
How many hours brings about the day,
How many days will finish up the year,
How many years a mortal man may live.
When this is known, then to divide the times: 30
So many hours must I tend my flock;
So many hours must I take my rest;
So many hours must I contemplate;
So many hours must I sport myself;
So many days my ewes have been with young;   35

---

9 then] *Eds.;* than F   **27 brings]** F; bring F2   **30 times]** F; time *Theobald*

5–8 Compare Hall: 'This deadly battle...
continued ten hours in doubtful victory. The
one part sometime flowing and sometime ebbing
...' (p. 256).

13 poise balance.

13 fell cruel.

14 molehill possibly a low rostrum that in
earlier scenes bore the throne and which was
used for the murder of York (see 1.4.67): an
emblem is thus created of the vanity of Henry's
power. In *Edward III* the king withdraws to
a 'little hill' (3.4.15) to rest from the battle.

22 swain shepherd (*OED* sv 4); Henry takes
literally the ancient metaphor of king as
shepherd: see Ezek. 34.2 ff., Jer. 23.1 ff., Plato,
Republic, I, 345, Aristotle, *Nicomachean Ethics*,
VIII, 11.

24 dials sundials.

24 quaintly skilfully.

26 hour here disyllabic (Cercignani, p. 228).

27 brings about completes; for the third
person plural in '-s' see Abbott 333.

33 contemplate meditate (*OED* sv 5).

34 sport divert, disport.

So many weeks ere the poor fools will ean;
So many years ere I shall shear the fleece:
So minutes, hours, days, months, and years,
Past over to the end they were created,
Would bring white hairs unto a quiet grave.   40
Ah what a life were this! How sweet, how lovely!
Gives not the hawthorn bush a sweeter shade
To shepherds looking on their silly sheep
Than doth a rich embroidered canopy
To kings that fear their subjects' treachery?   45
O yes, it doth; a thousandfold it doth.
And to conclude, the shepherd's homely curds,
His cold thin drink out of his leather bottle,
His wonted sleep under a fresh tree's shade –
All which secure and sweetly he enjoys –   50
Is far beyond a prince's delicates:
His viands sparkling in a golden cup,
His body couchèd in a curious bed
When care, mistrust, and treason waits on him.

Alarum. Enter a SON *that hath killed his father, at one door* [*with the dead man in his arms*]

SON Ill blows the wind that profits nobody: 55
     This man whom hand to hand I slew in fight
     May be possessèd with some store of crowns,

---

37 years] F *subst.*; Months *Rowe*   38 days,] F *subst.*; Days, Weeks *Rowe*   53 SD *with the dead man in his arms*] *This edn* (*following* O); *and a Father that hath kill'd his Sonne at another doore.* F

36–7 The absence of 'months' from Henry's catalogue (compare 38) led Walker to conjecture that, owing to compositorial eye-skip, a line was missing here, and Rowe plausibly substituted 'months' for 'years' in 27.

36 poor fools a phrase of endearment and not contempt.

36 ean give birth.

39 end they end for which they.

40 Compare Gen. 42.38: 'then ye shall bring my grey head with sorrow unto the grave'.

43 silly helpless, innocent (*OED* sv 1b and c).

44 canopy either that carried in a procession or, more probably (see 49 and 53), that over a bed.

47 curds coagulates made from milk.

48 thin lacking in body or alcoholic content (*OED* sv *adj* 4c).

50 secure free from care (*OED* sv *adj* 1).

51 delicates delicacies.

53 curious (1) full of cares, (2) elaborately decorated (*OED* sv 1 and 7).

54 When At which time.

54 waits attend (Abbott 333).

*54 SD–122 SD F offers two entrances for the Father that had killed his Son, here and 78 (see collation), and implies that the two pairs of actors exit together. This suggests that Shakespeare may have originally thought of the scene as being more of a tableau, possibly prefixed by a dumbshow. O, however, indicates that in performance the two pairs of actors entered and exited successively (see Textual analysis, p. 206 n.10).

55 Compare the proverb 'It is an ill wind that blows no man good' (Tilley W421).

57 with of (*OED* Possess 8).

57 crowns coins.

And I that haply take them from him now
May yet ere night yield both my life and them
To some man else, as this dead man doth me.   60
Who's this? O God, it is my father's face,
Whom in this conflict I unwares have killed.
O heavy times, begetting such events!
From London by the king was I pressed forth;
My father, being the Earl of Warwick's man,   65
Came on the part of York, pressed by his master;
And I, who at his hands received my life,
Have, by my hands, of life bereavèd him.
Pardon me, God, I knew not what I did –
And pardon, father, for I knew not thee.   70
My tears shall wipe away these bloody marks;
And no more words till they have flowed their fill.

KING HENRY O piteous spectacle! O bloody times!
Whiles lions war and battle for their dens,
Poor harmless lambs abide their enmity.   75
Weep, wretched man: I'll aid thee, tear for tear,
And let our hearts and eyes, like civil war,
Be blind with tears and break o'ercharged with grief.

Enter [a] FATHER [*that hath killed his son, at another door*] *bearing of*
[*the body*]

FATHER Thou that so stoutly hast resisted me,
Give me thy gold – if thou hast any gold –   80
For I have bought it with an hundred blows.
But let me see: is this our foeman's face?
Ah, no, no, no, it is mine only son!
Ah, boy, if any life be left in thee,

---

78 SD] *This edn (following* F's *53* SD); *Enter Father, bearing of his Sonne.* F   79 hast] F3; *hath* F   82 our] F; *a* Collier
MS

58 **haply** by chance.
61, 82 The text indicates that the faces of
the bodies are at first unrecognisable, perhaps
smeared with blood or covered by the visors of
helmets.
62 **unwares** unknowingly (*OED* sv 2).
63 **heavy** sorrowful.
64 **pressed forth** compulsorily enlisted.
65 **man** attendant.
66 **part** side.
68 **bereavèd** deprived.
69–70 Compare Luke 23.34: 'Then said
Jesus, "Father, forgive them, for they know not
what they do"'; and compare 1.4.94 ff.

71 **marks** stigmatic signs (*OED* Mark *sb*
11c).
72 **they...fill** I have finished crying,
although this may refer to the miraculous bleeding from the corpses of saints.
75 **abide** endure (*OED* sv 16).
77–8 'The meaning is here inaccurately expressed. The king intends to say that the state of
their "hearts and eyes" shall be like that of the
kingdom in a "civil war": all shall be destroyed
by a power formed within themselves' (Johnson).
78 **blind** blinded.
79 **stoutly** bravely.

Throw up thine eye! See, see, what showers arise,   85
Blown with the windy tempest of my heart
Upon thy wounds, that kills mine eye and heart!
O pity, God, this miserable age!
What stratagems, how fell, how butcherly,
Erroneous, mutinous, and unnatural,   90
This deadly quarrel daily doth beget!
O boy, thy father gave thee life too soon,
And hath bereft thee of thy life too late!
KING HENRY Woe above woe! Grief more than common grief!
O that my death would stay these ruthful deeds!   95
O pity, pity, gentle heaven, pity!
The red rose and the white are on his face,
The fatal colours of our striving houses:
The one his purple blood right well resembles,
The other his pale cheek methinks presenteth.   100
Wither one rose and let the other flourish!
If you contend, a thousand lives must wither.
SON How will my mother, for a father's death,
Take on with me and ne'er be satisfied?
FATHER How will my wife, for slaughter of my son,   105
Shed seas of tears, and ne'er be satisfied!
KING HENRY How will the country, for these woeful chances,
Misthink the king and not be satisfied!

---

89 stratagems] F3; Stragems F   92–3] soon . . . late F; -late . . . sone O   100 cheek] *Rowe²*; Cheekes F   105 my son] O F; her son Q2

85 **Throw up** Raise (*OED* Throw *v* 48c).
85–6 **See . . . heart** Compare the proverb 'After wind (thunder) comes rain' (Tilley T275) and 1.4.145–6.
87 **kills . . . [my] heart** proverbial (Dent KK2); for the third person plural termination in '-s' see Abbott 333.
89 ***stratagems*** bloody deeds (*OED* Stratagem 3).
89 **fell** cruel.
90 **Erroneous** Criminal (*OED* sv 2).
92–3 **thy . . . late** 'Thy father exposed thee to danger by "giving thee life too soon", and hath "bereft thee of life" by living himself too long' (Johnson).
92 **soon** readily (Schmidt).
93 **late** recently.
94 **above** upon.
95 **stay** put an end to.

95 **ruthful** lamentable (*OED* sv 2).
97 **red . . . white** symbolising life and death, perhaps the blood and water that came from the body of the dead Christ (John 19.34), as well as the two contending dynasties.
99 **purple** blood-red.
100 ***cheek** Rowe's emendation improves the symmetry of the rhetorical figure.
100 **presenteth** represents (Abbott 334).
102 Compare *1H6* 2.4.124–7.
102 **contend** make war.
104 **Take on with** Rage against (*OED* Take *v* 84j).
104 **be satisfied** find reparation or atonement (*OED* Satisfy 2).
106 **seas of tears** proverbial (Dent T82.1).
107 **chances** events.
108 **Misthink** Think ill of (*OED* sv 3).

SON Was ever son so rued a father's death?
FATHER Was ever father so bemoaned his son?   110
KING HENRY Was ever king so grieved for subjects' woe?
      Much is your sorrow; mine ten times so much.
SON I'll bear thee hence, where I may weep my fill.

[Exit with the body]

FATHER These arms of mine shall be thy winding-sheet;
      My heart, sweet boy, shall be thy sepulchre,   115
      For from my heart thine image ne'er shall go;
      My sighing breast shall be thy funeral bell;
      And so obsequious will thy father be,
      Mean for the loss of thee, having no more,
      As Priam was for all his valiant sons.   120
      I'll bear thee hence; and let them fight that will,
      For I have murdered where I should not kill.

Exit [with the body]

KING HENRY Sad-hearted men, much overgone with care,
      Here sits a king more woeful than you are.

Alarums. Excursions. Enter [PRINCE EDWARD]

PRINCE EDWARD Fly, father, fly, for all your friends are fled   125
      And Warwick rages like a chafèd bull!
      Away, for Death doth hold us in pursuit!

[*Enter* QUEEN MARGARET]

MARGARET Mount you, my lord; towards Berwick post amain:
      Edward and Richard, like a brace of greyhounds

---

113 SD] O *subst.*(*Exit* with his father.)*; not in* F   119 Mean] *Hulme;* Men F; *Even Capell;* E.'en *Collier MS;* Meet *conj. Sisson* (*New Readings*)   122 SD *with the body*] O *subst.* (with his sonne)*; not in* F   124 SD PRINCE EDWARD] *This edn* (*following* O)*; the Queen, the Prince, and Exeter.* F   127 SD] *This edn* (*following* O *at 124*)*; not in* F   128 Berwick] *Eds.;* Barwicke F

109 rued repented of (*OED* Rue *v* 5).
114–15 Compare Marlowe, *The Jew of Malta* 3.2.11: 'These arms of mine shall be thy sepulchre'.
114 winding-sheet shroud.
118 obsequious 'dutiful in performing funeral obsequies' (*OED* sv 1b).
119 *Mean Capell's emendation 'Even' for F's 'Men' has been widely accepted even though the graphic confusion is unlikely. However, Hulme (p. 234) argues that 'Men' represents 'Mean' (modern spelling) = (1) intermediary, employed as an agent (*OED* sv *adj*² and *adv*² 4), (2) poor, abject (*OED* *adj*¹ 2b and 2d).
120 In fact, according to Homer (*Iliad*,

XXIV, 239 ff.), Priam mourned mainly for Hector and not the remainder of his fifty sons.
123 overgone overwhelmed (*OED* 5).
***124, 127, 133** SD F offers a single massed entrance; O, from which these successive entrances derive (although that text, probably as a result of memorial error, brings Margaret on before her son), suggests that in performance tension was raised by a succession of entrances.
126 chafèd enraged.
127 hold . . . pursuit puts us to flight (*OED* 'Pursuit' 2b).
128 Berwick Berwick-on-Tweed in Northumberland on the Scottish border.
128 post amain ride at full speed.

Having the fearful flying hare in sight,   130
With fiery eyes sparkling for very wrath
And bloody steel grasped in their ireful hands,
Are at our backs; and therefore hence amain!

[*Enter* EXETER]

EXETER Away, for vengeance comes along with them.
        Nay, stay not to expostulate: make speed   135
        Or else come after. I'll away before.
KING HENRY Nay take me with thee, good sweet Exeter:
        Not that I fear to stay but love to go
        Whither the queen intends. Forward, away!

                                                        Exeunt

[**2.6**] *A loud alarum. Enter* CLIFFORD *wounded* [*, with an arrow in his neck*]

CLIFFORD Here burns my candle out; ay, here it dies,
        Which, whiles it lasted, gave King Henry light.
        O Lancaster, I fear thy overthrow
        More than my body's parting with my soul!
        My love and fear glued many friends to thee   5

133 SD] *This edn (following* O*); not in* F . 139 Whither] *Eds.;* Whether F   **Act 2, Scene 6**   2.6] *Capell; not in*
F   0 SD *with . . . neck*] O; *not in* F

131 **for very wrath** with pure anger.
135 **expostulate** remonstrate (*OED* sv 2).
139 **intends** directs her journey (*OED* Intend
6).

Act 2, Scene 6
*2.6 Historically Clifford died at Dintingdale
while fleeing from the same skirmish at
Ferrybridge – which preceded the battle of
Towton – in which Warwick's bastard brother
was killed (see 2.3.15 and 0 SD n. below). On 30
March 1461 Edward reached York. From the
gate of the city he removed the head of his
father and replaced it by others (Holinshed,
p. 278; Hall, p. 256) – Shakespeare invents
the detail that Clifford's head was so treated.
His return to London, his coronation, and the
investiture of his brothers as dukes took place in
June (Holinshed, p. 279; Hall, pp. 257–8). A
match with Bona of Savoy (90) was proposed,

but it seems that in 1464 Warwick's mission,
which the chroniclers describe (Holinshed,
p. 283; Hall, p. 263), was repeatedly postponed
and then cancelled (see Charles Ross, *Edward
IV*, 1974, p. 91).
0 SD *with . . . neck* This detail from O is to be
found in the chroniclers: 'the Lord Clifford . . .
suddenly with an arrow . . . without an head was
stricken into the throat' (Holinshed, p. 277;
Hall, p. 255; also *Mirror*, p. 191). Shakespeare
presumably instructed the players here on how
to do Clifford's death (see Hattaway, pp. 52–3).
1 **Here . . . out** Compare Job 21.17 'How oft
shall the candle of the wicked be put out', and
the proverbial 'candle of life' (Dent CC1).
3 **Lancaster** The house of Lancaster.
5 **My . . . fear** Love for me and fear of my
valour.
5 **glued** attached in sympathy or affection
(*OED* Glue v 2).

And now I fall, thy tough commixtures melts,
Impairing Henry, strength'ning misproud York.
The common people swarm like summer flies;
And whither fly the gnats but to the sun?
And who shines now but Henry's enemies? 10
O Phoebus, hadst thou never given consent
That Phaëthon should check thy fiery steeds,
Thy burning car never had scorched the earth!
And, Henry, hadst thou swayed as kings should do
Or as thy father and his father did, 15
Giving no ground unto the house of York,
They never then had sprung like summer flies;
I and ten thousand in this luckless realm
Had left no mourning widows for our death,
And thou this day hadst kept thy chair in peace. 20
For what doth cherish weeds but gentle air,
And what makes robbers bold but too much lenity?
Bootless are plaints and cureless are my wounds;
No way to fly nor strength to hold out flight;
The foe is merciless and will not pity, 25
For at their hands I have deserved no pity.
The air hath got into my deadly wounds
And much effuse of blood doth make me faint.

6 fall, thy] *Rowe;* fall. Thy F; die, that O; fall, the *conj. Johnson*   6 commixtures] F *subst.;* commixture O   8] O *subst., Theobald; not in* F   19 death] F; deathes O   24 out] F; our O   24 flight] F; fight *conj. Johnson*   26 For] F; And O

6 *fall, thy** Rowe's emendation of F's punctuation is supported by O's version of the line (see collation).
6 **tough** sticky, glutinous (*OED* sv 2).
6 **commixtures** compounds produced by the mingling of love and fear (5), hence, in this context, alliances.
6 **melts** For the third-person-plural in '-*s*' see Abbott 333.
7 **Impairing** Weakening.
7 **misproud** viciously proud (Schmidt).
*8 It is reasonable to insert this line from O as the image seems to be developed in 9 and 17.
9 **sun** Edward's badge – see 2.1.20 SD n.
11–13 See 1.4.33 n.
11 **Phoebus** Phoebus Apollo, the sun.
12 **Phaëthon** son to Phoebus: see 1.4.33 n.
12 **check** manage, rein (*OED* sv *v* 14b).
13 **car** chariot.

14 **swayed** ruled.
17 **sprung** multiplied.
19 **mourning widows** widows mourning (Abbott 419a).
20 **chair** throne.
21 **cherish** cultivate, nourish (*OED* sv 2b).
21 **gentle air** Compare the proverb 'As gentle as air' (Dent A88.1).
21 **gentle** light, mild (*OED* sv 6).
21 **air** breeze (*OED* sv *sb* 9).
23 **Bootless** Unavailing.
23 **plaints** lamentations.
23 **cureless** mortal.
24 **hold out** maintain (*OED* Hold *v* 41 f.).
27 Compare the proverb 'Fresh air is ill for the wounded man' (Tilley A93).
28 **effuse** pouring out.
28 **faint** feeble.

Come, York and Richard, Warwick and the rest:
I stabbed your fathers' bosoms – split my breast.   30

[*He faints.*] *Alarum and retreat. Enter* EDWARD [*now* DUKE OF
YORK], WARWICK, RICHARD, *and Soldiers,* MONTAGUE, *and*
[GEORGE]

EDWARD Now breathe we, lords: good fortune bids us pause
        And smooth the frowns of war with peaceful looks.
        Some troops pursue the bloody-minded queen
        That led calm Henry, though he were a king,
        As doth a sail, filled with a fretting gust,   35
        Command an argosy to stem the waves.
        But think you, lords, that Clifford fled with them?
WARWICK No, 'tis impossible he should escape;
        For, though before his face I speak the words,
        Your brother Richard marked him for the grave   40
        And wheresoe'er he is he's surely dead.
            Clifford groans [*and then dies*]
EDWARD Whose soul is that which takes her heavy leave?
RICHARD A deadly groan like life and death's departing.
EDWARD See who it is and, now the battle's ended,
        If friend or foe, let him be gently used.   45

30] F *subst.;* I stabde your fathers, now come split my brest. O   30 split] F; split, *conj. this edn*   30 SD.1 He faints.]
Rowe; not in F   30 SD.3 GEORGE] *Eds.; Clarence* F   39 For,] *Capell;* For F   41 SD *and...dies*] O; *not in*
F   42–4] O *subst.* (*Edw.* Harke, what soule... leaue? / *Rich.* A deadlie... departure. / *Edw.* See... is,
and... ended,); *Rich.* Whose... leaue? / A... departing. / See... is. / *Ed.* And... ended. F   43 and death's] F
subst.; in death *Hanmer*

30 O's version of the line (see collation) is
rhythmically superior.
30 SD.1 *retreat* a battlefield signal sounded
by drum or trumpet (Long, pp. 5, 6).
30 SD.2–3 MONTAGUE... GEORGE The
appearance of these names in the list after
'Soldiers' suggests that these two characters may
have been added as an afterthought. George,
who has lines in both F and O, may simply have
been omitted by Shakespeare, Montague whose
entrance is not recorded in O and who has lines
in neither text, may have been added simply to
swell the scene.
31 **breathe we** let us rest.
34 **led** dominated.
35 **fretting** a pun: 'apt to a sudden gust and
to the nagging impatience of a headstrong
woman' (Wilson).
36 **Command** Force.
36 **argosy** large merchant ship.
36 **stem** push forward through.

39 **his** Richard's.
40 **marked** (1) destined, (2) wounded, struck
(*OED* Mark v 12).
41 SD **and...dies* The exact moment of
Clifford's death is not indicated. It might be
effective in a production for him to expire
during the buffeting he receives later in the
sequence.
*42–4 O's distribution of these lines seems
superior to that of F in that it has Edward ask a
question to which Richard responds at 46. F's
reading may be due to compositorial confusion
and O's, possibly, to revision of foul paper copy
in rehearsal.
42 **heavy** sorrowful.
43 **departing** sundering (*OED* Depart v 3).
44–5 In fact Edward ordered that 'no
prisoner should be taken', i.e. that all the
Lancastrian prisoners be killed (Holinshed,
p. 278; Hall, p. 255).
45 **gently used** treated with honour.

RICHARD Revoke that doom of mercy, for 'tis Clifford
          Who, not contented that he lopped the branch
          In hewing Rutland when his leaves put forth,
          But set his murd'ring knife unto the root
          From whence that tender spray did sweetly spring –   50
          I mean our princely father, Duke of York.
WARWICK From off the gates of York fetch down the head,
          Your father's head, which Clifford placèd there;
          Instead whereof let this supply the room:
          Measure for measure must be answerèd.   55
EDWARD Bring forth that fatal screech-owl to our house
          That nothing sung but death to us and ours:
          Now death shall stop his dismal threat'ning sound
          And his ill-boding tongue no more shall speak.
WARWICK I think his understanding is bereft. –   60
          Speak, Clifford, dost thou know who speaks to thee?
          Dark cloudy death o'ershades his beams of life
          And he nor sees nor hears us what we say.
RICHARD O would he did! And so, perhaps, he doth:
          'Tis but his policy to counterfeit   65
          Because he would avoid such bitter taunts
          Which in the time of death he gave our father.
GEORGE If so thou think'st, vex him with eager words.
RICHARD Clifford, ask mercy and obtain no grace.
EDWARD Clifford, repent in bootless penitence.   70
WARWICK Clifford, devise excuses for thy faults.
GEORGE While we devise fell tortures for thy faults.

49 But] F; Did *Hudson*   54 this] F; his O   60 his] O; is F   68] *Pope;* If... think'st / Vex... Words. F

46 **doom** sentence.
47–50 The imagery is of a genealogical tree;
compare 2.2.165 n.
48 **when ... forth** in his early prime.
49 **But** But also – the sentence is constructed
as though 'contented' in 47 were a finite verb
rather than a participle.
50 **spray** shoot, twig.
54 **this ... room** Clifford's head take its
place.
55 Proverbial (Tilley M800); derived from
Mark 4.24: 'With what measure ye mete, it shall
be measured unto you' (Tilley M801).
55 **answerèd** required.
56–7 Compare the proverb 'The screeching
owl (raven) bodes death' (Dent R33).
56 **fatal ... house** the owl whose screech
heralded death in our family (Abbott 419a).

58 **dismal** fore-boding, sinister.
59 **ill-boding** foretelling ill.
60 **understanding** consciousness.
60 **bereft** taken from him, impaired.
65 **policy** craft.
65 **counterfeit** pretend.
68 **vex** torment.
68 **eager** Latinate sense = sharp, biting
(*OED* sv 1c).
69–74 For the Senecan trick of using
repeated words in stichomythia see T. S. Eliot,
Selected Essays, 1932, pp. 88–90.
70 **bootless** fruitless.
71 **faults** offences.
72 **fell** cruel.

RICHARD Thou did'st love York and I am son to York.

EDWARD Thou pitied'st Rutland; I will pity thee.

GEORGE Where's Captain Margaret to fence you now? 75

WARWICK They mock thee, Clifford: swear as thou wast wont.

RICHARD What, not an oath? Nay then, the world goes hard
When Clifford cannot spare his friends an oath.
I know by that he's dead; and, by my soul,
If this right hand would buy but two hours' life, 80
That I in all despite might rail at him,
This hand should chop it off and, with the issuing blood,
Stifle the villain whose unstanchèd thirst
York and young Rutland could not satisfy.

WARWICK Ay but he's dead. Off with the traitor's head, 85
And rear it in the place your father's stands.
And now to London with triumphant march,
There to be crownèd England's royal king;
From whence shall Warwick cut the sea to France
And ask the Lady Bona for thy queen: 90
So shalt thou sinew both these lands together
And, having France thy friend, thou shalt not dread
The scattered foe that hopes to rise again;
For though they cannot greatly sting to hurt,
Yet look to have them buzz to offend thine ears. 95
First will I see the coronation
And then to Brittany I'll cross the sea
To effect this marriage, so it please my lord.

EDWARD Even as thou wilt, sweet Warwick, let it be,

---

74 I will pity] F *subst.;* I'll not pity *conj. this edn* 76] O; They . . . *Clifford,* / Sweare . . . wont. F 80 buy but] O; buy F 82 This . . . chop] F; Ide cut O 85 Off] F2; Of F 91 sinew] F4; sinow F 96 the] F; thy *conj. Capell*

75 **fence** defend.
77 **world goes hard** Compare the proverb 'As hard as the world goes' (Dent w877.1).
80 ***buy but** F's omission of 'but' (the restoration of which improves the metre) was probably due to compositorial eye-skip.
81 **despite** contempt, scorn (*OED* sv *sb* 5a).
82 **This hand** His left hand.
83 **Stifle** Choke by pouring (blood) down the throat (*OED* sv 3).
83 **unstanchèd** insatiable.
85–6 It is possible that by some contrivance a property head was produced here (or at the end of the scene) to replace the head of York which

might have been displayed from the beginning of 2.2 (see 2.2.2 n.)
86 **rear** erect.
90 **Lady Bona** Third daughter of Louis, first Duke of Savoy and sister-in-law to Louis XI of France.
91 **sinew** join fast as with sinews.
92 **France** The king of France.
93 **scattered** cast down, defeated (hence desirous to 'rise again').
94 **greatly . . . hurt** For the transposition of the adverb from the end of the phrase, see Abbott 421.
95 **buzz** spread false rumours.

For in thy shoulder do I build my seat   100
And never will I undertake the thing
Wherein thy counsel and consent is wanting.
Richard, I will create thee Duke of Gloucester;
And, George, of Clarence; Warwick, as ourself,
Shall do and undo as him pleaseth best.   105
RICHARD Let me be Duke of Clarence, George, of Gloucester;
For Gloucester's dukedom is too ominous.
WARWICK Tut, that's a foolish observation:
Richard, be Duke of Gloucester. Now to London
To see these honours in possession.   110

               Exeunt

[3.1] *Enter [two KEEPERS] with cross-bows in their hands*

1 KEEPER Under this thick-grown brake we'll shroud ourselves,
For through this laund anon the deer will come:
And in this covert will we make our stand,
Culling the principal of all the deer.
2 KEEPER I'll stay above the hill, so both may shoot.   5

---

105 him] F; himself Q3   110 SD] F; *Exeunt. York's head is removed / Oxford*   **Act 3, Scene 1**   3.1] *Rowe; not in*
F   0 SD *two* KEEPERS] O; *Sinklo, and Humfrey* F   0 SD *cross-bows*] F *subst.*; bow and arrowes O   1 SH] *Malone*
subst.; Sink. F *subst.* (*throughout scene*)   1 thick-grown] *Pope*; thicke growne F   5 SH] *Malone subst.; Hum.* F
(*throughout scene*)

---

100 seat throne.

104 ourself Edward adopts the royal 'we'.

105 do … undo make and unmake men.

107 Refers to the disgrace and murder of
Humphrey, Duke of Gloucester, portrayed in
2H6, of Thomas of Woodstock, Duke of
Gloucester, uncle to Richard II, and of Hugh
Spenser, Duke of Gloucester, a favourite of
Edward II. Richard too met a violent death as
Richard III at Bosworth. These are listed by
Holinshed, p. 211 (Hall, p. 209).

Act 3, Scene 1

*3.1 The scene derives from the chroniclers'
reports that in 1465, about four years after the
battle of Towton (Boswell-Stone, p. 309), Henry,
'whether he was past all fear, or that he was not
well established in his wits and perfect mind, or
for that he could not long keep himself secret, in
disguised attire boldly entered into England
[where] he was known and taken of one Cantlow'
(Holinshed, p. 282; Hall, p. 262). The play

completely passes over the battle of Hexham in
1464 when the Lancastrians were defeated by
Montague (Holinshed, p. 281; Hall, p. 260).

0 SD KEEPERS Gamekeepers. In F, the
names of two members of Strange's company
who originally took these parts, 'Sinklo and
Humphrey', appear here and as SH's throughout
the scene; see Introduction, p. 59 and compare
2H6 4.2.0 SD.

0 SD cross-bows These properties served to
set the scene – see Hattaway, pp. 35 ff.

1 brake thicket. Shakespeare may have taken
the detail from Fabyan who noted 'King Henry
[was] taken in a wood in the north country'
(p. 654).

1 shroud conceal.

2 laund glade, clearing.

3 covert thicket.

3 stand 'hide' or cover from which to shoot.

4 Culling Picking out.

4 principal the best beast (*OED* sv B *sb* 6).

1 KEEPER That cannot be: the noise of thy cross-bow
          Will scare the herd and so my shoot is lost:
          Here stand we both, and aim we at the best;
          And, for the time shall not seem tedious,
          I'll tell thee what befell me on a day   10
          In this self place where now we mean to stand.
1 KEEPER Here comes a man: let's stay till he be past.

          Enter [KING HENRY, *disguised,*] *with a prayer-book*

KING HENRY From Scotland am I stol'n even of pure love
          To greet mine own land with my wishful sight.
          No, Harry, Harry, 'tis no land of thine;   15
          Thy place is filled, thy sceptre wrung from thee,
          Thy balm washed off wherewith thou wast anointed.
          No bending knee will call thee Caesar now,
          No humble suitors press to speak for right,
          No, not a man comes for redress of thee: 20
          For how can I help them and not myself?
1 KEEPER Ay, here's a deer whose skin's a keeper's fee:
          This is the quondam king; let's seize upon him.
KING HENRY Let me embrace thee, sour Adversity,
          For wise men say it is the wisest course.   25

---

7 scare] F3; scarre F   12 SD KING HENRY, *disguised,*] O *subst.; the King* F   17 wast] F3; was F   24 thee, sour
Adversity] *Singer, conj. Dyce;* the sower Aduersaries F; thee, sour adversities *Sisson (New Readings)*

7 **shoot** shot.
7 **lost** wasted.
8 **at the best** to our best advantage.
9 **for** so that.
11 **self** same.
12 **stay** wait.
12 SD ***disguised*** See 3.1 n. and Textual
analysis, p. 203 n.5.
13–14 Compare the chroniclers (see 3.1 n.)
who surmised that Henry may have been insane
at this time.
13 **even of pure** because of my absolute.
14 **wishful** yearning.
17 **balm** fragrant oil used at coronations and
often supposed to be the source of the monarch's
curative powers (see Thomas, pp. 230 and 236).
18 **Caesar** the type of the absolute ruler.
19 **press ... right** push forward to ask for
justice – with perhaps an ironic allusion to the
conspirators who murdered Caesar – see *JC*
3.1.27 ff.
19 ***press*** F's 'prease' may indicate a pronunciation with a long vowel (see Cercignani,
p. 73).

20 **of** from.
20 **man** single person.
21 **and** if.
22 **fee** The deer's head and skin were
customarily given to the gamekeeper – see
Harrison, *The Description of England*, 1587, II,
xix (cited Wilson).
23 **quondam** former.
24–5 Sisson (*New Readings*, II, 84) argues,
on graphic grounds, for 'adversities' (rather than
the commonly accepted 'adversity' [aduersitie])
as an emendation for F's 'Aduersaries'.
('Adversaries' is unlikely as it was generally
stressed on the first syllable.) However,
'adversity' seems preferable on grammatical
grounds. There may be an allusion to the wise
Son of Sirach in Ecclus 2.4.5: 'Whatsoever
cometh unto thee, receive it patiently, and be
patient in the change of thine affliction. For as
gold and silver are tried in the fire, even so are
men acceptable in the furnace of adversity'
(Noble). Compare the proverbs 'Adversity makes
men wise' (Tilley A42) and 'He is wise that can
be patient in adversity' (Dent A42.1).

2 KEEPER Why linger we? Let us lay hands upon him.

1 KEEPER Forbear awhile: we'll hear a little more.

KING HENRY My queen and son are gone to France for aid;
    And, as I hear, the great commanding Warwick
    Is thither gone to crave the French king's sister   30
    To wife for Edward. If this news be true,
    Poor queen and son, your labour is but lost,
    For Warwick is a subtle orator
    And Lewis a prince soon won with moving words.
    By this account, then, Margaret may win him,   35
    For she's a woman to be pitied much:
    Her sighs will make a batt'ry in his breast;
    Her tears will pierce into a marble heart;
    The tiger will be mild whiles she doth mourn;
    And Nero would be tainted with remorse   40
    To hear and see her plaints, her brinish tears.
    Ay, but she's come to beg, Warwick to give:
    She on his left side, craving aid for Henry,
    He on his right, asking a wife for Edward;
    She weeps and says her Henry is deposed,   45
    He smiles and says his Edward is installed;
    That she, poor wretch, for grief can speak no more
    Whiles Warwick tells his title, smooths the wrong,
    Inferreth arguments of mighty strength,
    And, in conclusion, wins the king from her   50
    With promise of his sister and what else
    To strengthen and support King Edward's place.
    O Margaret, thus 'twill be; and thou, poor soul,
    Art then forsaken, as thou went'st forlorn.

2 KEEPER Say what art thou that talk'st of kings and queens?   55

---

30 Is] F2; I: F   40 And F; A *conj.* Steevens in *Johnson Var.*   40 would] *Pope;* will F   55 that] O; *not in* F

27 **Forbear** Be patient.

31 **To** As a (Abbott 189).

32 **your...lost** Compare the proverb 'You lose your labour' (Dent L9).

37 **make...batt'ry** cause his heart to sound like the signal for an assault (see *OED* Battery 2).

38 Compare the proverbs 'Constant dropping will wear the stone' (Tilley D618) and 'A heart of marble' (Dent H311).

40 **Nero** The Roman emperor who was the type of hard-hearted cruelty. Among other atrocities he had his mother Agrippina murdered.

40 ***would** F's 'will' was probably caught by the compositor from the preceding lines.

40 **tainted...remorse** feel a pity contrary to his nature.

41 **plaints** lamentations.

41 **brinish** salt-tasting, bitter.

47 **That** With the result that.

47 **for** because of.

48 **tells his title** goes over Edward's claims.

48 **smooths** glosses over.

49 **Inferreth** Adduces.

51 **what** who knows what.

52 **place** high rank (*OED* sv *sb* 9).

55 **what** of what quality.

55 ***that** Emendation from O is justified on metrical grounds.

KING HENRY More than I seem and less than I was born to:
    A man at least, for less I should not be;
    And men may talk of kings, and why not I?
2 KEEPER Ay, but thou talk'st as if thou wert a king.
KING HENRY Why so I am, in mind: and that's enough.   60
2 KEEPER But if thou be a king, where is thy crown?
KING HENRY My crown is in my heart, not on my head;
    Not decked with diamonds and Indian stones,
    Nor to be seen: my crown is called Content –
    A crown it is that seldom kings enjoy.   65
2 KEEPER Well, if you be a king crownèd with content,
    Your crown Content and you must be contented
    To go along with us, for, as we think,
    You are the king King Edward hath deposed;
    And we his subjects, sworn in all allegiance,   70
    Will apprehend you as his enemy.
KING HENRY But did you never swear and break an oath?
2 KEEPER No, never such an oath, nor will not now.
KING HENRY Where did you dwell when I was king of England?
2 KEEPER Here in this country where we now remain.   75
KING HENRY I was anointed king at nine months old;
    My father and my grandfather were kings
    And you were sworn true subjects unto me:
    And tell me then, have you not broke your oaths?
1 KEEPER No, for we were subjects but while you were king.   80
KING HENRY Why, am I dead? Do I not breath a man?
    Ah, simple men, you know not what you sware:
    Look: as I blow this feather from my face
    And as the air blows it to me again,

---

57 for . . . not] F *subst.;* and more I cannot O   72 oath?] *Eds.;* Oath F   82 sware] *Cairncross, conj. Delius;* sweare F

63 Indian stones gems from India, probably pearls (compare *Oth.* 5.3.343).

64 my . . . Content Compare the proverb 'A mind content is a crown' (Tilley C623).

71 apprehend arrest.

75 country region.

76–9 These lines may derive from a report in Holinshed (p. 325) of remarks made by Henry not long before his death (see Appendix 1, p. 210).

76 See 1.1.112 n.

76 anointed crowned; see 17 n. above.

80 but only.

82 simple foolish, ignorant.

82 *sware an obsolete form of 'swore' (see collation).

83 as introduces an elaborate simile.

83 this feather Henry could pick it from the ground or, conceivably, from a dead bird brought on by the keepers.

84–8 Compare the proverb 'As wavering as feathers in the wind' (Dent F162); and see C. A. Patrides, '"The beast with many heads": Renaissance views on the multitude', *SQ* 16 (1965), 241–6.

Obeying with my wind when I do blow   85
And yielding to another when it blows,
Commanded always by the greater gust:
Such is the lightness of you, common men.
But do not break your oaths, for of that sin
My mild entreaty shall not make you guilty.   90
Go where you will, the king shall be commanded;
And be you kings: command, and I'll obey.

I KEEPER We are true subjects to the king: King Edward.

KING HENRY So would you be again to Henry
If he were seated as King Edward is.   95

I KEEPER We charge you, in God's name and the king's,
To go with us unto the officers.

KING HENRY In God's name lead; your king's name be obeyed:
And what God will, that let your king perform;
And what He will, I humbly yield unto.   100

Exeunt

[3.2] *Enter* KING EDWARD, [RICHARD, DUKE OF]
GLOUCESTER, [GEORGE, DUKE OF] CLARENCE, [*and*] LADY
[ELIZABETH] GREY

KING EDWARD Brother of Gloucester, at Saint Alban's field
This lady's husband, Sir Richard Grey, was slain,
His lands then seized on by the conqueror.
Her suit is now to repossess those lands
Which we in justice cannot well deny   5

---

88 you,] F; you *Eds.*   93] *Pope*; We...king, / King *Edward* F   100 He] *This edn;* he F   **Act 3, Scene
2   3.2**] *Pope; not in* F   0 SD] *This edn; Enter K. Edward, Gloster, Clarence, Lady Gray.* F   2 Richard] F; John
Pope   3 lands] O; Land F

85 **Obeying** Being ruled.
85 **with** by means of (Abbott 193).
85 **wind** breath.
88 **lightness** with the implication of fickle-ness.

Act 3, Scene 2
*3.2 Details in the scene reveal that the author turned to Holinshed's account of the wooing of the Lady Elizabeth which was derived from More's *History of Richard III* and found in the chapter on the reign of Edward V (Holinshed, p. 586; Hall, pp. 365–7; see 97–8 n.) Edward was privately married to Lady Grey on 1 May 1464 (Boswell-Stone, p. 310 n.).

There are close resemblances to 2.1 of the apocryphal *Edward III*.
2 **Sir Richard Grey** The chroniclers note that the Lady Elizabeth's husband was called Sir John Grey – Shakespeare may have caught the name from that of Sir Richard Woodville her father who is mentioned in the same paragraph (Holinshed p. 283; Hall, p. 264). Grey was knighted by Henry VI and fell for the Lancastrians – not the Yorkists (see 6–7 below) – at the second battle of St Albans (as is narrated in *R3* 1.3.126–9).
3 *lands O's reading is justified because the word is repeated in the next line.
4 **repossess** regain possession of.
5 **deny** refuse.

> Because in quarrel of the house of York,
> The worthy gentleman did lose his life.

GLOUCESTER Your highness shall do well to grant her suit:
> It were dishonour to deny it her.

KING EDWARD It were no less, but yet I'll make a pause.   10

GLOUCESTER [*Aside to Clarence*] Yea, is it so?
> I see the lady hath a thing to grant
> Before the king will grant her humble suit.

CLARENCE He knows the game: how true he keeps the wind!

GLOUCESTER [*Aside to Clarence*] Silence!   15

KING EDWARD Widow, we will consider of your suit;
> And come some other time to know our mind.

LADY GREY Right gracious lord, I cannot brook delay:
> May it please your highness to resolve me now,
> And what your pleasure is shall satisfy me.   20

GLOUCESTER [*Aside to Clarence*] Ay, widow? Then I'll warrant you
>   all your lands
> And if what pleases him shall pleasure you:
> Fight closer or, good faith, you'll catch a blow.

CLARENCE [*Aside to Gloucester*] I fear her not, unless she chance
>   to fall.

GLOUCESTER [*Aside to Clarence*] God forbid that, for he'll take
>   vantages.   25

KING EDWARD How many children hast thou, widow, tell me?

CLARENCE [*Aside to Gloucester*] I think he means to beg a child
>   of her.

---

8 SH] O *subst.; Rich.* F (*throughout scene*)   11] F *subst.; Glo.* I, is the wind in that doore? O   11, 15, 21, 24, 25, 27,
28 SD] *Capell; not in* F   18 SH] *Rowe subst.; Wid.* F (*throughout scene*)   23 blow] F; clap O   25 God forbid that]
F; Marie godsforbot man O

6 **in...of** in the cause of (*OED* Quarrel *sb³* 2); for the omission of an article as in archaic poetry see Abbott 82.

11, 25 O's versions of both lines (see collation) seem to offer examples of actor's 'gag' (see Hattaway, p. 90).

12 hath...grant must offer her virtue (Partridge, 'thing', p. 199).

14 game (1) the chase, (2) the sport of womanising.

14 keeps the wind stays downwind (like a hunting dog).

18 brook endure.

19 resolve me give me an answer.

20 pleasure will – there is a hint of sexual equivocation.

21 warrant guarantee; probably pronounced 'warn't' (Cercignani, p. 275).

22 And if If.

23–5 The lines combine images from fighting with bawdy puns.

23 closer nearer to the enemy to avoid his thrusts.

23 blow (1) hit, (2) coital thrust – O's 'clap' (gonorrhoea) provides another double-entendre.

24 fear...not do not fear for her.

24 fall (1) succumb to Edward's attack, (2) surrender her virtue (*OED* sv *v* 21 and 22).

25 vantages opportunities.

27 beg...her (1) petition the Court of Wards for the custody of a minor (*OED* Beg 5a), an office which could be exploited by the guardian for his own profit (*Shakespeare's England*, I, 386–7), (2) invite her to conceive a child by him.

GLOUCESTER [*Aside to Clarence*] Nay then, whip me: he'll rather
    give her two.
LADY GREY Three, my most gracious lord.
GLOUCESTER [*Aside to Clarence*] You shall have four, if you'll be
    ruled by him.   30
KING EDWARD 'Twere pity they should lose their father's lands.
LADY GREY Be pitiful, dread lord, and grant it then.
KING EDWARD Lords, give us leave: I'll try this widow's wit.
GLOUCESTER [*Aside to Clarence*] Ay, good leave have you, for you
    will have leave
    Till youth take leave and leave you to the crutch.   35
        [*Gloucester and Clarence retire*]
KING EDWARD Now tell me, madam, do you love your children?
LADY GREY Ay, full as dearly as I love myself.
KING EDWARD And would you not do much to do them good?
LADY GREY To do them good I would sustain some harm.
KING EDWARD Then get your husband's lands to do them good.   40
LADY GREY Therefore I came unto your majesty.
KING EDWARD I'll tell you how these lands are to be got.
LADY GREY So shall you bind me to your highness' service.
KING EDWARD What service wilt thou do me if I give them?
LADY GREY What you command that rests in me to do.   45
KING EDWARD But you will take exceptions to my boon.
LADY GREY No, gracious lord, except I cannot do it.
KING EDWARD Ay, but thou canst do what I mean to ask.
LADY GREY Why then, I will do what your grace commands.
GLOUCESTER [*Aside to Clarence*] He plies her hard, and much
    rain wears the marble.   50
CLARENCE [*Aside to Gloucester*] As red as fire! Nay then, her wax
    must melt.

---

28 then, whip me] F *subst.;* whip me then O   30 if] F; and O   31 lands] F *subst.;* land *Capell*   32 then] F; them
O   35 SD] *Johnson subst.; not in* F   50, 51, 82, 83, 107, 108 SD] *Dyce; not in* F

28 whip 'confound', 'hang' (*OED* sv *v* 11b) –
a mild oath.
32 pitiful compassionate.
33 give us leave retire so we may speak
privately (Dent L167.1).
33 try test.
33 wit intelligence, prudence.
34 good...you we are going gladly
(compare Kyd, *The Spanish Tragedy* 3.11.2).
34 have leave (1) speak alone, (2) take
liberties.
35 crutch (1) symbol of old age, (2) the
widow's crotch.

41 Therefore For that purpose.
44 service sexually equivocal – compare 20.
45 rests in me lies in my power.
46 boon request.
47 except unless.
47 do (1) perform, (2) fornicate.
50 plies works on.
50 much...marble compare the figure in
3.1.38.
51 As...fire Proverbial (Tilley F248); i.e.
the lady is blushing.
51 her...melt Compare the proverb 'To
melt like wax against the fire' (Dent W137.1).

LADY GREY Why stops my lord? Shall I not hear my task?
KING EDWARD An easy task: 'tis but to love a king.
LADY GREY That's soon performed because I am a subject.
KING EDWARD Why then, thy husband's lands I freely give thee.   55
LADY GREY I take my leave with many thousand thanks.
GLOUCESTER [*Aside to Clarence*] The match is made: she seals
            it with a curtsy.
                    [*Lady Grey turns to go*]
KING EDWARD But stay thee – 'tis the fruits of love I mean.
LADY GREY The fruits of love I mean, my loving liege.
KING EDWARD Ay, but I fear me in another sense.   60
        What love think'st thou I sue so much to get?
LADY GREY My love till death, my humble thanks, my prayers,
        That love which virtue begs and virtue grants.
KING EDWARD No, by my troth, I did not mean such love.
LADY GREY Why then, you mean not as I thought you did.   65
KING EDWARD But now you partly may perceive my mind.
LADY GREY My mind will never grant what I perceive
        Your highness aims at, if I aim aright.
KING EDWARD To tell thee plain I aim to lie with thee.
LADY GREY To tell you plain I had rather lie in prison.   70
KING EDWARD Why then, thou shalt not have thy husband's
            lands.
LADY GREY Why then, mine honesty shall be my dower:
        For by that loss I will not purchase them.
KING EDWARD Therein thou wrong'st thy children mightily.
LADY GREY Herein your highness wrongs both them and me.   75
        But, mighty lord, this merry inclination
        Accords not with the sadness of my suit:
        Please you dismiss me either with ay or no.
KING EDWARD Ay, if thou wilt say 'Ay' to my request;
        No, if thou dost say 'No' to my demand.   80
LADY GREY Then no, my lord. My suit is at an end.
GLOUCESTER [*Aside to Clarence*] The widow likes him not: she
            knits her brows.

57 curtsy] F2 *subst.;* Cursie F   57 SD] *This edn; not in* F

57 **seals** ratifies.   72 **honesty** chastity.
58 **stay thee** stop.   73 **that loss** loss of that.
58 **fruits of love** copulation.   76 **inclination** disposition.
59 **fruits of love** the devotion of a subject. 77 **sadness** seriousness.
68 **aim** guess.

CLARENCE [*Aside to Gloucester*] He is the bluntest wooer in
    christendom.
KING EDWARD [*Aside*] Her looks doth argue her replete with
    modesty;
    Her words doth show her wit incomparable;   85
    All her perfections challenge sovereignty:
    One way – or other – she is for a king
    And she shall be my love, or else my queen. –
    Say that King Edward take thee for his queen?
LADY GREY 'Tis better said than done, my gracious lord: 90
    I am a subject fit to jest withal
    But far unfit to be a sovereign.
KING EDWARD Sweet widow, by my state I swear to thee
    I speak no more than what my soul intends
    And that is to enjoy thee for my love.   95
LADY GREY And that is more than I will yield unto:
    I know I am too mean to be your queen
    And yet too good to be your concubine.
KING EDWARD You cavil, widow: I did mean my queen.
LADY GREY 'Twill grieve your grace my sons should call you
    father.   100
KING EDWARD No more than when my daughters call thee
    mother.
    Thou art a widow and thou hast some children,
    And, by God's mother, I, being but a bachelor,
    Have other some. Why, 'tis a happy thing
    To be the father unto many sons.   105
    Answer no more for thou shalt be my queen.

---

84 SD] *Johnson; not in* F   84, 85 doth] F; F2 do   101] *Pope;* No . . . Daughters / Call . . . Mother. F

83 **bluntest** rudest.
84 **doth** For the third-person-plural in '-*th*'
see Abbott 334.
84 **argue** prove.
84 **replete with** full of.
86 **challenge** lay claim to.
86 **sovereignty** (1) supremacy over their
kind, (2) kingship.
88 **love** mistress.
90 **'Tis . . . done** Proverbial (Tilley S116).
91 **subject** (1) topic, (2) citizen.
93 **state** sovereignty.

97–8 The lines derive from the second
account of the wooing, found in the life of
Edward V: 'she showed him plain that, as she
wist herself too simple to be his wife, so
thought herself too good to be his concubine'
(Holinshed, p. 586; Hall, p. 366).
97 **mean** humble, of low estate.
99 **cavil** raise frivolous objections.
99 **queen** The context evokes the word
'quean' (whore).
104 **other some** another set.
104 **happy** fortunate.

GLOUCESTER [*Aside to Clarence*] The ghostly father now hath
    done his shrift.
CLARENCE [*Aside to Gloucester*] When he was made a shriver, 'twas
    for shift.
KING EDWARD Brothers, you muse what chat we two have had.
GLOUCESTER The widow likes it not for she looks vexed.   110
KING EDWARD You'd think it strange if I should marry her.
CLARENCE To who, my lord?
KING EDWARD   Why, Clarence, to myself.
GLOUCESTER That would be ten days' wonder at the least.
CLARENCE That's a day longer than a wonder lasts.
GLOUCESTER By so much is the wonder in extremes.   115
KING EDWARD Well, jest on, brothers; I can tell you both
    Her suit is granted for her husband's lands.

      Enter a NOBLEMAN [SIR JAMES HARRINGTON]

HARRINGTON My gracious lord, Henry your foe is taken
    And brought your prisoner to your palace gate.
KING EDWARD See that he be conveyed unto the Tower. –   120
    And go we, brothers, to the man that took him
    To question of his apprehension. –
    Widow, go you along. – Lords, use her honourably.
                   Exeunt [*all but Gloucester*]
GLOUCESTER Ay, Edward will use women honourably –

---

110 vexed] *Cairncross, conj. Vaughan;* very sad F; sad F2   117 SD NOBLEMAN] F *subst.;* Messenger O   117
SIR . . . HARRINGTON] *This edn; not in* F   118 SH] *This edn;* Nob. F   119 your] F; as O   123 honourably] O
subst.; honourable F   123 SD] *Eds.; Exeunt. / Manet Richard.* F

107–8 To shrive a woman to her shift
(smock) was a common quibble on religious and
sexual confessions – compare *1H6* 1.2.119 and
see Hulme, pp. 122–3.
  107 **ghostly father** priest (but also alluding
knowingly to 104–5).
  107 **done his shrift** completed his spiritual
(and sexual) office.
  108 **shriver** confessor.
  108 **for shift** (1) as a trick, (2) in order to get
under her smock (see Partridge, p. 182).
  109 **muse** wonder.
  110 ***vexed** F's 'very sad' spoils the metre
and may have come about partly by eye-skip
from the 'had' of the previous line.
  112 **who** For 'who' rather than 'whom' see
Abbott 274.
  113–14 Referring to the proverbial 'nine
days' wonder' (Tilley W728).

115 **in extremes** in its last throes (Lat. *in*
extremis – *OED* Extreme 2b). However, *OED*
and most eds. gloss the phrase to mean 'to the
utmost degree' (*OED* 4).
  119 **your prisoner** F's 'your' (O reads 'as')
may well be due to eye-skip.
  120 **Tower** Tower of London.
  122 **apprehension** arrest.
  123 **use** treat.
  123 ***honourably** F' 'honourable' is probably
a misprint for 'honourablie' (as in O and the
next line although adjectives were used freely as
adverbs (Abbott 23).
  124 **use** copulate with.
  124 **honourably** A double-entendre, punning on 'on her' (see Partridge, pp. 155–6 and
compare *Ado* 3.4.27).

Would he were wasted, marrow, bones, and all,   125
That from his loins no hopeful branch may spring
To cross me from the golden time I look for!
And yet, between my soul's desire and me –
The lustful Edward's title burièd –
Is Clarence, Henry, and his son, young Edward,   130
And all the unlooked-for issue of their bodies
To take their rooms ere I can place myself –
A cold premeditation for my purpose!
Why then, I do but dream on sovereignty,
Like one that stands upon a promontory   135
And spies a far-off shore where he would tread,
Wishing his foot were equal with his eye,
And chides the sea that sunders him from thence,
Saying he'll lade it dry to have his way:
So do I wish the crown, being so far off,   140
And so I chide the means that keeps me from it,
And so, I say, I'll cut the causes off,
Flattering me with impossibilities.
My eye's too quick, my heart o'erweens too much,
Unless my hand and strength could equal them.   145
Well say there is no kingdom then for Richard:
What other pleasure can the world afford?
I'll make my heaven in a lady's lap
And deck my body in gay ornaments
And witch sweet ladies with my words and looks.   150

132 place] F; plant O   144 eye's] F3; Eyes F   150 witch] O; 'witch F

125 **wasted** with disease; syphilis, the 'bone ache' (*TC* 2.3.19), would be Gloucester's desired reward for Edward's lust – see 129.
125 **marrow** It was common to think of love consuming the 'marrow' (see *Ven.* 142); here the word is a metonym for manly mettle or semen (compare *AWW* 2.3.181).
126 A reference to the tree of Jesse, a common motif in church windows – on which is imposed a double-entendre.
127 **cross** debar.
127 **golden time** when Gloucester would wear the crown.
129 **burièd** eliminated.
131 **unlooked-** unbargained-.
132 **rooms** positions in the realm.
132 **place** establish; some eds. print O's 'plant' on the grounds that it picks up the

imagery of 126 (and contains a witty sexual quibble).
133 **cold premeditation** cheerless prospect.
137 **were ... with** occupied the place seen by.
139 **lade** drain by bailing.
141 **means** obstacles.
142 **cut ... off** murder those who stand in my way.
143–5 These lines might gain if read as if dashes were printed after 'with' and 'them'.
143 **me** myself.
144 **quick** alive.
144 **o'erweens** presumes.
148–52 The lines suggest Richard's sexual insecurity, and foreshadow some of the sentiments contained in *R3* 1.2.260–4.
150 **witch** bewitch.

O miserable thought! And more unlikely
Than to accomplish twenty golden crowns!
Why, Love forswore me in my mother's womb
And, for I should not deal in her soft laws,
She did corrupt frail Nature with some bribe   155
To shrink mine arm up like a withered shrub;
To make an envious mountain on my back
Where sits Deformity to mock my body;
To shape my legs of an unequal size;
To disproportion me in every part,   160
Like to a chaos or an unlicked bear-whelp
That carries no impression like the dam.
And am I then a man to be beloved?
O monstrous fault to harbour such a thought!
Then, since this earth affords no joy to me   165
But to command, to check, to o'erbear such
As are of better person than myself,
I'll make my heaven to dream upon the crown
And, whiles I live, t'account this world but hell
Until this head my misshaped trunk doth bear   170
Be round impalèd with a glorious crown.
And yet I know not how to get the crown
For many lives stand between me and home:
And I, like one lost in a thorny wood,
That rents the thorns and is rent with the thorns,   175

156 shrink . . . shrub] F *subst.;* drie . . . shrimpe O   161 or an] F; or F3   170] *This edn;* Vntill my mis-shap'd Trunke, that beares this Head, F; Until the head this mis-shap'd trunk doth bear *Hanmer*

152 accomplish obtain.

153 forswore abjured.

154 for so that.

157 envious spiteful (transferred epithet).

161 chaos formless mass.

162 unlicked . . . dam There was a popular belief, deriving from Pliny (*Nat. Hist.*, X, 63), that bear cubs were born misshapen and then licked into proper shape by their mother (see Tilley S284); compare *Metamorphoses*, XV, 416 ff.

162 carries . . . dam in no way bears the mother's form.

164 (1) **monstrous fault** unnatural error (*OED* Fault *sb* 5b), (2) prodigious vagina (compare *Wiv.* 5.5.8–11).

165–8 'Richard speaks here the language of nature. Whoever is stigmatised with deformity has a constant source of envy in his mind, and would counterbalance by some other superiority

these advantages which he feels himself to want' (Johnson Var.).

166 check rebuke (*OED* sv *v* 11).

166 o'erbear overthrow, put down (*OED* Overbear 2).

167 person appearance.

168–95 For a useful commentary on these lines see Mahood, p. 27.

***170** F's reading obviously makes little sense, but whether from authorial inadvertence or compositorial error we cannot tell.

171 impalèd encircled.

173 between . . . home proverbial (Dent H533.1).

173 home my goal (*OED* sv *adv.* 4) with, because of the context, the possibility that Richard is invoking the metaphor of home as grave (*OED* sb 4).

175 rents tears (*OED* Rent *v²*).

Seeking a way and straying from the way,
Not knowing how to find the open air
But toiling desperately to find it out,
Torment myself to catch the English crown;
And from that torment I will free myself,   180
Or hew my way out with a bloody axe.
Why, I can smile, and murder whiles I smile,
And cry, 'Content!' to that which grieves my heart,
And wet my cheeks with artificial tears,
And frame my face to all occasions.   185
I'll drown more sailors than the mermaid shall;
I'll slay more gazers than the basilisk;
I'll play the orator as well as Nestor,
Deceive more slyly than Ulysses could,
And, like a Sinon, take another Troy.   190
I can add colours to the chameleon,
Change shapes with Proteus for advantages,
And set the murderous Machiavel to school.

---

183 'Content!'] *This edn*; Content, F   193 murderous Machiavel] *Pope* (murth'rous); murtherous *Macheuill* F; aspiring *Catalin* O

176 a way a path.
178 find it out discover it.
182 Compare the proverb 'To smile in one's face and cut one's throat' (Tilley F16).
184 artificial feigned.
185 frame shape, compose (*OED* sv *v* 5b).
186–95 The tone of these lines is notably Marlovian.
186 mermaid siren, a figure of deception; sailors were charmed onto rocks by the false melodies of mermaids – see *Odyssey* XII, 39–54; *FQ* 2, 12, 17 and 30.
187 basilisk a fabulous 'royal' serpent that wore a crown (see Pliny, VIII, 78; XXIV, 66) and, according to later authorities, could kill with its look (Isidore, *Etymol.* XII, 4.6, 7); and see Dent B99.1.
188 play the orator proverbial (Dent O74.1).
188 Nestor The aged king of Pylos, present at the siege of Troy and noted for his eloquence (*Metamorphoses*, XIII, 80).
189 Ulysses King of Ithaca, hero of the the *Odyssey*, noted for his cunning; see *TC. passim*, and compare Golding's 'sly Ulysses' (*Metamorphoses*, XIII, 68, 115).
190 Sinon According to Virgil (*Aeneid* II, 13–267 – Sinon is not in Homer), the Greek who persuaded the Trojans to take the wooden horse into their city. The description of Sinon in *Lucr.* 1501–78 indicates that Shakespeare read Virgil in the original (A. K. Root, *Classical*

Mythology in Shakespeare, 1903, p. 107).
191 colours (1) hues, (2) shows of reason or rhetorical figures.
191 chameleon proverbially able to change its colours to match its surroundings (Pliny, XXVII, 8; *Metamorphoses*, XV, 453–4; Tilley C222).
192 Proteus Neptune's seal herd who could assume different shapes in order to escape being questioned (*Metamorphoses*, VIII, 916 ff.; Tilley S285).
193 set … school the phrase became proverbial (Dent M1.1).
193 *Machiavel The name popularly given to any ambitious, greedy, or ruthless power-seeker; see *1H6* 5.4.74 n. and compare 'Machevil' who appears as Prologue to Marlowe's *The Jew of Malta*. Richard adopts the role of the stage 'Machiavel', a vice-like figure whose immorality bore little resemblance to the pragmatic principles set out by the Florentine statesman Niccolò Machiavelli (1469–1527). O's 'Catalin[e]' probably derives from a memory lapse on the part of the reporter rather than from censorship – although it could be an (authorial?) correction of the anachronistic evocation of Machiavelli. (Catiline was an impoverished Roman patrician who conspired to bring about a general massacre in 65 BC.) Stephen Gosson had a now lost play, *Catiline's Conspiracies*, performed at the Theatre about 1578.

Can I do this and cannot get a crown?
Tut! Were it farther off, I'll pluck it down.   *Exit*   195

[3.3] *Flourish. Enter [to a chair of state]* LEWIS *the French king, his sister* BONA, *his Admiral, called* BOURBON; PRINCE EDWARD, QUEEN MARGARET, *and the* EARL OF OXFORD. *Lewis sits and riseth up again*

KING LEWIS Fair Queen of England, worthy Margaret,
Sit down with us: it ill befits thy state
And birth that thou shouldst stand while Lewis doth sit.
MARGARET No, mighty King of France: now Margaret
Must strike her sail and learn awhile to serve   5
Where kings command. I was, I must confess,
Great Albion's queen in former golden days;
But now mischance hath trod my title down
And with dishonour laid me on the ground
Where I must take like seat unto my fortune   10
And to my humble state conform myself.
KING LEWIS Why say, fair queen, whence springs this deep
despair?
MARGARET From such a cause as fills mine eyes with tears
And stops my tongue, while heart is drowned in cares.

---

195 I'll] F *subst.;* I'd *Collier MS*   **Act 3, Scene 3**   3.3] *Capell; not in* F   0 SD.1 *to . . . state*] *This edn; not in* F   11 state] *Dyce²; Seat* F

Act 3, Scene 3

*3.3 Shakespeare backtracks to 1462 when, after the battle of Towton, Henry sent his wife and Prince Edward from Scotland to France (Holinshed, p. 279; Hall, p. 257). He then moves from the moment after Edward's coronation (28 June 1461) when Warwick had said he would leave for France (2.6.89–90), to the account of the negotiations which took place in 1464, which were designed to give the new king 'affinity' in France, and which caused Warwick to turn against Edward (Holinshed, pp. 283–4; Hall, pp. 263–4). Warwick returned to France in 1470 which was when he encountered Margaret at the court of King Louis XI. He did not in fact devote himself to Henry's restoration until 1470 when Prince Edward of Lancaster was, according to the chroniclers, married to his daughter Anne (Holinshed, p. 295; Hall, p. 281: see 242 n.).

0 SD.1 *Flourish* As at 1.1.49 and 275, this is

placed ambiguously, proclaiming not only the entrance of King Lewis but the ambitions of Richard Crook-back at the end of the previous scene (Long, p. 29).

0 SD.2 *sister* sister-in-law. Bona's eldest sister Charlotte was the second wife of King Louis.

2 state rank.

3 Lewis possibly monosyllabic (Cercignani, p. 282).

5 strike her sail humble herself (Dent S24.3 – literally 'lower a sail in deference to a more important vessel').

7 Albion's England's.

8 mischance misfortune.

10 like . . . unto a position similar to.

11 *state F's 'Seat' was probably caught from the previous line and destroys the symmetry of the exchange which begins with the 'state-sit-stand' conceit of 2–3.

KING LEWIS Whate'er it be, be thou still like thyself　　　　15
　　　And sit thee by our side.
　　　　　　　　　　　Seats her by him.
　　　　　　　　　　　　　　Yield not thy neck
　　　To Fortune's yoke, but let thy dauntless mind
　　　Still ride in triumph over all mischance.
　　　Be plain, Queen Margaret, and tell thy grief;
　　　It shall be eased, if France can yield relief.　　　　20
MARGARET Those gracious words revive my drooping thoughts
　　　And give my tongue-tied sorrows leave to speak.
　　　Now therefore be it known to noble Lewis
　　　That Henry, sole possessor of my love,
　　　Is, of a king, become a banished man　　　　25
　　　And forced to live in Scotland a forlorn;
　　　While proud ambitious Edward, Duke of York,
　　　Usurps the regal title and the seat
　　　Of England's true-anointed lawful king.
　　　This is the cause that I, poor Margaret,　　　　30
　　　With this my son, Prince Edward, Henry's heir,
　　　Am come to crave thy just and lawful aid:
　　　And if thou fail us, all our hope is done.
　　　Scotland hath will to help, but cannot help;
　　　Our people and our peers are both misled,　　　　35
　　　Our treasure seized, our soldiers put to flight,
　　　And, as thou seest, ourselves in heavy plight.
KING LEWIS Renownèd queen, with patience calm the storm
　　　While we bethink a means to break it off.
MARGARET The more we stay the stronger grows our foe.　　　　40
KING LEWIS The more I stay the more I'll succour thee.

16–18] *Theobald subst.;* And … *him.* / Yeeld … yoake, / But … triumph, / Ouer … mischance. F　　21] *Rowe subst.;* Those … words / Reuiue … thoughts, F　　29 true-anointed] *Theobald;* true anoynted F　　38] *Rowe;* Renowned Queene, / With … Storme F

15 **be … thyself** always behave in a manner that befits your station.
17–18 **dauntless … mischance** The image derives from that of a deity in a chariot, crushing its foes beneath the wheels as described in Petrarch's *Trionfi*.
　18 **Still** Always.
　19 **grief** grievance.
　20 **France** the King of France.
　25 **of** from being.
　26 **in Scotland** Margaret is ignorant of the events of 3.1.

26 **forlorn** forsaken man.
33 **And if** If indeed (Abbott 105).
36 **treasure** treasure-chest (*OED* sv 3).
37 **heavy plight** sad condition.
38 **calm the storm** appease your passion.
39 **While** Until – a common Elizabethan use still prevalent in S. Yorkshire.
　39 **break it off** make the political perturbation cease (see *OED* Break *v* 28).
40 **stay** delay.
41 **stay** with a pun on 'stay' = 'support'.

MARGARET O, but impatience waiteth on true sorrow –
    And see where comes the breeder of my sorrow.

       Enter WARWICK

KING LEWIS What's he approacheth boldly to our presence?
MARGARET Our Earl of Warwick, Edward's greatest friend.   45
KING LEWIS Welcome, brave Warwick! What brings thee to
    France?
       He descends. She ariseth.
MARGARET Ay, now begins a second storm to rise
    For this is he that moves both wind and tide.
WARWICK From worthy Edward, King of Albion,
    My lord and sovereign and thy vowèd friend,   50
    I come, in kindness and unfeignèd love,
    First to do greetings to thy royal person
    And then to crave a league of amity,
    And, lastly, to confirm that amity
    With nuptial knot, if thou vouchsafe to grant   55
    That virtuous Lady Bona, thy fair sister,
    To England's king in lawful marriage.
MARGARET [*Aside*] If that go forward, Henry's hope is done.
WARWICK *Speaking to Bona.* And, gracious madam, in our king's
    behalf,
    I am commanded, with your leave and favour,   60
    Humbly to kiss your hand and, with my tongue,
    To tell the passion of my sovereign's heart
    Where Fame, late ent'ring at his heedful ears,
    Hath placed thy beauty's image and thy virtue.
MARGARET King Lewis and Lady Bona, hear me speak   65
    Before you answer Warwick. His demand
    Springs not from Edward's well-meant honest love
    But from deceit, bred by necessity:

---

42 waiteth . . . sorrow] F *subst.*; waiting, rues to Morrow *conj. Warburton in Theobald* 45 Our] F; Proud *conj.*
Vaughan 47 Ay] F *subst.*; [*Aside*] Ay *Wilson* 58 SD] *Capell; not in* F 59 *Pope;* And . . . Madame, *Speaking to*
Bona. / In . . . behalfe, F

42 **waiteth** attends.
43 **breeder** author.
44 **What's** Who's (Abbott 254).
46 SD *He descends* comes down from the
dias on which the throne stands.
47–8 These lines might be effectively
delivered as an aside.
51 **in . . . love** Compare 2 Cor. 4–6 'But in
all things we approve ourselves as the ministers
of God . . . by kindness . . . by love unfeigned'
(see Noble, pp. 82, 129).

53 **crave** request (*OED* sv 3).
54 **confirm** strengthen.
56 **sister** sister-in-law. She was sister to
Lady Charlotte, Lewis' queen.
58 **go forward** come to pass.
62 **passion** suffering caused by love.
63 **Fame** Report.
63 **late** recently.

For how can tyrants safely govern home
Unless abroad they purchase great alliance?   70
To prove him tyrant this reason may suffice,
That Henry liveth still; but, were he dead,
Yet here Prince Edward stands, King Henry's son.
Look therefore, Lewis, that by this league and marriage
Thou draw not on thy danger and dishonour: 75
For though usurpers sway the rule awhile,
Yet heavens are just and time suppresseth wrongs.
WARWICK Injurious Margaret.
PRINCE EDWARD   And why not 'Queen'?
WARWICK Because thy father Henry did usurp;
And thou no more art prince than she is queen.   80
OXFORD Then Warwick disannuls great John of Gaunt
Which did subdue the greatest part of Spain;
And, after John of Gaunt, Henry the Fourth
Whose wisdom was a mirror to the wisest;
And, after that wise prince, Henry the Fifth   85
Who by his prowess conquerèd all France:
From these our Henry lineally descends.
WARWICK Oxford, how haps it in this smooth discourse
You told not how Henry the Sixth hath lost
All that which Henry the Fifth had gotten?   90
Methinks these peers of France should smile at that.
But for the rest: you tell a pedigree
Of threescore and two years – a silly time
To make prescription for a kingdom's worth.

75 thy] F; thee *Johnson*   78 SH] O *subst.; Edw.* F

69 **tyrants** usurpers (*OED* Tyrant 1).
70 **purchase** obtain.
76 **sway** control.
77 **time...wrongs** Compare the proverb 'Time cures every disease' (Tilley T325).
78 **Injurious** Insulting (*OED* sv 2).
81 **disannuls** deprives of his title (*OED* Disannul 2).
81–2 **John...Spain** 'John of Gaunt, Duke of Lancaster [and great-grandfather to Henry VI], claimed Castile in right of his second wife Constance, elder daughter of Pedro the Cruel. The Duke, however, failed to dethrone John I, son of Pedro's bastard brother Henry II; and obtained but a few transient successes by his invasion of Spanish territory' (Boswell-Stone, p. 313). In 1601 the Admiral's Men were to present a now lost play by R. Hathway and W. Rankins called *The Conquest of Spain by John of Gaunt*.
82 **Which** Who (Abbott 265).
84 **mirror** model.
88 **haps it** does it happen.
88 **smooth** bland.
92 **tell** (1) number, (2) recount.
93 **threescore...years** from the deposition of Richard II in 1399.
93 **silly** trifling.
94 **prescription** a claim based on long use (*OED* sv 4b).

OXFORD Why, Warwick, canst thou speak against thy liege   95
    Whom thou obeyed'st thirty and six years,
    And not bewray thy treason with a blush?

WARWICK Can Oxford, that did ever fence the right,
    Now buckler falsehood with a pedigree?
    For shame! Leave Henry and call Edward king.   100

OXFORD Call him my king by whose injurious doom
    My elder brother, the Lord Aubrey Vere,
    Was done to death? And more than so, my father,
    Even in the downfall of his mellowed years,
    When nature brought him to the door of death?   105
    No, Warwick, no: while life upholds this arm,
    This arm upholds the house of Lancaster.

WARWICK And I the house of York.

KING LEWIS Queen Margaret, Prince Edward, and Oxford,
    Vouchsafe at our request to stand aside   110
    While I use further conference with Warwick.

                   They stand aloof

MARGARET Heavens grant that Warwick's words bewitch him not.

KING LEWIS Now, Warwick, tell me, even upon thy conscience,
    Is Edward your true king? For I were loath
    To link with him that were not lawful chosen.   115

WARWICK Thereon I pawn my credit and mine honour.

KING LEWIS But is he gracious in the people's eye?

WARWICK The more that Henry was unfortunate.

KING LEWIS Then further, all dissembling set aside,

---

109 and] F; and Lord *Hanmer*   115 chosen] F; heir O

---

96 thirty and six Henry came to the throne in 1422 and Warwick joined the Yorkists in 1455 (see *2H6* 5.1). However, he was born only in 1428 – the dates do not tally unless we assume that Oxford is ignoring Warwick's defection and referring to his age: the marriage embassy took place in 1463 when he was thirty-five.

97 bewray reveal.

98 fence defend.

99 buckler shield, defend.

101 injurious doom wrongful (*OED* sv 1) sentence.

102–104 Holinshed reports that in the first year of Edward IV's reign, 1462, the aged Earl of Oxford and his son, 'either through malice of their enemies or for that they had offended the king, were both ... attainted, and put to execution' (p. 279; Hall, p. 258).

103 more ... so what is more.

104 downfall decline, setting; compare *Tit.* 5.2.56–7: 'Hyperion's ... very downfall in the sea'.

105 door of death proverbial (Tilley D162).

111 use ... conference have ... conversation.

114 were would be.

115 lawful For adjectives used as adverbs see Abbott 1.

116 pawn pledge.

116 credit reputation.

117–18 Shakespeare may be remembering the account of the council called by Edward after the second battle of St Albans (Holinshed, p. 272; Hall, p. 254; see Appendix 1, pp. 213–14).

117 gracious acceptable, popular.

118 unfortunate associated with mishap (*OED* sv 2).

119 dissembling hypocrisy.

Tell me for truth the measure of his love   120
Unto our sister Bona.

WARWICK   Such it seems
As may beseem a monarch like himself.
Myself have often heard him say and swear
That this his love was an eternal plant
Whereof the root was fixed in virtue's ground,   125
The leaves and fruit maintained with beauty's sun,
Exempt from envy, but not from disdain,
Unless the Lady Bona quit his pain.

KING LEWIS Now, sister, let us hear your firm resolve.

BONA Your grant or your denial shall be mine.   130
        Speaks to Warwick Yet I confess that often ere this day
When I have heard your king's desert recounted,
Mine ear hath tempted judgement to desire.

KING LEWIS Then, Warwick, thus: our sister shall be Edward's.
And now forthwith shall articles be drawn   135
Touching the jointure that your king must make,
Which with her dowry shall be counterpoised. –
Draw near, Queen Margaret, and be a witness
That Bona shall be wife to the English king.

PRINCE EDWARD To Edward, but not to the English king.   140

MARGARET Deceitful Warwick, it was thy device
By this alliance to make void my suit:
Before thy coming Lewis was Henry's friend.

---

124 eternal] O; externall F   128 quit] F; Quite O   131] *Eds.;* Yet . . . day, *Speaks to War.* F   133 tempted] F;
tempered *Cairncross conj. Vaughan*   134] *Pope;* Then . . . thus: / Our . . . *Edwards.* F

120 **measure** degree (*OED* sv *v* 14).

122 **beseem** befit.

124–8 'Envy is always supposed to have some fascinating or blasting power, and to be out of the reach of envy is therefore a privilege belonging only to great excellence. I know not well why "envy" is mentioned here, or whose "envy" can be meant, but the meaning is that his love is superior to "envy", and can feel no blast but from the Lady's "disdain". Or, that if Bona refuse to "quit" or "requite" his pain, his "love" may turn to "disdain", though the consciousness of his own merit will exempt him from the pangs of "envy"' (Johnson). 'Envy', however, may mean here simply 'malice'.

124 *eternal i.e. heavenly. There may be a veiled reference to Matt. 15.13: 'Every plant which mine heavenly Father hath not planted,

shall be rooted up.' F's 'external', however, may stand – if we take it to mean 'visible' (*OED* sv 2).

126 **maintained** sustained, nourished.

127 **envy** malice (*OED* sv 1).

127 **disdain** aversion, contempt.

128 **quit . . . pain** reward his passion with her love.

129 **resolve** decision.

130 **grant** permission.

131 **Yet** But, although.

132 **desert** merit.

135 **articles** terms of agreement.

136 **Touching** Concerning.

136 **jointure** settlement of money or lands made upon a woman to support her in widowhood (*OED* sv 4).

137 **counterpoised** equally balanced.

141 **device** stratagem.

KING LEWIS And still is friend to him and Margaret.
    But if your title to the crown be weak –   145
    As may appear by Edward's good success –
    Then 'tis but reason that I be released
    From giving aid which late I promisèd.
    Yet shall you have all kindness at my hand
    That your estate requires and mine can yield.   150
WARWICK Henry now lives in Scotland at his ease
    Where, having nothing, nothing can he lose.
    And as for you yourself, our quondam queen,
    You have a father able to maintain you,
    And better 'twere you troubled him than France.   155
MARGARET Peace, impudent and shameless Warwick,
    Proud setter-up and puller-down of kings!
    I will not hence till, with my talk and tears,
    Both full of truth, I make King Lewis behold
    Thy sly conveyance and thy lord's false love,   160
        Post blowing a horn within
    For both of you are birds of self-same feather.
KING LEWIS Warwick, this is some post to us or thee.

        Enter the POST

POST *Speaks to Warwick* My lord ambassador, these letters are for
    you,
    Sent from your brother, Marquess Montague.
    To Lewis These from our king unto your majesty.   165
    To Margaret And, madam, these for you: from whom, I
    know not.
        They all read their letters
OXFORD I like it well that our fair queen and mistress
    Smiles at her news while Warwick frowns at his.

156 Warwick,] F *subst.;* Warwick, peace! F2   **160** SD] F *subst.; after 161* Capell   **163**] Pope; My ... Ambassador, / These ... you. *Speakes to Warwick,* F   **165–6**] *Eds.;* These ... Maiesty. *To Lewis.* / And ... you: *To Margaret* F   **166**] *Theobald;* And ... you: / From ... not. F

146 good success 'Success' meant 'result' (*OED* sv 1), either good or bad.
  148 late recently.
  150 estate rank.
  152 Compare the proverb 'They that have nothing need fear to lose nothing' (Dent N331); there may also, as at *R2* 5.5.40–1 and *Lear* 1.1.250, be an echo of 2. Cor. 6.10: 'having nothing, and yet possessing all things'.

153 quondam former.
  154 'This seems ironical. The poverty of Margaret's father is a very frequent topic of reproach' (Johnson).
  157 See 2.3.37 n.
  160 conveyance juggling, fraud (*OED* 11b).
  160 SD *Post* Express messenger.
  161 birds ... feather Compare 2.1.170 n. and Tilley B393.

PRINCE EDWARD Nay, mark how Lewis stamps as he were nettled.
    I hope all's for the best.   170
KING LEWIS Warwick, what are thy news? And yours, fair queen?
MARGARET Mine such as fill my heart with unhoped joys.
WARWICK Mine full of sorrow and heart's discontent.
KING LEWIS What, has your king married the Lady Grey
    And now, to soothe your forgery and his,   175
    Sends me a paper to persuade me patience?
    Is this th'alliance that he seeks with France?
    Dare he presume to scorn us in this manner?
MARGARET I told your majesty as much before:
    This proveth Edward's love and Warwick's honesty.   180
WARWICK King Lewis, I here protest in sight of heaven
    And by the hope I have of heavenly bliss
    That I am clear from this misdeed of Edward's –
    No more my king for he dishonours me,
    But most himself if he could see his shame.   185
    Did I forget that by the house of York
    My father came untimely to his death?
    Did I let pass th'abuse done to my niece?
    Did I impale him with the regal crown?
    Did I put Henry from his native right?   190
    And am I guerdoned at the last with shame?
    Shame on himself! For my desert is honour;
    And, to repair my honour, lost for him,

169–70] *As verse in Rowe; prose in* F   171] *Pope subst.;* Warwicke . . . Newes? / And . . . Queene. F   175 soothe] F; smooth *Rann*

170 **all's . . . best** proverbial (Dent A136.1).
172 **unhoped** unexpected.
173 **discontent** vexation.
175 **soothe** gloss over.
175 **forgery** deception.
176 **persuade** counsel (*OED* sv 3).
180 **proveth** shows the truth of.
181 **protest** proclaim.
183 **clear from** not guilty of.
185 Although he would do most harm to his own reputation, assuming that he could perceive this.
186–7 Holinshed reports that Richard Neville, Earl of Salisbury and father to Warwick – he appeared in *2H6* – was captured by the Lancastrians along with York at the battle of Wakefield in 1460 and later beheaded at Pontefract, his head being set over a town gate at York (p. 269; Hall, pp. 250-1). Warwick means that unless the Yorkists had rebelled, his father would not have been killed, but almost insinuates that they killed him.
186 **by** by means of.
187 **untimely** prematurely.
188 Holinshed reports that Edward 'would have deflowered' Warwick's 'daughter or his niece' (p. 284; Hall, p. 265).
188 **let pass** overlook
188 **abuse** injury (*OED* sv *sb* 5).
189 **impale him** encircle his brow, crown him.
190 **native right** claim to the crown to which he was born.
191 **guerdoned** rewarded.
192 **my desert** what I deserve.
193 **repair** restore.

I here renounce him and return to Henry. –
My noble queen, let former grudges pass   195
And henceforth I am thy true servitor.
I will revenge his wrong to Lady Bona
And replant Henry in his former state.
MARGARET Warwick, these words have turned my hate to love
And I forgive and quite forget old faults   200
And joy that thou becom'st King Henry's friend.
WARWICK So much his friend, ay, his unfeignèd friend,
That if King Lewis vouchsafe to furnish us
With some few bands of chosen soldiers,
I'll undertake to land them on our coast   205
And force the tyrant from his seat by war.
'Tis not his new-made bride shall succour him;
And as for Clarence, as my letters tell me,
He's very likely now to fall from him
For matching more for wanton lust than honour   210
Or than for strength and safety of our country.
BONA Dear brother, how shall Bona be revenged
But by thy help to this distressèd queen?
MARGARET Renownèd prince, how shall poor Henry live
Unless thou rescue him from foul despair?   215
BONA My quarrel and this English queen's are one.
WARWICK And mine, fair Lady Bona, joins with yours.
KING LEWIS And mine with hers and thine and Margaret's.
Therefore at last I firmly am resolved
You shall have aid.   220
MARGARET Let me give humble thanks for all at once.
KING LEWIS Then, England's messenger, return in post
And tell false Edward, thy supposèd king,

199] *Pope subst.;* Warwicke / These . . . Loue, F   221 Let] F; *(Kneeling)* Let *conj. This edn*

194 Warwick did not in fact desert Edward
for Henry until 1470 (Holinshed, p. 290; Hall,
p. 278).
  194 renounce disclaim allegiance to (*OED*
sv 3).
  195 grudges inveterate hatred.
  196 true servitor loyal servant.
  198 replant punning on 'Plantagenet' as at
1.1.48
  198 state royal position.
  200 forgive . . . forget Proverbial (Tilley
F597).
  200 faults offences.

204 bands companies, troops.
206 tyrant usurper.
206 seat throne.
208–10 Holinshed (p. 290) and Hall
(p. 280) report a league between Warwick and
Clarence in 1470 as well as a visit by the two of
them to Lewis.
209 fall from desert.
210 matching marrying.
210 for because of (Abbott 150).
210 wanton unrestrained.
216 quarrel cause.
222 in post with speed.

That Lewis of France is sending over masquers
To revel it with him and his new bride. 225
Thou seest what's passed: go fear thy king withal.
BONA Tell him, in hope he'll prove a widower shortly,
I'll wear the willow garland for his sake.
MARGARET Tell him my mourning weeds are laid aside
And I am ready to put armour on. 230
WARWICK Tell him from me that he hath done me wrong,
And therefore I'll uncrown him ere't be long.
[*Giving money*] There's thy reward; be gone.

Exit Post

KING LEWIS But, Warwick,
Thou and Oxford with five thousand men
Shall cross the seas and bid false Edward battle; 235
And, as occasion serves, this noble queen
And prince shall follow with a fresh supply.
Yet, ere thou go, but answer me one doubt:
What pledge have we of thy firm loyalty?
WARWICK This shall assure my constant loyalty: 240
That if our queen and this young prince agree,
I'll join mine eldest daughter and my joy
To him forthwith in holy wedlock bands.
MARGARET Yes, I agree, and thank you for your motion. –
Son Edward, she is fair and virtuous, 245
Therefore delay not: give thy hand to Warwick,
And, with thy hand, thy faith irrevocable
That only Warwick's daughter shall be thine.

---

226 passed] *Wilson;* past F   228 I'll] O; I F   233 SD *Giving money*] *This edn; not in* F   234 Thou] F; Thyself *Theobald*   243 wedlock] F *subst.;* wedlockes O

224 masquers participants in masques or allegorical entertainments of the sort performed at weddings; here the sense is ironic: soldiers.

225 it For this indefinite object see Abbott 226.

226 fear terrify.

228 *I'll* O's reading is confirmed by the accurate report of this speech at 4.1.100; compare 4.1.93.

228 wear...garland traditionally worn by forsaken women (Tilley W403).

229 weeds garments.

233 reward payment (*OED* sv *sb*²4c).

236 serves is opportune, favourable (*OED* Serve *v*¹ 25).

237 supply reinforcements (*OED* sv *sb* 5).

242 eldest Edward was betrothed (but not

married) to Anne Neville who was in fact Warwick's second daughter. Edward's death at Tewkesbury in 1471 (5.5) occurred before they could be married. (The chroniclers (Holinshed, p. 295; Hall, p. 281) report correctly that Anne was the second daughter, but tell us that the young couple were married.) Isabel, Warwick's older daughter, married Clarence. The error is repeated in O and at 4.1.118 and 4.2.12, but the relationships are correctly described in *R3* 1.1.153, although there too Shakespeare assumes that Edward had married Anne. (Anne married Richard of Gloucester in 1474.)

244 motion proposal.

248 Margaret is thinking of Edward's betrayal of the Lady Bona.

PRINCE EDWARD Yes, I accept her, for she well deserves it;
  And here, to pledge my vow, I give my hand.   250
    He gives his hand to Warwick
KING LEWIS Why stay we now? These soldiers shall be levied
  And thou, Lord Bourbon, our High Admiral,
  Shalt waft them over with our royal fleet.
  I long till Edward fall by war's mischance
  For mocking marriage with a dame of France.   255
     Exeunt [all but] Warwick
WARWICK I came from Edward as ambassador
  But I return his sworn and mortal foe:
  Matter of marriage was the charge he gave me
  But dreadful war shall answer his demand.
  Had he none else to make a stale but me?   260
  Then none but I shall turn his jest to sorrow.
  I was the chief that raised him to the crown
  And I'll be chief to bring him down again:
  Not that I pity Henry's misery,
  But seek revenge on Edward's mockery.   *Exit* 265

[4.1] *Enter* GLOUCESTER, CLARENCE, SOMERSET, *and*
MONTAGUE

GLOUCESTER Now tell me, brother Clarence, what think you
  Of this new marriage with the Lady Grey?
  Hath not our brother made a worthy choice?
CLARENCE Alas, you know, 'tis far from hence to France:

---

253 Shalt] F2; shall F **255** SD *all but*] *Eds.; Manet* F
Cairncross Act 4, Scene 1 4.1] *Rowe; not in* F **263** to . . . again] F *subst.;* again to bring him down *conj.*

---

251 stay delay.
253 waft convey by water (*OED sv v*[1] 2).
254 long till am impatient for the time when.
255 mocking (1) pretending to desire, (2) making a mock of.
258 Matter The business.
258 charge order.
259 demand request (*OED sv v* 6).
260 stale laughing-stock (*OED sv sb* 6).

Act 4, Scene 1
**4.1 See 3.3 n. Clarence's dissaffection to the king his brother is merely reported by Holinshed (p. 290); Hall had given Clarence a long speech in which Clarence complained of his treatment to Warwick (p. 271). Clarence's

marriage to Warwick's eldest daughter Isabel took place on 11 July 1469 (Boswell-Stone, p. 320; Holinshed, p. 290; Hall, p. 272). 'Somerset's' rebellion (122) is based on the double defection of Henry Beaufort, the third Duke who joined Edward's party in 1462 and then rejoined the Lancastrians (Holinshed, p. 280; Hall, p. 259): the 'Somerset' of Act 5 is Henry's brother Edmund the fourth Duke. The dispatch of Pembroke and Stafford against Warwick took place seven years later in 1469, the year of Clarence's marriage (Holinshed, p. 291; Hall, p. 273). Montague's loyalty to Edward (142), despite the importunity of Warwick his brother, is reported by both chroniclers (Holinshed, pp. 290–1; Hall, p. 271).

How could he stay till Warwick made return?   5
SOMERSET My lords, forbear this talk: here comes the king.

Flourish. Enter KING EDWARD [*attended*], LADY GREY [*now*
QUEEN ELIZABETH]; PEMBROKE, STAFFORD, HASTINGS
[*, and others*]: *four stand on one side, and four on the other*

GLOUCESTER And his well-chosen bride.
CLARENCE I mind to tell him plainly what I think.
KING EDWARD Now, brother of Clarence, how like you our choice
    That you stand pensive as half malcontent?   10
CLARENCE As well as Lewis of France or the Earl of Warwick
    Which are so weak of courage and in judgement
    That they'll take no offence at our abuse.
KING EDWARD Suppose they take offence without a cause,
    They are but Lewis and Warwick: I am Edward,   15
    Your king and Warwick's, and must have my will.
GLOUCESTER And shall have your will because our king –
    Yet hasty marriage seldom proveth well.
KING EDWARD Yea, brother Richard, are you offended too?
GLOUCESTER Not I, no: 20
    God forbid that I should wish them severed
    Whom God hath joined together; ay, and 'twere pity
    To sunder them that yoke so well together.
KING EDWARD Setting your scorns and your mislike aside,
    Tell me some reason why the Lady Grey   25
    Should not become my wife and England's queen. –
    And you too, Somerset and Montague,
    Speak freely what you think.

6 SD.1 *attended*] *Capell; not in* F   6 SD.1–2 *now* QUEEN ELIZABETH] *Rowe subst.; not in* F   6 SD.3 *and others*]
Capell; with souldiers O; *not in* F   9] *Pope;* Now ... Clarence, / How ... Choyce, F   10 malcontent] O *subst.;*
malecontent F   11] *Pope;* As ... France, / Or ... Warwicke, F   13 our] F; your *conj. Capell*   17 And] F; And
you *Rowe*   22–3] *Capell;* Whom ... together: / I ... them, / That ... together. F

5 **stay** wait.
6 **forbear** stop.
6 SD.3 **four stand ... other** It is impossible
to tell whether Shakespeare intended Queen
Elizabeth to be with the king (or to take her
place among the grouped courtiers), or whether
Gloucester etc. joined the tableau or stood apart.
For other symmetrical stage patterns in the plays
of the period see Hattaway, pp. 56–7.
8 **mind** intend.
10 *****malcontent** melancholy and discontented; F's 'malecontent' may indicate a pronunciation with four syllables.

12 **Which** Who (Abbott 265).
13 **abuse** ill-usage (*OED* sv *sb* 5).
16 **will** (1) way, (2) sexual gratification.
18 **hasty ... well** Compare the proverb
'Marry in haste and repent at leisure' (Tilley
H196).
21–3 Gloucester adds sexual innuendo to
phrases from the marriage service: 'Those
whom God hath joined together, let no man put
asunder.'
23 **yoke** are coupled (like oxen).
24 **mislike** disaffection (*OED* sv *sb* 3).

CLARENCE Then this is mine opinion: that King Lewis
    Becomes your enemy for mocking him   30
    About the marriage of the Lady Bona.
GLOUCESTER And Warwick, doing what you gave in charge,
    Is now dishonoured by this new marriage.
KING EDWARD What if both Lewis and Warwick be appeased
    By such invention as I can devise?   35
MONTAGUE Yet to have joined with France in such alliance
    Would more have strengthened this our commonwealth
    'Gainst foreign storms than any home-bred marriage.
HASTINGS Why, knows not Montague that of itself
    England is safe, if true within itself?   40
MONTAGUE But the safer when 'tis backed with France.
HASTINGS 'Tis better losing France than trusting France.
    Let us be backed with God and with the seas
    Which he hath giv'n for fence impregnable
    And, with their helps, only defend ourselves: 45
    In them and in ourselves our safety lies.
CLARENCE For this one speech Lord Hastings well deserves
    To have the heir of the Lord Hungerford.
KING EDWARD Ay, what of that? It was my will and grant,
    And for this once my will shall stand for law.   50
GLOUCESTER And yet methinks your grace hath not done well
    To give the heir and daughter of Lord Scales
    Unto the brother of your loving bride;

29–30] *Pope;* Then . . . opinion: / That . . . Enemie, / For . . . Marriage / Of . . . Bona. F   **29 mine**] F; my O   **33**
this new] F; this *Cairncross*   **41 But**] F; But all *conj. Vaughan;* But sure *conj. Oxford*   **42 losing**] *This edn (conj.*
Vaughan); vsing F

32 **gave . . . charge** commissioned.
35 **invention** stratagem.
39–40 **of . . . itself** An ancient patriotic
commonplace repeated throughout the sixteenth
century: see A. R. Braunmuller (ed.), *John,*
1989, 5.7.117–18, p. 297.
41 **backed with** supported by.
42 ***losing** This, Vaughan's conjecture for F's
'vsing', is supported by an equivalent line in
O: 'We need not France nor any alliance with
them.'
44 **fence** defence (*OED* sv *sb* 3).
45 **only** alone.
48 In fact it was Hastings' son Edward who
married Mary, daughter of Sir Thomas, Lord
Hungerford (Thomson, p. 148).
50 Compare the proverb 'What the king wills,
that the law wills' (Dent K72); the end of the

sixteenth century saw a protracted debate over
the validity of proclamations (see Williams,
pp. 36–7; R. Eccleshall, *Order and Reason in*
Politics, 1978, p. 94).
51–2, 56–7 'It must be remembered that till
the Restoration the heiresses of great estates
were in the wardship of the king who, in their
minority, gave them up to plunder and after
matched them to his favourites. I know not when
liberty gained more than by the abolition of the
Court of Wards' (Johnson).
52–7 The new queen's brother, Lord
Anthony Rivers, married Elizabeth, daughter of
the Lord Scales who appears in *2H6* 4.5, while
'Sir Thomas Grey, son to Sir John Grey, the
queen's first husband, was created Marquess
Dorset and married to Cicily, heir to the Lord
Bonville' (Holinshed, p. 284; Hall, p. 264).

> She better would have fitted me or Clarence;
> But in your bride you bury brotherhood.   55
>
> CLARENCE Or else you would not have bestowed the heir
> Of the Lord Bonville on your new wife's son
> And leave your brothers to go speed elsewhere.
>
> KING EDWARD Alas, poor Clarence! Is it for a wife
> That thou art malcontent? I will provide thee.   60
>
> CLARENCE In choosing for yourself you showed your judgement
> Which, being shallow, you shall give me leave
> To play the broker in mine own behalf;
> And to that end I shortly mind to leave you.
>
> KING EDWARD Leave me or tarry, Edward will be king   65
> And not be tied unto his brother's will.
>
> Q. ELIZABETH My lords, before it pleased his majesty
> To raise my state to title of a queen,
> Do me but right, and you must all confess
> That I was not ignoble of descent –   70
> And meaner than myself have had like fortune.
> But as this title honours me and mine,
> So your dislikes, to whom I would be pleasing,
> Doth cloud my joys with danger and with sorrow.
>
> KING EDWARD My love, forbear to fawn upon their frowns: 75
> What danger or what sorrow can befall thee
> So long as Edward is thy constant friend
> And their true sovereign whom they must obey?
> Nay, whom they shall obey, and love thee too,
> Unless they seek for hatred at my hands;   80
> Which if they do, yet will I keep thee safe
> And they shall feel the vengeance of my wrath.
>
> GLOUCESTER [*Aside*] I hear, yet say not much but think the more.

61] *Pope;* In . . . selfe, / You . . . iudgement: F   66 brother's] *Rowe subst.;* Brothers F; brothers' *conj. this edn*   67
SH] O (*Queen.*); *Lady Grey.* F   83 SD] *Johnson; not in* F

57 **Lord Bonville** William, Lord Harrington and Bonville, captured by Margaret and executed after the second battle of St Albans, 1461.

58 **go speed** seek their marital fortunes.

60 **malcontent** discontented.

63 **play the broker** act as go-between.

64 **mind** intend.

70 In fact Elizabeth was the first commoner to become a queen of England: she was daughter of Sir Richard Woodville by Jacquetta of Luxemburg, widow of the Duke of Bedford and sister-in-law to Henry V (Holinshed, p. 586; Hall, p. 365).

71 **meaner** people of lowlier birth.

73 **dislikes** disapproval (*OED* Dislike *sb* 1).

74 **danger** apprehension.

83 Compare the proverb 'Though he said little he thought the more' (Tilley I.367).

Enter a POST

KING EDWARD Now, messenger, what letters, or what news
            From France?   85
POST My sovereign liege, no letters and few words
            But such as I, without your special pardon,
            Dare not relate.
KING EDWARD Go to, we pardon thee: therefore in brief
            Tell me their words as near as thou canst guess them.   90
            What answer makes King Lewis unto our letters?
POST At my depart, these were his very words:
            'Go tell false Edward, thy supposèd king,
            That Lewis of France is sending over masquers
            To revel it with him and his new bride.'   95
KING EDWARD Is Lewis so brave? Belike he thinks me Henry. –
            But what said Lady Bona to my marriage?
POST These were her words, uttered with mild disdain:
            'Tell him, in hope he'll prove a widower shortly,
            I'll wear the willow garland for his sake.'   100
KING EDWARD I blame not her; she could say little less:
            She had the wrong. – But what said Henry's queen,
            For I have heard that she was there in place?
POST 'Tell him', quoth she, 'my mourning weeds are done
            And I am ready to put armour on.'   105
KING EDWARD Belike she minds to play the Amazon. –
            But what said Warwick to these injuries?
POST He, more incensed against your majesty
            Than all the rest, discharged me with these words:
            'Tell him from me that he hath done me wrong   110
            And therefore I'll uncrown him ere't be long.'

84–5] *As verse in Capell; prose in* F   89–91] *Capell;* Goe...thee: / Therefore...words, / As...them. /
What...Letters? F   89 Go to] *Pope;* Goe too F   93 'Go] *Eds.;* Goe F   93 thy] O; the F   95 bride.'] *Eds.;*
Bride. F   104] *Pope;* Tell...she) / My...done, F

87–8 Messengers could feel threatened if
they brought bad news: compare the proverb
'Messengers should neither be headed nor
hanged' (Tilley M905).
89 *Go to An exclamation of impatience.
90 guess conjecture; remember (compare
MV 1.3.54).
92 depart departure (Abbott 451).
93 *thy O's reading is supported by 3.3.223
which issued from Lewis' own lips; compare
3.3.228.
96 so brave possessed of so much bravado.
96 Belike Perhaps.

100 See 3.3.228 n.
103 in place present (*OED* Place *sb* 19b).
104 done done with, worn out (*OED* Done
pple adj 1).
106 minds intends.
106 Amazon One of a mythical race of
woman warriors supposed to live near the
Euxine in what is now southern Russia; see
Simon Shepherd, *Amazons and Warrior Women:
Varieties of Feminism in Seventeenth-Century
Drama*, 1981.
107 injuries insults.
109 discharged dismissed.

KING EDWARD Ha? Durst the traitor breathe out so proud words?
   Well, I will arm me, being thus forewarned:
   They shall have wars and pay for their presumption. –
   But say, is Warwick friends with Margaret? 115
POST Ay, gracious sovereign, they are so linked in friendship
   That young Prince Edward marries Warwick's daughter.
CLARENCE Belike the elder: Clarence will have the younger. –
   Now, brother king, farewell and sit you fast;
   For I will hence to Warwick's other daughter 120
   That, though I want a kingdom, yet in marriage
   I may not prove inferior to yourself. –
   You that love me and Warwick, follow me.
         Exit Clarence, and Somerset follows
GLOUCESTER [*Aside*] Not I; my thoughts aim at a further matter:
   I stay not for the love of Edward but the crown. 125
KING EDWARD Clarence and Somerset both gone to Warwick?
   Yet am I armed against the worst can happen
   And haste is needful in this desp'rate case. –
   Pembroke and Stafford, you in our behalf
   Go levy men and make prepare for war: 130
   They are already, or quickly will be, landed;
   Myself in person will straight follow you.
         Exeunt Pembroke and Stafford
   But ere I go, Hastings and Montague,
   Resolve my doubt: you twain, of all the rest,
   Are near'st to Warwick by blood and by alliance: 135
   Tell me if you love Warwick more than me;
   If it be so, then both depart to him:
   I rather wish you foes than hollow friends.
   But if you mind to hold your true obedience,

116] *Pope subst.*; I . . . Soueraigne, / They . . . friendship, F 116 they are] F; theare O 118] *Pope;*
Belike . . . elder; / *Clarence* . . . younger. F 124] *Pope;* Not I: / My . . . matter: F 124 SD] *Rowe (after* Not I
Oxford); *not in* F 125 for the] F; for *Pope* 135 near'st] O *subst.;* neere F

113 **armed . . . forewarned** Compare the
proverb 'Forewarned is forearmed' (Tilley H54).
 118 **elder** For the same mistake, see
3.3.242 n.
 119 **sit you fast** hold fast to your throne.
Clarence was next in line of succession.
 120–2 Clarence married Isabel Neville in
1469: see 3.3.242 n.
 121 **want** lack – although there may be a
pun on 'want' = 'desire' – see 4.6.57.
 123 'That Clarence should make this speech
in the king's hearing is very improbable, yet I do
not see how it can be palliated. The king never

goes out, nor can Clarence be talking to a
company apart, for he answers immediately to
that which the post says to the king' (Johnson).
 127 **armed against** prepared for (*OED* Arm
v^1, 2c).
 130 **prepare** preparation (Abbott 451).
 132 **straight** immediately.
 138 Compare the proverb 'It is better to have
an open foe than a dissembling friend' (Dent
410).
 138 **hollow** false.
 139 **mind** intend.

Give me assurance with some friendly vow   140
That I may never have you in suspect.
MONTAGUE So God help Montague, as he proves true.
HASTINGS And Hastings, as he favours Edward's cause.
KING EDWARD Now, brother Richard, will you stand by us?
GLOUCESTER Ay, in despite of all that shall withstand you.   145
KING EDWARD Why so, then am I sure of victory!
Now therefore let us hence and lose no hour
Till we meet Warwick with his foreign power.

Exeunt

[4.2] *Enter* WARWICK *and* OXFORD *in England, with French Soldiers*

WARWICK Trust me, my lord, all hitherto goes well:
The common men by numbers swarm to us.

Enter CLARENCE *and* SOMERSET

But see where Somerset and Clarence comes. –
Speak suddenly, my lords, are we all friends?
CLARENCE Fear not that, my lord.   5
WARWICK Then, gentle Clarence, welcome unto Warwick –
And welcome, Somerset: I hold it cowardice
To rest mistrustful where a noble heart

Act 4, Scene 2   4.2] *Capell; not in* F   2 men] *This edn; people* F; sort *Oxford*   2 by…us] F; swarm by numbers to us *Pope;* swarm to us by numbers *Hudson*   5 Fear] F *subst.;* Fear you *conj. Cairncross*

141 in suspect under suspicion (Abbott 451); suspect was accented on the second syllable (Cercignani, p. 38).
145 despite spite.
145 that who.
148 power army.

Act 4, Scene 2
*4.2 See 3.3 n. Edward was captured (see 4.3) on 26 July 1469 (Boswell-Stone, p. 323; Holinshed, p. 293; Hall, p. 275), although Warwick's vaunting of his popularity derives from the chroniclers' account of his return to England from exile in France the next year (Holinshed, p. 296; Hall, p. 282).
0 SD in England This locality note in a stage direction is typical of authorial copy: see Textual analysis, p. 206 and W. W. Greg, *The Editorial Problem in Shakespeare*, 1951, p. 116; compare *2H6* 4.6.0 SD.

1–18 R. B. McKerrow, 'A note on the "Bad Quartos" of *2 and 3 Henry VI*', *RES* 13 (1937), 64–72 demonstrated that the compositor of these lines must have consulted a copy of an edition of O, probably Q3. This helps justify the emendations at 2, 12, and 15 below.
1 hitherto thus far.
2 *men As the line is in a passage which has been contaminated by O (see 1–18 n. above), it is legitimate to restore the metre of the line by rejecting F and O's 'people'. For the phrase 'common men' see 3.1.88, *H5*, 4.7.74, 4.8.79 etc.
2 by in great.
3 comes for the singular inflection see Abbott 336.
4 suddenly immediately.
5 Fear not You may be sure of.
6 gentle noble.
8 rest remain.

Hath pawned an open hand in sign of love;
Else might I think that Clarence, Edward's brother,   10
Were but a feignèd friend to our proceedings.
But come, sweet Clarence, my daughter shall be thine.
And now what rests but in night's coverture,
Thy brother being carelessly encamped,
His soldiers lurking in the towns about   15
And but attended by a simple guard,
We may surprise and take him at our pleasure?
Our scouts have found the adventure very easy:
That as Ulysses and stout Diomede
With sleight and manhood stole to Rhesus' tents   20
And brought from thence the Thracian fatal steeds,
So we, well covered with the night's black mantle,
At unawares may beat down Edward's guard
And seize himself – I say not slaughter him
For I intend but only to surprise him.   25
You that will follow me to this attempt,
Applaud the name of Henry with your leader.
                    They all cry, 'Henry!'

---

12 But ... Clarence] *Cairncross;* But welcome sweet *Clarence* F, O; But welcome, Clarence *Capell*   15 towns] *conj.*
Thirlby in Theobald; town F *subst.*

---

9 pawned staked, pledged.

12 *come Emendation of F's 'welcome' restores the metre. F's reading may have been carried over from 6–7 above or have been recalled from 5.1.108 by a reporter.

13 rests remains.

13 coverture protective cover.

14 carelessly without fear or apprehension.

15 lurking idling (*OED* Lurk *v* 1b).

15 *towns Theobald's emendation is justified by the plural in the same phrase in 15 of the next scene.

16 simple small, insignificant (*OED* sv *adj* 7).

17 at ... pleasure whenever we wish.

18 adventure hazard, venture.

19 Ulysses see 3.2.189 n.

19 stout valiant.

19 Diomede (three syllables) King of Argos and, according to Homer's *Iliad*, the bravest hero among the Greeks after Achilles.

20 sleight trickery – the attribute of Ulysses (see 3.2.189) as manhood was of Diomede.

20–1 Rhesus ... steeds It had been predicted by the oracle that if the white horses of

Rhesus, prince of Thrace, should drink from the River Xanthus, Troy would not fall. Therefore Ulysses and Diomede went by night to kill Rhesus in his camp and capture his horses in order to prevent the prophecy coming true (see *Iliad*, X; *Metamorphoses*, XIII, 122–6, 306–10; the Latin commentary, based on Servius, on *Aeneid*, I, 496–73 (see J. A. K. Thomson, *Shakespeare and the Classics*, 1952, p. 94).

21 fatal fraught with destiny (*OED* sv 5).

22 night's black mantle proverbial (Dent MM7).

23 At unawares Suddenly.

25 surprise capture.

26–7 O's version of these lines reads 'Courage, my soldiers, now or never!/ But follow me now and Edward shall be ours. / ALL A Warwick! A Warwick!' which may indicate familiarity with Hall's report that when Warwick landed in 1470 'all the towns and all the country adjacent was in a great roar ... crying "King Henry! King Henry! A Warwick! A Warwick!"' (p. 283).

Why then, let's on our way in silent sort:
For Warwick and his friends, God and Saint George!

Exeunt

[4.3] *Enter three* WATCHMEN *to guard [King Edward's] tent*

1 WATCHMAN Come on, my masters, each man take his stand:
The king by this is set him down to sleep.
2 WATCHMAN What, will he not to bed?
1 WATCHMAN Why, no; for he hath made a solemn vow
Never to lie and take his natural rest   5
Till Warwick or himself be quite suppressed.
2 WATCHMAN Tomorrow then belike shall be the day
If Warwick be so near as men report.
3 WATCHMAN But say, I pray, what nobleman is that
That with the king here resteth in his tent?   10
2 WATCHMAN 'Tis the Lord Hastings, the king's chiefest friend.
3 WATCHMAN O is it so? But why commands the king
That his chief followers lodge in towns about him
While he himself keeps in the cold field?
2 WATCHMAN 'Tis the more honour because more dangerous.   15
3 WATCHMAN Ay, but give me worship and quietness:
I like it better than a dangerous honour.

Act 4, Scene 3   4.3] *Capell; not in* F   0 SD *King Edward's*] *Eds.; the Kings* F   1 SH WATCHMAN] *This edn;*
Watch. F (*throughout scene*)   9 nobleman] F4; Noble man F   14 keeps] F; keepeth *Theobald;* keeps *here* Hanmer;
keeps state *conj.* Oxford

28 **sort** manner (*OED* sv *sb*² 21b).
29 **Saint George** The patron saint of
England.

Act 4, Scene 3
*4.3 See 4.2 n. Warwick's proclamation of
Henry VI (49) took place in 1470 (Holinshed,
p. 296; Hall, p. 282), the year after the capture
of Edward.
    0 SD **tent** Tents were erected on the
Elizabethan stage (Hattaway, p. 38) but it is
likely that here a curtained discovery space was
used as in *2H6* 3.2 (Hattaway, p. 28; see also
Textual analysis, p. 206).
    1 **stand** station, post.
    2 **by this** by this time.
    2 **set him down** settled (in a chair – see 27
SD.4–5 below).

3–6 Shakespeare has invented these details
for stage effect: in the chronicles Warwick
persuaded Edward that he wanted peace before
he, 'in the dead of the night, with an elect
company of men of war, . . . set on the king's
field, killing them that kept the watch; and
ere the king was ware . . . at a place called
Wolney . . . he was taken prisoner and brought to
the Castle of Warwick' (Holinshed, p. 293; Hall,
p. 275).
    6 **suppressed** vanquished (*OED* Suppress
1b).
    13 **lodge** sleep.
    13 **about** around.
    14 **keeps** remains.
    15 Compare the proverb 'The more danger
the more honour' (Tilley D35).
    16 **worship** honour, dignity.

If Warwick knew in what estate he stands
'Tis to be doubted if he would waken him.
1 WATCHMAN Unless our halberds did shut up his passage.   20
2 WATCHMAN Ay, wherefore else guard we his royal tent
But to defend his person from night-foes?

Enter WARWICK, CLARENCE, OXFORD, SOMERSET, *and*
French Soldiers, silent all

WARWICK This is his tent, and see where stand his guard.
Courage, my masters! Honour now or never!
But follow me, and Edward shall be ours.   25
1 WATCHMAN Who goes there?
2 WATCHMAN Stay, or thou diest.

Warwick and the rest cry all, 'Warwick, Warwick!' and set upon the
guard, who fly, crying, 'Arm, Arm!', Warwick and the rest following
them. The Drum playing and Trumpet sounding, enter WARWICK,
SOMERSET, *and the rest, bringing the* KING *out in his gown, sitting in*
a chair. RICHARD [*of* GLOUCESTER] *and* HASTINGS *fly over the*
stage.

SOMERSET What are they that fly there?
WARWICK Richard and Hastings. Let them go; here is the duke.
KING EDWARD 'The duke'? Why, Warwick, when we parted   30
Thou call'dst me king.
WARWICK   Ay, but the case is altered.
When you disgraced me in my embassade,
Then I degraded you from being king
And come now to create you Duke of York.

---

27 SD.3 *them*] F; *them.* / 4.4 Oxford   29] *As verse in Capell; prose in* F   30 KING . . . parted] *Pope subst.; K.*
Edw. . . . Duke? / Why . . . parted, F   34 *now to create*] F; *to new create conj. Johnson*

---

18 **estate** state, condition.
18 **he** the king.
19 **doubted** feared.
20 **halberds** battle-axes on long poles, or halberdiers (*OED* Halberd 2).
20 **shut up his** bar (Warwick's).
22, 27 SDD Presumably Warwick and his men entered by one stage door, exited by another, and re-entered through the discovery space. Richard and Hastings may have come from the discovery space and leapt down into the play-house yard from the stage.
25 **But** Simply.
27 SD Although there is a line's break after 'them' (27.3) in F's printing of this stage direction, there seems no need to begin a new scene here. Warwick and Somerset re-enter after their first appearance at 22 above, and on the stage the

action forms a continuous sequence. O offers no evidence of a scene break and the division in F which occurs in a very uncrowded column may the result of defective casting off.
27 SD.3 **The . . . sounding** There is no way of telling whether this is theatrical short-hand for a battle 'off' (Hattaway, p. 61) or part of a processional entrance. Long (p. 27) considers the direction to signify an entrance and prints a suitable '*simple cavalquot*' (p. 271)
27 SD.4 **gown** night-gown (*OED* sv *sb* 2).
31 **the . . . altered** proverbial (Tilley C111).
32 **embassade** ambassadorial errand.
33 **degraded** deposed (*OED* Degrade 2).
34 **now . . . create** Edward, of course, had become Duke of York on the death of his father, so Johnson's conjecture 'to new-create' is attractive.

Alas, how should you govern any kingdom   35
That know not how to use ambassadors,
Nor how to be contented with one wife,
Nor how to use your brothers brotherly,
Nor how to study for the people's welfare,
Nor how to shroud yourself from enemies?   40
KING EDWARD Yea, brother of Clarence, art thou here too?
Nay then I see that Edward needs must down. –
Yet, Warwick, in despite of all mischance,
Of thee thyself and all thy complices,
Edward will always bear himself as king: 45
Though Fortune's malice overthrow my state,
My mind exceeds the compass of her wheel.
WARWICK Then, for his mind, be Edward England's king,
                    Takes off his crown
But Henry now shall wear the English crown
And be true king indeed: thou but the shadow. –   50
My lord of Somerset, at my request
See that forthwith Duke Edward be conveyed
Unto my brother, Archbishop of York.
When I have fought with Pembroke and his fellows
I'll follow you and tell what answer   55
Lewis and the Lady Bona send to him. –
Now, for a while farewell, good Duke of York.
               They [begin to] lead him out forcibly
KING EDWARD What fates impose, that men must needs abide;
It boots not to resist both wind and tide.
                    [Exit, guarded, with Somerset]
OXFORD What now remains, my lords, for us to do   60
But march to London with our soldiers?

41] *Steevens;* Yea ... Clarence, / Art ... too? F   55 tell] F; tell him there *Dyce²*   57 SD *begin to*] *This edn; not in*
F   59 SD] *Capell subst.; Exeunt.* F; *Exeunt* some with *Edward.* O

36, 38 **use** treat.
40 **shroud** conceal.
42 **down** fall (by the turning of Fortune's
wheel – see 46–7).
44 **complices** accomplices.
46 **state** sovereignty.
47 **compass** circular extent (Dame Fortune
was customarily depicted turning a wheel; see
W. Farnham, *The Medieval Heritage of Elizabethan
Tragedy*, 1936, *passim*, and Frederick Kieffer,
Fortune and Elizabethan Tragedy, 1983.)
48 **for** as regards (Abbott 149).

50 **shadow** image, portrait, or player (*OED* sv
6b); compare *1H6* 2.3.35; *R2* 4.1.297–9.
53 **brother ... York** George Neville (1433?–
76) who was also chancellor.
58–9 There may be an allusion here to
Clytemnestra's speech in Seneca's *Agamemnon*,
138–44.
58 **abide** endure.
59 Compare the proverb 'To sail against
wind and tide' (Dent W435.1).
59 **boots** avails.

WARWICK Ay, that's the first thing that we have to do,
   To free King Henry from imprisonment
   And see him seated in the regal throne.

                                                    Exeunt

[4.4] *Enter* RIVERS *and* [QUEEN ELIZABETH *weeping*]

RIVERS Madam, what makes you in this sudden change?
Q. ELIZABETH Why, brother Rivers, are you yet to learn
   What late misfortune is befall'n King Edward?
RIVERS What, loss of some pitched battle against Warwick?
Q. ELIZABETH No, but the loss of his own royal person.   5
RIVERS Then is my sovereign slain?
Q. ELIZABETH Ay, almost slain, for he is taken prisoner;
   Either betrayed by falsehood of his guard
   Or by his foe surprised at unawares;
   And, as I further have to understand,   10
   Is new committed to the Bishop of York,
   Fell Warwick's brother and by that our foe.
RIVERS These news I must confess are full of grief,
   Yet, gracious madam, bear it as you may:
   Warwick may lose that now hath won the day.   15
Q. ELIZABETH Till then fair hope must hinder life's decay,
   And I the rather wain me from despair
   For love of Edward's offspring in my womb:
   This is it that makes me bridle passion

---

64 throne.] F *subst.;* throne, / Come let vs haste awaie, and hauing past these cares, *I* le post to *Yorke,* and see how *Edward* fares. O   64 SD] O *subst.; exit.* F   Act 4, Scene 4   4.4] Capell; *not in* F   o SD QUEEN ELIZABETH] Theobald *subst.;* Lady Gray. F   o SD *weeping*] *This edn; not in* F   1 you in] F; in you *Collier MS*   2 SH] O (*Queen.*); Gray. F (*throughout scene*)   4] Pope; What . . . battell / Against . . . Warwicke? F   11 new] F; now *Rowe*   16 life's] *Rowe subst.;* liues F   17 wain] F *subst.;* wean *Rowe*

63–4 See collation and Textual analysis, p. 202.

Act 4, Scene 4
*4.4 In 1470, a year after Edward's capture (see 4.2 n.), Elizabeth sought sanctuary at Westminster where she gave birth to a son, Edward (Holinshed, p. 300; Hall, p. 285). O reverses the order of 4.4 and 4.5 – a change which is more accurate chronologically (see 4.5 n.) – but offers a particularly mangled version of the scene (see Appendix 2, p. 219).

   1 makes . . . in is the cause of. Schmidt ('Make' 2) argues that there are here two accusatives, the second being the prepositional phrase, but it may be preferable to accept Collier's reading 'in you'.

   1 change change of mood, or possibly changefulness, caprice (*OED* sv *sb* 4b).
   3 late recent.
   4 What Why (Abbott 253).
   8 falsehood treachery.
   9 surprised captured (*OED* Surprise *v* 2b).
   9 at unawares unexpectedly.
   11 Bishop Archbishop (see 4.3.53n.).
   12 by that therefore.
   17 Wain me convey myself.
   19 passion an outburst of emotion.

And bear with mildness my misfortune's cross: 20
Ay, ay, for this I draw in many a tear
And stop the rising of blood-sucking sighs,
Lest with my sighs or tears I blast or drown
King Edward's fruit, true heir to th'English crown.
RIVERS But, madam, where is Warwick then become?   25
Q. ELIZABETH I am informèd that he comes towards London
          To set the crown once more on Henry's head.
          Guess thou the rest: King Edward's friends must down.
          But to prevent the tyrant's violence –
          For trust not him that hath once broken faith –   30
          I'll hence forthwith unto the sanctuary
          To save at least the heir of Edward's right.
          There shall I rest secure from force and fraud.
          Come, therefore, let us fly while we may fly:
          If Warwick take us we are sure to die.   35

                                             Exeunt

[4.5] *Enter* [GLOUCESTER], LORD HASTINGS, *and* SIR
WILLIAM STANLEY [*with Soldiers*]

GLOUCESTER Now, my Lord Hastings and Sir William Stanley,
          Leave off to wonder why I drew you hither
          Into this chiefest thicket of the park.
          Thus stands the case: you know our king, my brother,

---

20 misfortune's] *Pope;* misfortunes F   25] *Pope subst.;* But Madam, / Where . . . become? F   26 informèd] *Rowe;*
informed F *subst., Theobald*   **Act 4, Scene 5**   4.5] *Capell; not in* F   0 SD.1 GLOUCESTER] 0 *subst.; Richard*
F   0 SD.2 *with Soldiers*] *Capell subst.; not in* F   4 stands] F2; stand F

---

20 **cross** vexation, mischance.
21 **draw** in constrain.
22 **blood-sucking** every sigh was supposed
to draw a drop of blood from the heart; compare
2H6 3.2.61.
23 **blast** blight, wither.
25 **is . . . become** has betaken himself, gone.
28 **down** fall; compare 4.3.42 n.
29 **prevent** forestall.
29 **tyrant's** usurper's.
30 **trust . . . faith** Compare the proverb 'He
that once deceives is ever suspected' (Tilley
D180).
31 **sanctuary** At Westminster (Hall, p. 285)
Elizabeth was immune from arrest; for the
Tudor legislation that sought to abolish this
right, see Williams, pp. 277–8.
32 **right** claim to the throne.
33 **fraud** faithlessness (*OED* sv 1).

Act 4, Scene 5
  *4.5 Edward recovered his liberty only four
months after being captured (Holinshed, p. 293;
Hall, p. 275) and before his wife took sanctuary
(see 4.4 n.). Shakespeare fuses this escape with
his flight from Warwick, who landed from
France in September 1470 (see 4.6.78–9;
Holinshed, p. 299; Hall, p. 283).
  0 SD.2 **with Soldiers** That the lords do not
enter alone is indicated by 12 and 16 below.
  2 **Leave off** Cease.
  2 **to wonder** For the infinitive used as an
object, see Abbott 355.
  3 **chiefest** largest.
  3 **park** enclosed hunting domain (*OED* sv
sb 1).
  4, 18 **case** circumstances.

Is prisoner to the bishop here, at whose hands   5
He hath good usage and great liberty
And, often but attended with weak guard,
Comes hunting this way to disport himself.
I have advertised him by secret means
That if about this hour he make this way   10
Under the colour of his usual game
He shall here find his friends with horse and men
To set him free from his captivity.

Enter KING EDWARD, *and a* HUNTSMAN *with him*

HUNTSMAN This way, my lord, for this way lies the game.
KING EDWARD Nay this way, man, see where the huntsmen
    stand. –   15
  Now, brother of Gloucester, Lord Hastings, and the rest,
  Stand you thus close to steal the bishop's deer?
GLOUCESTER Brother, the time and case requireth haste;
  Your horse stands ready at the park corner.
KING EDWARD But whither shall we, then?
HASTINGS   To Lynn, my lord,   20
  And shipped from thence to Flanders.
GLOUCESTER Well guessed, believe me, for that was my meaning.
KING EDWARD Stanley, I will requite thy forwardness.
GLOUCESTER But wherefore stay we? 'Tis no time to talk.
KING EDWARD Huntsman, what say'st thou? Wilt thou go along?   25
HUNTSMAN Better do so than tarry and be hanged.
GLOUCESTER Come then, away! Let's ha'no more ado.

---

8 Comes] F2; Come F   14] *Pope;* This...Lord, / For...Game. F   15–17] F *subst.;* No this waie
huntsman, see where the / Keepers stand. Now brother and the rest, / What, are you prouided to depart? o   15]
Pope; Nay...man, / See...stand. F   16 Lord Hastings] F; Hastings *Cairncross*   21 And] F; *King Edward* And
Wilson   21 shipped] F (shipt); ship F2   21 Flanders] F; Flanders? *Riverside conj. Cartwright*   21 And] F; [*To
Gloucester*] And *Riverside*   22 SH] F *subst.;* GLOUCESTER [*aside*] *Oxford subst.*   25] *Pope;* Huntsman...thou? /
Wilt...along? F

5 **bishop** The Archbishop of York (see
4.3.53).
 9 **advertised** accented on the second syllable
(Cercignani, p. 41).
  10 **make** should come.
  11 **colour** semblance.
  11 **game** hunting.
  14 **game** quarry.
  16 The line is unmetrical but closely resembles 4.7.1 which is regular. This may

indicate some compositorial error.
  17 **close** concealed.
  19 **horse** horses.
  20 **then** a discourse marker, not an adverb.
  20 **Lynn** King's Lynn, a port in Norfolk.
  22 **guessed** conjectured, reasoned.
  22 **meaning** intention (*OED* sv 1).
  23 **requite** reward.
  23 **forwardness** zeal.
  25 **go along** join us.

KING EDWARD Bishop, farewell. Shield thee from Warwick's
          frown
       And pray that I may repossess the crown.

                                                    Exeunt

[4.6] *Flourish. Enter* WARWICK [*and*] CLARENCE [*with the crown,
and then*] KING HENRY THE SIXTH, SOMERSET, *young* HENRY
[EARL *of* RICHMOND], OXFORD, MONTAGUE, *and* [*the*]
LIEUTENANT [*of the Tower*]

KING HENRY Master lieutenant, now that God and friends
       Have shaken Edward from the regal seat
       And turned my captive state to liberty,
       My fear to hope, my sorrows unto joys,
       At our enlargement what are thy due fees?   5
LIEUTENANT Subjects may challenge nothing of their sovereigns;
       But if an humble prayer may prevail
       I then crave pardon of your majesty.
KING HENRY For what, lieutenant? For well using me?
       Nay, be thou sure I'll well requite thy kindness   10
       For that it made my imprisonment a pleasure,
       Ay, such a pleasure as encagèd birds
       Conceive when, after many moody thoughts,

28] *Pope subst.;* Bishop farwell, / Sheeld . . . frowne, F   Act 4, Scene 6   4.6] *Capell; not in* F   0 SD.1–2
WARWICK . . . SOMERSET] *This edn; King Henry the sixt, Clarence, Warwicke, Somerset* F; *Warwike and Clarence, with the
Crowne . . . and Oxford, and Summerset* O   0 SD.3 EARL *of* RICHMOND] O; *not in* F   0 SD.4 *of the Tower*] *Rowe; not
in* F   11 made my] F; *made Pope*   11 imprisonment] F; *prisonment Hudson*

Act 4, Scene 6
 *4.6 Henry, 'apparelled in a long gown of
blue velvet', was delivered from the Tower by
Warwick in October 1470. He made Warwick
'governor' of the realm and Clarence 'his fellow
associate', but in the chronicles it was Parliament and not Warwick who ordered that Edward
be proclaimed a traitor, his goods be confiscate,
and Clarence be designated as Henry's heir
(Holinshed, p. 301; Hall, pp. 285–6). Holinshed
(pp. 302–3) tells the tale of the meeting of
Henry VI with the future Henry VII (Hall, p.
287), and both chroniclers record how, after the
battle of Tewkesbury (5.4–5), the young
Richmond was sent to Brittany for his own safety
in September 1471 (Holinshed, p. 328; Hall, p.
303). O reverses the order of 4.6 and 4.7 and
offers a severely cut version of this scene.
 *0 SD O's version of the entrance (see

collation) may preserve certain details of this
processional entry.
   0 SD.4 LIEUTENANT Acting commandant,
designated by the Constable of the Tower (see
Thomson, p. 186).
   5 enlargement liberation.
   5 due fees On their release prisoners paid
their keepers for food and services provided
during their imprisonment – compare Heywood,
A Woman Killed With Kindness 2.2.10 ff. and
Shakespeare's England, II, 507–8.
   6 challenge claim as their due.
   7 prayer petitioner (*OED* sv *sb*²); disyllabic
(Cercignani, p. 357).
     10 requite repay.
     11 For that Because.
     13 Conceive Begin to feel.
     13 moody gloomy (*OED* sv 4).

At last by notes of household harmony
They quite forget their loss of liberty. –   15
But, Warwick, after God, thou set'st me free
And chiefly therefore I thank God and thee:
He was the author, thou the instrument.
Therefore, that I may conquer Fortune's spite
By living low where Fortune cannot hurt me,   20
And that the people of this blessèd land
May not be punished with my thwarting stars,
Warwick, although my head still wear the crown,
I here resign my government to thee,
                    [*Handing him a commission*]
For thou art fortunate in all thy deeds.   25
WARWICK Your grace hath still been famed for virtuous,
And now may seem as wise as virtuous
By spying and avoiding fortune's malice,
For few men rightly temper with the stars.
Yet in this one thing let me blame your grace   30
For choosing me when Clarence is in place.
CLARENCE No, Warwick, thou art worthy of the sway,
To whom the heavens in thy nativity
Adjudged an olive branch and laurel crown,
As likely to be blest in peace and war;   35
And therefore I yield thee my free consent.
WARWICK And I choose Clarence only for Protector.
KING HENRY Warwick and Clarence, give me both your hands.
Now join your hands and with your hands your hearts

24 SD] *This edn; not in* F

14 **household** familiar, homely (*OED* sv 6c).
18 **author** instigator, first mover (*OED* sv 1d); for contemporary beliefs concerning the mechanisms of providence, see Thomas, pp. 92 ff.
18 **instrument** agent.
19 ff. Shakespeare opposes Henry's fatalistic belief in the power of Fortune wielded through the stars with Warwick's belief that virtue may overcome Fortune.
19 **spite** malice.
20 **low** i.e. from where, by the turning of Fortune's wheel, he could fall no further; compare 4.3.46.
22 **thwarting stars** adverse fortune.
24 **government** authority (*OED* sv 3).
25 **fortunate** favoured by Fortune.
26 **still** always.
26 **famed** reputed.

26 **virtuous** perhaps Warwick is sarcastically invoking the older meaning still current in Shakespeare's time, 'full of manly courage' (*OED* sv 1).
28 **spying** discovering.
29 'Few men conform their "temper" to their destiny, which King Henry did when, finding himself unfortunate, he gave the management of public affairs to more prosperous hands' (Johnson).
31 **in place** here, available.
32 **sway** rule.
33 **nativity** conjunction of stars, horoscope.
34 Explained in the following line.
37 **only** alone (Abbott 420).
37 **Protector** Regent.
39 **with ... hearts** Compare the proverb 'With heart and hand' (Dent H339).

> That no dissension hinder government.   40
> I make you both Protectors of this land
> While I myself will lead a private life
> And in devotion spend my latter days
> To sin's rebuke and my Creator's praise.

WARWICK What answers Clarence to his sovereign's will?   45

CLARENCE That he consents, if Warwick yield consent,
>   For on thy fortune I repose myself.

WARWICK Why then, though loath, yet must I be content.
>   We'll yoke together, like a double shadow
>   To Henry's body, and supply his place –   50
>   I mean in bearing weight of government
>   While he enjoys the honour and his ease;
>   And, Clarence, now then it is more than needful
>   Forthwith that Edward be pronounced a traitor
>   And all his lands and goods be confiscate.   55

CLARENCE What else. And that succession be determinèd?

WARWICK Ay, therein Clarence shall not want his part.

KING HENRY But with the first of all your chief affairs
>   Let me entreat – for I command no more –
>   That Margaret your queen and my son Edward   60
>   Be sent for to return from France with speed;
>   For till I see them here, by doubtful fear
>   My joy of liberty is half eclipsed.

CLARENCE It shall be done, my sovereign, with all speed.

KING HENRY My lord of Somerset, what youth is that   65
>   Of whom you seem to have so tender care?

SOMERSET My liege, it is young Henry, Earl of Richmond.

---

55 be] *Malone; not in* F

---

43 **latter** final.

47 **repose myself** rely (*OED* Repose v^2 5).

49 **yoke** join.

50 **supply** fill.

52 **honour** respect due to the office of kingship.

53–7 These lines do not appear in O, possibly as a result of censorship. Parliament 'adjudged [Edward] a traitor to the country and an usurper of the realm. His goods were confiscate and forfeited' (Holinshed, p. 301; Hall, p. 286).

55 ***be** Malone's emendation is justified on metrical grounds (although it is possible that the following word, 'confiscate', was accented on the second syllable – Cercignani, p. 40).

55 **confiscate** For the omission of 'ed' after 't' in participles, see Abbott 342.

56 **What else** Assuredly.

57 **want** lack.

57 **his part** Clarence stood to inherit the throne from the childless Edward if the Lancastrian claim were set aside and Edward attainted for treason.

62 **doubtful** mistrustful.

66 **so tender** such loving.

67 **Henry** Henry Tudor, future Henry VII, whose accession in 1485 ended the Wars of the Roses. He had been brought up by his uncle Jasper Tudor, Earl of Pembroke, in Wales. Somerset was his uncle, and through the Somersets he laid claim to the throne.

KING HENRY Come hither, England's hope.
                    Lays his hand on his head
                                                If secret powers
         Suggest but truth to my divining thoughts,
         This pretty lad will prove our country's bliss.   70
         His looks are full of peaceful majesty,
         His head by nature framed to wear a crown,
         His hand to wield a sceptre, and himself
         Likely in time to bless a regal throne.
         Make much of him, my lords, for this is he   75
         Must help you more than you are hurt by me.

                         Enter a POST

WARWICK What news, my friend?
POST That Edward is escapèd from your brother
         And fled, as he hears since, to Burgundy.
WARWICK Unsavoury news! But how made he escape?   80
POST He was conveyed by Richard, Duke of Gloucester,
         And the Lord Hastings who attended him
         In secret ambush on the forest side
         And from the bishop's huntsmen rescued him –
         For hunting was his daily exercise.   85
WARWICK My brother was too careless of his charge.
         But let us hence, my sovereign, to provide
         A salve for any sore that may betide.
                     Exeunt [all but] Somerset, Richmond, and Oxford
SOMERSET My Lord, I like not of this flight of Edward's,
         For doubtless Burgundy will yield him help   90
         And we shall have more wars befor't be long.
         As Henry's late presaging prophecy
         Did glad my heart with hope of this young Richmond,
         So doth my heart misgive me, in these conflicts,
         What may befall him to his harm and ours.   95
         Therefore, Lord Oxford, to prevent the worst

68–9] *Pope;* Come ... Hope: / *Layes ... Head.* / If ... truth / To ... thoughts F   **88** SD *Exeunt all but*] *Eds.; Manet* F

69 **divining** foretelling the future.
78 **your brother** George Neville, Archbishop of York.
81 **conveyed** carried away secretly.
82 **attended** looked out for (*OED* Attend 13).
83 **forest side** outskirts of the forest (*OED* Side *sb*¹, 6b).

88 Compare the proverb 'There is a salve for every sore' (Tilley s84).
88 **betide** develop.
89 **like ... of** am alarmed by (Abbott 177).
96 **to ... worst** Compare the proverb 'It is good to fear the worst' (Dent w912).
96 **prevent** forestall.

Forthwith we'll send him hence to Brittany
Till storms be past of civil enmity.
OXFORD Ay, for if Edward repossess the crown
    'Tis like that Richmond with the rest shall down.   100
SOMERSET It shall be so: he shall to Brittany.
    Come, therefore, let's about it speedily.

Exeunt

[4.7] *Flourish. Enter* [KING] EDWARD, GLOUCESTER, HASTINGS,
and [*a troop of Hollanders with a Drummer*]

KING EDWARD Now, brother Richard, Lord Hastings, and the
        rest,
    Yet thus far Fortune maketh us amends
    And says that once more I shall interchange
    My wanèd state for Henry's regal crown.
    Well have we passed and now repassed the seas   5
    And brought desirèd help from Burgundy.
    What then remains, we being thus arrived
    From Ravenspurgh Haven before the gates of York,
    But that we enter, as into our dukedom?
        [*Hastings knocks on the gates*]
GLOUCESTER The gates made fast? Brother, I like not this,   10

Act 4, Scene 7   4.7] *Capell; not in* F   0 SD.1 KING] *Eds.; not in* F   0 SD.2 *a troop of Hollanders*] O *subst.;*
Souldiers F   0 SD.2 *with a Drummer*] *This edn; not in* F   4 wanèd] *Steevens subst.;* wained F   8 Ravenspurgh
Haven] F *subst.; Ravenspurg/Pope*   8 before] F; 'fore *conj. Steevens*   9 SD] *This edn; not in* F   10] *Pope;*
The . . . fast? / Brother . . . this. F

100 **like** likely.
100 **down** fall.

Act 4, Scene 7
***4.7** Holinshed and Hall record that in 1471
Charles the Bold of Burgundy refused to offer
Edward aid openly but helped him 'underhand'
with money and ships (Holinshed, p. 303; Hall,
p. 290). Hall (pp. 291–2), but not Holinshed,
gives us the arguments used by Edward to have
the gates of York opened to him. Both chroniclers underline the perjury of Edward who
swore before York to use the citizens courteously
and to be faithful to Henry (see Introduction,
p. 18; Holinshed, p. 305; Hall, p. 292). It was
actually at Nottingham that Edward met Sir
Thomas Montgomery (see 40 n.), and the
chroniclers report that Edward there proclaimed

himself king (compare 70–1; Holinshed, p. 306;
Hall, p. 292).
    0 SD.2 ***a troop of Hollanders** This detail
from 0 accords with 'desirèd help from
Burgundy' (6) and with 'blunt Hollanders'
(4.8.2). However, Fabyan notes that Edward
landed at Ravenspurgh 'with a small company of
Flemings and other' (p. 660).
    3 **interchange** exchange.
    8 **Ravenspurgh Haven** at the mouth of the
Humber. The line is unmetrical and, as Pope's
emendation implies, 'Haven' may be a compositorial insertion.
    ***9 SD** This piece of business can be inferred
from 16 below. For the use of stage doors for
city gates see Hattaway, pp. 24–6.
    10 **made fast** locked.

> For many men that stumble at the threshold
> Are well foretold that danger lurks within.

KING EDWARD Tush man, abodements must not now affright us.
> By fair or foul means we must enter in
> For hither will our friends repair to us.   15

HASTINGS My liege, I'll knock once more, to summon them.
> [*He knocks and the Drummer sounds*]

> *Enter on the walls, the* MAYOR OF YORK, *and his brethren [the*
> *Aldermen]*

MAYOR My lords, we were forewarnèd of your coming
> And shut the gates for safety of ourselves,
> For now we owe allegiance unto Henry.

KING EDWARD But, master Mayor, if Henry be your king,   20
> Yet Edward at the least is Duke of York.

MAYOR True, my good lord, I know you for no less.

KING EDWARD Why, and I challenge nothing but my dukedom
> As being well content with that alone.

GLOUCESTER [*Aside*] But when the fox hath once got in his nose   25
> He'll soon find means to make the body follow.

HASTINGS Why, master Mayor, why stand you in a doubt?
> Open the gates; we are King Henry's friends.

MAYOR Ay, say you so? The gates shall then be opened.
> *He descends*

GLOUCESTER A wise stout captain and soon persuaded!   30

HASTINGS The good old man would fain that all were well,
> So 'twere not long of him; but, being entered,
> I doubt not, I, but we shall soon persuade
> Both him and all his brothers unto reason.

16] F *subst.;* Sound vp the drum and call them to the wals. O   16 SD.1] *This edn; not in* F   16 SD.2–3 *the Aldermen*] *Dyce; not in* F   17] *Pope;* My Lords, / We . . . comming, F   25 SD] *Rowe²; not in* F   29 SD] F; *Exit* Maire O   30 soon persuaded] F; persuaded soon *Pope*   34 SD *Enter . . . Mayor*] F *subst.;* The Maire opens the dore, O   34 SD *with . . . hand*] O *subst.; not in* F   34 SD *below*] *Capell; not in* F

---

11 **stumble . . . threshold** proverbial for ill luck (Tilley T259).
> 12 **foretold** forewarned.
> 13 **abodements** omens.
> 15 **repair** return.
> *16 SD.1 This piece of business can be inferred from O's version of 16 (see collation).
> 16 SD.2 **on the walls** the tiring-house balcony or music room would have served for the scene where, as Hall narrates (p. 291), the citizens 'began to common [commune] with him from the walls'; see also the collation to 29 SD and 34 SD.

18 **of** concerning (Abbott 174).
> 23 **challenge** lay claim to.
> *25–6 The lines could be an aside directed to Edward or Hastings. Compare the proverb 'When the fox has got in his nose, he will soon make the body follow' (Tilley F655).
> 30 **stout** valiant (ironical).
> 31 'The mayor is willing we should enter so he may not be blamed' (Johnson).
> 32 **long of** on account of.

Enter the Mayor [with the keys in his hand] and two Aldermen [below]

KING EDWARD So, master Mayor: these gates must not be shut   35
    But in the night or in the time of war.
    What, fear not, man, but yield me up the keys,
        Takes his keys
    For Edward will defend the town and thee
    And all those friends that deign to follow me.

March. Enter [SIR JOHN] MONTGOMERY, *with Drum and Soldiers*

GLOUCESTER Brother, this is Sir John Montgomery,   40
    Our trusty friend, unless I be deceived.
KING EDWARD Welcome, Sir John. But why come you in arms?
MONTGOMERY To help King Edward in his time of storm
    As every loyal subject ought to do.
KING EDWARD Thanks, good Montgomery; but we now forget   45
    Our title to the crown and only claim
    Our dukedom till God please to send the rest.
MONTGOMERY Then fare you well for I will hence again:
    I came to serve a king and not a duke. –
    Drummer, strike up and let us march away.   50
        The drum begins to march
KING EDWARD Nay stay, Sir John, a while and we'll debate
    By what safe means the crown may be recovered.
MONTGOMERY What talk you of debating? In few words,
    If you'll not here proclaim yourself our king,
    I'll leave you to your fortune and be gone   55
    To keep them back that come to succour you.
    Why shall we fight if you pretend no title?
GLOUCESTER Why, brother, wherefore stand you on nice points?
    Resolve yourself and let us claim the crown.

39 SD SIR JOHN] O; *not in* F   **45–7**] Pope; Thankes . . . *Mountgomerie:* / But . . . Crowne, / And . . . Dukedome, /
Till . . . rest. F   **57** shall] F; should O   **59**] O *subst.; not in* F

   39 deign think it fit.
   40 Sir John Thus in both F and O, although
the chroniclers call him Sir Thomas (Holinshed,
p. 306; Hall, p. 292). This is more likely to be
an authorial than a compositorial error.
   49 The chroniclers report Montgomery's
boast that he 'would serve no man but a king'
(Holinshed, p. 306; Hall, p. 292).

   50 SD *march* sound a march beat.
   51 debate discuss.
   57 pretend claim.
   58 stand . . . points dwell on such petty
scruples.
   *59 This line from O is necessary as the king
seems to respond to Gloucester's 'claim'.

KING EDWARD When we grow stronger, then we'll make our
    claim: 60
    Till then 'tis wisdom to conceal our meaning.
HASTINGS Away with scrupulous wit! Now arms must rule.
GLOUCESTER And fearless minds climb soonest unto crowns. –
    Brother, we will proclaim you out of hand:
    The bruit thereof will bring you many friends.   65
KING EDWARD Then be it as you will; for 'tis my right
    And Henry but usurps the diadem.
MONTGOMERY Ay, now my sovereign speaketh like himself;
    And now will I be Edward's champion.
HASTINGS Sound, trumpet; Edward shall be here proclaimed.   70
    Come, fellow soldier, make thou proclamation.
        [Gives him a paper.] Flourish. Sound
SOLDIER *[Reads]* Edward the Fourth, by the Grace of God, King
    of England and France, and Lord of Ireland, etc.
MONTGOMERY And whosoe'er gainsays King Edward's right,
    By this I challenge him to single fight.   75
        Throws down his gauntlet
    Long live Edward the Fourth!
ALL Long live Edward the Fourth!
KING EDWARD Thanks, brave Montgomery, and thanks unto you
    all:
    If fortune serve me, I'll requite this kindness.

60] *Pope;* When . . . stronger, / Then . . . Clayme: F   **71** fellow soldier] F; fellow-soldier *Cambridge*   **71** SD
Gives . . . paper.] Capell; not in F   **72–5]** F *subst.;* Edward the fourth by the grace of God, king of England and
France, and Lord of Ireland, and whosoeuer gainsaies king *Edwards* right: by this *I* challenge him to single fight,
long liue *Edward* the fourth. o   **72** SD] *Capell;* not in F   **76]** o *subst.;* not in F   **78]** *Steevens;*
Thankes . . . *Mountgomery,* / And . . . all: F

61 meaning intention.

62 scrupulous over-nice, cautious (*OED*
sv 1).

62 wit argument, intellect.

64 out of hand immediately (Dent HH1).

65 bruit report.

67 diadem crown.

69 champion defender of the royal title.

70 trumpet trumpeter.

71–6 There seem to be signs that F's text
was modified in performance (see 73 n. and
collation). It is difficult to tell whether 'fellow'
in 71 means 'comrade' and is addressed to
Montgomery, or whether it designates the
common soldier who, according to F, reads the
proclamation. The Oxford editors argue that
the SH at 72 was inserted because the word was
wrongly construed in the latter sense (Wells and
Taylor, p. 204). o gives a prose version of the
whole proclamation to Montgomery.

71 SD Flourish. Sound This seems to be
a duplication, the *'Flourish'* having been added
(in the margin); it may, however, indicate that
music was sounded both before and after 71.

73 etc. This suggests either that the text of a
full proclamation is to be supplied (compare *2H6*
1.4.21 SD.2) or that Montgomery interrupts this
part of the formalities. (F's version suggests
that the moment may have been comic – if the
soldier was semi-literate).

74–5 Montgomery acts the part of the king's
champion at a coronation; Holinshed (p. 400)
offers a full description of the role as performed
at the coronation of Richard III.

74 gainsays denies.

76 o indicates that in performance the line
was pronounced before being echoed by all on
stage.

79 serve favour (*OED* sv v 25a).

Now, for this night, let's harbour here in York   80
And when the morning sun shall raise his car
Above the border of this horizon,
We'll forward towards Warwick and his mates,
For well I wot that Henry is no soldier.
Ah, froward Clarence, how evil it beseems thee   85
To flatter Henry and forsake thy brother!
Yet, as we may, we'll meet both thee and Warwick. –
Come on, brave soldiers: doubt not of the day
And, that once gotten, doubt not of large pay.

> *[Flourish. March.] Exeunt*

[4.8] *Flourish. Enter the* KING [HENRY], WARWICK [*bearing a letter*], MONTAGUE, CLARENCE, OXFORD, *and* [EXETER]

WARWICK   What counsel, lords? Edward from Belgia
With hasty Germans and blunt Hollanders

---

89 SD *Flourish. March.*] *This edn; not in* F   **Act 4, Scene 8**   **4.8**] *Capell; not in* F   **0** SD.1–2 *bearing a letter*] *This edn following* 0 (*Enter one with a letter to* Warwike. / *after 76 of 4.6 which precedes this scene in that text*)   **0** SD.2 EXETER] *Capell;* Somerset F   **1** SH] F *subst.;* KING HENRY *conj. Johnson*   **2** hasty] F *subst.,* 0; lusty *conj. Walker;* hardy *conj. Cartwright*

80 harbour take up our quarters.
81 car Phoebus' chariot.
82 horizon accented on the first syllable (Cercignani, p. 40).
83 forward march on.
83 mates fellows (contemptuous).
84 wot know.
85 froward perverse.
85 evil ill.
88 doubt fear.
88 day outcome of the day's battle.
89 doubt ... of expect.
*89 SD I have added a flourish, to amplify the exit of one king and provide a musical challenge to the second who enters with his own flourish at the beginning of the next scene (compare 5.3.24 SD and Long, pp. 29–30).

Act 4, Scene 8
*4.8 The central episode of the scene, Henry's capture on 11 April 1471 at the bishop's palace in London, is narrated by both chroniclers (Holinshed, p. 311; Hall, p. 294) although it is Hall who notes how Somerset and others fled, 'leaving King Henry alone as an host [victim] that should be sacrificed'. However, Shakespeare, possibly in order 'to prevent the

juxtaposition of scenes before the walls of York and Coventry' (Wilson, p. 189), diverts Edward's journey from 'York' (4.7) to 'Coventry' (5.1) via 'London' – which simply indicates that it was dramatic theme and theatrical pattern rather than geographic or historical importance which were important in the theatres of the time (compare 33 n. below). Edward's challenge to Warwick at Coventry (5.1) took place before he captured Henry (Holinshed, pp. 306–7; Hall, p. 293).

0 SD.2 *EXETER Sanders, following Wilson and others, thinks that 33 ff. originally constituted a separate scene (Sanders, p. 259, 4.8.32 SD n.). However, substituting Exeter for Somerset not only regularises the SD with the SHH at 37 etc. but accords with the fact that Somerset had left London some days before Exeter arrived – see Boswell-Stone, p. 333 n. 4. This is more likely to be an authorial error than to derive from contamination from 0 which runs 4.6 and 4.8 together.

1 Belgia The Netherlands.
2 hasty rash, quick-tempered (*OED* sv 4).
2 blunt rude, uncivilised, harsh (*OED* sv 4a and b).

Hath passed in safety through the Narrow Seas
And with his troops doth march amain to London;
And many giddy people flock to him.   5
KING HENRY Let's levy men and beat him back again.
CLARENCE A little fire is quickly trodden out
     Which, being suffered, rivers cannot quench.
WARWICK In Warwickshire I have true-hearted friends
     Not mutinous in peace yet bold in war;   10
     Those will I muster up; and thou, son Clarence,
     Shalt stir in Suffolk, Norfolk, and in Kent
     The knights and gentlemen to come with thee. –
     Thou, brother Montague, in Buckingham,
     Northampton, and in Leicestershire shalt find   15
     Men well inclined to hear what thou command'st. –
     And thou, brave Oxford, wondrous well beloved
     In Oxfordshire shalt muster up thy friends. –
     My sovereign with the loving citizens,
     Like to his island girt in with the ocean   20
     Or modest Diane circled with her nymphs,
     Shall rest in London till we come to him. –
     Fair lords, take leave and stand not to reply. –
     Farewell, my sovereign.
KING HENRY Farewell, my Hector, and my Troy's true hope.   25
CLARENCE In sign of truth, I kiss your highness' hand.
     [*He kisses the king's hand*]
KING HENRY Well-minded Clarence, be thou fortunate.

---

6 SH] F *subst.; Oxf.* O; WARWICK *conj. Johnson*   12 stir] *Pope* stirre vp F   17 beloved] *Hart subst.;* belou'd, F   18 Oxfordshire,] *Hart;* Oxfordshire F   26, 28, 29 SD] *This edn following Johnson (at 29); not in* F

---

3 **Narrow Seas** The English Channel.
4 **amain** at full speed.
5 **giddy** fickle.
6 Johnson's reattribution of the line to Warwick and Malone's to Oxford have been widely followed on the grounds that it is out of character with the king and that Henry is not being directly addressed. But 35–6 suggest that he has acquired some degree of boldness and speaks out.
7–8 Compare the proverb 'Of one little spark is made a great fire' (Ecclus 11.32; Tilley S714).
8 **being suffered** if unchecked or ignored.
11 **son** son-in-law (see 4.2.12).
12 ***stir** incite (*OED* sv *v* 7); F's 'stir up' is unmetrical, and the 'up' may have been caught from the previous line.

21 Compare Phoebe (Diana, goddess of chastity) with her 'troop of nymphs that guarded her about' (*Metamorphoses*, II, 553).
23 **stand** wait.
25 **Hector** the greatest champion of the Trojans.
25 **Troy's** i.e. London's, because London ('Troy-Novant') was supposed to have been founded by Brutus, legendary grandson of the Trojan hero Aeneas. See Geoffrey of Monmouth, *Historia Regum Britanniae*, ed. A. Griscom, 1929, I, XI, pp. 238–9 and *FQ*, 3, 9, 44–6.
25 **true hope** For the Virgilian allusion, see 2.1.51 n.
27 **Well-minded** Virtuously disposed (dramatic irony).

MONTAGUE Comfort, my lord; and so I take my leave.

    [He kisses the king's hand]

OXFORD And thus I seal my truth and bid adieu.

    [He kisses the king's hand]

KING HENRY Sweet Oxford and my loving Montague   30

    And all at once, once more a happy farewell.

WARWICK Farewell, sweet lords, let's meet at Coventry.

    Exeunt [by different doors, all but King Henry and Exeter]

KING HENRY Here at the palace will I rest awhile.

    Cousin of Exeter, what thinks your lordship?

    Methinks the power that Edward hath in field   35

    Should not be able to encounter mine.

EXETER The doubt is that he will seduce the rest.

KING HENRY That's not my fear; my meed hath got me fame:

    I have not stopped mine ears to their demands

    Nor posted off their suits with slow delays;   40

    My pity hath been balm to heal their wounds,

    My mildness hath allayed their swelling griefs,

    My mercy dried their water-flowing tears;

    I have not been desirous of their wealth,

    Nor much oppressed them with great subsidies,   45

    Nor forward of revenge – though they much erred.

    Then why should they love Edward more than me?

    No, Exeter, these graces challenge grace:

    And when the lion fawns upon the lamb

---

31 farewell.] F; farewell. *Exit / Oxford*   32–32 SD Coventry. / *Exeunt*] F *subst.*; Couentrie. / *All.* Agreed. *Exeunt Omnes.* O; Coventry. / *Exeunt [severally]* / 4.10 [*Enter King Henry and the Duke of Exeter*] Oxford   32 SD *by . . . doors*] *This edn; not in* F   32 SD *all . . . Exeter*] Capell; *not in* F   43 tears] F *subst.*; eyes *conj.* Capell

29 **seal . . . truth** confirm my loyalty.

31 **at once** together.

*32 SD–33 **palace** The dialogue indicates that Warwick leaves from a different door from the rest. There is therefore no need to begin a new scene here as various editors following Wilson have done (Wilson was following the arguments of P. A. Daniel, *Time-Analysis of Shakespeare's Plays*, 1877–9, p. 321). Even if Henry were to exit at 31 as Oxford suggests, his reappearance after only one line would be awkward. F's '*Exeunt*' (32) would seem to refer just to the lords, and the compositor left no space afterwards as he usually did between scenes. O offers no guidance as it cuts the sequence between Henry and Exeter.

33 **palace** that of the Bishop of London (Holinshed, p. 311; Hall, p. 285), although an audience need not be troubled by the fact that

Edward was unlikely to have got south so quickly – the line, along with 22, may be read to suggest that Henry rests at some other palace en route to London.

35 **power** army.

37 **doubt** fear.

38 **meed** merit, worth (OED *sv* 3).

38 **fame** a good reputation.

40 **posted off** put off.

43 **water-flowing** flowing like water, copious (Schmidt).

45 **subsidies** particular property taxes exacted by the monarch; see Williams for subsidies raised by Elizabeth I (pp. 73–5).

46 **forward of** eager for.

48 **challenge grace** lay claim to favour.

49 A recollection of Isa. 11.6: 'The wolf also shall dwell with the lamb, and the leopard shall lie with the kid, and the calf, and the lion.'

The lamb will never cease to follow him.   50
        Shout within, 'A Lancaster! A Lancaster!'
EXETER Hark, hark, my lord! What shouts are these?

Enter [KING] EDWARD and his Soldiers [, with GLOUCESTER, and
                            others]

KING EDWARD Seize on the shame-faced Henry, bear him hence;
        And once again proclaim us King of England. –
        You are the fount that makes small brooks to flow:
        Now stops thy spring, my sea shall suck them dry   55
        And swell so much the higher by their ebb. –
        Hence with him to the Tower; let him not speak.
                    Exit [Exeter] with King Henry [guarded]
        And, lords, towards Coventry bend we our course,
        Where peremptory Warwick now remains.
        The sun shines hot and, if we use delay,   60
        Cold biting winter mars our hoped-for hay.
GLOUCESTER Away betimes, before his forces join,
        And take the great-grown traitor unawares.
        Brave warriors, march amain towards Coventry.
                                              Exeunt

50 SD 'A Lancaster! A Lancaster!'] F; 'A York! A York!' *conj. Johnson*   52 SD *with . . . others*] *Riverside following* O
(*Edward* and his traine); *not in* F   57 SD *Exeter . . . guarded*] *Riverside; not in* F   59 Where . . . remains] F *subst.;*
Whither . . . repairs *conj. this edn.*

51 SD *within* i.e. within the tiring-house.
51 SD 'A Lancaster! A Lancaster!' The
shouts announce the arrival of the Yorkist party,
and some eds. have altered the text to 'A York!
A York!'. But we can either conjecture that this
was Edward's simple ruse, a misleading cry to
gain admittance, or that guards were trying to
raise the watch, having recognised Edward. (A =
to (*à*)).
52 **shame-faced** modest, shy (*OED* sv 1), an
etymological misinterpretation of 'shamefast'.
55 **Now . . . spring** Now that the source of
power runs dry.
58–9 The lines have been used to support

the argument that 33 ff. constitute a separate
scene (see headnote). But they can be explained
equally by considering them as evidence of
'dramatic foreshortening' (Sisson, *New Readings*,
II, 85); 59 may also be corrupt (see collation).
59 **peremptory** dictatorial (*OED* sv 5).
59 **remains** has taken up his abode (*OED*
Remain 4b).
60–1 Compare the proverb 'Make hay while
the sun shines' (Tilley H235).
62 **betimes** quickly.
63 **take** capture.
64 **amain** swiftly.

[5.1] *Enter* WARWICK, *the Mayor of Coventry, two* MESSENGERS, *and others upon the walls*

WARWICK Where is the post that came from valiant Oxford?
         How far hence is thy lord, mine honest fellow?
1 MESSENGER By this at Dunsmore, marching hitherward.
WARWICK How far off is our brother Montague?
         Where is the post that came from Montague?   5
2 MESSENGER By this at Daintry, with a puissant troop.

                Enter [SIR THOMAS] SOMERVILLE

WARWICK Say, Somerville, what says my loving son,
         And, by thy guess, how nigh is Clarence now?
SOMERVILLE At Southam I did leave him with his forces,
         And do expect him here some two hours hence.   10
                [A drum sounds a march]
WARWICK Then Clarence is at hand – I hear his drum.
SOMERVILLE It is not his, my lord. Here Southam lies:
         The drum your honour hears marcheth from Warwick.
WARWICK Who should that be? Belike unlooked-for friends.
SOMERVILLE They are at hand and you shall quickly know.   15

     March. Flourish. Enter [KING] EDWARD, RICHARD [OF
            GLOUCESTER], *and Soldiers*

KING EDWARD Go, trumpet, to the walls and sound a parle.

Act 5, Scene 1   **5.1]** *Pope; not in* F   **6 SD SIR THOMAS]** *This edn; not in* F; SIR JOHN *Capell*   **6 SD SOMERVILLE]**
Eds.; Someruile F; *Summerfield* O   **10 SD]** *This edn; not in* F

Act 5, Scene 1
***5.1** See 4.8 n. Edward challenged Warwick at Coventry on 29 March 1471, but Warwick refused to join battle because he distrusted Clarence's loyalty (Holinshed, pp. 306–7; Hall, p. 293). Clarence was reconciled to his brother, and both chroniclers (Holinshed, p. 309; Hall, p. 293) report that the three brothers of York sought to win Warwick back to their cause (21–52). The scene knits together events at Coventry and the preparations for the battle of Barnet (fought on 14 April): both chroniclers (Holinshed, p. 312; Hall, p. 295) list the nobles on Warwick's side at that battle – those that Shakespeare shows entering Coventry. Having challenged Warwick a second time at Coventry, Edward turned south to London, in which direction Warwick followed him as far as Barnet (Holinshed, pp. 309–11; Hall, pp. 293–5).
1, 5 post messenger.

3, 6 By this By now.
3 Dunsmore Between Coventry and Daventry.
6 Daintry The local pronunciation of Daventry, a town in Northamptonshire.
6 puissant powerful.
6 SD *SIR THOMAS Thomson reports that this was the Somerville intended. Sir Thomas Aston-Somerville, who lived near Evesham, died in 1500.
7 son son-in-law, i.e. Clarence.
9 Southam Ten miles SE of Coventry.
12–13 Somerville points in the direction of Southam to indicate that it lies SE of Coventry while Warwick lies SW.
14 Belike As it seems.
14 unlooked-for unexpected, unwelcome.
16 trumpet trumpeter.
16 parle summons to a meeting to discuss terms.

GLOUCESTER See how the surly Warwick mans the wall.
WARWICK O unbid spite, is sportful Edward come?
        Where slept our scouts or how are they seduced
        That we could hear no news of his repair?   20
KING EDWARD Now, Warwick, wilt thou ope the city gates,
        Speak gentle words, and humbly bend thy knee,
        Call Edward king and at his hands beg mercy,
        And he shall pardon thee these outrages.
WARWICK Nay rather wilt thou draw thy forces hence,   25
        Confess who set thee up, and plucked thee down,
        Call Warwick patron and be penitent,
        And thou shalt still remain the Duke of York.
GLOUCESTER I thought at least he would have said 'the king',
        Or did he make the jest against his will?   30
WARWICK Is not a dukedom, sir, a goodly gift?
GLOUCESTER Ay, by my faith, for a poor earl to give;
        I'll do thee service for so good a gift.
WARWICK 'Twas I that gave the kingdom to thy brother.
KING EDWARD Why then, 'tis mine, if but by Warwick's gift.   35
WARWICK Thou art no Atlas for so great a weight,
        And, weakling, Warwick takes his gift again;
        Henry is my king, Warwick his subject.
KING EDWARD But Warwick's king is Edward's prisoner:
        And, gallant Warwick, do but answer this: 40
        What is the body when the head is off?
GLOUCESTER Alas, that Warwick had no more forecast

---

24 outrages.] Pope; Outrages? F   38 Henry] O subst.; And Henry F   42 forecast] F subst.; foresight O

18 unbid spite unwelcome vexation.
18 sportful lustful: Edward was notorious for his lasciviousness.
20 repair coming, arrival.
21, 25 wilt thou if you will.
25 draw withdraw (OED sv v 37).
26 set ... up installed you on the throne.
27 patron protector.
30 Gloucester seems to have diagnosed a parapraxis. Warwick by his slip has revealed that he cannot bear the thought of the erstwhile duke as his monarch.
32 earl (lower in rank than a duke).
33 do ... service render the dues of a feudal tenant to his lord (ironical) – see OED Service sb 8b.

34 See 4.6.37.
36 Atlas In punishment for his revolt against the Titans, this giant was condemned to support the heavens on his shoulders (Metamorphoses, II, 377 ff.); later Atlas was portrayed as bearing the earth.
38 *Henry F's 'And Henry' is probably dittography, caught from the previous line.
41 Compare the proverb 'If the head is off, no beast can live' (Dent H257.1).
42–6 The whole speech may be directed to Warwick (or perhaps only the last two lines).
42 forecast forethought, prudence (accented on the second syllable); O's reading, 'foresight' may, however, be correct – 'forecast' appears nowhere else in Shakespeare.

But whiles he thought to steal the single ten,
The king was slyly fingered from the deck!
You left poor Henry at the bishop's palace,   45
And ten to one you'll meet him in the Tower.
KING EDWARD 'Tis even so; [*to Warwick*] yet you are Warwick
        still.
GLOUCESTER Come, Warwick, take the time, kneel down, kneel
        down.
        Nay, when? Strike now or else the iron cools.
WARWICK I had rather chop this hand off at a blow   50
        And with the other fling it at thy face
        Than bear so low a sail to strike to thee.
KING EDWARD Sail how thou canst, have wind and tide thy friend,
        This hand, fast wound about thy coal-black hair,
        Shall, whiles thy head is warm and new cut off,   55
        Write in the dust this sentence with thy blood:
        'Wind-changing Warwick now can change no more.'

        Enter OXFORD, *with drum and colours*

WARWICK O cheerful colours! See where Oxford comes!
OXFORD Oxford, Oxford, for Lancaster!
        [*He and his forces enter the city*]
GLOUCESTER The gates are open: let us enter too.   60
KING EDWARD So other foes may set upon our backs.
        Stand we in good array, for they no doubt
        Will issue out again and bid us battle;

47 SD] *Oxford; not in* F   48] *Pope; Come Warwicke, / Take ... downe:* F   53] *Pope; Sayle ... canst, /*
Haue ... friend, F   57 SD] F; O *adds & al crie,*   57, 66, 71, 75 SDD] *colours* F *subst.;* souldiers O   59 SD] *Capell;*
Exit. O; *not in* F

43 **single** mere.
43 **ten** the highest non-court card in a pack
of cards.
44 **fingered ... deck** filched from the pack.
45 **bishop's palace** The palace of the
Bishop of London (see 4.8.33).
47 **still** always.
48 **take the time** seize the opportunity –
compare the proverb 'Take time when time
comes' (Dent T312).
49 **when** (exclamation of impatience).
49 **Strike ... cools** Combining the proverb
'Strike while the iron is hot' (Tilley I94), with a
pun on strike = yield (see 3.3.5 n.).
52 **Than** be so humble as to pay homage to
you – see 3.3.5 n.

52 **strike** punning on the phrase 'strike
(lower) one's sail'.
53 **have ... friend** Compare the proverb
'Sail with the wind and tide' (Dent W429).
57 **Wind-changing** (I) Inconstant, (2)
Director of the wind.
57 **change** transfer his allegiance.
57 SD–76 SD This series of entrances may
well have been made into the playhouse yard, so
that the soldiers could ascend and 'pass over' the
stage, exiting through the playhouse doors which
signified the gates of the city (Hattaway, p. 25).
61 **So** Then (Abbott 66).
61 **backs** forces in the rear (*OED* Back *sb*
11).
62 **array** display of order (*OED* sv 2).
63 **bid** offer.

If not, the city being but of small defence,
We'll quickly rouse the traitors in the same.   65
[Oxford appears aloft]
WARWICK O welcome Oxford, for we want thy help.

Enter MONTAGUE, *with drum and colours*

MONTAGUE Montague, Montague, for Lancaster!
[He and his forces enter the city]
GLOUCESTER Thou and thy brother both shall buy this treason
Even with the dearest blood your bodies bear.
[Montague appears aloft]
KING EDWARD The harder matched, the greater victory: 70
My mind presageth happy gain and conquest.

Enter SOMERSET, *with drum and colours*

SOMERSET Somerset, Somerset, for Lancaster!
[He and his forces enter the city]
GLOUCESTER Two of thy name, both Dukes of Somerset,
Have sold their lives unto the house of York,
[Somerset appears aloft]
And thou shalt be the third, if this sword hold.   75

Enter CLARENCE, *with drum and colours*

WARWICK And lo, where George of Clarence sweeps along
Of force enough to bid his brother battle;
With whom an upright zeal to right prevails
More than the nature of a brother's love.

65, 69, 74 SDD] *This edn; not in* F   67, 72 SDD] *Malone; Exit.* O; *not in* F   68 buy] F; abie O; bye *Oxford*   75 if]
F; and O   78 whom an] *Rowe;* whom, an F2; whom, in F

64 of small defence weakly fortified.
65 rouse start (an animal from its lair).
*65, 69, 74 SDD Alternatively Oxford, Montague, and Somerset may have remained within the tiring-house, with Warwick delivering line 66 to Oxford 'within'.
66 want need.
68 buy pay the penalty for (*OED* sv 3), an aphetic form of 'aby' which is recorded in O.
69 dearest most vital.
70 Compare the proverb 'The more danger the more honour' (Tilley D35).
71 happy fortunate.
73 Edmund, second Duke of Somerset, killed (1455) at the first battle of St Albans (whose

head Richard threw down at 1.1.16), and his son Henry, third Duke of Somerset, beheaded after the battle of Hexham (1464) which Shakespeare does not dramatise (see 3.1 n.). Somerset's defection from Edward was shown in 4.1 and 4.2 which portray events of 1470.
76 sweeps along like a proud peacock – compare *1H6* 3.3.6.
77 Of force enough With sufficient troops.
78 *whom an Rowe's emendation is necessary to the sense.
78 to towards.
78 to right for justice.
79 nature natural inclination.
79 brother's love love for a brother.

CLARENCE Clarence, Clarence for Lancaster!　　　　　　　　　　80

KING EDWARD *Et tu, Brute?* Wilt thou stab Caesar too?
　　　A parley, sirrah, to George of Clarence!

*[Sound a parley; and Gloucester and Clarence whisper together, and then
　　Clarence takes his red rose out of his hat and throws it at Warwick.]*

WARWICK Come Clarence, come: thou wilt, if Warwick call.

CLARENCE Father of Warwick, know you what this means?
　　　Look here I throw my infamy at thee:　　　　　　　　85
　　　I will not ruinate my father's house,
　　　Who gave his blood to lime the stones together,
　　　And set up Lancaster. Why trowest thou, Warwick,
　　　That Clarence is so harsh, so blunt, unnatural,
　　　To bend the fatal instruments of war　　　　　　　　90
　　　Against his brother and his lawful king?
　　　Perhaps thou wilt object my holy oath:
　　　To keep that oath were more impiety
　　　Than Jephthah's when he sacrificed his daughter.
　　　I am so sorry for my trespass made　　　　　　　　95
　　　That, to deserve well at my brother's hands,
　　　I here proclaim myself thy mortal foe
　　　With resolution, wheresoe'er I meet thee –
　　　As I will meet thee if thou stir abroad –

80–3 SH] O *subst.; not in* F　　94 Jephthah's] *Rowe*² *subst.; Iephah* F

*80–2 I have included these lines from O as the omission of at least 80 destroys the succession of war-cries (see 67 and 72 above). They may have been omitted from F as a consequence of compositorial eye-skip or, less probably, they may represent a revision. *Et tu, Brute* ('and you, Brutus') is the first printed occurrence of what seems to have been a stage catch-phrase – see A. Humphries (ed.), *Julius Caesar*, 1984, pp. 24–5. (Other references to Caesar are to be found at 3.1.18 and 5.5.53.)

*82 SD This SD from O presumably records some original business and mimes out details from Holinshed, p. 308 (Hall, p. 293). Holinshed has a marginal note: 'The dissimulation of the Duke of Clarence'. It clarifies 85 below (see Alan Dessen, *Elizabethan Stage Conventions and Modern Interpreters*, 1984, pp. 54–5). It may be that the best theatrical effect would be achieved by having Clarence throw the rose after 84.

82 SD.2 *takes...hat* signifying the end of his Lancastrian allegiance.

84 Father Father-in-law (see 3.3.242 n.).

86–92 These lines derive from Hall's account of how a 'damsel' was sent to Clarence who

was a refugee in France to persuade him that it was not 'natural...to him...to...take part against the house of York...and to set up again the house of Lancaster' (p. 281).

86 ruinate bring to ruin.

87 lime cement.

88 trowest thou do you believe.

89 blunt 'stupid, insensible of paternal fondness' (Johnson).

90 bend direct (*OED* 17).

92–4 Compare the proverb 'An unlawful oath is better broken than kept' (Dent O7).

92 object urge as an objection.

*94 Jephthah's Rowe's emendation to the possessive is justified grammatically. (The Geneva Bible's spelling of the name is 'Ipthtáh'.) The story of Jephthah the Israelite judge, who vowed to sacrifice the first thing to emerge from the doors of his house in return for victory over the Ammonites and who then had to sacrifice his daughter who had come out to meet him, is told in Judges 11.20 ff.

95 trespass made sin committted.

99 stir abroad move outside the walls (of Coventry).

To plague thee for thy foul misleading me.   100
And so, proud-hearted Warwick, I defy thee
And to my brothers turn my blushing cheeks. –
Pardon me, Edward, I will make amends. –
And, Richard, do not frown upon my faults,
For I will henceforth be no more unconstant.   105

KING EDWARD Now welcome more, and ten times more beloved
    Than if thou never hadst deserved our hate!

GLOUCESTER Welcome, good Clarence, this is brother-like.

WARWICK O passing traitor, perjured and unjust!

KING EDWARD What, Warwick, wilt thou leave the town, and
    fight?   110
    Or shall we beat the stones about thine ears?

WARWICK Alas, I am not cooped here for defence:
    I will away towards Barnet presently
    And bid thee battle, Edward, if thou dar'st.

KING EDWARD Yes, Warwick, Edward dares, and leads the way. – 115
    Lords, to the field! Saint George, and victory!

*Exeunt [King Edward and his company below, Warwick and his company
aloft]. March. [Enter below as out of the city] Warwick and his
company [and] follow [King Edward]*

[5.2] *Alarum, and excursions. Enter [KING] EDWARD bringing forth*
WARWICK *wounded*

KING EDWARD So, lie thou there. Die thou, and die our fear,
    For Warwick was a bug that feared us all.

---

102 brothers] O; brother F   110] *Pope;* What *Warwicke,* / Wilt...fight? F   116 SD.1–3 *King...alofi.*
Enter...city...and...King Edward] Pelican; not in F   116 SD.3 *follow] Eds.; followes* F   Act 5, Scene 2   5.2]
Capell; not in F   0 SD] F *subst.;* Alarmes, and then enter *Warwike* wounded. O

102 *brothers O's plural is justified by
103–4.
104 faults offences.
109 passing supreme, surpassing.
111 about...ears proverbial (Dent E.F3).
112 Alas Truly (used in defiance).
112 cooped enclosed, prepared.
113 Barnet about ten miles north of London
in Hertfordshire. Shakespeare gives the impression that Barnet is close to Coventry.
113 presently immediately.
*116 SD A ceremonial exit of this kind marks
the division between a scene of words and one of
action.

Act 5, Scene 2
*5.2 In the chroniclers there is no report of
an encounter between Edward and Warwick at
the battle of Barnet (14 April 1471), nor does
either chronicler report who killed Warwick and
Montague (Holinshed, p. 314; Hall, p. 296).
Margaret, having gathered an army in France to
support her husband, set sail for England, but
was fatally delayed for lack of a favourable wind
(Holinshed, p. 315; Hall, p. 297).
0 SD O's SD (see collation) does not imply that
Edward killed Warwick (see 5.2 n.).
2 bug ' "bugbear", a terrific being' (Johnson);
compare the proverbial phrase 'bugs to scare
babes' (Dent B703).
2 feared frightened.

Now, Montague, sit fast: I seek for thee
That Warwick's bones may keep thine company.   *Exit*
WARWICK Ah, who is nigh? Come to me, friend or foe,   5
    And tell me who is victor, York or Warwick?
    Why ask I that? My mangled body shows,
    My blood, my want of strength; my sick heart shows
    That I must yield my body to the earth
    And, by my fall, the conquest to my foe.   10
    Thus yields the cedar to the axe's edge,
    Whose arms gave shelter to the princely eagle,
    Under whose shade the ramping lion slept,
    Whose top-branch overpeered Jove's spreading tree,
    And kept low shrubs from winter's powerful wind.   15
    These eyes that now are dimmed with death's black veil
    Have been as piercing as the midday sun
    To search the secret treasons of the world;
    The wrinkles in my brows, now filled with blood,
    Were likened oft to kingly sepulchres: 20
    For who lived king but I could dig his grave
    And who durst smile when Warwick bent his brow?
    Lo, now my glory smeared in dust and blood.
    My parks, my walks, my manors that I had,
    Even now forsake me; and of all my lands   25
    Is nothing left me but my body's length.

---

7 that? My] F *subst.*; that my *Cairncross*   7 shows,] F *subst.*; shows? *Cairncross*

---

3 **sit fast** take up a secure position; watch out.

11–14 Compare the comparison of Ashur, the highest god of the Assyrians, to a cedar 'with thick shadowing branches ... his height was exalted above all the trees of the field ... All the fowls of the heaven make their nests in his boughs, and under his branches did all the beasts of the field bring forth their young, and under his shadow dwelt all mighty nations' (Ezek. 31.3–6).

11 **cedar** In the hierarchy of trees, the tallest and therefore the prince among the evergreens; compare 14 n.

12 **arms** branches (*OED* Arm *sb* 7).

12 **the ... eagle** Richard, Duke of York; compare 2.1.92.

12 **eagle** king among birds.

13 **the ... lion** Henry VI on whose coat of arms three lions rampant (springing up) appeared; compare 4.8.49.

13 **ramping** fierce.

14 **overpeered** towered over.

14 **Jove's ... tree** The oak, peerless among deciduous trees; compare Virgil, *Georgics*, III, 332, 'magna Iovis ... quercus' (the great oak of Jove), and Golding's *Metamorphoses*, I, 121 'Jove's broad tree in field'.

15 **kept** protected (*OED* Keep *v* 14).

18 **search** seek to discover (*OED* sv *v* 11b).

24 'This mention of his "parks" and "manors" diminishes the pathetic effect of the foregoing lines' (Johnson).

24 **parks** hunting grounds.

24 **walks** tracts of forest land (*OED* Walk *sb* 10).

25–7 and ... dust The *topos* that compared the extent of a living prince's lands with the size of his grave was common: see *R2* 3.3.153–4, *1H4* 5.4.87–92; also Ovid, *Amores*, 3.9.33, 40; Juvenal, *Satires*, X, 172–3; and the proverb 'Six feet of earth make all men equal' (Dent F582).

Why, what is pomp, rule, reign, but earth and dust?
And live we how we can, yet die we must.

Enter OXFORD *and* SOMERSET

SOMERSET Ah, Warwick, Warwick! Wert thou as we are,
    We might recover all our loss again.   30
    The queen from France hath brought a puissant power:
    Even now we heard the news. Ah, could'st thou fly!
WARWICK Why then I would not fly. Ah, Montague,
    If thou be there, sweet brother, take my hand
    And with thy lips keep in my soul awhile.   35
    Thou lov'st me not: for, brother, if thou did'st,
    Thy tears would wash this cold congealèd blood
    That glues my lips and will not let me speak.
    Come quickly, Montague, or I am dead.
SOMERSET Ah, Warwick, Montague hath breathed his last,   40
    And to the latest gasp cried out for Warwick,
    And said, 'Commend me to my valiant brother.'
    And more he would have said and more he spoke,
    Which sounded like a canon in a vault
    That mought not be distinguished: but at last   45
    I well might hear, delivered with a groan,
    'O farewell, Warwick!'
WARWICK Sweet rest his soul: fly, lords, and save yourselves
    For Warwick bids you all farewell – to meet in heaven.
                        [He dies]
OXFORD Away, away, to meet the queen's great power.   50
                   Here they bear away his body. Exeunt

---

44 canon] *McKerrow;* Cannon F; clamor O   48] O *subst.;* Sweet . . . Soule: / Flye . . . selues, F   49 farewell –]
Rann subst.; farewell, F   49 SD] O; *not in* F

28 **die we must** proverbial (Dent M505).

31 **puissant** mighty.

33 After this line O inserts versions of 2.1.53 and 2.3.3–5.

35 **with . . . while** kiss me: the soul of a dying man was supposed to fly out of the mouth; compare *2H6* 3.2.396–7 and Ovid, *Tristia,* 3.3.61–2.

41 **latest** final.

44 ***canon** part song, 'the idea being that the hollow reverberations make the words indistinguishable' (McKerrow). O's 'clamour',

however, might equally be substituted for F's 'cannon' (see collation).

45 **mought** could (Abbott 312).

49 The line is hypermetric; Shakespeare conceivably wrote a couplet (the first line ending with 'farewell') and had Warwick die in the middle of the second line, so that the audience was left to supply 'or else in hell'.

50 For O's expansion of this one line to six see Appendix 2, p. 220.

50 SD On an open stage all bodies had to be carried off in view of the audience.

[5.3] *Flourish. Enter* KING EDWARD *in triumph, with* RICHARD [OF GLOUCESTER], CLARENCE, [*with Soldiers*]

KING EDWARD Thus far our fortune keeps an upward course
　　　　　And we are graced with wreaths of victory;
　　　　　But in the midst of this bright-shining day
　　　　　I spy a black suspicious threatening cloud,
　　　　　That will encounter with our glorious sun   5
　　　　　Ere he attain his easeful western bed –
　　　　　I mean, my lords, those powers that the queen
　　　　　Hath raised in Gallia have arrived our coast
　　　　　And, as we hear, march on to fight with us.
CLARENCE A little gale will soon disperse that cloud   10
　　　　　And blow it to the source from whence it came;
　　　　　Thy very beams will dry those vapours up,
　　　　　For every cloud engenders not a storm.
GLOUCESTER The queen is valued thirty thousand strong
　　　　　And Somerset, with Oxford, fled to her: 15
　　　　　If she have time to breathe, be well assured
　　　　　Her faction will be full as strong as ours.
KING EDWARD We are advertised by our loving friends
　　　　　That they do hold their course toward Tewkesbury.
　　　　　We, having now the best at Barnet field,   20
　　　　　Will thither straight, for willingness rids way;

Act 5, Scene 3　　　5.3] *Capell; not in* F　　　0 SD.2 *with Soldiers*] 0 *subst.; and the rest* F

Act 5, Scene 3
*5.3 See 5.2. Shakespeare telescopes events between the battle of Barnet on 14 April and 3 May when Edward learned of the Lancastrians' purpose to do battle with him at Tewkesbury (Boswell-Stone, p. 338; Holinshed, p. 318; Hall, pp. 299–300).
　0 SD *in triumph* triumphantly like a Roman victor whose brows would be girt with an actual crown of laurel (see 2).
　2 Exactly the same line occurs in Marlowe, *The Massacre at Paris* 794.
　5 **encounter with** confront in battle (*OED* Encounter *v* 1b).
　5 **sun** the Yorkist badge – see 2.1.20 SD n.
　7 **powers** troops.
　8 **Gallia** France.

8 **arrived** landed on (*OED* Arrive *v* 1).
12 **very** mere.
12 **beams** of the Yorkist sun.
13 Compare the proverb 'All clouds bring not storms' (Tilley C443).
13 **engenders** conceives.
14 **valued** estimated.
16 **breathe** rest, recuperate.
18 **advertised** informed (accented on the second syllable – Cercignani, p. 41).
19 **Tewkesbury** A town in Gloucestershire where the Avon and Severn meet.
20 **best** victory.
21 **straight** at once.
21 **rids way** covers the ground quickly (*OED* Rid *v* 8b).

And as we march our strength will be augmented
In every county as we go along.
Strike up the drum; cry, 'Courage!' and away!

> [*Flourish. March.*] *Exeunt*

[**5.4**] *Flourish. March. Enter the* QUEEN [MARGARET], *young* [PRINCE] EDWARD, SOMERSET, OXFORD, [*with Drum and Soldiers*]

MARGARET Great lords, wise men ne'er sit and wail their loss
But cheerly seek how to redress their harms.
What though the mast be now blown overboard,
The cable broke, the holding anchor lost,
And half our sailors swallowed in the flood –   5
Yet lives our pilot still. Is't meet that he
Should leave the helm and, like a fearful lad,
With tearful eyes add water to the sea
And give more strength to that which hath too much,
Whiles, in his moan, the ship splits on the rock,   10
Which industry and courage might have saved?

---

22 augmented] *Eds. following* O*; augmented:* F   23–4] F *subst.; Come lets goe, for if we slacke this faire / Bright Summers daie, sharpe winters / Showers will marre our hope for haie.* O   24 SD *Flourish. March.*] *Oxford; not in* F   **Act 5, Scene 4**   5.4] *Capell; not in* F   0 SD.2–3 *with Drum and Soldiers*] O *subst.; and Souldiers* F   4 holding anchor] *Kittredge; holding-Anchor* F

23–4 See collation, and Textual analysis, p. 203.

*24 SD The addition of a final flourish and march is justified by 24; compare 4.7.89 SD.

Act 5, Scene 4

*5.4 Hall reports that when news came to Margaret of the defeat at Barnet she in fact, 'dismayed with fear, fell to the ground, her heart ... pierced with sorrow' (p. 297). However, he later tells how Somerset urged her to do battle immediately, and how the queen and her son at Tewkesbury 'rode about the field, encouraging their soldiers' (p. 300). O's expanded version of the SD at the end of the scene reveals knowledge of the chronicles (see 82 SD n.).

0 SD.2–3 *with ... Soldiers* This detail from O indicates that, as was common, the visible signs of battle were amplified with music.

1–50 For O's reduced and essentially different version of these lines see Appendix 2, p. 220.

1–31 Baldwin locates the origin of the figure

of the ship of state in Horace (*Odes*, 1.14), but they derive more directly from Arthur Brooke's *Romeus and Juliet*, 1562, 1359–80 (see Appendix 1, p. 217); compare *R2* 3.2.178–9.

1–2 wise ... harms Compare the proverb 'One must not bemoan a mischief but find out a remedy for it' (Tilley M999a).

2 cheerly cheerfully.

4 *holding anchor 'Holding' is probably a participial adjective which means 'the last anchor to hold' and does not designate a special sort of anchor. *Shakespeare's England*, however, glosses the phrase as 'an unusual substitute for "sheet-anchor"' i.e. a large anchor used for emergencies (I, 162).

6 pilot Henry VI. According to *OED* Shakespeare was the first to use this metaphor.

6 meet suitable.

7 fearful frightened.

8 Compare the proverb 'To cast water into the sea' (Tilley W106).

10 in at, during (Abbott 161).

11 industry labour.

11 saved prevented.

Ah, what a shame; ah, what a fault were this!
Say Warwick was our anchor, what of that?
And Montague our top-mast, what of him?
Our slaughtered friends the tackles, what of these? 15
Why, is not Oxford here another anchor,
And Somerset another goodly mast,
The friends of France our shrouds and tacklings?
And, though unskilful, why not Ned and I
For once allowed the skilful pilot's charge? 20
We will not from the helm to sit and weep
But keep our course, though the rough wind say no,
From shelves and rocks that threaten us with wrack.
As good to chide the waves as speak them fair.
And what is Edward, but a ruthless sea, 25
What Clarence but a quicksand of deceit,
And Richard, but a ragged fatal rock?
All these the enemies to our poor bark.
Say you can swim: alas, 'tis but awhile;
Tread on the sand: why, there you quickly sink; 30
Bestride the rock: the tide will wash you off,
Or else you famish – that's a three-fold death.
This speak I, lords, to let you understand,
If case some one of you would fly from us,
That there's no hoped-for mercy with the brothers 35
More than with ruthless waves, with sands, and rocks.
Why, courage then! What cannot be avoided
'Twere childish weakness to lament or fear.
PRINCE EDWARD Methinks a woman of this valiant spirit
Should, if a coward heard her speak these words, 40
Infuse his breast with magnanimity
And make him, naked, foil a man-at-arms.

---

18 The] F; These *conj. Walker*   **27** ragged] *Rowe*; raged F   **35** brothers] F *subst.*; brothers York *Oxford*   **39** SH]
This edn; Prince. F (*throughout scene*)

15 tackles ropes.
18 of from.
18 shrouds ropes that formed part of the standing rigging of a ship and which served to brace the mast laterally.
18 tacklings rigging.
19 Ned Edward, Prince of Wales, her son.
20 charge responsibility.
21 from leave.
23 shelves sandbanks.
23 wrack shipwreck (*OED* sv *sb*² 2).
24 speak . . . fair address them politely.

27 *ragged** jagged (*OED* sv 2).
28 bark vessel.
34 If case If it should happen that.
37–8 What . . . fear Compare the proverb 'What cannot be cured must be endured' (Dent C922).
41 magnanimity greatness of heart, fortitude (*OED* sv 2).
42 naked unarmed (*OED* sv 4).
42 foil defeat.
42 man-at-arms heavily armed soldier on horseback.

I speak not this as doubting any here;
For did I but suspect a fearful man
He should have leave to go away betimes   45
Lest in our need he might infect another
And make him of like spirit to himself.
If any such be here, as God forbid,
Let him depart before we need his help.

OXFORD Women and children of so high a courage   50
And warriors faint! Why, 'twere perpetual shame.
O brave young prince, thy famous grandfather
Doth live again in thee: long mayst thou live
To bear his image and renew his glories.

SOMERSET And he that will not fight for such a hope,   55
Go home to bed and, like the owl by day,
If he arise, be mocked and wondered at.

MARGARET Thanks, gentle Somerset; sweet Oxford, thanks.

PRINCE EDWARD And take his thanks that yet hath nothing else.

Enter a MESSENGER

MESSENGER Prepare you, lords, for Edward is at hand   60
Ready to fight; therefore be resolute.

OXFORD I thought no less; it is his policy
To haste thus fast to find us unprovided.

SOMERSET But he's deceived; we are in readiness.

MARGARET This cheers my heart to see your forwardness.   65

OXFORD Here pitch our battle; hence we will not budge.

Flourish, and march. Enter [KING] EDWARD, GLOUCESTER,
CLARENCE, *and Soldiers*

KING EDWARD Brave followers, yonder stands the thorny wood
Which by the heavens' assistance and your strength
Must by the roots be hewn up yet ere night.
I need not add more fuel to your fire,   70

---

66 SD GLOUCESTER] *Eds.; Richard* F; *Glo. Hast.* O

44 **fearful** frightened.
45 **leave** permission.
45 **betimes** immediately.
51 **faint** faint-hearted.
52 **grandfather** Henry V.
54 **image** likeness.
55 **hope** prince of great hope, saviour (*OED*
sv *sb* 4b).
56–7 **like . . . at** Compare the proverb 'To be

like an owl to wonder at' (Dent O94.1) and
Metamorphoses, II, 742–52.
59 **his thanks** the thanks of one who.
62 **policy** cunning.
63 **unprovided** unprepared.
65 **forwardness** zeal, ardour.
66 **pitch our battle** set our troops in battle
formation.
70 **add . . . fire** proverbial (Tilley F785).

For well I wot ye blaze to burn them out:
Give signal to the fight, and to it, lords!
MARGARET Lords, knights, and gentlemen, what I should say
My tears gainsay: for every word I speak
Ye see I drink the water of my eye.   75
Therefore, no more but this: Henry, your sovereign,
Is prisoner to the foe, his state usurped,
His realm a slaughter-house, his subjects slain,
His statutes cancelled, and his treasure spent;
And yonder is the wolf that makes this spoil.   80
You fight in justice: then, in God's name, lords,
Be valiant, and give signal to the fight.

[*Alarums to the battle. The Yorkists fly, then the chambers be discharged.*
Then enter KING EDWARD, CLARENCE, *and the rest, and*
make a great shout and cry, 'For York! For York!' And then the
queen is taken, and the prince, and Oxford and Somerset.] *Exeunt*

[5.5] *Flourish. Enter* [KING] EDWARD, GLOUCESTER,
CLARENCE [*and Soldiers; with*] QUEEN [MARGARET], OXFORD,
[*and*] SOMERSET [, *prisoners*]

KING EDWARD Now here a period of tumultuous broils.
Away with Oxford to Hammes Castle straight;

75 my eye] F; mine eies O   82 SD.1–4 *Alarums . . . Somerset*] O subst.; *Alarum, Retreat, Excursions.* F   **Act 5,**
Scene 5   5.5] *Capell; not in* F   0 SD.1–3 KING . . . *prisoners*] Capell; *Edward, Richard, Queene, Clarence, Oxford,*
Somerset F

71 **wot** know.
74–5 Compare Ps. 80.5: 'Thou hast fed
them with the bread of tears, and given them
tears to drink with great measure.'
74 **gainsay** forbid.
77 **state** sovereignty.
80 **spoil** destruction.
81–2 For O's essentially different version of
these lines see Appendix 2, p. 220.
*82 SD O's version amplifies the terse direc-
tions of F, showing how the Yorkists suffered a
preliminary reverse. The chroniclers describe
this as a tactical retreat (Holinshed, p. 319; Hall,
p. 300; see Appendix 1, p. 216.)
82 SD.1 *chambers* small cannon without
carriages used to fire salutes or, as here, in the
playhouses (see Hattaway (ed.), *1H6*, p. 19).

Act 5, Scene 5
*5.5 Somerset was executed in the market-

place at Tewkesbury (Holinshed, p. 320; Hall,
p. 301); Oxford was at Barnet but not at
Tewkesbury, and it was not until 1474 that he
surrendered and was imprisoned at Hammes
(Holinshed, p. 329; Hall, p. 304). Edward's
proclamation and the death of Prince Edward
are narrated by both chroniclers, although both
make plain that the king did not stab him himself (Holinshed, p. 320; Hall, p. 301). Sources
contemporary with the events agree that Prince
Edward was in fact killed in the fighting (Charles
Ross, *Edward IV*, 1974, p. 172 n.).
1–17 For O's essentially different version of
these lines see Appendix 2, pp. 220–1.
1 **period** end.
2 **Hammes** A town on the Somme (modern
Ham) where Oxford was sent after being
captured at St Michael's Mount in Cornwall in
1474, three years after the battle of Tewkesbury
(Holinshed, p. 329; Hall, p. 304).

For Somerset, off with his guilty head.
Go bear them hence; I will not hear them speak.
OXFORD For my part, I'll not trouble thee with words. 5

[*Exit guarded*]

SOMERSET Nor I, but stoop with patience to my fortune.

[*Exit guarded*]

MARGARET So part we sadly in this troublous world
To meet with joy in sweet Jerusalem.
KING EDWARD Is proclamation made that who finds Edward
Shall have a high reward, and he his life? 10
GLOUCESTER It is, and lo where youthful Edward comes.

Enter [*Soldiers with*] *the* PRINCE [EDWARD]

KING EDWARD Bring forth the gallant; let us hear him speak.

[*Edward struggles with his captors*]

What, can so young a thorn begin to prick?
Edward, what satisfaction canst thou make
For bearing arms, for stirring up my subjects, 15
And all the trouble thou hast turned me to?
PRINCE EDWARD Speak like a subject, proud ambitious York.
Suppose that I am now my father's mouth:
Resign thy chair and, where I stand, kneel thou
Whilst I propose the self-same words to thee, 20
Which, traitor, thou wouldst have me answer to.
MARGARET Ah that thy father had been so resolved!
GLOUCESTER That you might still have worn the petticoat
And ne'er have stol'n the breech from Lancaster.
PRINCE EDWARD Let Aesop fable in a winter's night: 25
His currish riddles sorts not with this place.

---

5 SD] O *subst.; not in* F   6 SD O *subst.; Exeunt.* F   11 SD] Capell; *Enter the Prince.* F   12 SD] *This edn; not in* F

3 **For** As for.
8 **sweet Jerusalem** 'the holy city new Jerusalem' of Rev. 21.2, i.e. heaven.
10 **he ... life** This guarantee of safety for the young prince augments the horror of his ensuing murder.
13 Compare the proverb 'It early pricks that will be a thorn' (Tilley T232); the figure fits the rose badges worn by both parties.
14 **satisfaction** atonement.
18 **mouth** mouthpiece.
19 **chair** throne.
22 **resolved** resolute (*OED* sv 4).

23 **still** always.
23–4 **worn ... breech** Compare the proverb 'She wears the breeches' (Tilley B645).
24 **breech** breeches (*OED* sv 1a).
25 **Aesop** the famous sixth-century BC Greek composer of fables about animals, who was reputed to be hunch-backed – a jibe at Gloucester's deformity.
26 **currish** (1) concerning beasts, (2) dog-like, mean-spirited, cynical – which in its Greek etymology means 'dog-like'.
26 **sorts not** are not appropriate; for the verb form see Abbott 333.

GLOUCESTER By heaven, brat, I'll plague ye for that word.

MARGARET Ay, thou wast born to be a plague to men.

GLOUCESTER For God's sake, take away this captive scold.

PRINCE EDWARD Nay, take away this scolding crook-back rather.   30

KING EDWARD Peace, wilful boy, or I will charm your tongue.

CLARENCE Untutored lad, thou art too malapert.

PRINCE EDWARD I know my duty: you are all undutiful.
　　　　　Lascivious Edward, and thou, perjured George,
　　　　　And thou, misshapen Dick, I tell ye all   35
　　　　　I am your better, traitors as ye are,
　　　　　And thou usurp'st my father's right and mine.

KING EDWARD Take that, thou likeness of this railer here.
　　　　　　　　　　　Stabs him

GLOUCESTER Sprawl'st thou? Take that to end thy agony.
　　　　　　　　　　　Stabs him

CLARENCE And there's for twitting me with perjury.   40
　　　　　　　　Stabs him. [The prince dies]

MARGARET O, kill me too!

GLOUCESTER Marry, and shall.   *Offers to kill her*

KING EDWARD Hold, Richard, hold, for we have done too much.

GLOUCESTER Why should she live to fill the world with words.
　　　　　　　　　　　[Margaret faints]

KING EDWARD What, doth she swoon? Use means for her
　　　recovery.   45
　　　　　　　[One wrings the queen by the nose]

GLOUCESTER *[Drawing Clarence aside]* Clarence, excuse me to the
　　　king, my brother.
　　　I'll hence to London on a serious matter:
　　　Ere ye come there, be sure to hear some news.

---

33 you are all] F; you're *Pope*   38 thou] Q3; the F   39 SD] *Eds.*; Rich. stabs him. F   40 SD] *This edn; Clar. stabs*
him. F   44, 45, 46 SDD] *This edn; not in* F

28 **plague** calamity, scourge (for the latter sense, see *1H6* 1.2.129 n.) The plagues which were sent as a visitation upon mankind are described in Rev. 9.
　31 **charm** put a spell on, silence (Dent CC9).
　32 **Untutored** Boorish (*OED* sv 1).
　32 **malapert** saucy.
　35 **Dick** A common designation for any base fellow; here possibly with an obscene connotation (compare *LLL* 5.2.464–5).
　37 **right** legal claim.
　38 **thou ... here** 'Thou that resemblest thy railing mother' (Johnson).

39 **Sprawl'st thou?** Are those the convulsions of death?
　39 **agony** throes of death.
　40 **perjury** See 2.2.81 n.; Clarence's act of perjury and murder of Edward haunts him in his dream before death (*R3* 1.4.55).
　42 **Marry ... shall** Indeed I will (Dent M699.1); a mild oath invoking the Virgin Mary.
　44 **fill ... words** 'Prophetic of her future role' (Wilson).
　*45 SD Wringing someone by the nose was a means of restoring circulation (see *2H6* 3.2.34).
　48 **be sure to** be confident that you will.

CLARENCE What? What?

CLOUCESTER Tower. The Tower!   *Exit*   50

MARGARET O Ned, sweet Ned, speak to thy mother, boy!
Can'st thou not speak? O traitors! Murderers!
They that stabbed Caesar shed no blood at all,
Did not offend, nor were not worthy blame,
If this foul deed were by to equal it: 55
He was a man; this, in respect, a child;
And men ne'er spend their fury on a child.
What's worse than murderer that I may name it?
No, no, my heart will burst and if I speak –
And I will speak that so my heart may burst.   60
Butchers and villains, bloody cannibals,
How sweet a plant have you untimely cropped!
You have no children, butchers! If you had,
The thought of them would have stirred up remorse;
But if you ever chance to have a child   65
Look in his youth to have him so cut off
As, deathsmen, you have rid this sweet young prince.

KING EDWARD Away with her, go bear her hence perforce.

MARGARET Nay, never bear me hence: dispatch me here;
Here sheathe thy sword; I'll pardon thee my death.   70
What, wilt thou not? – Then, Clarence, do it thou.

CLARENCE By heaven, I will not do thee so much ease.

MARGARET Good Clarence, do; sweet Clarence, do thou do it.

CLARENCE Didst thou not hear me swear I would not do it?

MARGARET Ay, but thou usest to forswear thyself: 75

50] F; The Tower man, the Tower, Ile root them out O   66 off,] O; off. F

---

50 O's version of the line makes the meaning clearer but destroys the suggestion that
Gloucester speaks in a stage whisper to the
uncomprehending Clarence.

53–4 For a review of attitudes to the murder
of Caesar, see Mildred E. Hartsock, 'The com-
plexity of *Julius Caesar*', *PMLA* 81 (1966), 56–7.

55 were … it it had taken place and then could
be compared with it.

56 respect comparison.

61 cannibals savages (*OED* Cannibal 1b).

62 untimely prematurely.

63–4 Compare the proverb 'He that has no
children knows not what love is' (Dent C341).

63 You … children In fact Edward had
several, and Clarence one son; with this sentiment compare *Mac.* 4.3.216.

64 remorse pity (*OED* sv 3).

65–7 'The condition of this warlike queen
would move compassion could it be forgotten
that she gave York, to wipe his eyes in his
captivity, a handkerchief stained with his young
child's blood' (Johnson).

67 deathsmen slaughterers.

67 rid killed (*OED* sv v 6c).

68 perforce by force.

69 dispatch kill.

70 Here In my body.

72 do … ease give you so much pleasure.

75 thou … thyself you are a habitual
perjurer.

'Twas sin before but now 'tis charity.
What, wilt thou not? Where is that devil's butcher,
        Richard?
Hard-favoured Richard? Richard, where art thou
Thou art not here? Murder is thy alms-deed;
Petitioners for blood thou ne'er put'st back.   80

KING EDWARD Away, I say; I charge ye bear her hence.
MARGARET So come to you and yours as to this prince!
[*Attendants, bearing the body of Prince Edward, lead out Queen Margaret*
                                forcibly]
KING EDWARD Where's Richard gone?
CLARENCE To London all in post – [*aside*] and, as I guess,
To make a bloody supper in the Tower.   85
KING EDWARD He's sudden if a thing comes in his head.
Now march we hence; discharge the common sort
With pay and thanks and let's away to London
And see our gentle queen how well she fares:
By this, I hope, she hath a son for me.   90

                                                          Exeunt

---

77–8 What . . . Richard?] F *subst.;* Whears the Diuels butcher, hardfauored *Richard*, O   77 devil's butcher] F
(diuels butcher); Devil-butcher *Theobald*   78 thou] *Hudson subst.;* thou? F   79 here?] *Hudson;* heere F   82 SD]
This edn; Exit Queene. F   84 SD] *Oxford; not in* F   88 let's . . . to] F; let vs towards O   90 SD] O; *Exit.* F

---

77 The line is unmetrical – although 'Where
is' and 'devil's' may be monosyllabic – and some
eds. have followed O's omission of 'Richard'. I
see no need to emend, however, given that the
metrical irregularity might serve as an index of
Margaret's excitement.
77 **devil's butcher** 'a butcher set on by the
devil' (Johnson). Theobald, however, emended
to 'devil-butcher', considering that Shakespeare
intended a 'kill-devil': for that term see
Marlowe, *Doctor Faustus*, ed. J. Jump, 1962, A
text, iv, 50–1.
78–9 *art . . . art are you that you are.
78 **Hard-favoured** Ugly.
79 **alms-deed** act of charity (*OED* sv 2).
80 **put'st back** rejected.
82 Margaret's curse comes to fruition in *R3*
where she adopts an unhistorical role as a figure
of revenge.
82 **come to** befall.

84 **all . . . post** at full speed.
*84 SD As McKerrow points out, the
chroniclers recorded that Richard murdered
Henry in the Tower (Holinshed, p. 324; Hall,
p. 303), but they followed Sir Thomas More in
pointing out that this was done without Edward's
assent (Holinshed, p. 362; Hall, p. 343; see 5.6
headnote). Line 86 seems a more appropriate
response to the first half of 84 than to the whole
of Clarence's speech.
85 **bloody supper** For feasts of death elsewhere in the trilogy, see Hattaway (ed.), *1H6*,
p. 30 and *2H6*, pp. 31–2.
86 Edward studiously refuses to take the hint
that Gloucester plans to murder King Henry.
86 **sudden** impetuous.
87 **common sort** ordinary soldiers.
90 **By this** By this time – Edward's son had
been born in fact six months before the battle of
Tewkesbury.

[5.6] *Enter* HENRY THE SIXTH, *and* GLOUCESTER, *with the Lieutenant on the walls*

GLOUCESTER Good day, my lord. What, at your book so hard?
KING HENRY Ay, my good lord – my lord I should say rather:
    'Tis sin to flatter. 'Good' was little better:
    'Good Gloucester' and 'good devil' were alike
    And both preposterous: therefore, not 'good lord'.   5
GLOUCESTER Sirrah, leave us to ourselves; we must confer.

                                                    [Exit Lieutenant]

KING HENRY So flies the reckless shepherd from the wolf;
    So first the harmless sheep doth yield his fleece
    And next his throat unto the butcher's knife.
    What scene of death hath Roscius now to act?   10
GLOUCESTER Suspicion always haunts the guilty mind;
    The thief doth fear each bush an officer,
KING HENRY The bird that hath been limèd in a bush
    With trembling wings misdoubteth every bush:

Act 5, Scene 6   **5.6**] *Capell; not in* F   **0** SD.2 *on the walls*] F *subst.; in the Tower* O   **6** SD] *Rowe; not in* F   7
reckless] *Hanmer;* wreaklesse F   **10** Roscius] *Pope; Rossius* F; *Rosius* O; Richard *Theobald conj. Warburton*

Act 5, Scene 6
***5.6** Henry died in the Tower on 21 or 22 May 1471, killed, 'as the constant fame ran', by Richard with a dagger (Holinshed, p. 324; Hall, p. 303). (Modern authorities cannot be certain that Richard was in fact the murderer but agree that the act must have been done on Edward's behalf; see Charles Ross, *Edward IV*, 1974, p. 175.) The scene is largely Shakespeare's invention and serves to establish the character of Richard in preparation for *R3*. However, Shakespeare is again indebted to More's 'Description of Richard III' found in the chronicles at the beginning of their accounts of the reign of Edward V (compare 3.2 n.).

0 SD.2 ***on the walls*** O's SD 'in the Tower' may indicate that the scene was played on the stage proper rather than in the rear gallery. However, it is more likely that O's phrase designated this same gallery, as in *1 Contention* TLN, 485, 488, 1727. Alternatively, O may here report a theatrical revision. Playing the scene aloft as F suggests, however, allows Richard to leave at the end of the scene and appear below at the beginning of the next without making an awkward re-entrance.

1 book prayer-book (*OED* 4b).
3 '**Tis ... flatter** Compare Dan. 11.32: 'And

such as wickedly break the covenant, shall he cause to sin by flattery.'
3 better (than flattery).
4 were would be.
5 preposterous inverting the natural order of things.
6 Sirrah Used to an inferior.
6 confer talk.
7 Compare John 10.11: 'an hireling ... shepherd ... seeth the wolf coming, and he leaveth the sheep and fleeth, and the wolf catcheth them and scattereth the sheep'.
7 *reckless careless, heedless.
10 What tragic scene do you wish me now to play?
10 *Roscius** The celebrated Roman comic actor (d.62 BC), whom the Elizabethans incorrectly took as the prototype tragedian (see *Ham.* 2.2.391).
11 Compare the proverb 'Who is guilty suspects everybody' (Tilley F117).
11 Suspicion Apprehension of evil (*OED* sv 4).
12 Proverbial (Tilley T112).
13–14 Compare the proverb 'Birds once limed fear all bushes' (Tilley B394).
13 limèd caught with bird-lime (a glutinous, sticky substance smeared upon twigs).
14 misdoubteth suspects.

And I, the hapless male to one sweet bird,   15
Have now the fatal object in my eye
Where my poor young was limed, was caught, and killed.
GLOUCESTER Why, what a peevish fool was that of Crete
That taught his son the office of a fowl!
And yet, for all his wings, the fool was drowned.   20
KING HENRY I, Daedalus; my poor boy, Icarus,
Thy father, Minos that denied our course;
The sun that seared the wings of my sweet boy,
Thy brother Edward; and thyself, the sea
Whose envious gulf did swallow up his life.   25
Ah, kill me with thy weapon, not with words:
My breast can better brook thy dagger's point
Than can my ears that tragic history.
But wherefore dost thou come? Is't for my life?
GLOUCESTER Think'st thou I am an executioner?   30
KING HENRY A persecutor I am sure thou art;
If murdering innocents be executing,
Why then, thou art an executioner.
GLOUCESTER Thy son I killed for his presumption.
KING HENRY Hadst thou been killed when first thou didst
      presume   35
Thou hadst not lived to kill a son of mine.
And thus I prophesy: that many a thousand
Which now mistrust no parcel of my fear,

---

15 male] F *subst.;* maile O; make *conj. Oxford*   20 fool] F *subst.;* Fowle O

---

15 **male** father (Schmidt; compare 2.1.42, *2H4* 3.2.130).

15 **bird** offspring, chick – unless it is taken as a reference to Margaret, in which case Oxford's conjecture of 'make' (mate) for 'male' may be acceptable.

16 **object** sight (*OED* sv *sb* 2).

16 **eye** mind's eye.

17 **Where** When.

18 **peevish** mischievous, harmful (*OED* 2).

18 **fool...Crete** the cunning Athenian craftsman Daedalus who, in order to escape imprisonment at Minos' hands in Crete, equipped his son Icarus with wings attached to his body which melted when he flew near the sun with the result that he fell into the sea (see Ovid, *Ars Amatoria*, II, 21–100); for this and related passages, see Armstrong, p. 38.

19 **office** function.

19 **fowl** 'Fool' and 'fowl' may have been pronounced similarly (see collation and Cercignani, p. 198; see also Weston Babcock, 'Fools, fowls . . .' *SQ* 2 (1951), 211–19).

20 **for all** in spite of.

22 **denied** forbade.

22 **Minos** See 18 n. above.

23 **sun** another reference to the Yorkist badge.

25 **envious** malignant.

25 **gulf** (1) whirlpool (*OED* sv 3), (2) voracious gullet (*OED* 3b).

27 **brook** endure.

28 **history** narrative, tale.

38 'Who suspect no part of what my fears presage' (Johnson).

And many an old man's sigh, and many a widow's,
And many an orphan's water-standing eye –   40
Men for their sons', wives for their husbands',
Orphans for their parents' timeless death –
Shall rue the hour that ever thou wast born.
The owl shrieked at thy birth – an evil sign;
The night-crow cried, aboding luckless time;   45
Dogs howled and hideous tempests shook down trees;
The raven rooked her on the chimney's top
And chattering pies in dismal discords sung;
Thy mother felt more than a mother's pain
And yet brought forth less than a mother's hope,   50
To wit, an indigested and deformèd lump,
Not like the fruit of such a goodly tree.
Teeth hadst thou in thy head when thou wast born
To signify thou cam'st to bite the world;
And if the rest be true, which I have heard,   55
Thou cam'st –
GLOUCESTER I'll hear no more: die, prophet, in thy speech,
                    Stabs him
For this, amongst the rest, was I ordained.
KING HENRY Ay, and for much more slaughter after this,
O God forgive my sins, and pardon thee!   *Dies*   60
GLOUCESTER What, will the aspiring blood of Lancaster
Sink in the ground? I thought it would have mounted.
See how my sword weeps for the poor king's death!

---

41 sons'...husbands'] *This edn;* Sonnes, Wiues for their Husbands F   42 Orphans] F; And orphans F2   46
tempests] O; Tempest F   47 rooked her] F, O *subst.;* rocked her *Johnson;* croaked *Capell*   48 discords] F *subst.;*
discord O   51 indigested and deformèd] F *subst.;* indigest deformèd *Malone*   56 cam'st –] F; camst into the
world O; cam'st in the World with thy legs forward *Theobald*   57] *Pope;* Ile ... more: / Dye ... speech, F   62 in]
F; into *conj. Oxford*

40 **water-standing** flooded with tears.
42 **timeless** untimely (*OED* 1).
44 **owl** the sceech-owl or barn owl, a bird of ill-omen as in Isa. 34.14–15.
45 Proverbial (Dent R33).
45 **night-crow** the name given by poets to a bird supposed to croak in the night and to be of evil omen.
45 **aboding** presaging.
47 **rooked her** crouched, cowered.
48 **pies** magpies (considered to be unlucky).
48 **dismal** sinister.
51 **indigested** shapeless (echoing Ovid's description of chaos as *rudis indigestaque moles* (*Metamorphoses,* I, 7)).

52 Compare Matt. 7.18: 'A good tree cannot bring forth evil fruit.'
56 See collation. Theobald's insistence that Henry should utter what Richard quotes at 71 is logical but not perhaps dramatically or psychologically necessary.
57 SD The chroniclers report that Richard killed Henry with a dagger (see headnote), but Richard invokes his 'sword' at 63.
61–2 The mock apocalyptic tone recalls one of the last lines of Marlowe's Faustus: 'See, see where Christ's blood streams in the firmament' (*Doctor Faustus* XIX, 146; compare Rev. 19.13).
63 **sword** See 57 SD above.

O may such purple tears be alway shed
From those that wish the downfall of our house!   65
If any spark of life be yet remaining,
Down, down to hell, and say I sent thee thither –
                Stabs him again
I that have neither pity, love, nor fear.
Indeed 'tis true that Henry told me of,
For I have often heard my mother say   70
I came into the world with my legs forward.
Had I not reason, think ye, to make haste
And seek their ruin that usurped our right?
The midwife wondered and the women cried,
'O Jesus bless us, he is born with teeth!'   75
And so I was, which plainly signified
That I should snarl, and bite, and play the dog.
Then, since the heavens have shaped my body so,
Let hell make crook'd my mind to answer it.
I had no father, I am like no father;   80
I have no brother, I am like no brother;
And this word 'love', which greybeards call divine,
Be resident in men like one another
And not in me: I am myself alone.
Clarence, beware: thou keep'st me from the light;   85
But I will sort a pitchy day for thee,

---

75 Jesus] F, O *subst.;* Jesu *Cairncross*   80] O *subst.; not in* F   81 brother ... brother] F *subst.;* brothers ... brothers
O   82 'love'] *Eds.;* [Loue] F   85 keep'st] F3; keptst F; keptst O

64 **purple** blood-red.

64 **tears** i.e., drops of blood; 'purple tears' occurs also in *Ven.* 1054.

67 Iden expresses the same sentiment when killing Cade (*2H6* 4.10.72).

69 **that** what.

70–7 For beliefs concerning monstrous births, see Thomas, *passim.*

71 See 56 n.

73 **right** claim to the throne.

74 **wondered** marvelled.

75 Compare *R3* 4.4.49 and the proverb, spoken when any prince was born with teeth, 'The thorn comes forth with his point forwards' (Tilley T234).

75 **Jesus** Although this form occurs only four times in the canon compared with 21 occurrences of 'Jesu' there seems no justification for emendation.

77 **play the dog** compare 5.5.26 n.

79 **answer** correspond to.

*80 This line from O which does not appear in F and which serves to build up a rhetorical climax at 84 may well have been omitted because of compositorial eye-skip, or added in performance – it is proleptic, in that Gloucester may be planning his murder of Clarence (*R3* 1.4).

82 Compare 1 John, 4.7: 'Beloved, let us love one another, for love cometh of God.'

83 **like** who resemble.

84 **I ... alone** Richard only comes to feel the force of this in his recognition speech in *R3* – see 5.3.184.

86 **sort ... thee** Compare the proverb 'It will be a black day for somebody' (Tilley D88).

86 **sort** assign, arrange (*OED* sv *v* 1).

86 **pitchy** black.

> For I will buzz abroad such prophecies
> That Edward shall be fearful of his life
> And then, to purge his fear, I'll be thy death.
> Henry and his son are gone; thou, Clarence, next,   90
> And by one and one I will dispatch the rest,
> Counting myself but bad till I be best.
> I'll throw thy body in another room,
> And triumph, Henry, in thy day of doom.

Exit [with the body]

[5.7] *Flourish. Enter* KING [EDWARD], QUEEN [ELIZABETH],
CLARENCE, GLOUCESTER, HASTINGS, [a] *Nurse* [with the
YOUNG PRINCE], *and Attendants*

KING EDWARD   Once more we sit in England's royal throne
> Repurchased with the blood of enemies:
> What valiant foemen, like to autumn's corn,
> Have we mowed down in tops of all their pride:
> Three Dukes of Somerset, threefold renowned   5
> For hardy and undoubted champions;
> Two Cliffords, as the father and the son;

90–1] O *subst.*; King *Henry*, and the Prince his Son are gone, / *Clarence* thy turne is next, and then the rest, F; King *Henry*, and the Prince his sonne are gone, / And *Clarence* thou art next must follow them, / So by one and one dispatching all the rest. Q3   90 Clarence] O; Clarence, art *Oxford*   94 triumph,] *Eds.*; Triumph F   94 SD *with the body*] *Capell; not in* F   **Act 5, Scene 7**   5.7] *Capell; not in* F   o SD.1 ELIZABETH] O; *not in* F   o SD.2–3 *with*... PRINCE] O; *not in* F   4 tops] F; top *Rowe*   5 renowned] Q3; renowmd O; Renowne F   6 undoubted] F, O *subst.*; redoubted *conj. Capell*

87 **buzz abroad** spread about.

88 **of** for (Abbott 174).

89 **purge** 'cure by lancing' (Wilson); compare *Mac.* 5.2.28.

*90–1 It is almost certain that F was badly contaminated here by Q3, the compositor of which seems to have padded his copy as a result of imperfect casting off (see collation). O's version is metrically superior and rhetorically more forceful.

91 Richard is shown contriving Clarence's downfall and murder in *R3* 1.1 and 1.3–4.

92 **bad . . . best** Compare the proverb 'Bad is the best' (Dent B316).

92 **bad** wretched, insignificant (*OED* sv 1).

94 **triumph . . . doom** Compare the proverb 'Death's day is doomsday' (Dent D161).

94 **triumph** exult.

94 **of doom** on which you face your maker.

Act 5, Scene 7

*5.7 Margaret was not in fact ransomed until October 1475, more than four years after the battle of Tewkesbury – the chroniclers report this, however, immediately after their account of the battle (Holinshed, p. 321; Hall, p. 301).

2 **Repurchased** Regained.

3 **corn** wheat.

4 **in tops** at the height.

5 **threefold** in three ways (*OED adv.* 1).

5 *renowned F's 'Renowne' exemplifies a common d/e error.

6 **undoubted** fearless (Schmidt; compare *1H6* 3.3.41): Wilson offers 'unquestionable' citing *OED* 2; Capell's conjecture 'redoubted' is attractive as this usage of 'undoubted', although confirmed by O, is rare.

6 **champions** men of valour (*OED* Champion *sb* 1).

7 **as** namely.

And two Northumberlands – two braver men
Ne'er spurred their coursers at the trumpet's sound;
With them, the two brave bears, Warwick and Montague,   10
That in their chains fettered the kingly lion
And made the forest tremble when they roared.
Thus have we swept suspicion from our seat
And made our footstool of security. –
Come hither, Bess, and let me kiss my boy. –   15
Young Ned, for thee thine uncles and myself
Have in our armours watched the winter's night –
Went all afoot in summer's scalding heat –
That thou might'st repossess the crown in peace:
And of our labours thou shalt reap the gain.   20
GLOUCESTER [*Aside*] I'll blast his harvest, if your head were laid;
For yet I am not looked on in the world.
This shoulder was ordained so thick to heave,
And heave it shall some weight, or break my back:
Work thou the way – and that shalt execute.   25
KING EDWARD Clarence and Gloucester, love my lovely queen,
And kiss your princely nephew, brothers both.
CLARENCE The duty that I owe unto your majesty
I seal upon the lips of this sweet babe.
ELIZABETH Thanks, noble Clarence; worthy brother, thanks.   30

21 if] F; *and* O   21, 33 SDD] *Rowe; not in* F   25 way –] *Capell;* way, F   25 that shalt] F; thou shalt O; that shall F3; this shall *conj. Johnson*   25 shalt] F; shall *Brooke*   30 SH] O *subst.;* Cla. F   30 Thanks] O, *Theobald;* Thanke F

9 **coursers** chargers.
10 **bears** alluding to Warwick's badge, a bear chained to a ragged staff – see *2H6* 5.1.144–5.
13–14 'For the idea of making of enemies a footstool as a symbol of security, see Ps. 110.1: "The Lord said unto my Lord: sit thou at my right hand until I make thine enemies thy footstool".' (Noble).
13 **suspicion** anxiety, apprehension (*OED* sv 4).
13 **seat** throne.
14 Almost identical ('on' for 'of') with Marlowe, *The Massacre at Paris*, 744.
17 **watched** stayed awake.
20–1 Compare John 4.37–8: '. . . one soweth and another reapeth. I sent you to repay that whereon ye bestowed no labour: other men laboured, and ye are entered into their labours.'
21 **blast** blight.
21 **his** the young prince's.
21 **head** (1) Edward's head, (2) a head of wheat.

21 **laid** (1) put to rest in the grave, (2) flattened by storm.
22 **looked on** respected.
23 **thick** compactly.
23 **heave** swell up (*OED v* 23).
24 And it will raise the weight of the crown or it will kill me (as a horse is killed).
25 'I believe we should read "and *this* shall [see collation] execute". Richard, laying his hand on his forehead, says, "Work thou the way – ", then, bringing down his hand and beholding it, "– and *this* shall execute." Though "that" may stand, the arm being included in the shoulder' (Johnson).
25 **Work . . . way** Devise a way.
25 **thou** i.e. himself.
25 **that** i.e. this task.
29 **seal** confirm.
*30 SH O's reading is confirmed by 26 above.
30 'A typical formal chiasmus' (Cairncross).
30 **brother** brother-in-law.

GLOUCESTER And that I love the tree from whence thou
      sprang'st,
      Witness the loving kiss I give the fruit.
      [*Aside*] To say the truth, so Judas kissed his master
      And cried 'All hail!' when as he meant all harm.
KING EDWARD Now am I seated as my soul delights,   35
      Having my country's peace and brothers' loves.
CLARENCE What will your grace have done with Margaret?
      Reignier, her father, to the King of France
      Hath pawned the Sicils and Jerusalem,
      And hither have they sent it for her ransom.   40
KING EDWARD Away with her and waft her hence to France!
      And now what rests but that we spend the time
      With stately triumphs, mirthful comic shows,
      Such as befits the pleasure of the court. –
      Sound, drums and trumpets! Farewell, sour annoy!   45
      For here, I hope, begins our lasting joy.
                            [*Flourish. March.*] *Exeunt*

FINIS

38 Reignier] *Rowe; Reynard* F   45 Farewell] F *subst.;* farewell to O   46 SD] *This edn; Exeunt omnes* F

31–2 Compare the proverb 'Many kiss the child for the nurse's sake' (Tilley C312).
31 **tree** (family of York).
33 **so . . . master** see Matt. 26.48–9.
34 **All hail** This is the salutation used by Judas in the plays from the York and Chester cycles that present the betrayal. In Matt. and Mark Judas is made to say 'Hail, Master'. The phrase occurs again in *R2* 4.1.169; compare Armstrong, pp. 93, 96.
34 **when as** while on the contrary.

35 **my soul delights** compare Isa. 55.2: 'let your soul delight in fatness'.
39 **the Sicils** Naples and Sicily.
40 **it** the money borrowed.
41 **waft** convey by water.
42 **rests** remains.
43 **triumphs** joyful celebrations.
44 **befits** For the singular form of the verb, see Abbott 333.
45 **sour** bitter.
45 **annoy** vexation, trouble (*OED* sv *sb* 1).

TEXTUAL ANALYSIS

The first edition of *3 Henry VI* appeared in 1595[1] as an octavo. The title-page reads: *The true Tragedie of Richard Duke of Yorke, and the death of good King Henrie the Sixt, with the whole contention betweene the two Houses Lancaster and Yorke, as it was sundrie times acted by the Right Honourable the Earle of Pembrooke his seruants* (O).[2] It was printed by P[eter] S[hort] for Thomas Millington who also published the first quarto of *2 Henry VI*.[3] The next edition was a quarto (Q2),[4] printed from a copy of the octavo in 1600 by W[illiam] W[hite], also for Millington. In 1619 Thomas Pavier, to whom Millington had transferred his rights in the play on 19 April 1602,[5] combined it with a version of *2 Henry VI*, printing the two plays with a joint title derived from the title-pages of O and Q2: *The Whole contention betweene the two Famous Houses, Lancaster and Yorke.*[6] This extensively edited text[7] appeared in an undated quarto form (Q3)[8] as part of a set of ten plays printed by William Jaggard who, four years later, was to print the First Folio of Shakespeare's works (F). This edition was the first to bear Shakespeare's name on its title-page, but there is no reason to assume that the variant readings it offers derive from anyone other than printing-shop editors or compositors.

---

1 It was not entered on the Stationers' Register, although this was not uncommon (see W. W. Greg, *Some Aspects and Problems of London Publishing between 1550 and 1650*, 1956, ch. 4); Millington's entry of *2H6* on 12 March 1594 specifically describes the action of *2H6*.

2 I have referred to this text in the collation and elsewhere as O, but, as the two reprints that derive from it are quartos, I have used 'quarto' to designate this family of texts. For an argument that O offers the original title of *3H6* see Wells and Taylor, *Textual Companion*, p. 199. I would conjecture that this title was used only when the play was being toured.

3 The Octavo was probably issued as an unbound pamphlet and sold for 8 pence, a higher than average price for a publication of this kind: see Francis R. Johnson, 'Notes on English retail book-prices, 1550–1640', *The Library* 5 (1950), 83–112.

4 The title is *The True Tragedie of Richarde Duke of Yorke, and the death of good King Henrie the sixt: With the whole contention betweene the two Houses, Lancaster and Yorke; as it was sundry times acted by the Right Honourable the Earle of Pembrooke his seruantes.*

5 The entry reads 'The first and Second pte of henry the vj[t] ij bookes'. This has commonly been interpreted to designate *2* and *3H6*. But as *1H6* was certainly in existence by this time, it is either a mistake or, possibly, an entry which covers all three parts of the play, *2H6* and *3H6* being considered as one play. In the collective entry of new plays for F in 1623 we find 'The thirde parte of Henry ye Sixt'.

6 The fact that the phrase 'the whole contention...' was used by Millington in O and Q2 to designate that part of the action that occurs in *3H6* (the word 'contention' is used at 1.2.6) would militate against the assumption that *2* and *3H6* were originally known under a 'contention' title; compare Wells and Taylor, *Textual Companion*, pp. 177–8.

7 Wells and Taylor, *Textual Companion*, pp. 198, 205.

8 This too was set up from a copy of O. See Peter W. M. Blayney, '"Compositor B" and the Pavier quartos: Problems of identification and their implication', *The Library* 27 (1972), 179–206; Peter W. M. Blayney, 'The Compositors of the Pavier quartos', *The Library* 31 (1976), 143–5; S. W. Reid, 'The Compositors of the Pavier quartos', *The Library* 31 (1976), 392–4. The quarto texts are collated in vol. 40 of The Cambridge Shakespeare, ed. W. A. Wright, 1895.

If, as it would seem, F derives from Shakespeare's manuscript or 'foul papers' (sharing some readings with the quarto texts), three conjectures are possible: that F was set up basically from an authorial manuscript but with some reference to a quarto text, that certain quarto passages derive in part from a manuscript identical or related to that used for the preparation of F, or, finally, that copy for o was annotated by someone (a player?) with memories of performance based on a version of the text recorded in the foul papers. The first is the most likely.[1]

These quarto texts are about a third shorter than the text which was printed in the folio edition which appeared some seven years after Shakespeare's death. There it is entitled *The third Part of Henry the Sixt, with the death of the Duke of Yorke*. The Henry VI plays are placed among the history plays after *Henry V*, in the order, that is, of monarchical reign and not the order of composition by Shakespeare. *3 Henry VI* occupies pp. 147–72 of the volume. The texts had been prepared by John Heminge and Henry Condell, Shakespeare's fellow players, and printed in the workshop of William Jaggard.

The texts in the subsequent seventeenth-century folios (1632, 1664, 1685) are based ultimately on this first edition. Although F2 offers a number of metrical regularisations (see collation), these represent only conjectures emanating from the printing house responsible for that text.

The quarto texts bear all the signs of deriving from a playhouse.[2] The stage directions are often fuller (see, for example, 1.1.0 SD, 5.1.82 SD), they generally indicate which scenes require 'extras' (soldiers, etc.) and, on occasion, they iron out irregularities that are to be found in the folio text.[3] They contain short passages of dialogue or 'gag' that were probably improvised in rehearsal or performance (see, for example, 3.2.11 which enlivens F's 'Yea, is it so [?]' with the proverbial 'I, is the wind in that doore?',[4] and 3.2.35 which expands F's 'and God forbid that' to 'Marie godsforbot man'). Lines are displaced from their contexts: 'But *Hercules* himselfe must yeeld to ods' (2.1.53) and 'And so the valiant *Montague* gaue vp the ghost' (2.3.22) appear in o's version of 5.2.[5] The dull repetition of o's

> KING HENRY Let me but raigne in quiet whilst I liue.
> YORK Confirme the crowne to me and to mine heires
>   And thou shalt raigne in quiet whilst thou liu'st   (o, sig. A5ʳ)

is seemingly due to an actor forgetting Henry's line 'Let me for this my life-time reign as king' (1.1.171). On two occasions lines are added to round a scene off:

> Come let vs haste awaie, and hauing past these cares,
> *I*le post to *Yorke*, and see how *Edward* fares.   (o, sig. D6ʳ)

---

1 See below.
2 See Date and occasion, p. 60.
3 See 2.5.54 SD–122 SD n.
4 See Tilley W419.
5 Sigs. E2ᵛ and E3ʳ.

and

> Come lets goe, for if we slacke this faire
> Bright Summers daie, sharpe winters
> Showers will marre our hope for haie.   (o, sig E3ᵛ)

replace scene endings in F that lack final couplets (4.3.63–4 and 5.3.23–4).

The octavo text is therefore now commonly agreed to be a memorial recon-struction of London performances[1] – rather than, as scholars of earlier gener-ations thought, a source or early draft of the text found in the folio.[2] The text is also shortened[3] and a few characters are omitted: Lord Stafford from 4.1, the Watchmen from 4.3, the Lieutenant from 4.6, and the 'brethren' of the Lord Mayor of York in 4.7.[4]

There is some evidence of direct consultation of the chronicles:[5] these would seem to suggest that Shakespeare was at hand to tell the players what to do. On the other hand, there are many mistakes, especially dynastic, as in *2 Henry VI*,[6] and in o's version of York's assignment of tasks to his sons.[7] Peter Alexander demonstrated how, in particular, o's version of 4.1.47–57,[8] which describes the relationships between the queen's relatives, could have been written only by a reporter who did not understand the facts of the case.[9] These texts also contain echoes of plays by Shakespeare and others[10] which supports the case for memorial reconstruction and almost certainly destroys the case of those who would see the play as an early draft. Besides being considerably shorter, the quarto texts show signs that the play was possibly, as we would expect, subject to

---

1 This was first demonstrated by Peter Alexander, *Shakespeare's 'Henry VI' and 'Richard III'*, 1929, and Madeleine Doran, *Henry VI, Parts II and III: Their Relation to the Contention and the True Tragedy*, 1928; see also Marco Mincoff, '*Henry VI Part III* and the *True Tragedy*', *ES* 42 (1961), 273–88; and A. S. Cairncross, 'Pembroke's Men and some Shakespearian piracies', *SQ* 11 (1960), 335–49. From the near congruity of their lines in both texts, I concur with Alexander that the players who took the parts of Clifford and Warwick were largely responsible for setting up the text. Madeleine Doran, however, and Scott McMillin ('Casting for Pembroke's Men: The *Henry VI* quartos and *The Taming of A Shrew*', *SQ* 23 (1972), 141–59), suggest that the compilers were a group of actors. See also Date and occasion, pp. 57–60. Alexander's assumptions and conclusions are challenged but not convincingly overthrown by Steven Urkowitz, '"If I mistake in these foundations which I build upon": Alexander's analysis of *Henry VI Parts 2 and 3*', *ELR* 18 (1988), 230–56.
2 Dr Johnson, however, considered them to have been taken down by a reporter over various performances (V, 225).
3 Margaret's speech deploring the disinheritance of Prince Edward (1.1.217–227) is cut, Henry's 54-line soliloquy at the opening of 2.5 is reduced to 13 lines, Richard's 71-line soliloquy at the end of 3.2 to a mere 30 lines.
4 Bourbon is not listed in o's opening SD in 3.3, but his presence is indicated in dialogue later in the scene (sig. D3ʳ).
5 See notes to 2.1.177–81, 3.1.12 SD, 4.2.26–27 SD, 5.1.82 SD, 5.4 n., 5.4.82 SD.
6 See Hattaway (ed.), *2H6*, pp. 234–5. In 2.3, o reports the death of Warwick's father (sig. C1ʳ) rather than his brother (see 2.3.15 n.)
7 1.2.36–41, and see 2.3.15 n.
8 See Appendix 2, p. 221.
9 Alexander, pp. 63–4.
10 See Appendix 2, pp. 221–3.

revision in performance,[1] especially in the fourth act where certain scenes are transposed.[2] The clumsy juxtaposition in O of 4.3 and 4.5, however, which deal with King Edward's capture and release respectively, suggests that the re-arrangement is more likely to derive from memory lapses:[3] F interposes 4.4 in which Edward's consort hears of her husband's loss of office, a simple device which both suggests the passage of time and makes for dramatic contrast. On the other hand, O's fusing of 4.6 and a truncated version of 4.8 which creates a juxtaposition of Henry's blessing of Henry Tudor with the arrival of Edward, generates effective dramatic irony.

The omissions in the quartos, in other words, are not to be accounted for simply by lapses in memory. For although these texts are commonly known as 'bad quartos', it may well be that behind them lie 'good acting versions', cut or adapted for a smaller playing company.[4] At 1.1.120−4, for example, O supplies lines that serve to make Henry much less confident in his confrontation with York.[5] There is, however, no way of telling whether this and other revisions were made with or without Shakespeare's authority,[6] and if they were, there is no compelling argument that allows a modern editor to decide whether the author's second thoughts are to be preferred over his first. Only occasionally have I included passages that appear solely in the quarto texts into my own version of the play, but, in the commentary, I have alerted readers and directors to their presence in Appendix 2. It may well be decided that a quarto version of part of a sequence would suit a particular modern revival.

F therefore stands revealed as the only authoritative text for the play as a whole, although there is no doubt that O records details of staging of per-formances with which Shakespeare was probably associated.[7]

We must now consider what may have happened to the transmission of copy from manuscript to printed book. The text of a Renaissance play was subject to alteration or corruption at up to seven stages: by the author (or authors) while still in preliminary drafts; by authors or scribes preparing a 'fair copy' for delivery to a company;[8] by an adapter connected with the company by whom it was

---

1 See, for example, 1.1.14 n., 2.3.7−13 n., 2.5.54 SD−122 SD n., 2.6.42−4 n., 3.2.193 n., 4.2.26−27 SD n., 4.7.71−6 n., 5.1.80−2 n., 5.2.50 n., 5.4.1−50 n., 5.4.81−5 n., 5.5.1−17 n., 5.6.0 SD n., 5.6.80 n.
2 The sequence in O runs 4.1−3, 4.5, 4.4, 4.7, 4.6, 4.8; there are similar transpositions in *1 Contention*; see Hattaway (ed.), *2H6*, p. 216.
3 This was suggested by A. Hart, *Stolne and Surreptitious Copies*, 1942, pp. 121 ff.
4 See Scott McMillin, 'Casting for Pembroke's Men: the *Henry VI* quartos and *The Taming of a Shrew*', *SQ* 23 (1972), 141−59; Robert E. Burkhart, *Shakespeare's Bad Quartos*, 1975, pp. 29−54.
5 See Appendix 2, p. 218; compare Wells and Taylor, *Textual Companion*, p. 200. It is conceivable that the O version, which suggests that two men may have equal claims on the throne, was censored. However, for this to have happened, the new version would have had to be written into F, which is unlikely.
6 For an account of various kinds of textual 'piracy' see Wells and Taylor, *Modernizing Shakespeare's Spelling*, p. 110 n.
7 Hattaway, pp. 52−3.
8 See Fredson Bowers, *On Editing Shakespeare*, 1966.

performed; by the book-holder (who doubled as a prompter)[1] annotating the foul papers[2] or preparing a copy for performance; by an editor preparing copy for the printer;[3] by the compositors; and by the proof-reader. It is logical to look for evidence of changes of these kinds in reverse order and so produce a theory about the nature of the copy used by the compositors who turned the manuscript into the printed texts that survive. As a preliminary, we should note that proof-readers did not always check proofs against copy, that their aim was simply to correct typographical inaccuracies or irregularities, and that they might well thereby introduce corruption by correction. In the case of *3 Henry VI*, there are three non-textual variants as well as four textual variants in 5.7 which is printed on a part-page (q4^v); all of these are obvious and reference to copy would not have been required.[4]

It was established by Charlton Hinman that *3 Henry VI* was, like the remainder of the histories, set by two compositors, A and B who, in Jaggard's shop, were responsible for setting most of the folio. Spelling tests (A preferred the forms 'doe', 'goe', 'heere'; B the forms 'do', 'go', 'here') and the tracing of individual pieces of type allowed Hinman to assign A, working from case x, and B, working for the most part from from case y, the following stints:[5]

Ax set 04^r–06^v	pp. 147–52	1.1.1 –2.1.75
By set p1^r–p3^v	pp. 153–8	2.1.76 –3.2.1
Ax set p4^r–p5^r	pp. 159–61	3.2.2 –3.3.151
By set p5^v	p. 162	3.3.152–4.1.4
Ax set p6^{r-v}	pp. 163–4	4.1.5 –4.3.40
Bx set q1^r	p. 16[5]	4.3.41 –4.6.15
Ax set q1^v–q3^v	pp. 16[6]–70	4.6.16 –5.5.43
By set q4^{r-v}	pp. 171–2	5.5.44 –5.7.46

This analysis accounts for spelling inconsistencies that seemed to earlier scholars to point to manuscript copy, either produced by more than one hand or written by more than one author.

The next stage in our investigation must be to decide whether the copy used by the compositors derives from a manuscript used in the playhouse or not. Evidence of theatrical stage directions, added presumably by the book-holder, would suggest that the text passed through such a stage: we must decide whether the copy was a holographic (or possibly scribal) text marked up by the book-

---

1 W. W. Greg, *The Shakespeare First Folio*, 1955, p. 100.
2 Greg, *First Folio*, p. 109.
3 These have been studied by S. W. Reid, 'The editing of Folio *Romeo and Juliet*', *SB* 35 (1982), 43–66, and by Eleanor Prosser, *Shakespeare's Anonymous Editors* (1981).
4 Charlton Hinman, *The Printing and Proof-Reading of the First Folio of Shakespeare*, 2 vols., 1963, I, 275–6.
5 Hinman, *Printing and Proof-Reading*, II, 68–72, 108–17; the setting of *3H6* was interrupted when the compositors returned to set the end of *R2* and *1* and *2H4* which had not been printed, probably because of a dispute over copyright with Matthew Law (Hinman, II, 523).

holder in preparation for the copying out of the prompt-book, or was a scribal copy of a fully annotated prompt-book.[1] The possibly misplaced 'flourish' at both 1.1.275 SD and 4.7.71 SD suggests that the word could have been added in the margin of the manuscript – but this could have been done either by the author (or scribe) or the book-holder. At 2.2.89–92 lines which are patently Edward's are assigned in both F and O to Clarence, which might suggest that an error was made in the prompt-book with subsequent contamination of F by O. However, this could equally be an authorial (or scribal) error which was not picked up by the book-holder. There are, but really only in 3.3, more than the usual number of stage directions which amplify implicit directions in the text[2] – but then the nature of the action of the scene requires them. They are therefore likely to be authorial. There are, on the other hand, no mentions of important properties like the arrow that pierces Clifford's neck (2.6.0 SD) or the roses which serve to distinguish the two factions (1.1.0 SD.4 and 49 SD.2). It is therefore reasonable to assume that if a prompt-book was used as copy it was a manuscript only partially marked up and not a document newly prepared by a scribe.[3]

We must now look to F to see whether it presents positive signs of authorial copy[4] to support our hypothesis further. It does. It contains descriptive stage directions like those at 1.1.169 and 1.1.207 SD: *He stamps with his foot, and the soldiers show themselves*[5] and *Sennet. Here they come down*;[6] at 4.1.6 the stage direction calls for a symmetrical stage grouping;[7] there is a locality note at 4.2.0 SD: '*Enter Warwicke and Oxford in England*';[8] and there is a description at 4.3.0 SD that explains the action (rather than any scenic provision): *Enter three* WATCHMEN *to guard* [*King Edward's*] *tent.*[9] Necessary entrances and exits are missing,[10] permissive (see '*. . . Exeter, and the rest*' at 1.1.49.2 SD), or incorrect

1 Greg lists all the stage directions and ascribes 'the very full provision of noises' to the book-holder (*First Folio*, pp. 181–2), but the nature of the action surely demands them. Wilson disagreed with Greg on the grounds that the names of actors for characters etc. indicated that the manuscript would not have passed through the hands of a book-holder ('The copy for *2* and *3 Henry VI* 1623', *3H6*, pp. 117–22). Cairncross argues, unnecessarily, that the copy was a scribal transcript of foul papers (pp. xxiii–xxiv).

2 See the SDD at 0, 16, 26, 46, 59, 111, 131, 160, 163–6, 250.

3 The work of a book-holder may be discerned by comparing the stage directions of the quarto editions of *Richard II*, which derive ultimately from foul papers, with those in the Folio text, which derives from a prompt-book. See A. Gurr (ed.), *Richard II*, 1984, pp. 176–9.

4 Greg, *First Folio*, pp. 124 ff.

5 O reads here 'Enter Souldiers' (sig. A5'); see also 5.3.OSD: '*Enter . . .* EDWARD *in triumph.*'

6 For a discussion of 'Here' in stage directions which Greg and others took to be a characteristic of Nashe, see Greg, *First Folio*, index; compare Hattaway (ed.), *1H6*, p. 191; see also 3.3.0 SD.

7 See Hattaway, p. 56.

8 Compare 3.3.0 SD and 4.3.27 SD.

9 See Richard Hosley, 'More about "tents" on Bosworth Field', *SQ* 7 (1956), 458–9.

10 See, for example, 1.1.34 SD, 186 SD, 188 SD, 190 SD, 212 SD.2, etc. There is a repeated entrance for the 'Father that hath kill'd his sonne' in 2.5 (54 SD.2 and 78 SD; see 2.5.54 SD–122 SD). There is no way of telling whether the former represents a massed entry (see Greg, *Editorial Problem, passim*) for the sequence, or a revision (as Alexander Leggatt, *Shakespeare's Political Drama*, 1988, p. 247 n., argues – on the grounds of theatrical effectiveness; see also Wells and Taylor, *Textual Companion*, p. 198).

(Somerset for Exeter at 4.8.0); Montague is a 'ghost' character[1] at 2.6.30 SD, and Bourbon, Pembroke, Stafford, and Sir William Stanley are given no lines at all;[2] speech prefixes are patently incorrect,[3] inconsistent,[4] or designate both names and roles,[5] and actors' names appear in both stage directions and speech headings: 'Gabriel [Spencer]' (1.2.47 SD, 1.2.49 SH) and '[John] Sinklo' and 'Humphrey [Jeffes?]' (3.1.0 SD).[6] The proclamation at 4.7.73 is incomplete.

It is probable, however, that the compositors consulted a copy of O or Q on occasion when their manuscript was unclear or damaged, almost certainly Q3.[7] McKerrow argued that 4.2.1–18 must have derived from a quarto text,[8] but as most of these lines are spoken by Warwick, and the actor who took that part was probably one of the reporters, the case is not proven.

It is also possible that O records some cuts made by a censor or by the company to avoid censorship.[9] For example, Margaret's reflection in F on the tyrannical policies of Edward (3.3.66–70), the passages (4.6.1–37 and 53–7) which record the way in which Henry elected to keep his crown but resign his power,[10] and the proclamation of Edward's treachery and the confiscation of his land and goods, do not appear in O. (The same kind of intervention to remove mention of the eclipse of monarchical power seems to have occurred in performances of *2 Henry VI*.[11]) However, these passages may well have been omitted simply as part of the process of abridging the play.

The conclusion must be, therefore, that the basic copy for F's version of *3 Henry VI*, as for *2 Henry VI*, was holographic with some possible annotation.[12] There was also some reference to Q3 on occasion in order to make good illegible passages of the foul papers.

---

1 See Greg, *First Folio*, pp. 112, 195.

2 See 3.3, 4.1, 4.3, and 4.5; of the four, only Pembroke is cut from O.

3 See 1.1.69, 2.2.133, and 5.7.30, all of which are corrected in O.

4 Both *'Yorke'* and *'Plant.'* are to be found in 1.1 (see Greg, *Editorial Problem*, p. 103).

5 Margaret is generally *'Queene'* but *'Marg.'* throughout 3.3; Lady Grey is *'Wid.'* throughout 3.2, *'Gray'* throughout 4.4.

6 Greg, *Editorial Problem*, p. 40.

7 For a general survey of Q > F transmission, see J. K. Walton, *The Quarto Copy for the First Folio of Shakespeare*, 1971, Wells and Taylor, *Textual Analysis*, pp. 198–9; Cairncross offers an inherently unlikely suggestion that the compositors constructed a 'galley' from alternate sides of Q2 and Q3 (p. xxxii). For probable examples of Q3 > F contamination, see 4.2.1–18 n., 5.6.90–1 n. Further significant concurrences between Q3 and F can be derived from Wells and Taylor, *Textual Analysis*, pp. 200–6 – there is a concentration in 2.2.

8 R. B. McKerrow, 'A note on the "bad quartos" of 2 and *3 Henry VI*', *RES* 13 (1937), 64–72; see the notes to these lines.

9 Compare 1.2.40 n., 4.6.53–7 n.; Cairncross, pp. xv–xvi, and see Janet Clare, '"Greater themes for insurrection's arguing": Political censorship of the Elizabethan and Jacobean stage', *RES* 38 (1987), 169–83.

10 In O, Henry seems to hand over the crown (sig. D8ʳ).

11 See Hattaway (ed.), *2H6*, 4.5.0 SD–4.6.5; compare p. 204 n. 5 above.

12 Greg, *Editorial Problem*, p. 55, describes it thus: 'an author's fair copy which the book-keeper had annotated to serve as a prompt-book without troubling to make vague directions specific'. This is also the basic conclusion of Cairncross, (p. xviii) and Wells and Taylor (*Textual Companion*, pp. 197–8).

APPENDIX 1: EXAMPLES FROM SHAKESPEARE'S SOURCES

Longer extracts from these texts are to be found in Bullough and Boswell-Stone

1 Characters of Henry

1.1 King Henry VI thus readepted [regained] (by the means only of the Earl of Warwick) his crown and dignity royal in ... 1471, newly, after so many overthrows, beginning to reign, likely within short space to fall again and to taste more of his accustomed captivity and usual misery. This ill chance and misfortune, by many men's opinions, happened to him because he was a man of no great wit, such as men commonly call an innocent man, neither a fool neither very wise, whose study always was more to excel, either in godly living and virtuous example, than in worldly regiment or temporal dominion, in so much that, in comparison to the study and delectation that he had to virtue and godliness, he little regarded but in manner despised all worldly power and temporal authority which seldom follow or seek after such persons as from them fly or disdain to take them. But his enemies ascribed all this to his coward stomach, affirming that he was a man apt to no purpose nor meet for any enterprise, were it never so small. But whosoever despiseth or dispraiseth that which the common people allow and marvel at, is often taken of them for a mad and undiscrete person; but, notwithstanding the vulgar opinion, he that followeth, loveth, and embraceth the contrary, doth prove both sad [serious] and wise (verifying Solomon's proverb the wisdom of this world is foolishness before God). Other there be[1] that ascribe his infortunity only to the stroke and punishment of God, affirming that the kingdom which Henry IV, his grandfather, wrongfully got and unjustly possessed against King Richard II and his heirs, could not by very divine justice long continue in that injurious stock; and that therefore God, by His divine providence, punished the offence of the grandfather in the son's son.   (Hall, pp. 285–6)

1.2 King Henry was of stature goodly, of body slender, to which proportion all other members were correspondent: his face beautiful, in the which continually was resident the bounty of mind with which he was inwardly indued. He did abhor of his own nature all the vices, as well of the body as of the soul, and from his very infancy he was of honest conversation and pure integrity, no knower of

---

1 See Introduction (p. 11) for a discussion of this characteristic method of offering alternative explanations.

evil and a keeper of all goodness, a despiser of all things which be wont to cause the minds of mortal men to slide, fall, or appair [decay]. Beside this, patience was so radicate in his heart that of all the injuries to him committed (which were no small number), he never asked vengeance nor punishment; but, for that, rendered to almighty God, his creator, hearty thanks, thinking that by this trouble and adversity his sins were to him forgotten and forgiven. What shall I say, that this good, this gentle, this meek, this sober and wise man did declare and affirm that those mischiefs and miseries partly came to him for his own offence, and partly for the heaping of sin upon sin, wretchedly by his ancestors and forefathers; wherefore, he little or nothing esteemed or in any wise did torment or macerate himself, whatsoever dignity, what honour, what state of life, what child, what friend he had lost or missed, but if it did but sound an offence toward God, he looked on that and not without repentance, both mourned and sorrowed for it. These and other like offices of holiness caused God to work miracles for him in his lifetime (as old men said).   (Hall, p. 303)

1.3 This king having enjoyed as great prosperity as favourable fortune could afford and as great troubles on the other side as she frowning could pour out, yet in both the states he was patient and virtuous, that he may be a pattern of most perfect virtue as he was a worthy example of Fortune's inconstancy. He was plain, upright, far from fraud, wholly given to prayer, reading of scriptures and alms-deeds; of such integrity of life that the bishop which had been his confessor ten years avouched that he had not all that time committed any mortal crime; so continent as suspicion of unchaste life never touched him, and having in Christmas a show of young women with their bare breasts laid out presented before him, he immediately departed with these words, 'Fie, fie, for shame; forsooth you be to blame.'

Before his marriage he liked not that women should enter his chamber, and for this respect he committed his two brethren by the mother's side, Jasper and Edmund, to most honest and virtuous prelates to be brought up. So far he was from covetousness that when the executors of his uncle the Bishop of Winchester, surnamed the rich cardinal, would have given him two thousand pounds, he plainly refused it, willing them to discharge the will of the departed, and would scarcely condescend at length to accept the same sum of money toward the endowing of his colleges in Cambridge and Eton. He was religiously affected (as the time then was) that at principal holidays he would wear sackcloth next his skin. Oath he used none, but in most earnest matters these words, 'Forsooth and forsooth'.

He was so pitiful [full of pity] that when he saw the quarter of a traitor against his crown over Cripplegate he willed it to be taken away with these words: 'I will not have any christian [man] so cruelly handled for my sake.' Many great offences he willingly pardoned and, receiving at a time a great blow by a wicked man which compassed his death, he only said, 'Forsooth, forsooth, ye do foully to smite a king anointed so.' Another also which thrust him into the side with a sword when he was prisoner in the Tower, was by him pardoned when he was restored to his state and kingdom. Not long before his death, being demanded why he had so long held the crown of England unjustly, he replied: 'My father was King of England,[1] quietly enjoying the crown all his reign, and his father, my grandsire, was also King of England, and I, even a child in my cradle, was proclaimed and crowned without any interruption, and so held it forty years well-near, all the states doing homage unto me as to my antecessors; wherefore I may say with King David, "The lot is fallen unto me in a fair ground; yea, I have a goodly heritage; my help is from the Lord which saveth the upright in heart." '

(Holinshed, pp. 325–6)

2 The period

2.1 When Queen Margaret heard that the king was taken,[2] she, with her son and eight persons, fled to . . . Wales, and was robbed by the way in Lancashire of all her goods, to the value of ten thousand marks; from thence she went into Scotland. Thus you see what fruits the tree of civil discord doth bring forth: that evil tree which, whilst some have taken pain to plant and some to prune and nourish, for others confusion (to whom they have given a taste of those apples which it bare, far more bitter than coloquintida) themselves have been forced to take such share as befell them by lot. For, as it is not possible that a common fire whose heat and flame is universally spread should spare any particular place (for so should it not be general), no more is it likely that in civil commotions, rebellions, insurrections, and partakings in conflicts and pitched fields (specially under ringleaders of great countenance and personage such as be the peers and states of kingdoms), any one should, though perhaps his life, yet (a thousand to one) not save his blood unspilt nor his goods unspoiled. (Holinshed, p. 261)

2.2 Thus far touching the tragical state of this land under the rent regiment of King Henry who (beside the bare title of royalty and naked name of king) had little appertaining to the port of a prince. For whereas the dignity of princedom standeth in sovereignty, there were of his nobles that imbecilled his prerogative by sundry practices, specially by main force, as seeking either to suppress, or to exile, or to obscure, or to make him away. Otherwise what should be the meaning of all those foughten fields from time to time most miserably falling out both to prince, peer, and people? As at St Albans, at Bloreheath, at Northampton, at Banbury, at Barnet, and at Wakefield, to the effusion of much blood and pulling on of many a plague which otherwise might have been avoided.

(Holinshed, pp. 272–3)

---

1 See 3.1.76–8.
2 At the battle of Northampton in 1460, not shown in the play.

3 The battle of Wakefield

3.1 The Duke [of York] by small journeys, came to his castle of Sandal, beside Wakefield, on Christmas Eve, and there began to assemble his tenants and friends. The queen, being thereof ascertained, determined to couple with him while his power was small and his aid not come. And so, having in her company the prince her son, the Dukes of Exeter and Somerset, the Earl of Devonshire, the Lord Clifford, the Lord Ross, and in effect all the lords of the north part, with eighteen thousand men, or as some write, twenty and two thousand, marched from York to Wakefield, and bade base to [challenged] the duke, even before his castle; he, having with him not fully five thousand persons, determined incontinent to issue out and to fight with his enemies; and although Sir Davy Hall, his old servant and chief counsellor, advised him to keep his castle and to defend the same with his small number till his son the Earl of March were come with his power of Marchmen and Welsh soldiers; yet he would not be counselled, but in a great fury said, 'Ah, Davy, Davy, hast thou loved me so long, and now wouldst have me dishonoured? Thou never saw me keep fortress when I was Regent in Normandy, when the dauphin himself with his puissance came to besiege me, but like a man, and not like a bird included in a cage, I issued and fought with mine enemies to their loss ever (I thank God) and to my honour. If I have not kept myself within walls for fear of a great and strong prince, nor hid my face from any man living, wouldst thou that I, for dread of a scolding woman whose weapon is only her tongue and her nails, should incarcerate myself and shut my gates? Then all men might of me wonder and all creatures may of me report dishonour, that a woman hath made me a dastard, whom no man ever to this day could yet prove a coward. And surely my mind is rather to die with honour than to live with shame; for of honour cometh fame, and of dishonour riseth infamy. Their great number shall not appal my spirits but encourage them; for surely I think that I have there as many friends as enemies which, at joining, will either fly or take my part. Therefore, advance my banner in the name of God and St George; for surely I will fight with them, though I should fight alone.'

The Earl of Salisbury and other his friends, seeing his courage, resolved themselves to his opinion and ordered their men, and set them forth in warlike fashion for their most advantage. The Duke of Somerset and other of the queen's part, knowing perfectly that if the duke got the victory their days were minished and their livings left bare, like men quickened and exasperate, for the safeguard of their lives and defence of their goods, determined to abide the chance and to espy their most advantage, and so appointed the Lord Clifford to lie in the one stale [ambush] and the Earl of Wiltshire in the other, and they themselves kept the main battle.

The Duke of York with his people descended down the hill in good order and array, and was suffered to pass forward toward the main battle; but when he was in the plane ground between his castle and the town of Wakefield, he was environed on every side, like a fish in a net or a deer in a buck-stall [large net], so that he, manfully fighting, was within half an hour slain and dead, and his whole army discomfited; and with him died of his trusty friends, his two bastard uncles, Sir John and Sir Hugh Mortimers, Sir Davy Hall his chief counsellor, Sir Hugh Hastings, Sir Thomas Neville . . . and two thousand and eight hundred other, whereof many were young gentlemen and heirs of great parentage in the south part, whose lineages revenged their deaths within four months next and immediately ensuing . . .

While this battle was in fighting, a priest called Sir Robert Aspall, chaplain and schoolmaster to the young Earl of Rutland, second son to the above-named Duke of York, scarce of the age of twelve years, a fair gentleman and a maidenlike person, perceiving that flight was more safeguard than tarrying, both for him and his master, secretly conveyed the earl out of the field by the Lord Clifford's band toward the town; but, ere he could enter into a house, he was by the said Lord Clifford espied, followed, and taken, and, by reason of his apparel, demanded what he was. The young gentleman, dismayed, had not a word to speak, but kneeled on his knees, imploring mercy and desiring grace, both with holding up his hands and making dolorous countenance, for his speech was gone for fear. 'Save him', said his chaplain, 'for he is a prince's son and peradventure may do you good hereafter.' With that word, the Lord Clifford marked him and said, 'By God's blood, thy father slew mine, and so will I do thee and all thy kin'; and, with that word, stuck the earl to the heart with his dagger, and bade his chaplain bear the earl's mother and brother word what he had done and said. In this act the Lord Clifford was accounted a tyrant and no gentleman: for the property of the lion, which is a furious and an unreasonable beast, is to be cruel to them that withstand him, and gentle to such as prostrate or humiliate themselves before him.

Yet this cruel Clifford and deadly blood-supper, not content with this homicide or child-killing, came to the place where the dead corpse of the Duke of York lay, and caused his head to be stricken off, and set on it a crown of paper, and so fixed it on a pole, and presented it to the queen, not lying far from the field, in great despite and much derision, saying: 'Madam, your war is done. Here is your king's ransom'; at which present was much joy and great rejoicing; but many laughed then that sore lamented after – as the queen herself and her son. And many were glad then of other men's deaths, not knowing that their own were near at hand – as the Lord Clifford and other. But surely man's nature is so frail that things passed be soon forgotten and mischiefs to come be not foreseen.

After this victory by the queen and her part obtained, she caused the Earl of Salisbury, with all the other prisoners, to be sent to Pomfret and there to be beheaded, and sent all their heads, and the Duke's head of York, to be set upon poles over the gate of the city of York, in despite of them and their lineage; whose children shortly revenged their father's quarrel, both to the queen's extreme perdition and the utter undoing of her husband and son. This end had the valiant lord, Richard Plantagenet, Duke of York, and this fine [end] ensued of his too much hardiness. (Hall, pp. 250–1)

3.2 Some write[1] that the duke was taken alive and in derision caused to stand upon a molehill, on whose head they put a garland instead of a crown, which they had fastened and made of sedges or bulrushes; and, having so crowned him with that garland, they kneeled down afore him (as the Jews did unto Christ) in scorn, saying to him, 'Hail, king without rule; hail, king without heritage; hail, duke and prince without people or possessions.' And at length, having thus scorned him with these and diverse other the like despiteful words, they struck off his head which, as ye have heard, they presented to the queen.

Many deemed that this miserable end chanced to the Duke of York as a due punishment for breaking his oath of allegiance unto his sovereign lord King Henry; but others held him discharged thereof, because he obtained a dispensation from the pope,[2] by such suggestion as his procurators made unto him, whereby the same oath was adjudged void as that which was received unadvisedly, to the prejudice of himself and disinheriting of all his posterity.

(Holinshed, p. 269)

4 The proclamation of Edward IV in 1461[3]

This prudent young prince, minding to take time when time served, called a great council both of the lords spiritual and temporal, and to them repeated the title and right that he had to the crown, rehearsing also the articles concluded between King Henry and his father, by their writings signed and sealed and also confirmed by act of parliament, the breaches whereof he neither forgot nor left undeclared. After the lords had considered of this matter, they determined by authority of the said council that, because King Henry had done contrary to the ordinances in the last parliament concluded and was insufficient of himself to rule the realm, he was therefore to be deprived of all kingly estate, and incontinently was Edward, Earl of March, son and heir to Richard, Duke of York, by the lords in the said council assembled, named elected, and admitted for king and governor of the realm.

On which day, the people of the earl's part, being in their muster in St John's field and a great number of the substantial citizens there assembled to behold their order, the Lord Falconbridge, who took the musters, wisely anon declared to the people the offences and breaches of the late agreement committed by King Henry VI, and demanded of the people whether they would have him to rule and reign any longer over them. To whom they with whole voice answered, 'Nay, nay.' Then he asked them if they would serve, love, honour, and obey the Earl of March as their only king and sovereign lord; to which question they answered, 'Yea, yea', crying 'King Edward' with many great shouts and clapping of hands in assent and gladness of the same.

1 In the margin 'Whethamsted' i.e. John Whethamstede (d. 1465), Abbot of St Albans. Holinshed has just offered a version of the text found in Hall.
2 In the margin 'A purchase of God's curse with the pope's blessing.'
3 See Introduction, p. 12, and 3.3.117–18n.

The lords were shortly advertised of the loving consent which the commons frankly and freely had given. Whereupon incontinently they all with a convenient number of the most substantial commons reparted to the Earl at Baynard's Castle, making just and true report of their election and admission, and the loving assent of the commons. The earl, after long pausing, first thanked God of His great grace and benefit towards him showed, then the lords and commons for their favour and fidelity; notwithstanding, like a wise prince, he alleged his insufficiency for so great a room and weighty burden, as lack of knowledge, want of experience, and diverse other qualities to a governor appertaining. But yet in conclusion, being persuaded by the Archbishop of Canterbury, the Bishop of Exeter, and other lords then present, he agreed to their petition and took upon him the charge of the kingdom, as forfeited to him by breach of the covenants established in parliament. (Holinshed, p. 272; Hall, p. 253)

5 Edward IV

This King Edward was such a prince of governance and behaviour in the time of peace (for in the time of war each must be other's enemy) that there was never any king in this realm attaining the crown by war and battle so heartily beloved with the more substance of his people, nor he himself so specially favoured in any part of his life as at the time of his death; which favour and affection, yet after his death, by the cruelty, mischief, and trouble of the tempestuous world that followed, highly towards him more increased. At such time as he died, the displeasure of those that bore him grudge for King Henry VI sake (whom he deposed) was well assuaged and in effect quenched within the space of twenty two years, which is a great part of a man's life; and some were reconciled and grown into his favour of the which he was never strange when it was with true heart demanded. He was goodly of personage and princely to behold, of heart courageous, politic in counsel, and in adversity nothing abashed, in prosperity rather joyful than proud, in peace just and merciful, in war sharp and fierce, in the field bold and hardy, and yet nevertheless no further than reason and policy would adventure; whose wars, whosoever circumspectly and advisedly considereth, he shall no less commend his wisdom and policy where he avoided them than his manhood where he vanquished them. He was of visage full-faced and lovely, of body mighty, strong and clean made; with over-liberal and wanton diet he waxed somewhat corpulent and burly, but nevertheless not uncomely. He was in youth greatly given to fleshly wantonness, from the which health of body, in great prosperity and fortune (without an especial grace), hardly refraineth. This fault little grieved his people, for neither could any one man's pleasure stretch or extend to the displeasure of very many, nor a multitude be grieved by a private man's fantasy or voluptuousness, when it was done without violence. And in his latter days he left all wild dalliance and fell to gravity, so that he brought his realm into a wealthy and prosperous estate: all fear of outward enemies were clearly extinguished, and no war was in hand, nor none toward, but such as no man looked for. The people were toward their prince not in a constrained fear, but in a true loving and wilful obedience amongst themself, and the commons were in good peace. The lords whom he knew at variance, he in his death bed (as he thought) brought to good concord, love, and amity.

(Hall, pp. 345–6, adapted from Sir Thomas More's *The History of King Richard the Third*; Holinshed, pp. 360–1)

6 Richard Duke of Gloucester

Richard, Duke of Gloucester, the third son . . . was in wit and courage egal [equal] with [George, Duke of Clarence], but in beauty and lineaments of nature far underneath both, for he was little of stature, evil-featured of limbs, crook-backed, the left shoulder much higher than the right, hard-favoured of visage – such as in estates is called a warlike visage, and among common persons a crabbed face. He was malicious, wrathful, and envious, and, as it is reported, his mother the duchess had much also in her travail, that she could not be delivered of him uncut, and that he came into the world the feet forward, as men be born outward, and, as the fame [rumour] ran, not untoothed. Whether that men of hatred reported above the truth, or that nature changed his course in his beginning, which, in his life, many things unnaturally committed, this I leave to God his judgment. He was none evil captain in war, as to the which his disposition was more inclined to than to peace. Sundry victories he had and some overthrows, but never for default of his own person, either for lack of hardiness or politic order. Free he was of his dispenses and somewhat above his power liberal: with large gifts he got him unsteadfast friendship; for which cause he was fain to borrow, pill, and extort in other places, which got him steadfast hatred. He was close and secret, a deep dissimumler, lowly of countenance, arrogant of heart, outwardly familiar where he inwardly hated, not letting to kiss whom he thought to kill, dispiteous and cruel; not alway for evil will, but often for ambition and to serve his purpose; friend and foe were all indifferent where his advantage grew – he spared no man's death whose life withstood his purpose.

He slew in the Tower King Henry VI, saying 'Now is there no heir male of King Edward III but we of the house of York'; which murder was done without King Edward his assent, which would have appointed that butcherly office to some other rather than to his own brother.

(Hall, pp. 342–3; adapted from Sir Thomas More's *The History of King Richard the Third*)

7 The battle of Tewkesbury

King Edward had ever good espials to advertise him still what his enemies did and which way they took. At length he came with all his army into a village called Cheltenham, like a five miles distant from Tewkesbury, where he had certain knowledge that his enemies were already come to Tewkesbury and were encamped there, proposing to abide in that place and to deliver him battle . . .

Edward was put to his shifts how (to any advantage) to assault his enemies. Nevertheless he, being well furnished with great artillery, the same was aptly lodged to annoy the enemies that they received great damage thereby; and the Duke of Gloucester, who lacked no policy, galled them grievously with the shot of arrows . . . The passages were so cumbersome that it was not possible to come upon any even hand to join at hand-blows.

The Duke of Gloucester, upon a politic purpose (as some have written), recoiled back with all his company,[1] which, when the Duke of Somerset perceived, either moved therewith or because he was too sore annoyed with the shot in that place where he and his fore-ward stood, like a knight more courageous than circumspect, came out of his strength with his whole battle and advanced himself . . . The king or (as other have) the Duke of Gloucester, taking the advantage that he adventured for, turned face to face unto the Duke of Somerset his battle and, winning the hedge and ditch of him, entered the close, and with great violence put him and his people up towards the hill from whence they were descended . . .

The Duke of Somerset seeing this unfortunate chance, as some write, turned to the middle-ward, and there finding the Lord Wenlock [who had not advanced with him but was] standing still, after he had reviled him and called him traitor, with his axe he struck the brains out of his head. The Duke of Gloucester, pursuing after them that fled with the Duke of Somerset to their camp where the rest of their army stood, entered the trench, and after him the king, where he bore himself so knightly that thereupon the queen's part went to wrack and was put to flight, the king and other falling in chase after them so that many were slain . . .

After the field was ended, proclamation was made that whosoever could bring forth Prince Edward alive or dead should have an annuity of a hundred pounds during his life, and the prince's life to be saved if he were brought back alive. Sir Richard Crofts [who had captured the prince], nothing mistrusting the king's promise, brought forth his prisoner Prince Edward, being a fair and well-proportioned young gentleman; whom, when King Edward had well advised, he demanded of him how he durst so presumptuously enter into his realm with banner displayed.

Whereupon the prince boldly answered, saying, 'To recover my father's kingdom and heritage, from his father and grandfather to him, and from him after him to me, lineally descended.' At which words King Edward said nothing, but with his hand thrust him from him or, as some say, struck him with his gauntlet, whom incontinently George Duke of Clarence, Richard Duke of Gloucester, Thomas Grey, Marquess Dorset, and William Lord Hastings that stood by, suddenly murdered: for the which cruel act the more part of the doers in their latter days drank of the like cup, by the righteous justice and due

---

1 See 5.4.82 SD n.

punishment of God. His body was homely interred with the other simple corpses in the church of the monastery of the black monks in Tewkesbury.

(Holinshed, pp. 318–20; Hall, p. 300)

8 Arthur Brooke, *Romeus and Juliet*, 1359–1380[1] (See 5.4.1–31)

A wise man in the midst of troubles and distress
Still stands not wailing present harm but seeks his harm's redress;
As when the winter flaws with dreadful noise arise
And heave the foamy swelling waves up to the starry skies,
So that the bruisèd bark, in cruel seas betossed,
Despaireth of the happy haven in danger to be lost.
The pilot bold a-helm cries, 'Mates, strike now your sail',
And turns her stem into the waves that strongly her assail.
Then, driven hard upon the bare and wrackful shore,
In greater danger to be wracked than he had been before,
He seeth his ship full right against the rock to run,
But yet he doth what lieth in him the perilous rock to shun.
Sometimes the beaten boat, by cunning government,
The anchors lost, the cables broke, and all the tackle spent,
The rudder smitten off, and overboard the mast,
Doth win the long desirèd port, the stormy danger past.
But if the master, dread and over-pressed with woe,
Begin to wring his hands and lets the guiding rudder go,
The ship rents on the rock or sinketh in the deep,
And eke the coward drenchèd is: so, if thou still beweep
And seek not how to help the changes that do chance,
The cause of sorrow shall increase, thou cause of thy mischance.

---

1 Modernised from Bullough, I, 321.

APPENDIX 2: ASPECTS OF *THE TRUE TRAGEDY* (O)

1 Passages from O[1] the substance of which does not appear in F

1.1 1.1.120−4

NORTHUM[BERLAND]   Peace thou and give king *Henry* leaue to speake.
KING   Ah *Plantagenet*,[2] why seekest thou to depose me?
Are we not both both [*sic*] *Plantagenets* by birth,
And from two brothers lineallie discent?
Suppose by right and equitie thou be king,   (O, sig. A4^{r-v})

1.2 1.4.1−6

YORKE   Ah *Yorke*, post to thy castell, save thy life,
The goale is lost thou house of *Lancaster*,
Thrise happie chance is it for thee and thine,
That heauen abridgde my daies and cals me hence,
But God knowes what chance hath betide my sonnes: (O, sig. A8^v)

1.3 2.3.7−13

ED[WARD]   . . . That we maie die vnlesse we gaine the daie:
What fatall starre malignant frownes from heauen
Vpon the harmelesse line of *Yorkes* true house?
                    Enter *George*.
GEORGE   Come brother, come, lets to the field againe,
For yet theres hope inough to win the daie:
Then let vs backe to cheere our fainting Troupes,
Lest they retire now we haue left the field.
WAR[WICK]   How now my lords: what hap, what hope of good?   (O, sig. C1^v)

1.4 2.3.15−22

RICH[ARD]   . . . Thy noble father in the thickest thronges,
Cride still for *Warwike* his thrise valiant son,
Vntill with thousand swords he was beset,
And manie wounds made in his aged brest,

---

1 Quotations are taken from the Shakespeare Quarto Facsimile, ed. W. W. Greg, 1958.
2 The Oxford editors, who incorporate this version into their text, read 'York' for 'Plantagenet' here on the grounds that it seems to have been caught from the following line.

And as he tottering sate vpon his steede,
He waft his hand to me and cride aloud:
Richard, commend me to my valiant sonne,
And still he cride *Warwike* reuenge my death,
And with those words he tumbled off his horse,
And so the noble Salsbury gaue vp the ghost.   (o, sig. CI^v)

1.5 3.3.1–43. These lines would seem to have been supplied as part of the process of abridgement:

LEWES Welcome *Queene* Margaret to the Court of *France*,
      It fits not *Lewis* to sit while thou does stand,
      Sit by my side, and here *I* vow to thee,
      Thou shalt haue aide to repossesse thy right,
      And beat proud Edward from his vsurped seat.
      And place king *Henry* in his former rule.
QUEEN I humbly thanke your royall maiestie.
      And pray the God of heauen to blesse thy state,
      Great king of *France*, that thus regards our wrongs.   (o, sig. C8^v)

1.6 4.4. In o the order of 4.5 and 4.4 are reversed. The following is the equivalent of 4.4:

                    Enter the *Queene* and the Lord *Riuers*.

RIUERS Tel me good maddam, why is your grace
       So passionate of late?
QUEEN Why brother *Riuers*, heare you not the newes,
      Of that successe king *Edward* had of late?
RIU What? losse of some pitcht battaile against *Warwike*,
    Tush, feare not faire *Queen*, but cast those cares aside.
    King *Edwards* noble mind, his honours doth display:
    And *Warwike* maie loose, though then he got the day.
QUEEN If that were all, my griefes were at an end:
      But greater troubles will I feare befall.
RIU What, is he taken prisoner by the foe,
    To the danger of his royall person then?
QUEEN I, theares my griefe, king *Edward* is surprisde,
      And led awaie, as prisoner vnto *Yorke*.
RIU The newes is passing strange I must confesse:
    Yet comfort your selfe, for *Edward* hath more friends,
    Then *Lancaster* at this time must perceiue,
    That some will set him in his throne againe.
QUEEN God grant they maie, but gentle brother come,
      And let me leane vpon thine arme a while,
      Vntill I come vnto the sanctuarie,
      There to preserue the fruit within my wombe,
      K. *Edwards* seed true heir to *Englands* crowne. *Exit.*   (o, sig. D6^v–D7^r)

1.7 5.2 The following is spoken after Warwick's death (5.2.49):

> OXF[ORD] Come noble *Summerset*, lets take our horse,
> And cause retrait be sounded through the campe,
> That all our friends that yet remaine aliue,
> Maie be awarn'd and saue themselves by flight.
> That done, with them weele post vnto the *Queene*,
> And once more trie our fortune in the field. *Ex ambo.*   (O, sig. E3ʳ)

1.8 5.4.1–50

> QUEE[N] Welcome to *England*, my louing friends of *France*,
> And welcome *Summerset*, and *Oxford* too.
> Once more haue we spread our sailes abroad,
> And though our tackling be almost consumde,
> And *Warwike* as our maine mast ouerthrowne,
> Yet warlike Lords raise you that sturdie post,
> That beares the sailes to bring vs vnto rest,
> And *Ned* and *I* as willing Pilots should
> For once with carefull mindes guide on the sterne,
> To bear vs through that dangerous gulfe
> That heretofore hath swallowed vp our friends.
> PRINCE And if there be, as God forbid there should,
> Amongst vs a timorous or fearefull man,
> Let him depart before the battels ioine,
> Least he in time of need intise another,
> And so withdraw the souldiers harts from vs.
> *I* will not stand aloofe and bid you fight,
> But with my sword presse in the thickest thronges,
> And single *Edward* from his strongest guard,
> And hand to hand enforce him for to yeeld,
> Or leaue my bodie as witnesse of my thoughts.   (O, sig. E3ᵛ)

1.9 5.4.1 – 5.5.16

> QUEEN ... Then on Gods name Lords togither cry saint *George.*
> ALL Saint *George* for *Lancaster.*
> Alarmes to the battlell, *Yorke* flies, then the chambers be discharged. Then enter the king,
> *Cla* & *Glo.* & the rest, & make a great shout, and crie, for *Yorke*, for *Yorke*, and then
> the *Queene* is taken, & the pince, and *Oxf.* & *Sum.* and then sound and enter all
> againe.
> EDW[ARD] Lo here a period of tumultuous broiles,
> Awaie with Oxford to *Hames* castell straight,
> For *Summerset* off with his guiltie head.
> Awaie I will not hear them speake.
> OXF[ORD] For my part Ile not trouble thee with words.
>   *Exit* Oxford.
> SUM[MERSET] Nor *I*, but stoope with patience to my death.
>   *Exit Sum.*

EDW Now *Edward* what satisfaction canst thou make,
         For stirring up my subjects to rebellion?   (sig. E4ᵛ)

2 O's version of 4.1.47–56

Hall and F correctly assign the three heiresses to Hastings, the queen's brother, and the queen's son. O misses the point of the passage, omitting all reference to the queen's relatives (see Textual analysis, p. 203).

> CLA[RENCE] For this one speech the Lord *Hastings* wel deserues,
>   To haue the daughter and heire of the Lord *Hungerford*.
> EDW[ARD] And what then? It was our will it should be so?
> CLA I, and for such a thing too the Lord *Scales*
>   Did well deserue at your hands, to haue the
>   Daughter of the Lord *Bonfield*, and left your
>   Brothers to go seeke elsewhere, but in
>   Your madnes, you burie brotherhood.   (O, sig. D3ᵛ–D4ʳ)

3 Recollections of lines from other plays which may have contaminated the memorial reconstruction from which O derives[1]

All of these plays could have belonged to Strange's or Pembroke's Men.

3.1 *1 Henry VI*

(a)   [Not in F; see 1.1.124 collation]

Compare: And from two brothers lineallie discent   (O, sig. A4ᵛ)[2]

With: From whence you spring, by Lineall Descent   (*1H6* 3.1.165)

(b)   To shrinke mine Arme vp like a wither'd Shrub   (*3H6* 3.2.156)

Compare: To drie mine arme vp like a withered shrimpe   (O, sig. C8ʳ)

With: And large proportion of his strong knit Limbes.
            Alas, this is a Child, a silly Dwarfe:
            It cannot be, this weake and writhled shrimpe   (*1H6* 2.3.20–2)

3.2 *2 Henry VI*

(a)   Mount you my Lord   (*3H6* 2.5.128)

Compare: Take horse   (O, sig. C3ᵛ)

With: my Lord, away, take horse   (*2H6* 4.4.54)

---

1 Some of these were first listed by Alexander, *Shakespeare's Henry VI and Richard III*, pp. 91 ff. and by Hart, *Stolne and Surreptitious Copies*. Like Alexander, Cairncross (pp. 182–5) offers some further examples which I do not accept.
2 Compare the first quarto of *2H6*, TLN 737 (and see Hattaway (ed.), *2H6*, p. 237).

(b)   (in all despight)   (*3H6* 2.6.81)

Compare   in all contempt   (O, sig. C5ʳ)

With   with all contempt   (*2H6* 5.1.209)

(c)   Richard, I will create thee Duke of Gloucester,
           And George of Clarence   (*3H6* 2.6.103–4)

Compare: We here create thee Duke of *Clarence*, and girt thee with the sword
                                                                 (O, sig. C5ʳ)

With: Lord Marques kneel down,
           We heere create thee the first Duke of Suffolke,
           And girt thee with the Sword.   (*2H6* 1.1.60–2)

3.2.1 *1 Contention* (the 'bad quarto' of *2 Henry VI*)

(a)   And he that throws not up his cap for joy
           Shall, for the fault, make forfeit of his head.   (*3H6* 2.1.196–7)

Compare: And he that casts not vp his cap for ioie,
           Shall for the offence make forfeit of his head.   (O, sig. B6ʳ)

With: . . . he that breakes a sticke of *Glosters* groue,
           Shall for th'offence, make forfeit of his head.   (*1 Cont.* TNL 226–7)[1]

(b)   Away! For vengeance comes along with them.
           Nay, stay not to expostulate: make speed   (*3H6* 2.5.134–5)

Compare: Awaie my Lord for vengance comes along with him;
           Nay stand not to expostulate make hast   (O, sig. C3ᵛ)

With: Away my Lord, and flie to London straight,
           Make hast, for vengeance comes along with them,
           Come stand not to expostulate, lets go.   (*1 Cont.* TLN 2194–6)

3.3 *Richard III*

(a)   But what art thou whose heavy looks foretell   (*3H6* 2.1.43)

Compare: But what art thou? that lookest so heauilie?   (O, sig. B3ᵛ)

With: Why looks your grace so heavily   (*R3* 1.4.1)

(b)   While I use further conference with Warwick.   (*3H6* 3.3.111)

Compare: Till I doe talke a word with *Warwike*.   (O, sig. D1ᵛ)

With: I must talk a word with you.   (*R3* 4.4.199)

(c)   O traitors! Murderers! . . . bloody cannibals,   (*3H6* 5.5.52, 61)

Compare: Traytors, Tyrants, bloudie Homicides,   (O, sig. E5ʳ)

With: A bloody tyrant and a homicide;   (*R3* 5.3.246)

---

1 Quotations are taken from W. Montgomery (ed.), *The First Part of the Contention 1594*, 1985.

3.4 *Titus Andronicus*

(a)	let former grudges pass	(*3H6* 3.3.195)
Compare:	pardon what is past	(O, sig. D2^v)
With:	pardon what is past	(*Tit.* 1.1.431)
(b)	Comes hunting this way	(*3H6* 4.5.8)
Compare:	Should come a hunting in this forrest heere	(O, sig. D6^r)
With:	To see the general hunting in this forest	(*Tit.* 2.3.59)

3.5 Kyd, *The Spanish Tragedy*[1]

(a)	Though Fortune's malice overthrow my state,	(*3H6* 4.3.46)
Compare:	let fortune doe her worst,	(O, sig. D5^v)
With:	let Fortune do her worst	(*Sp.Tr.* 1.3.19)
(b)	But sound the trumpets and about our task.	(*3H6* 2.1.200)
Compare:	But forward to effect these resolutions.	(O, sig. B6^r)
With:	But live t'effect thy resolution.	(*Sp.Tr.* 3.2.47)

3.6 Kyd(?), *Soliman and Perseda*[2]

(a)	O speak no more, for I have heard too much.	(*3H6* 2.1.48)
Compare:	O speake no more, for I can heare no more.	(O, sig. B3^v)
With:	Ah, stay, no more, for I can hear no more.	(*S&P* 2.2.28)
(b)	Their power, I think, is thirty thousand strong	(*3H6* 2.1.177)
Compare:	Their power *I* gesse them fifty thousand strong	(O, sig. B5^v)
With:	Their horse, I deem them fifty thousand strong	(*S&P* 3.1.48)
(c)	Richard, enough	(*3H6* 1.2.35)
Compare:	*I*, saist thou so boie? why then it shall be so.	(O, sig. A7^r)
With:	Ay, say'st thou so? Why, then it shall be so.	(*S&P* 4.1.242)

---

1 Quotations are taken from Philip Edwards (ed.), *The Spanish Tragedy*, 1959.
2 This play is of unknown auspices.

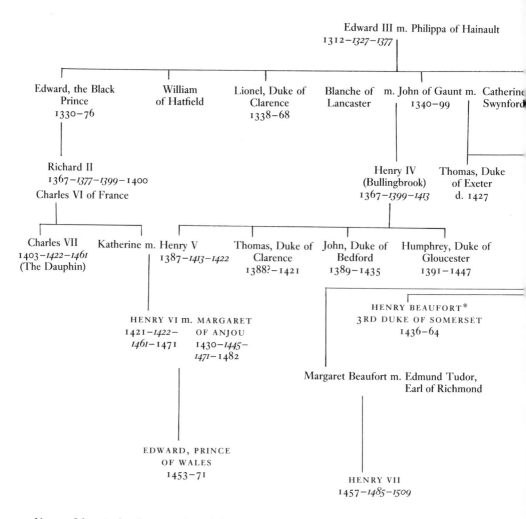

Edward III m. Philippa of Hainault
1312–*1327–1377*

Edward, the Black Prince 1330–76 — William of Hatfield — Lionel, Duke of Clarence 1338–68 — Blanche of Lancaster m. John of Gaunt m. Catherine Swynford 1340–99

Richard II 1367–*1377–1399*–1400 Charles VI of France — Henry IV (Bullingbrook) 1367–*1399–1413* — Thomas, Duke of Exeter d. 1427

Charles VII 1403–*1422–1461* (The Dauphin) — Katherine m. Henry V 1387–*1413–1422* — Thomas, Duke of Clarence 1388?–1421 — John, Duke of Bedford 1389–1435 — Humphrey, Duke of Gloucester 1391–1447

HENRY VI m. MARGARET 1421–*1422–1461*–1471 OF ANJOU 1430–*1445–1471*–1482

HENRY BEAUFORT* 3RD DUKE OF SOMERSET 1436–64

Margaret Beaufort m. Edmund Tudor, Earl of Richmond

EDWARD, PRINCE OF WALES 1453–71

HENRY VII 1457–*1485–1509*

Names of those in the play appear in capitals
Italicised dates are those of reigns.
*See Notes to List of characters, pp. 67–71 above.

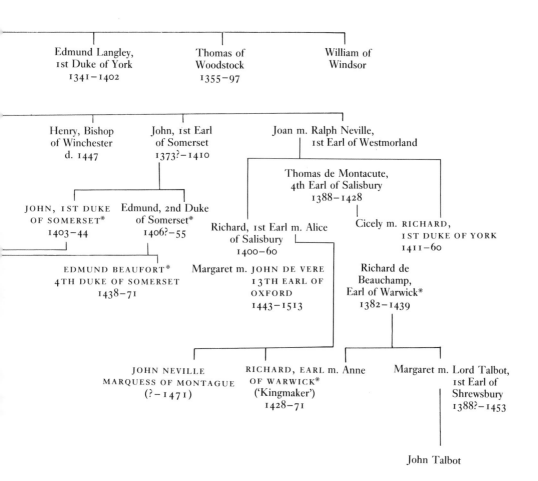

Edmund Langley,
1st Duke of York
1341–1402

Thomas of
Woodstock
1355–97

William of
Windsor

Henry, Bishop
of Winchester
d. 1447

John, 1st Earl
of Somerset
1373?–1410

Joan m. Ralph Neville,
1st Earl of Westmorland

Thomas de Montacute,
4th Earl of Salisbury
1388–1428

JOHN, 1ST DUKE
OF SOMERSET*
1403–44

Edmund, 2nd Duke
of Somerset*
1406?–55

Richard, 1st Earl m. Alice
of Salisbury
1400–60

Cicely m. RICHARD,
1ST DUKE OF YORK
1411–60

EDMUND BEAUFORT*
4TH DUKE OF SOMERSET
1438–71

Margaret m. JOHN DE VERE
13TH EARL OF
OXFORD
1443–1513

Richard de
Beauchamp,
Earl of Warwick*
1382–1439

JOHN NEVILLE
MARQUESS OF MONTAGUE
(?–1471)

RICHARD, EARL m. Anne
OF WARWICK*
('Kingmaker')
1428–71

Margaret m. Lord Talbot,
1st Earl of
Shrewsbury
1388?–1453

John Talbot

Table 1   THE HOUSE OF LANCASTER

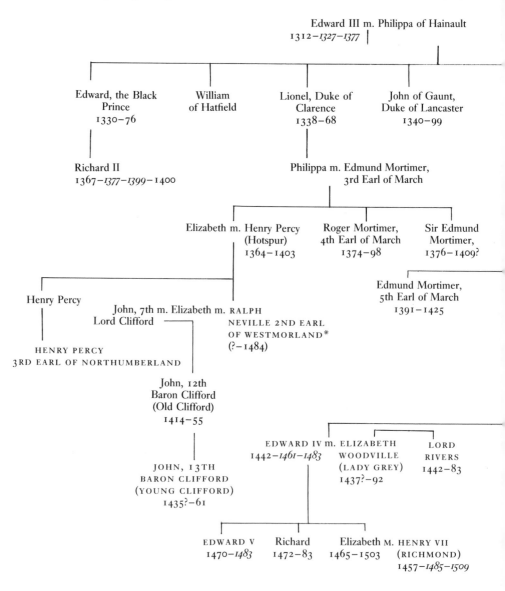

Names of those in the play appear in capitals.
Italicised dates are those of reigns.
*See Notes to List of characters, p. 68 above.

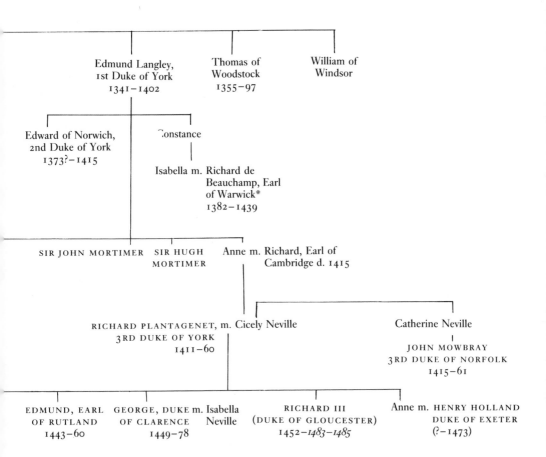

Table 2   THE HOUSES OF YORK AND MORTIMER

READING LIST

A selection of critical texts central to the study of the play is listed here. The list also includes relevant works of reference, as well as some books and articles which might be found useful for further study.

Alexander, Peter. *Shakespeare's Henry VI and Richard III*, 1929

Baldwin, T. W. *Shakspere's 'Small Latine & Lesse Greeke'*, 2 vols., 1944

Berman, Ronald S. 'Fathers and sons in the *Henry VI* plays', *SQ* 13 (1962), 487–97

Berry, Edward. 'Twentieth-century Shakespeare criticism: the histories' in Stanley Wells (ed.), *The Cambridge Companion to Shakespeare Studies*, 1986, pp. 249–56

    Patterns of Decay: Shakespeare's Early Histories, 1975

Blanpied, John W. *Time and the Artist in Shakespeare's English Histories*, 1983

Boswell-Stone, W. G. *Shakespeare's Holinshed, the Chronicle and the Historical Plays Compared*, 1896

Brockbank, J. P. 'The frame of disorder – *Henry VI*', in J. R. Brown and B. Harris (eds.), *Early Shakespeare*, 1961

Brooke, Nicholas. 'Marlowe as provocative agent in Shakespeare's early plays', *S.Sur. 14* (1961), 34–44

Brownlow, F. W. *Two Shakespearean Sequences*, 1977

Bullough, G. *Narrative and Dramatic Sources of Shakespeare*, III, 1960

Bulman, James C. *The Heroic Idiom of Shakespearean Tragedy*, 1985

    'Shakespeare's Georgic histories', *S.Sur. 38* (1985), 37–47

Campbell, Lily B. *Shakespeare's 'Histories': Mirrors of Elizabethan Policy*, 1947

Champion, L. *Perspective in Shakespeare's English Histories*, 1980

    The Noise of Threatening Drum: Dramatic Strategy and Political Ideology in Shakespeare and the English Chronicle Plays, 1990

Clare, Janet. '"Greater themes for insurrection's arguing": political censorship of the Elizabethan and Jacobean stage', *RES* 38 (1987), 169–83

Clemen, Wolfgang. 'Some aspects of style in the *Henry VI* plays', in P. Edwards, I.-S. Ewbank, G. K. Hunter (eds.), *Shakespeare's Styles: Essays in Honour of Kenneth Muir*, 1980, pp. 9–24

Colman, E. A. M. *The Dramatic Use of Bawdy in Shakespeare*, 1974

Cox, John D. *Shakespeare and the Dramaturgy of Power*, 1989

Dean, P. 'Shakespeare's Henry VI trilogy and Elizabethan "romance" histories: the origins of a genre', *SQ* 33 (1982), 34–48

Dessen, Alan C. *Elizabethan Stage Conventions and Modern Interpreters*, 1984

Eccleshall, Robert. *Order and Reason in Politics: Theories of Absolute and Limited Monarchy in Early Modern England*, 1978

Edmond, Mary. 'Pembroke's Men', *RES* 25 (1974), 129–36

Fleischer, Martha Hester. *The Iconography of the English History Play*, 1974

George, D. 'Shakespeare and Pembroke's Men', *SQ* 32 (1981), 305–23

Goy-Blanquet, D. 'Images de la monarchie dans le théâtre historique de Shakespeare', in E. Konigson (ed.), *Les Voies de la création théâtrale, VIII: théâtre, histoire, modèles*, 1980

    Le Roi mis à nu: l'histoire d'Henri VI de Hall à Shakespeare, 1986

Griffiths, Ralph. *The Reign of King Henry VI*, 1981

Hammond, A. C. *The Early Shakespeare*, 1967

Hattaway, Michael. *Elizabethan Popular Theatre*, 1982

Hawkins, Sherman. 'Structural pattern in Shakespeare's histories', *SP* 88 (1991), 16–45

Hinchcliffe, Judith. *King Henry VI, Parts 1, 2, and 3*, Garland Shakespeare Bibliographies, 1986

Hodgdon, B. 'Shakespeare's directorial eye: a look at the early history plays', in S. Homan (ed.), *Shakespeare's 'More than Words can Witness'*, 1980, pp. 115–29

Holderness, G., Potter, N., and Turner, J. *Shakespeare: The Play of History*, 1988

Honigmann, E. A. J. *Shakespeare: The 'Lost Years'*, 1985

    Shakespeare's Impact on his Contemporaries, 1982

Hunter, G. K. 'Truth and art in history plays', *S.Sur.* 42 (1990), 15–24.

Jackson, Sir Barry. 'On producing *Henry VI*', *S.Sur.* 6 (1953), 49–52

Jones, Emrys. *The Origins of Shakespeare*, 1977

    Scenic Form in Shakespeare, 1971

Kastan, David Scott. 'Proud majesty made a subject: Shakespeare and the spectacle of rule', *SQ* 37 (1986), 459–75

    Shakespeare and the Shapes of Time, 1982

Kay, C. McG. 'Traps, slaughter, and chaos: a study of Shakespeare's *Henry VI* plays', *Studies in the Literary Imagination* 5 (1972), 1–26

Kelly, F. L. 'Oaths in Shakespeare's *Henry VI* Plays', *SQ* 24 (1973), 357–71

Kelly, H. A. *Divine Providence in the England of Shakespeare's Histories*, 1970

Leggatt, Alexander. *Shakespeare's Political Drama*, 1988

Long, J. H. *Shakespeare's Use of Music: The Histories and the Tragedies*, 1971

McFarlane, K. B. *England in the Fifteenth Century*, 1982

McKerrow, R. B. 'A note on the "Bad Quartos" of *2* and *3 Henry VI*', *RES* 13 (1937), 64–72

McMillin, Scott. 'Casting for Pembroke's Men: the *Henry VI* Quartos and *The Taming of A Shrew*', *SQ* 23 (1972), 141–59

Manheim, M. *The Weak King Dilemma in the Shakespearean History Play*, 1973

Pitt-Rivers, Julian. *The Fate of Shechem*, 1977, chap. 1, 'The anthropology of honour'

Rackin, Phyllis. *Stages of History: Shakespeare's English Chronicles*, 1990

Reese, M. M. *The Cease of Majesty*, 1961

Rhodes, E. L. *Henslowe's Rose: The Stage and Staging*, 1976

Ribner, Irving. *The English History Play in the Age of Shakespeare*, revised edn, 1965

Riggs, D. *Shakespeare's Heroical Histories: Henry VI and its Literary Tradition*, 1971

Ross, Charles. *Edward IV*, 1974

Saccio, Peter. *Shakespeare's English Kings: History, Chronicle, and Drama*, 1977

Shepherd, Simon. *Marlowe and the Politics of Elizabethan Theatre*, 1986

Smidt, K. *Unconformities in Shakespeare's History Plays*, 1982

Sprague, A. C. *Shakespeare's Histories: Plays for the Stage*, 1964

Talbert, E. W. *Elizabethan Drama and Shakespeare's Early Plays: An Essay in Historical Criticism*, 1963

Tennenhouse, Leonard. *Power on Display: The Politics of Shakespeare's Genres*, 1986

Thomas, K. V. *Religion and the Decline of Magic*, 1971

Tillyard, E. M. W. *Shakespeare's History Plays*, 1944

Urkowitz, Steven. 'Good news about "bad" quartos', in M. Charney (ed.), *'Bad' Shakespeare: Revaluations of the Shakespeare Canon*, 1988

Vale, Malcolm. *War and Chivalry: Warfare and Aristocratic Culture in England, France and Burgundy at the End of the Middle Ages*, 1981

Warren, Roger. '"Contrarieties agree": an aspect of dramatic technique in *Henry VI*', *S.Sur. 37* (1984), 75–83

Watkins, Ronald. 'The only Shake-Scene', *PQ* 54 (1975), 47–67

Wells, Stanley, and Taylor, Gary. *William Shakespeare: A Textual Companion*, 1987

Wilders, John. *The Lost Garden: A View of Shakespeare's English and Roman History Plays*, 1978

Williams, Penry. *The Tudor Regime*, 1979

Williamson, Marilyn L. '"When men are rul'd by women": Shakespeare's first tetralogy', *Shakespeare Studies* 19 (1978), 41–60

Winny, J. *The Player King: A Theme of Shakespeare's Histories*, 1968

Yates, Frances A. *Astraea: The Imperial Theme in the Sixteenth Century*, 1975